RESISTANCE IN THE DESERT

Resistance in the Desert

Moroccan Responses to French Imperialism
1881-1912

ROSS E. DUNN

Illustrated by Jeanne Dunn

CROOM HELM LIMITED
THE UNIVERSITY OF WISCONSIN PRESS

Part of Chapter 4 has appeared as an article:

Ross E. Dunn
'The Trade of Tafilalt: Commercial Change in Southeast Morocco on the
    Eve of the Protectorate'
African Historical Studies, 4, no. 2 (1971), pp. 271-304 Published by
The African Studies Center, Boston University
Copyright 1971 by the Board of Trustees of Boston University

Part of Chapter 2 has appeared as an article:

Ross E. Dunn
'Berber Imperialism: The Ait Atta Expansion in Southeast Morocco'
Ernest Gellner and Charles Micaud, eds.
Arabs and Berbers: From Tribe to Nation in North Africa Lexington,
Mass.: D.C. Heath and Company, 1972 London: Gerald Duckworth
Publishers, 1972 pp. 85-107

Published in the United Kingdom and Continent of Europe by
Croom Helm Ltd
2-10 St John's Road, London SW11

ISBN 0 85664-453-6

Published in the United States of America and Canada by
The University of Wisconsin Press
Box 1379, Madison, Wisconsin 53701

ISBN 0-299-07360-2, LC 76-52597

First printing 1977

Printed in Great Britain
by Redwood Burn Ltd, Trowbridge and Esher

CONTENTS

MAPS

TABLES

A NOTE ON TRANSLITERATION

The transliteration method used in this book is designed to accommodate
the general reader more than the specialist, especially since a great many
names of places, tribes, and individuals are introduced. I have followed a
simplified version of standard English transliteration of Arabic terms.
Special diacritics have been eliminated with the exception of *hamza*,
indicated by an apostrophe, where it appears in the middle of a word; and
ع , indicated by '. The consonant *gaf* (چ or ڭ) of Moroccan usage is
indicated by 'g' and has a hard sound, as in 'girl'. With a few exceptions I
have avoided Arabic plurals and resorted to the device of adding '-s' to the
singular form. English transliteration is also used for names of tribes and
individuals (excepting 'Oufkir' rather than 'u Fakir'). I have rejected use
of French spellings of proper and tribal names because they are confusing
to non-French readers. Place names are spelled as they appear on standard
French maps of Morocco and Algeria. Pronunciation of words in
Moroccan or Algerian dialect differs in some cases from the transliterated
form. I have, though, used the written language as my model in almost all
cases.

Since most Berber names and terms appear in sections dealing with the
Ait 'Atta, I have adopted the phonetic spellings developed by David M.
Hart, who has done field work among this tribe. Again, however, I have
dropped most diacritics.

For those who may be interested the Glossary of Special Terms and
Tribal Names gives the full English transliteration of the Arabic or Berber.

ACKNOWLEDGEMENTS

This book is a revised and enlarged version of a doctoral dissertation submitted to the University of Wisconsin in 1968. I am grateful to a number
of institutions for supporting my research in Europe and Morocco. A
National Defense Foreign Language Fellowship financed the first year of
thesis research in 1966-7. Grants from the Program in Comparative World
History and the African Studies Program at Wisconsin permitted me to
extend my field trip an additional four months. A grant from San Diego
State University Foundation helped pay for a much needed return to
Morocco during the summer of 1969. While doing research on a separate
project in 1971-2 under a grant from the Social Science Research Council,
I was permitted time to make further revisions in the manuscript.

I would like to acknowledge my thanks to some of the individuals who
helped along the way. The staffs of numerous libraries and archives stood
ready and willing to guide my sometimes fumbling explorations through
catalogues and documents. I am especially indebted to the staffs of the
Service Historique de l'Armée in Vincennes, the Archives d'Outre-Mer in
Aix-en-Provence, and the Bibliothèque Générale in Rabat. In both 1967
and 1969 the government of Morocco gave me their authorization to do
field research in the provinces of Ksar-es-Souk and Oujda. A number of
provincial and local officials received me with great cordiality and did
much to facilitate my collection of oral data. I owe special thanks to my
informants, who were so willing to share their country's past, and usually
their table, with one so starved for knowledge. Qa'id Saddiqui Seddiq and
Chahid Bouaalem of Boudenib took an unusually enthusiastic interest in
my research on their Dawi Mani' ancestors and faithfully answered many
queries by mail after I had left.

Two professors at the University of Wisconsin advised me in the
preparation of the dissertation. Largely because of his excellent teaching
Stuart Schaar excited my interest in North Africa. He first suggested the
possibilities of the thesis topic and counselled me during the research.
Philip Curtin read the drafts of all the thesis chapters and during my years
in graduate school taught me most of whatever I may have learned about
writing. David Hart was largely responsible for introducing me to the cultural world of Morocco's mountains and deserts, and he has been consistently and extraordinarily generous in sharing his deep knowledge of
North African peoples. Ernest Gellner of the London School of Economics

and Political Science thoroughly critiqued the thesis soon after its completion, and he has inspired my protracted rewriting of it far more than he probably realizes. I am grateful to several other individuals for reading parts of the manuscript at one stage or another or for offering helpful ideas: Germain Ayache, Kenneth Brown, Dale Eickelman, Muhammad Gessous, Daniel Nordmann, Lawrence Rosen, David Seddon, Peter von Sivers, and John Waterbury, who have all shared their knowledge without, I think, getting nearly as much in return. This is especially true of Edmund Burke, whose critical judgement has never wavered under the weight of friendship. None of the individuals or institutions who helped in the preparation of this book bear any responsibility for my failure to listen or understand.

Marion Leitner typed the manuscript and did some scrupulous editing at no extra charge. Both the maps and the illustrations are the work of my wife Jeanne Dunn.

ABBREVIATIONS

Af. Fr.	*Bulletin du Comité de l'Afrique Française*
AGGA	Archives du Gouvernement Général de l'Algérie. Footnote references are listed by (1) series and carton number, (2) dossier title, (3) document title.
AMG	Archives du Ministère de la Guerre, Service Historique de l'Armée. Reference are listed by (1) series and carton number, (2) dossier title, (3) document title.
	Alg. Series A–B Algérie
	MM Mission Militaire
	Sit. pol. Situation politique et militaire
AN	Archives Nationales
BSGA	*Bulletin de la Société de Géographie d'Alger*
BSGAO	*Bulletin de la Société de Géographie et d'Archéologie d'Oran*
BSGP	*Bulletin de la Société de Géographie* (Paris)
CHEAM	Centre des Hautes Etudes sur l'Afrique et l'Asie Moderne
Doc. Dip.	*Documents Diplomatiques: Affaires du Maroc, 1901-1912*
FO	Foreign Office Political Correspondence
M & L	H.M.P. de la Martinière and N. Lacroix, *Documents pour servir à l'étude du Nord-Ouest africian,* 4 vols., Gouvernement Général de l'Algérie, Algiers, 1894-1897
Ren. Col.	*Renseignements Coloniaux*
ROMM	*Revue de l'Occident Musulman et de la Méditerranée*

INTRODUCTION

In the historical literature of the years leading to World War One the 'Moroccan Question' figures large in the evolution of Great Power rivalries. Historians preoccupied with the diplomatic issues have generally treated Morocco as one of the important 'factors' over which European ministers of state brooded, but not as one of the nations with a critical stake in the outcome of the struggle. A number of writers have described the fate of the sultan and his government in confronting colonial pressures, but the history of Morocco that emerges is hardly more than a chronicle of floundering reactions to European initiatives and incursions. In the early 1960s Jean-Louis Miège published *Le Maroc et l'Europe*, which drew upon a wealth of documentation to demonstrate for the first time that the population of Morocco, both urban and rural, was undergoing profound economic and social transformations during the nineteenth century. Following Miège's lead, other historians began to examine the Moroccan experience in the years before the Protectorate not as an adjunct to the great drama unfolding in Europe but as a case study of change in a non-Western society being buffeted by a host of external influences. These historians have set aside the generalities and stereotypes which characterized nineteenth-century Morocco as 'medieval' or 'anarchic' in order to examine the crisis of European power in terms of Morocco's own institutions and internal historical processes, both in the towns and among the rural tribes.

A crisis of European power was taking place in one form or another almost everywhere in Africa during the late nineteenth century. As in the Moroccan case historians have in recent years been examining the era of imperialism as an event primarily in African rather than European history, paying particular attention to the development of resistance movements and to the impact of European conquest on African social, political, and economic institutions.

The setting of this book is the southeastern region of Morocco, which France's Army of Africa, advancing from neighboring Algeria, conquered and occupied between 1881 and 1912. A number of writers have described this offensive, but invariably within the framework of European or Franco-Algerian history. Their interest has been in the development of the French African empire, problems of colonial warfare, or the evolution of diplomatic or legal issues relative to the demarcation of the Algero-

Moroccan border. This book does outline the origins, aims, and stages of French expansion into southeastern Morocco, but it is not essentially a study in European diplomatic or colonial history. Rather it examines the decades of French conquest as an episode in African history. The events described here, though taking place in a region admittedly off the beaten path of world history, make for a case study of African response to European conquest. This book, then, is primarily about political institutions in rural North Africa and how they functioned under the stress of European conquest and commercial penetration, about resistance movements and why they failed, and about continuity and change among a third world people during the early stages of the colonial era. It is secondarily about the tribes and oasis communities of southeastern Morocco and what they did when the French army marched in.

Southeastern Morocco constitutes no distinct geographical entity. It is defined for the purposes of this study in terms of the limits of French military activity from 1881 to 1912, that is, from the Mountains of the Ksour (western Saharan Atlas) and the Zousfana-Saoura River in the east to the Ziz River in the west (see Maps 1 and 9). Most of this region falls within the semiarid belt lying between the High Atlas and the Sahara Desert. It is a land of steppes and denuded mountains, broken up here and there by green oases. Its population, which may have numbered in the neighborhood of 200,000 in the late nineteenth century, engaged in either the herding of sheep or camels or the cultivation of date palms and certain grains and produce. Before the French occupation these people were divided politically into a number of tribes and oasis communities, some of them Arabic-speaking, others Berber. A few oases were large and densely populated, but in the nineteenth century there were no agglomerations that could be called cities in the sense Tangier, Rabat, or Marrakech were. The population was entirely rural, and with the exception of a comparatively few merchants, officials, and men of religion, everyone worked full time to produce food from the sun-drenched land.

The region's rural character and its distance from the great urban centers of Morocco or Algeria might suggest that before the twentieth century it was nothing more than a social and economic backwater on the outer periphery of North Africa. Two factors, however, opposed its isolation. First, two important routes in the trans-Saharan commercial system traversed the region, linking it with the wider world of both North and West Africa. One of these north-south routes passed through the oasis of Figuig, which before 1830 was a busy entrepôt on the desert fringe, serving caravans operating between the western portions of the Turkish Regency of Algiers and the Western and Central Sudan. In the years following France's occupation of Algeria Figuig declined as a trans-Saharan center, though it remained an important regional market place throughout the nineteenth century. Moreover, traders from the Southeast, while confining most of their trans-Atlas operations to Morocco, travelled to markets in French Algeria on occasion.

Much better known in African history than the Figuig route was the more westerly track passing through the oasis complex of Tafilalt and joining black Africa with the urban centers of both Morocco and Algeria. Prior to the nineteenth century Tafilalt's immense palm grove sheltered the city of Sijilmasa, one of the greatest and certainly the most famous northern emporium of the trans-Saharan trade. The flourishing days of Sijilmasa, when its name was closely associated with the West African gold and slave trade and consequently with the great political movements in North African history, extended from the ninth to the sixteenth century. Following the destruction of the Songhay Empire of West Africa in the 1590s, Sijilmasa gradually deteriorated, though it was not finally abandoned to ruin until the early nineteenth century. From then until the arrival of the French, Tafilalt continued to play a reduced but still significant part in the Saharan trade. More important, it served as the principle date basket for central Morocco, especially the imperial city of Fez. In short, the position of southeastern Morocco astride those two main lines of trade put its population in close touch with the currents of change in North African history, perhaps closer than groups living in mountainous areas much nearer but less accessible to the cities.

The second factor opposing the Southeast's isolation was the strong political bond between Tafilalt and the centers of dynastic power in Morocco. Since the ninth century the control of Sijilmasa and its commercial revenue was crucial to any group wishing to seize and retain the rulership of Morocco. Thus, the tribes and communities of Tafilalt and a wide surrounding area were frequently enmeshed in dynastic politics, sometimes supporting the incumbent sultan, sometimes making common cause with pretenders and rebels. In the 1630s Tafilalt was thrust into an even more prominent position when one of its native sons, Mawlay 'Ali Sharif, launched a new dynastic movement for which he claimed legitimacy by his status as a *sharif* (plural *shurfa*), or descendant of the Prophet Muhammad. The 'Alawi family, as Mawlay 'Ali Sharif's lineage became known, successfully supplanted the crumbling Sa'adian dynasty and established its power in the cities north of the Atlas. Yet Tafilalt remained the ideological headquarters of the new dynasty and the homeland of the 'Alawi *shurfa*, the kinsmen of the sultan. It also continued to be a breeding ground for court intrigue and conspiracy. Though the legitimacy of the 'Alawis was generally accepted in Morocco, no rule of primogeniture governed the succession. Consequently, members of the *shurfa* lineage, many of whom lived in Tafilalt, frequently vied with one another for the positions of strength necessary to depose a weak sultan or to assure themselves of the succession. A sultan's death invariably unleashed a factional struggle in which the populations of the Tafilalt area were likely to become involved. Thus, from the seventeenth to the twentieth century the political dispositions of the tribes and communities of the Southeast were of constant concern to the sultan as well as to other power elements in the country. Conversely, political crises generated in central Morocco and the imperial cities quickly reverberated in the Southeast.

Over the centuries, then, commercial and political interchange between central Morocco and the Saharan periphery was regular and often intense, and it produced broad, enduring relationships between groups and individuals on both sides of the Atlas. Nevertheless, the people of the Southeast existed most of the time beyond the sultan's sphere of political and fiscal control. They, like the inhabitants of other desert regions or of the mountains, accepted the sultan as sovereign of the Muslim community, but they avoided paying taxes, submitting to central administrators, or contributing conscripts to the royal army unless coerced into doing so. Two of the 'Alawi rulers, Mawlay Isma'il (1673-1727) and Mawlay Hasan (1873-1894) undertook energetic centralizing campaigns to bring mountainous or fringe areas under their authority. But these centralizing efforts had only transitory effects in the Southeast. Until the establishment of the French Protectorate the population remained a congeries of tribes and oasis villages, independent of over-arching government and, for the most part, of one another.

These two central facts, autonomy but not isolation, characterized the condition of the Southeast on the eve of the French conquest. From these facts derive the two principle themes of this book. The first is the interaction between the inhabitants of the region and of Morocco as a whole, including the central government (*makhzan*), during three decades of crisis brought on by European military, economic, and political pressures. Some French writers of the colonial period have suggested that the government and the population of the country north of the Atlas were indifferent to and largely ignorant of the events of colonial conquest on the Saharan periphery and that, conversely, the economic and political crisis affecting central and coastal Morocco had few reverberations in the far south. A major aim of this book is to show that on the contrary communication and political exchange across the Atlas was notably intense during the conquest period and that European provocations and pressures, no matter where they occurred, often rippled from one end of Morocco to another. It is true that these pressures exposed the profound weaknesses and inadequacies of the government to provide effective leadership and administration. But they also threw into relief the complex institutions and relationships which melded all Moroccans into a social and economic organism. In the past scholars of pre-Protectorate Morocco have laid great stress on the problem of determining the nature, extent, and limits of the Moroccan state from the standpoint of Western definitions. This book emphasizes the political interplay, whatever its form, between the sultan and his far-flung subjects, as well as the social and economic factors which encouraged the intertwining of groups and individuals across natural and ethnic frontiers.

The second major theme centers on the autonomous and politically fragmented people of the Southeast and their confrontation with the French army. Notwithstanding the various influences of the *makhzan* on the tribes and villages of the region, they could not look to it for significant military aid or political direction when facing the French. In large measure they were obliged to deal with the European challenge much as did populations in other parts of Africa which did not possess central institutions or ethnic homogeneity. Southeastern Morocco, a distinct theatre of colonial conquest, offers a distinct case study of response by a diverse, multitribal population.

Studies of African response elsewhere on the continent have generally stressed problems centering on resistance or revolt. While this book deals extensively with resistance, it argues that the population of southeastern Morocco cannot be categorized as either resisters or collaborators. Rather trade, negotiation, and collaboration went on simultaneously with resistance, adding up to a collective response over three decades that was multifarious, fluctuating, and inconsistent. This diversity of response will be explored and explained with two central facts in mind. First, political, social, and economic institutions, as well as historical experience, varied considerably from one tribe or oasis community to another. The population's complex response to the colonial challenge, therefore, related not only to French or *makhzan* actions but also to the separate, overlapping, and sometimes conflicting interests of numerous groups within the region. Second, the extreme uncertainty of economic life in the pre-Sahara obliged every individual to put the defense of economic resources ahead of loyalty to standing political or social ties. Both before and after the arrival of the French the collective political actions of tribal or *qsar*-dwelling groups were in large measure contingent upon economic considerations. The economic effects of the colonial conquest upon the population were

great, but they were also highly ambiguous. This ambiguity encouraged
individuals and cooperating groups to protect, and if possible enlarge their
local resources in water, land, crops, or herds by maintaining the greatest
possible flexibility in their political relations and by entering into large-
scale alliances or movements with only the most tentative of commitments. In his study of the multitribal Maji Maji revolt against the Germans
in Tanganyika, John Iliffe states:

> A division of African reactions into negative resistance and prudent
> collaboration is no longer adequate, and many responses can instead
> be explained as rational calculations of interest and probable conse-
> quence.
> . . . a very complex pattern emerges, a pattern of local initiatives and
> local bargains, an interplay between European and African aims in
> which colonial policy as an isolate formulated by governor or colonial
> office, is only one among a number of variables.[1]

So it was in southeastern Morocco, where diverse, conflicting, and critical
local interests, together with the policies and actions of the French and of
the Moroccan government, gave the crisis of conquest its kaleidoscopic,
multicentered character.

The book is in two parts. Part One presents a description of political,
social, and economic life in southeastern Morocco in the later nineteenth
century. As a study in the history of rural North Africa this book aims to
put the tribes and communities of the Southeast, rather than the French
army or the Moroccan government, on center stage. This approach represents a departure from much of the historical writing on Morocco, which
concentrates predominantly on either colonial enterprises or the ideas and
actions of the urban-based élite and which pushes the patterns of dynamic
change in the countryside into a blurry background. The principle aim of
Part One is to establish clearly and concretely both the distinct identities
and the interrelations of the major groups of the region by presenting in
some detail the diversity and complexity of their institutions and histories.
Only in this way can the stage be set for demonstrating the variety, fluidity,
and inconsistency of their response to *makhzan* initiatives and to the French
conquest. Chapter 1 is an introduction to the geography and people of the
region and to the pattern of *makhzan* influence in its affairs. Chapters 2
and 3 present more detailed ethnographic profiles of five communities of
the Southeast which played preeminent roles in the events of 1881 to 1912.
Two of them are transhumant pastoral tribes whose grazing lands cover
much of the region. The other three are important oasis communities.

Chapter 4 discusses the commercial network which linked the tribes and oasis-dwellers of the region to one another and to the world beyond the pre-Sahara.

The chapters of Part Two are divided into four time periods, each one corresponding to a distinct phase of evolving crisis in southeastern Morocco. The four chapters span the period from 1881 to 1912 because these two dates mark important turning points in relations between the people of the Southeast and the French. The insurrection of Abu 'Amama (Bou Amama) in western Algeria in 1881 triggered the initial French military penetration into southern Oranie (as the French termed the territory south of Oran province). The army advanced gradually southward and westward into Moroccan territory during the following thirty-one years. The declaration of the Protectorate in 1912 opened a new era for all of Morocco. That year also marked the beginning of a period of colonial consolidation in the Southeast as well as a hiatus of several years in significant military expansion in the pre-Saharan region.

The period of this study coincides with three critical decades of European conquest and popular response throughout the African continent. Chapter 9 will therefore advance some general observations about the nature of response and change during the initial phase of Africa's colonial experience in the light of the Moroccan case.

Morocco's Road to Colonialism: Key Events, 1873-1912[2]

The conquest of the Southeast was played out against a backdrop of deepening crisis and accelerating transformation throughout the entire country. During the course of the nineteenth century, European industrial expansion carried southward across the Mediterranean in the form of greatly increased trade with the independent countries of North Africa. The rulers of Morocco, as well as of Tunisia and Egypt, were ill-prepared to manage the internal economic and fiscal effects of this trade and to resist European pressures for special commercial and political privileges. In the 1850s and 1860s the Moroccan government signed trade agreements with Britain, Spain, and France which effectively deprived it of jurisdiction over its own customs administration and over Europeans residing in the country, as well as their Moroccan *protégés*. A brief war with Spain in 1859-60, in which Spanish forces occupied the city of Tetouan, exposed Morocco's grave military weakness and left the *makhzan* saddled with an enormous war indemnity. When Algerian army units began pressing against the southeastern frontier in 1881, Morocco's sovereignty was already in doubt owing to the proliferation of European influence in the ports and the coastal hinterlands. During the last two decades of the century, the

growth of external trade became more and more a one-sided affair with
Moroccan exports declining and European goods pouring into the country.
The result was perpetual monetary crisis, rampant inflation, deterioration
of craft industries, and exacerbation of poverty in the countryside. The
only Moroccans to benefit from these economic traumas were members of
the palace èlite and a small but growing class of professional merchants,
who thrived on speculations and on contacts with European commercial
interests.

Sultan Mawlay Hasan, who ascended the throne in 1873, attempted to
strengthen the state against European pressures by introducing a number
of reforms modelled on European ideas and technology. Like certain other
African rulers of the nineteenth century, he believed that a cautious policy
of defensive westernization would encourage the powers to protect his
sovereignty or even allow him to regain a measure of control over the
forces of change. His program centered on reform of the monetary system,
the army, and the administrative apparatus, since no recovery was possible
without a stabilized currency and an efficient tax-gathering system.
Throughout his reign he moved incessantly from one region to another,
collecting taxes and tribute, suppressing rebellions, and strengthening ties
with local leaders. In the face of French Algerian expansionism he revitalized relations between the *makhzan* and the tribes and villages of the
eastern and Saharan frontier lands and in 1893 led a massive army expedition to Tafilalt. On the international level he became aware of Morocco's
strategic importance in Euro-Mediterranean diplomacy, especially after
1869 when the Suez Canal was opened. At first, he appealed to Great
Britain to guarantee his independence and support his reforms. Failing in
that effort, he attempted to balance out the influence of all the major
powers by refusing to favor one more than another.

The reform program cost the state treasury a great deal but in the end
bore little fruit. Most of the country's religious and political leadership
opposed the innovations as infringements of Muslim tradition and law.
More important, none of the European powers was willing to condone any
changes in the economic sector which might reduce the privileges they had
already gained. France was distinctly uncooperative, knowing that her
eventual creation of an empire spanning North Africa would depend upon
the enduring weakness and vulnerability of the *makhzan*. After the occupation of Tunisia in 1881 French expansionists became increasingly
impatient to complete the empire by adding Morocco.

Mawlay Hasan died suddenly in 1894 while pursuing his centralizing
campaign in the Marrakech region. The succession of his fourteen year old
son, Mawlay 'Abd al-'Aziz, could have unleashed a severe dynastic struggle

among members of the royal family. However, Ba Ahmad ibn Musa, one of Mawlay Hasan's ministers (*vizirs*), extinguished opposition before it had time to coalesce. Establishing his power center in Marrakech, Ba Ahmad governed the country as regent for six years. He was an able politician and attempted to continue the policies of Mawlay Hasan, but he was obliged to concentrate most of his efforts on holding the administrative apparatus together and checking tribal rebellions.

Mawlay 'Abd al-'Aziz took over the reins of government in 1900. In character and ability he was a kind of distorted image of his father, intelligent and disposed to innovation and reform, yet regrettably lacking in persistence, energy, and will. Mawlay Hasan himself had failed to stem the tide of European penetration; 'Abd al-'Aziz was utterly engulfed by it. Instead of selectively employing Western technology to strengthen the state, he displayed a frivolous fascination for it, surrounding himself with oddities and gadgets of the machine age, which an unending line of European salesmen eagerly introduced to the court. In contrast to his father, he asserted little control over his ministers and officials, who engaged incessantly in factional intrigues, graft, and private speculations that incensed the population and eroded the state treasury. At the same time the sultan came increasingly under the influence of a coterie of European advisors, most of them British adventurers.

France's gift to the new sultan was the seizure of Touat, the vast oasis complex in the north central Sahara. This action, which began in December, 1899, marked the first major incursion by a Christian power onto territory commonly recognized as within the 'Alawi domain. The ease with which the French army secured the submission of Touat revealed Morocco's military and diplomatic impotence as nothing had done since the war with Spain in 1859-60. The event prompted a strong reaction throughout the country. 'Abd al-'Aziz made a protest to the European powers, but none of them considered the issue diplomatically important enough to risk a confrontation with France.

Jolted temporarily by the Touat crisis, 'Abd al-'Aziz launched a reform plan of his own in 1901 with the aid and encouragement of Great Britain. The crux of the program was the creation of a uniform, universal tax, the *tartib*. All koranic taxes were to be abolished and replaced by a single levy on agriculture. The new tax was to be extended to all, including the political and religious elites, who were traditionally exempt. The idea may have been a modern one, but it was not grounded in Moroccan realities. Those who might have benefited from the change condemned it as an abrogation of Muslim law, while the privileged groups attacked it as an infringement of their rights. The old revenue system was abolished, the new one was still-born. Consequently, the *makhzan* collected almost no revenue at all for a period of two years.

The debacle of the reform, together with growing economic distress and the blatant manifestation of European influence at court, left 'Abd al-'Aziz with a rapidly shrinking base of popular support. In the fall of 1902 a major revolt broke out in the Northeast under the leadership of Jilali al-Zarhuni, better known as Abu Himara. At first posing as Mawlay Muhammad, the sultan's older brother, Abu Himara rallied enough support among the tribes to threaten an offensive against Fez. The *makhzan* army managed to contain the revolt during the course of 1903, but Abu Himara held large areas of the Northeast in submission for seven years. Until 1909 he represented to the European powers, especially France, the most obvious symbol of the *makhzan*'s ineffectualness in preserving law and order.

The revolt also had the effect of discouraging the British government from further misguided tutorship of Moroccan reform. In return for recognition of her special rights in Egypt, Britain was willing to concede the Moroccan field to France. The *entente cordiale* of April, 1904, which formalized this arrangement, put France in a much stronger diplomatic position for a final assault on the remaining shreds of Moroccan sovereignty. In October she worked out an additional agreement with Spain, which recognized a Spanish sphere of influence in rural northern Morocco but which reaffirmed French preeminence everywhere else. The same month she began to draw up a new reform proposal which called for what amounted to a virtual protectorate over the *makhzan*.

In the later nineteenth century the rulers of Tunisia and Egypt passed the point of no-return on the road to colonialism by contracting large debts with European financial interests. In 1901 'Abd al-'Aziz followed suit by borrowing 7,500,000 francs from a group of French banks. Other loans inexorably followed, notably one in 1904 for 62,000,000 francs which conceded to France the right to put its own officials in Moroccan ports to collect 60 percent of the customs receipts.

The *entente cordiale*, the loans, and the seeming catalepsy of 'Abd al-'Aziz in the face of the crisis produced an upsurge of anti-European protest, first in the cities, then in the countryside. Europeans were assaulted and in some instances killed, a mass force of four to five thousand Moroccans attacked the French garrison at Taghit in the Southeast, the religious scholars (*'ulama*) of Fez called for the replacement of European advisors by Muslim Turkish ones, and opposition elements began to make overtures to Germany to protect the country from France.

Germany at first reacted moderately to the *entente cordiale* but soon came to the conclusion that France was planning to isolate her diplomatically and to ignore her economic and commercial interests in Morocco, which had been growing steadily during the previous three decades. In March, 1905, Kaiser Wilhelm visited Tangier in a dramatic demonstration of support for Morocco's independence and for the continuation of free trade. In May the *makhzan*, now greatly encouraged by the German intervention, formally rejected France's reform plan. On the broad diplomatic front, Germany aimed to reassert her influence among the powers, humiliate the anti-German government of Théophile Delcassé, and drive a wedge between France and Great Britain by bringing the question of Moroccan sovereignty into the open. The threat of a severe confrontation with Germany convinced France to agree to Berlin's proposal for an international meeting to work out Morocco's future status. Germany, however, greatly overestimated the willingness of the other powers to support her in restraining France. Consequently, the Conference of Algeciras, which sat from January to April, 1906, produced an agreement leaving France in a preponderant position in Morocco. The Act of Algeciras created a Franco-Spanish police force, a Moroccan state bank financed by the powers and dominated by France, and a number of other institutions which effectively terminated the *makhzan*'s control over internal security and economic policy. Because of popular pressure, 'Abd al-'Aziz delayed for several months before signing the Act. But with German support gone, the anti-French forces in the *makhzan* could no longer bring much influence to bear on the sultan.

Shielded by the Act, France discarded her policy of 'peaceful penetration' in favor of a series of military interventions ostensibly launched to protect the Algerian frontier or French citizens residing in Morocco. In the Southeast the army occupied the oasis of Béchar in 1903, then in a succession of 'police actions' pushed gradually westward in the direction of Tafilalt. In March, 1907, following the murder of a French physician in Marrakech, troops marched across the Algerian border and summarily occupied the city of Oujda. In July an expeditionary force landed at Casablanca after Moroccans killed a number of European construction workers. These two towns subsequently served as beachheads for military penetration into the Bani Znasan territory in the Northeast and into the Atlantic hinterland known as the Chaouia (Shawiya). To Moroccans these actions must have appeared as an invasion of the country from three different directions.

By signing the Act of Algeciras 'Abd al-'Aziz wrote off whatever support remained to him outside of his palace coterie. By 1907 opposition elements were calling upon Mawlay 'Abd al-Hafid, the sultan's brother and governor (*khalifa*) of Marrakech, to lead a popular rebellion. 'Abd al-Hafid's most powerful supporters were the Berber chieftains, notably Madani al-Glawi, who had autarkic control over the central and western High Atlas. The landing of French troops at Casablanca signalled the start of the revolt. On August 16 'Abd al-Hafid had himself proclaimed sultan by the *'ulama* of Marrakech and immediately declared a *jihad*, or holy war, against the French. In September 'Abd al-'Aziz left Fez for Rabat, fearing for his own safety. The following January the *'ulama* of Fez declared for 'Abd al-Hafid on condition that he would repudiate the Act of Algeciras, drive the French and Spanish (who controlled enclaves in the north) from the country, and put an end to special privileges for foreigners.

The dynastic struggle between the two brothers lasted until August, 1908, when 'Abd al-'Aziz was deserted by his remaining troops and forced to abdicate. 'Abd al-Hafid managed to generate a great deal of popular support for his pretendership by taking an intransigent stand against European penetration and supporting armed resistance. The Chaouia tribes rose against the French expeditionary force and in the Southeast a pan-tribal throng attacked French units on two occasions in 1908. The fighting of 1907-8 represented at the same time a civil conflict and a movement of countrywide resistance against European military incursions.

The Hafidiya, as the new régime was called, got off to a promising start. Besides defeating his brother, 'Abd al-Hafid captured Abu Himara, the pretender of the Northeast, formed a new *makhzan* in coalition with the High Atlas chiefs, and began to reassert government authority in the hinterlands of the major cities. Unfortunately, he also inherited all the financial, military, and diplomatic handicaps of his brother's government. The French army was still expanding in the Southeast, the Chaouia, and the territory west of Oujda. In 1909 the Spanish began advancing into Moroccan territory from their enclaves at Melilla and Ceuta. Moreover, the forces of economic and social change introduced from Europe in the nineteenth century had long since run out of control. 'Abd al-Hafid ultimately had no choice but to follow in his brother's footsteps by asking the powers for recognition and by contracting a new loan to reconstruct the administration and army. The price of European cooperation was his compliance with the Act of Algeciras, recognition of the *makhzan's* international debts, and acceptance of temporary French or Spanish occupation of Moroccan territory. When the sultan agreed to these conditions in agreements with France and Spain in 1910, his popular support rapidly dwindled. Furthermore, the heady months of *jihad* had muffled the deep-seated tensions existing between the government and the tribes. When 'Abd al-Hafid began collecting taxes more efficiently and more ruthlessly than his brother had done, these tensions quickly surfaced.

The Hafidiya moved into its final act early in 1911 when the tribes around Fez, reacting to the exactions of *makhzan* tax collectors and to an ill-conceived program of military reform, rose up and beseiged the city. In April Mawlay Zayn al-Abadin, another brother of the sultan, was proclaimed sultan in Meknes with the support of the neighboring tribes. By this time the French were diplomatically disposed to take matters into their own hands. In May an expeditionary force marched from the Atlantic coast to Fez with the official aim of supporting the sultan and protecting European residents. In June another column fought its way to Meknes and forced Zayn al-Abadin to surrender. In September lines of communication were secured between Fez, Meknes, and Rabat. With the conquest of central Morocco already well underway 'Abd al-Hafid signed the Treaty of Fez in March, 1912, turning the *makhzan* over to France. In August he abdicated and left the country, following his brother into oblivion.

It took the French army, now under the command of General Lyautey, the first Resident-General of the Protectorate, most of the remaining months of 1912 to stabilize its position in Morocco. In May, following a mutiny of Moroccan military units in Fez, the tribes in the area rose up and invested the city a second time. The army suppressed this rebellion only by conquering and occupying a wide area around Fez. In the south the situation was even more fluid owing to the resistance activities of Mawlay Ahmad al-Hiba, a son of the deceased Saharan resistance leader Shaykh Ma al-'Aynayn. In the spring of 1912 al-Hiba had himself proclaimed rightful sultan and launched a *jihad* in the Sous region south of the western High Atlas. He then marched on Marrakech, accumulating a mass following as he advanced over the mountains. He managed to control the city and its hinterland for about a month in the late summer. On September 6, however, a French column moving south from Casablanca defeated the mass force he sent out to meet it. Al-Hiba immediately retreated to the Sous, leaving Marrakech to the Protectorate.

Having achieved control of the four imperial cities — Rabat, Fez, Meknes, and Marrakech — the new French administration was ready to proceed to reconstitute and reorganize the *makhzan*, which thenceforth would serve as the legal though largely substanceless executor of colonial directives. In a sense General Lyautey set out to carry on the work of Mawlay Hasan, subduing independent tribes, reforming the administration and army, and introducing the modern ideas and technology of the West.

This brief overview has merely capsulized the major milestones in

Morocco's progress toward colonial submission. The weave of history during these critical decades is much tighter and more intricate than a chronology of diplomatic and political events can reveal. This book aims to examine more closely the complexities of the political, military, and economic crisis in the southeastern region.

Notes

1. John Iliffe, *Tanganyika under German Rule, 1905-1912* (Cambridge, 1969), pp. 6, 7.
2. For this section I have drawn heavily on Edmund Burke's doctoral dissertation, 'Moroccan Political Responses to French Penetration, 1900-1912' (Princeton University, 1970), and on a subsequently revised and enlarged version of the manuscript now published as *Prelude to Protectorate in Morocco: Precolonial Protest and Resistance, 1860-1912* (Chicago, 1976). This work, which deals largely with central Morocco and with the *makhzan*, is the first to present a detailed reconstruction and analysis of internal history during the critical years before the Protectorate. Other general works which treat all or part of the 1878-1912 period are: Jamil M. Abun-Nasr, *A History of the Maghrib* (Cambridge, 1971); Jean Brignon *et al.*, *Histoire du Maroc* (Paris, 1967); Pierre Guillen, *L'Allemagne et le Maroc de 1870 à 1905* (Paris, 1967); Jean-Louis Miège, *Le Maroc et l'Europe* (Paris, 1961-1963), vols. 3 and 4; Henri Terrasse, *Histoire du Maroc* (Casablanca, 1950), vol. 2.

PART I THE SOUTHEAST ON THE EVE OF THE FRENCH CONQUEST

1 THE PEOPLE OF THE DESERT FRINGE

The Three Rivers

The Algero-Moroccan frontier region which the French army conquered between 1881 and 1912 is a deprived, desolate land of crags and barren steppes, its aridness symbolized by the great funnels of dust which hot winds push aimlessly back and forth across the desert. The severity of the landscape is modified only in the vicinity of a few wadis, or irregularly flowing rivers, where greener vegetation can survive. The Ziz, the Guir, and the Zousfana, which are born on the slopes of Atlas peaks and flow southward into the desert, are the three longest and agriculturally most important of these rivers. They bisect the narrow belt of territory that forms the climatic transition between mountain and desert waste and is usually referred to as 'pre-Saharan.' The Ziz and the Zousfana generally delineate the western and eastern limits of the frontier zone. The three rivers, lying approximately parallel to each other, provide good reference points for a geographical overview of the region. A traveler who descends each of them in turn would be able to glimpse most of the major topographical features of the region.

The Wad Ziz has its source in the eastern High Atlas south of the Jebel Ayachi range. It flows eastward to a point near the town of Rich, then turns southward away from the mountains. Just north of Ksar-es-Souk, a present-day provincial capital, the river empties onto the vast pre-Saharan steppe, where weaker streams vanish not far from the base of the mountains. Continuing southward, it cuts a deep gorge into the land. About forty miles from Ksar-es-Souk the gorge levels out, and the river enters a broad alluvial plain called Tafilalt.[1] Hundreds of thousands of palm trees covering an area approximately thirteen miles long and nine miles wide blanket this densely populated region. In the nineteenth century the Ziz usually flowed as far as Tafilalt even during the summer, albeit at a reduced level. In flood season it might flow further south into the desert, sometimes reaching the lonely oasis of Taouz, an important watering place twenty-five miles from the edge of Tafilalt. The Wad Gheris, which issues from the Atlas west of Ksar-es-Souk, also flows through Tafilalt, paralleling the Ziz on the west.

The Wad Guir also starts in the High Atlas, but further to the east, where the mountains begin to taper off and become fragmented. Here the range splits into two major sections, one of them thrusting northeastward but soon dissipating in the Dahra, the high plains of eastern Morocco. The other branch extends due eastward and almost links up with the Saharan Atlas chain of Algeria. The river issues from the mountain country onto the steppe just south of the oasis of Tazzouguert, then it turns westward, passing by the oasis of Boudenib and a few smaller population centers. Resuming its southward course, it passes through a totally unpopulated region dominated by treeless steep-sided buttes. Near the village of Abadla it fans out in numerous channels over an alluvial plain where the Dawi Mani' Arabs congregate to plant and harvest grain. South of the plain the river narrows into a single channel again and continues to a rendezvous with the Wad Zousfana at Igli. Since the mountains near the source of the Guir are lower in elevation than those further west, the volume of water and frequency of flow is less in this wadi than in the Ziz. Still, the gorges and rocky shelves of the upper Guir channel the water well enough to send it as far south as the plain of Abadla on the average of eighty-two days out of the year.[2]

Between the lower courses of the Guir and the Ziz stretches the Hammada of the Guir, a broad plateau. Steep escarpments border the Hammada on the east and west, making access to it extremely difficult in many places.

The Wad Zousfana, the third major artery, is fed by rains falling in the western end of the Mountains of the Ksour, the largest, driest, and western-most chain of the Saharan Atlas. Its peaks tend to be extremely fragmented and to run parallel to one another, giving the appearance of isolated masses rising out of a continuous plain. The Jebel Beni Smir, the Jebel Grouz, and the Jebel Maïs are the most important masses on the western side, the peaks of the Beni Smir going above 6,500 feet. The only major population center in this region is the oasis of Figuig, which is nestled in a depression just west of the upper course of the Zousfana.

Except when rain is especially heavy in the mountains, the river does not flow above ground south of Figuig until it reaches the vicinity of Taghit. This oasis is the principal one in a district of small settlements known collectively as the Beni Goumi. The water surfaces here for about nine miles, then descends again, giving evidence of a continuously flowing subterranean bed along the entire length of the Zousfana valley.

The Jebel Béchar and other minor mountain chains flank the Zousfana on the west, screening it from the Guir valley. The principal route of communication between the Zousfana and the Guir goes through a narrow pass between the northern tip of the Jebel Béchar and a lesser massif, the Jebel Antar. To the east of the Zousfana lies the great Erg Occidental, a land of massive sand dunes extending all the way to the Mzab in south

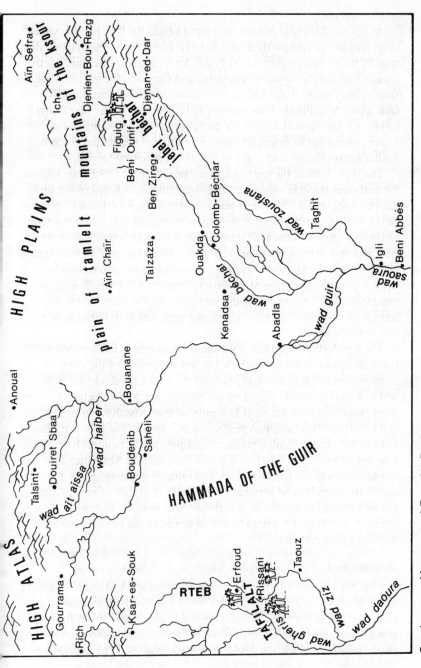

Southeastern Morocco and Frontier Region

central Algeria.

At Igli the Zousfana and the Guir join to form the Wad Saoura, which continues in a southeasterly direction to Gourara, the northern most district of the great oasis complex of Touat. About thirty settlements line the eastern bank of the Saoura between Igli and Gourara. These oases survive from ground water in the Saoura bed, numerous springs, and floods on the Guir which periodically flow south of Igli.[3] The narrow corridor of habitation and palm groves formed by the valleys of the Zousfana and the Saoura was a kind of desert lifeline connecting the population centers of northwestern Algeria with those of Touat in the central Sahara.

The High Atlas in the west and, to a lesser degree, the Saharan Atlas in the east once stood as barriers to easy communication between the pre-Saharan zone and the Mediterranean world. The plain of Tamlelt, however, lies between the extremities of these two chains and offers an open door to the high plains. These plains, usually though inaccurately called the High Plateaus, stretch from the Atlas to the Moroccan and Algerian coastal belt. The present Algero-Moroccan frontier bisects the plains, which extend across both eastern Morocco and Oran Province. Small wadis in this region flow only at infrequent intervals, and the only permanent sources of water are the open springs and wells which serve the local camel and sheep herders.[4]

The simplest criterion for determining the northern limits of the Sahara is the change in volume of rainfall. By this measure all of the Ziz-Guir-Zousfana region, with the exceptions of the mountain elevations, falls within a zone of aridity that does not become much more extreme as one moves south into the desert. A line running approximately through Figuig and Boudenib delineates two rainfall zones. North of the line, including most of the Moroccan high plains, annual precipitation ranges between four and eight inches. South of the line, including the northern Sahara, yearly rainfall is less than four inches. Rainfall is not only sparse, but evaporation tends to be very rapid. Moreover, the range of precipitation can be extremely variable, so that the amount of water flowing in the riverbeds or filling the springs from one season to the next can never be predicted with certainty.[5]

Tent-dwellers

The harsh environment of southeastern Morocco was still not so arid as to preclude human adaptation to it. Indeed, during the later nineteenth century, in the neighborhood of two hundred to two hundred and fifty thousand people inhabited the region, surviving, and in good years thriving, on the resources which the sparse rains made available. The population practiced both agricultural and pastoral economies, sometimes a combination of both. Agriculture depended entirely on irrigation. Therefore, it was limited to the banks of wadis, to alluvial plains, or to the vicinity of springs, where the water flowed continually or at frequent intervals either above or below ground. In short, only a very small percentage of the total land surface of the region was arable.

Most of the energy of the sedentary populations was devoted to the cultivation of date palms, which thrived in the intense heat as long as irrigation water was sufficient. In the upper reaches of the Ziz and the Guir the inhabitants grew olives, walnuts, and other products of a mountain climate. The date palm was king southward from a line running approximately through Ksar-es-Souk and Figuig.[6] The notable exception to this rule was the Guir valley south of Saheli and including the Abadla plain, where dates could not mature because of the saline quality of the water and its insufficiency during the summer.[7] In addition to dates, which was the chief dietary staple, the oases produced barley, corn, wheat, alfalfa (for feeding animals), and various fruits and vegetables. The dates matured in the fall, and grain was harvested in the spring.

Rainfall on the great stretches of steppe country produced enough pasturage to support herds of sheep, goats, and camels. These stock, which provided meat, milk, wool, and hides, fed on esparto grass and artemisia, which was the dominant vegetation of the steppe, as well as on certain grasses which sprang up in particular areas after rainfall.[8] Pastoralism was transhumant rather than truly nomadic. That is, flocks and herds made two basic seasonal moves each year. They did not circulate continuously over a vast area as did, for example, the Regibat or Sha'amba camel nomads of the Sahara. The seasonal displacements corresponded, of course, to the changing availability of pasture and water. The general pattern was to move either northward or to higher altitude in the summer and southward or to lower altitude in the winter. The transhumant population did not, however, base its economy exclusively on livestock. Some groups owned grain fields and palm groves as well. In fact, the need to be in a particular location for planting or harvest in some cases determined seasonal transhumance patterns. A few groups lived in houses rather than in tents part of the year and maintained groves and gardens around these dwellings.

Though it is important to keep in mind that pastoralism and agriculture were not mutually exclusive occupations, the contrast in style of living between the tent-dwelling and the sedentary population is clear enough to permit a division of the society on this basis in discussing the fundamental elements of social organization.

In looking at the ethnographic map of the Ziz-Guir-Zousfana region,
one notices a rather abrupt frontier between the territory of Berber-
speaking and Arabophone pastoral populations. The Berber heartland of
central and southern Morocco extends eastward as far as the extremity of
the High Atlas and the Hammada of the Guir. The major tribes of the
Berber borderlands were the Ait Seghrushin, the Ait Izdig, and the Ait
'Atta. The first language of all these tribes was Tamazight, one of
Morocco's three Berber tongues. For political or commercial reasons some
men spoke Arabic as well.[9]

Arabophone tribes dominated the high plains of eastern Morocco, the
lower Guir valley, and the Zousfana-Saoura corridor. Eastward of the
frontier zone Arabic was spoken all the way across central Algeria and the
northern Sahara. The major tribes in the zone were the Bani Gil and
Awlad al-Nasir on the high plains, the Dawi Mani' and the Awlad Jarir in
the lower Guir and Zousfana regions, and three small groups in the Mountains of the Ksour.

In terms of size, territorial spread, and economic activity these transhumant groups exhibited a considerable range of diversity. The sketch map
(Map 2) indicates the general location of each of them. The map and the
introductory description of these tribes refers in time to the late nineteenth century, that is, immediately prior to the French conquest.

Ait 'Atta

This tribe may have numbered more than 50,000 people in the nineteenth
century, making it one of the largest in Morocco. Its territory included the
entire pre-Saharan belt and parts of the southern High Atlas from the
Hammada of the Guir in the east to the Dra valley in the west. The Ait
Khabbash and the Ait Umnasf, two major subtribes of the Ait 'Atta,
dominated the pasture lands surrounding the lower Ziz valley.

Ait Izdig

Their territory stretched from the Tizi-n-Telrhemt pass in the High Atlas
all the way south to the Rteb. They therefore controlled more than one
hundred miles of the great caravan route from Fez to Tafilalt. Other sections of the tribe inhabited the upper Guir region. By 1900 the Ait Izdig
were on the way to complete sedentarization, although part of the tribe
continued to live in tents and make short seasonal moves around the upper
Guir and the Ziz valleys. The sedentary groups inhabited villages along
these two rivers and cultivated mainly olive trees or date palms, depending
on the latitude.[10]

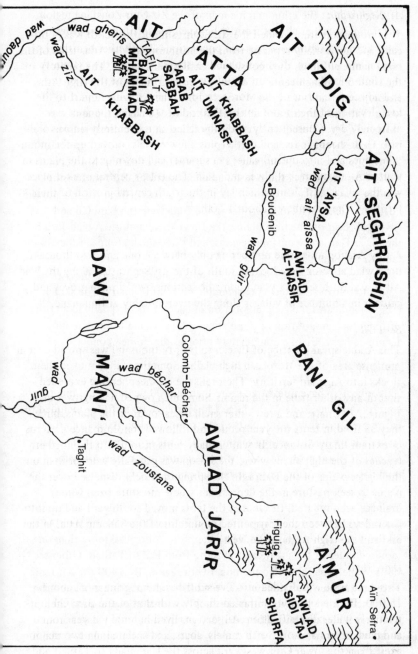

Tribes of Southeastern Morocco and Frontier Region

Ait Seghrushin

This group, sometimes called the Ait Seghrushin of the South was politically and territorially separate from the northern, Middle Atlas tribe of the
same name, although they considered each other cousins. The territory of
the southern branch centered on the far eastern ridges of the High Atlas
and adjacent sections of the Moroccan high plains. Owing in part to the
low elevation of the mountains on this end of the chain, the area was
extremely dry. Consequently, the tribe relied almost entirely on pastoralism. Their sheep, goats, and cattle (plus a few camels) moved up the mountain slopes and into upland valleys in summer and down onto the plains in
winter. A few cultivated olives and grain. The tribe's central market place
was the village of Talsint, which lay in the south central portion of their
territory. They numbered about 12,000.[11]

Awlad al-Nasir

A tiny Arabophone tribe numbering only between one and two thousand,
the Awlad al-Nasir were located south of the Ait Seghrushin along the Wad
Ait Aïssa. Both sedentary and nomadic sections owned palm groves and
gardens in a number of villages along the river, notably at Bouanane.[12]

Bani Gil

This Arabic-speaking tribe of fifteen to twenty thousand was spread over an
immense area of the Moroccan high plains. Sometimes they moved their
flocks into Algerian territory. Their reliance on sheepherding exceeded
that of any other tribe in the region. Some men owned palm groves in
Figuig, Aïn Chaïr, and a few other small oases south of the plains, but
they all lived in tents the year round and followed transhumance patterns
of extraordinary distance. In winter many tents moved into the northern
reaches of the high plains where the season was generally warmer than on
the higher plains of the Dahra. In the spring the flocks dispersed over the
plains to seek pasture in the depressions where moisture from winter
drainage accumulated. In summer the tents moved southward and up into
the valleys between the fragmented mountains of the Saharan Atlas in the
east and the High Atlas in the west.[13]

Dawi Mani'

This Arab tribe was divided into five subtribes, numbering in all about
15,000. Their economy contrasted sharply with that of the Bani Gil in its
relatively wider diversification. All sections lived in tents the year round
and made seasonal moves with camels, goats, and sheep along two major
axes: from the lower Guir westward across the Hammada to Tafilalt and

from the lower Guir eastward to the Zousfana. A large percentage of the tribe owned date palms in Tafilalt or along the Zousfana. Most of the tribe also grew barley and wheat on the Abadla plain along the Guir. Their reliance on grain production was much greater than that of any other pastoral group in the region.[14]

Awlad Jarir

This group of about 5,000 camel and sheepherders had a close political association with the Dawi Mani'. Their territory was sandwiched between that of the Dawi Mani' and the Bani Gil. It extended from the region of Béchar across the Jebel Béchar to the upper Zousfana, and sometimes further east. The Awlad Jarir harvested dates at Béchar and a few smaller centers and planted grain along the Zousfana. But their economy rested heavily on their camel herds.

Saharan Atlas Tribes

A small section of the Amur, cousins of the pastoralists which inhabited the Jebel Amour in central Algeria, practiced short range transhumance with sheep in the Mountains of the Ksour northeast of Figuig. Some of them had palm trees in Figuig and other oases. Two mini-tribes, the Shurfa and the Awlad Sidi Taj, shared this region with the Amur and moved their flocks between the mountains and the pre-Saharan pastures north of the Erg Occidental.[15]

The internal social structure of all these tribes followed a pattern found almost everywhere in rural North Africa and the Sahara. Social relations between individuals and between groups within a tribe were articulated in terms of patrilineal descent, that is, descent through the male line. The tribe may be defined as the ultimate group which claimed descent from a common ancestor. In some cases the identity of this apical ancestor was known, and legends about his life were preserved. For example, the Ait 'Atta were the 'people of Dadda 'Atta,' a warrior who presumedly lived about the sixteenth century. The Awlad al-Nasir were the 'children of al-Nasir', and the Dawi Mani' were the 'kinsmen of al-Mani'.' In other cases the founder of the tribe was forgotten. The Ait Seghrushin were the 'people of the jackal-that-was-made-dry', the name referring to a legend about an exploit of a venerated holy man. In any case all the members of the tribe regarded one another as agnatic kin. It was the idiom of kinship rather than place names by which a man was socially identified. It did not matter whether this kinship was real or fictive as long as a man's claim to be a member of the agnatic group was accepted. Kinship served as a unifying principle to hold together people having common economic, social, or political interests. Tribes grew for the most part through the absorption of newcomers into the genealogical structure rather than through the proliferation of descendants. The values and sentiments surrounding this putative bond were no stronger nor weaker than if the tie were one of blood.[16]

Each tribe ordered and expressed its network of internal kin relationships in terms of a hierarchy of kin groups of continually decreasing genealogical range. According to a kind of official model of relationships, small groups of kin 'nested' together to form larger groups, which, in turn, aggregated to form still larger groups, until at last the entire tribe was encompassed. The basic kinship unit (beyond the nuclear family) was the patrilineage (Arabic, *'adm*; Berber, *ighs*). Each member of this group usually knew his precise genealogical relationship with all the other members. That is, each member could usually name in succession the line of ancestors between himself and the founder of the lineage, whose name the group usually took. The Awlad Yusif, for example, were all the people descended from Yusif, the apical ancestor. Lineages were most often four to six generations deep, the average for almost all Moroccan tribes.

The number of levels of segmented kin groupings occurring between the lineage and the tribe as a whole varied from one group to another. The Awlad al-Nasir had none, the Ait 'Atta had as many as seven. At these intermediate levels the members of each group recognized common descent, but exact genealogical relationships were unknown. That is, people remembered the name of the ancestor who defined the group, but they could not name all the generations between him and the founder of their particular lineage. Each tribe had its own set of generic names for the segments at these intermediate levels. The terms 'clan' or 'subtribe' will generally be used here.

The French military officers who wrote most of the descriptions of the pastoral groups of the frontier region had the habit of describing a tribe's internal structure in terms of a pyramid of kin segments (*fractions* and *sous-fractions*) without explaining the social or political functions of these groupings or taking into account other modes of social organization crosscutting the bonds of kinship. Today the anthropologist or historian has at his disposal a substantial body of theory and comparative material (most of it from tribes outside North Africa) dealing with societies having what are termed segmentary lineage systems.[17] This theory can be usefully applied in investigating social and political processes in Moroccan or Algerian tribes. It would, however, be both inaccurate and misleading to describe the institutions and mechanisms of these groups in terms of broad

generalizations or to assume that all tribes with segmentary kinship structures function in essentially similar ways. A look at the tribes of southeastern Morocco reveals a remarkable diversity in social organization and
action, most of which cannot be explained purely in terms of interaction
between kin groups. Therefore, with this brief explanation of the segmentary model as a starting point, the uses and the limitations of kinship in
politics and economic life will be dealt with in the following chapter with
reference to the Dawi Mani' and the Ait 'Atta.

Qsar-dwellers

The transition from steppe to oasis was abrupt, since all agricultural life
huddled close to the wadis, the wells, and the springs. On the steppe lands
population density per square mile was extremely low. In the oases it
was higher than in any other region of Morocco. The great majority of the
population of the pre-Sahara lived year-round in the oases. The herding
groups ranged far and wide in search of meager vegetation, but the oasis-
dwellers practiced extremely intensive cultivation over an area no greater
than the network of flowing irrigation channels could reach.

The highly ramified kinship structures of the pastoralists gave way in
the oases to residence and class distinctions as the major factors in social
organization. The qsar (French, ksar; plural, ksour), or walled village, was
the unit of residence in all the oases of the region. The size of these villages varied greatly, but the walls usually formed a square and were broken
by a single entranceway. Inside, the residents occupied closely packed, two
or three story mud brick dwellings. The qsar was always located near a
water source, and the inhabitants cultivated the surrounding land. This
type of residence was designed not only for defense against outside attack
but also for maximum exploitation of the available economic resources.
The population was small enough to ensure subsistence from the agricultural resources it possessed, but large enough to supply sufficient labor to
maintain them. The qsar was a self-contained agricultural unit, comparable
to the duwar in pastoral groups.[18]

Within the qsar the society was grouped in patrilineages whose range
varied greatly, depending on the social class in question. In many villages
agnatic kinship relations did not extend beyond the walls, and the individual identified with a particular lineage in a particular qsar, not with a tribe.
In some cases he might also identify with a distinct cluster of qsar-s, or
district, such as the Rteb or the Beni Goumi. Four groups in the region,
although entirely sedentary or close to it, could be classified as tribes
because the members of each, though occupying several villages, claimed
descent from a common ancestor. The Bani Mhammad (French, Beni

M'hammed) and the 'Arab Sabbah of the lower Ziz valley each occupied a number of *qsar-s* in a contiguous area. The same was true of the Ait 'Aysa (French, Aït Aïssa), who resided along the Wad Ait Aïssa-Haïber, although a few of them continued to live in tents during the late nineteenth century. Also in this category were the Arabic-speaking Ghananma (French, Ghenanema), who occupied several *qsar-s* in the Saoura valley. As was already mentioned, some of the Ait Izdig of the Ziz and Guir valleys and the Awlad al-Nasir also lived in houses year-round by the end of the century.

The division of society into distinguishable social classes was much more pronounced among the *qsar*-dwelling sector of the population than among the transhumant groups. A visitor to any of the oasis communities of the region would be able to distinguish as many as six categories: *shurfa, murabtin*, common cultivators, *haratin*, slaves, and Jews.[19]

The two categories possessing the most prestigeous standing in the community were the *shurfa* and the *murabtin* (Arabic singular, *sharif* and *murabit*; French, *cherif* or *cheurfa, marabout* or *marabouts*). The *shurfa* were those individuals accepted by the community as being descended from the Prophet Muhammad, normally through the line of either Mawlay Idris of Fez or Mawlay 'Ali Sharif of Tafilalt. The former was the founder of the first Arab dynasty in Morocco in the eighth century. The latter was the progenitor of the 'Alawi dynasty, which came to power in the seventeenth century. *Shurfa* were scattered widely throughout Morocco. They exercised broad influence in political and social life and were entitled to a number of special privileges and immunities. They were normally addressed as Mawlay (pronounced Mulay).

Murabtin were the descendants of reputed holy men who were revered as saints. The living members of a saint's lineage were responsible for maintaining his tomb and for receiving the offerings in money and kind which devotees brought to it. Sometimes *murabtin* families established special centers, called *zawiya-s*, which served as sanctuaries, schools for rudimentary Koranic learning, headquarters of religious brotherhoods (*tariqa-s*), pilgrimage sites, and agencies for political mediation and arbitration. Some *zawiya-s* served all of these functions, others only one or two of them. The *shaykh* or head of the *zawiya* was usually a living saint in his own right. Sometimes other members of the family were as well. *Murabtin* were given the title of 'Si' or 'Sidi,' and their lineages were referred to as 'Awlad Sidi so and so.' *Sharif* and *murabit* were not mutually exclusive social categories. Some men could claim both titles if they had the appropriate social and genealogical qualifications.

Shurfa and *murabtin* groups were scattered throughout southeastern

Morocco. The greatest concentration of *shurfa* was in the Wad Ifli district
of Tafilalt, which was the homeland of the 'Alawi dynasty. Here, *shurfa*
families were grouped in sublineages which lived together in particular
qsar-s. Elsewhere in the region, *shurfa* kin groups constituted the major
element in a village or simply contributed a few families. The number of
murabtin lineages in the entire region was about twenty, eight of them
being in Tafilalt. The groups most widely known in the late nineteenth
century were the Awlad Sidi al-Ghazi of Tafilalt, the Awlad Abu Ziyan of
Kenadsa (near the lower Wad Guir), and the Awlad Sidi Mawlay Karzaz of
the Saoura valley. Both *shurfa* and *murabtin* were rather rigidly endoga-
mous. A son might be permitted to marry outside the group, but a
daughter never was since this would mean the loss of the holy descent line
in her progeny.

The basic ingredient which separated *shurfa* and *murabtin* from the rest
of the population was their possession of *baraka*, the quality of divine
grace.[20] The presence of *baraka* in a person was partially determined by
his line of descent, although the quality did not necessarily have to be
inherited. Evidence of it was also seen in the way he behaved. Exemplary
piety, erudition, aristocratic deportment, and distinctive dress were all
signs of its presence. It was commonly believed that *baraka* radiated from
its detainer and that physical contact or proximity with the man could
have a benign effect. The extent of a person's *baraka* in the eyes of others
could rise or fall depending on his success or failure in adhering to the
characteristic code of conduct. As will be seen in later chapters, it was
men of *baraka*, especially *murabtin*, whom the rest of the society employed
to legitimize social and political actions, to protect commerce, and to
arbitrate and mediate conflict.

The difficulty of describing in a precise manner the social characteristics of *shurfa* and *murabtin* should be pointed out. Many individuals, and
sometimes whole tribes, represented themselves as *shurfa* without offering
any genealogical credentials. Their behavior alone might determine
whether or not their assertion was accepted. Conversely, many bona fide
members of *shurfa* or *murabtin* lineages did not choose to behave in distinctive ways, and, consequently, no one expected them to shine with holy
benediction. In many borderline cases a man's inclusion in either category
was a highly subjective matter.

The largest class in the oasis-dwelling population were the Arabic or
Berber-speaking agriculturalists. They were independent property owners
and took an active part in the government and administration of their
qsar-s. Between the Ziz and the Zousfana valleys this class was known as
ahrar (Arabic singular, *harrar* or *hurr*) meaning 'freeborn.' The free cultiva-

tors of the region were not, with the exception of the Bani Mhammad, the 'Arab Sabbah, the Ait 'Aysa, and the Ghananma organized in tribes, but they had a strong sense of lineage solidarity. The *ahrar* group always distinguished themseves from the lower, *haratin* class by pointing to their lineage organization and to their white skins. In fact, many cultivators, as well as pastoralists, were very swarthy, owing to centuries of intermixing with black African slaves and their descendants. But in southeastern Morocco, indeed throughout North Africa and the Sahara, a man's 'whiteness' was determined less by the color of his skin than by his patrilineal descent. If his forefathers were white Arabs or Berbers, then he was too.

A fourth category, the *haratin* (singular, *hartani*), carried on most of the menial labor in the oases and had low social standing in the eyes of the three classes already noted. The origin of the *haratin* is still a subject of debate. Some believe them to be the descendants of people who came into the region as early as neolithic times. Others identify them as descendants of West African slaves who intermarried with the Berber and Arab population.[21] Most of them had dark skin and Negroid features. In the eyes of the 'white' groups they were the Moroccan equivalent of the 'hewer of wood and drawer of water,' but they were in no sense enslaved. They usually worked for a fifth or less of the crops which they planted and harvested. The term *khammas*, which refers to a man who worked at least ideally, for a fifth of the yield, was often used as a synonym for *hartani*. Some *haratin* worked and owned their own land, though this was the exception. They usually occupied a quarter in the *qsar*, if not the entire village, but they had no strong lineage organization and normally traced their descent no more than three generations. The *haratin* represented a substantial portion of the total sedentary population of the region, a majority in some places.[22]

By the end of the nineteenth century the number of slaves living in the region had probably dwindled to a few hundred owing to the decline of the trans-Saharan slave trade from West Africa. The transhumant groups owned most of them, employing them as domestics or as shepherds. Slaves were usually integrated into the families they served and often had strong personal ties with their masters. For this reason a slave could have higher social standing in the eyes of the 'white' Arabs and Berbers than did the toiling *hartani*.

Several *qsar-s* in the region had Jewish residents, who occupied a special quarter called the *mallah*. Tafilalt had the largest concentration. Other groups were found along the Ziz and the upper Guir and in Figuig. The Jews did not participate in the institutional life of Muslims, but neither were they persecuted in normal times. All of them had to have the protection of a Muslim patron, who would intercede for them in their dealings with the Muslim community. As almost everywhere else in Morocco, they specialized in commerce, silversmithing, and shoemaking.

A division of the *qsar*-dwelling population into these six categories is a useful guideline, but it does not mean to imply a simple typology of vertical stratification with *shurfa* and *murabtin* at the top and Jews at the bottom. To work out such a typology would present difficulties. A number of factors had to be considered in determining a man's place in the social framework: religion (Muslim or Jew), status as freeman or slave, ancestry and depth of known genealogy, occupation, and skin color. Sometimes the social categories and the roles connected with them overlapped. A man whose ancestors were *shurfa* might have the social and economic status comparable to that of a common cultivator. A *hartani* might have the same social position as a slave. Moreover, the precise meaning of names to indicate categories might change from one locality to another, or the same name might be used to refer to groups which did not have similar social positions. For example, in the valley of the Wad Dra in south central Morocco the term *haratin* had a much more restricted meaning than in Tafilalt. In the Dra the great majority of the sedentary population had strongly Negroid features, but their social position relative to other groups was similar to that of the *ahrar* of Tafilalt. Furthermore, the meaning of all these terms could be highly subjective and could vary depending on which category was using them.[23]

In the social and economic setting of southeastern Morocco the natural environment imposed itself upon the course of all human relations. The insufficiency as well as the extreme unevenness of rainfall put narrow limits on the range of production and dictated an economy characterized not only by scarcity but also, and more important, by perennial uncertainty. The problem of outwitting a fickle environment was an underlying and pervading preoccupation of every tribe and *qsar*. Prosperity was not unknown. In some years crops or stock yields were high enough to permit trade or storage of surpluses and a welcome increase in the standard of living. The good years, though, could never be foreseen, for drought, flood, disease, locust, warfare, and a host of minor disasters made their rounds in a habitual but always incalculable cycle. The expression *in sha' Allah*, 'if God so wills,' bespoke the unpredictability of life in an environment whose capriciousness could never be brought under control.

The only way a man could improve the economic odds in his favor from one year to the next was to accumulate alternative sources of supply. He could do this by diversifying his resources. Instead of growing only

dates, he could plant barley or raise sheep. If one resource failed, the other
might not. He could also cover himself by drawing on the aid of his close
kinsmen, by pooling his resources with those of his neighbors, or by
expanding his circle of relations through marriage ties. Of course, whom-
ever he called on for help in a bad year would, in a reverse situation, call
on him. Everyone in the society was obliged to plan for contingencies in
one way or another if he were to avoid the effects of nature's volatility.

A certain degree of continuous cooperation among people was essential
in order to maintain the balance between labor and production. The *duwar*
and the *qsar* both represented the units of production best adapted to
ensure maximum exploitation of the resources at hand. Even so, mutual
advantage more than kinship or residential proximity motivated this cooperation. The individual's search for a more secure economic stake consistently took precedence over the preservation of standing ties and
commitments. A man's willingness to aid an unlucky cousin did not preclude his taking undue advantage of him when the gains to be had out-
weighed the possible losses. In pastoral groups the continually fluctuating
size and composition of herding units, irrespective of close kinship ties,
reflected the ease with which people made their social relationships conform to their changing economic lot. The practice of viewing social relations in terms of the economic advantages or disadvantages they carried
with them gave the interaction of groups at all levels a character of extraordinary tentativeness and fluidity. The impact which this economy of
uncertainty had on the political life of the region had much to do with the
society's responses to the French conquest.

The Desert Fringe and the *Makhzan*

Until the French conquest, the separate tribes and oasis communities of
the Southeast had not known the inconveniences of central government
for a number of centuries. The Turkish regents who ruled Algeria before
the arrival of the French in 1830 had never extended their government
much beyond the Mediterranean littoral. Their influence south of the high
plains of Oranie was limited to taxation on trade goods entering the
northern towns and to occasional punitive forays.[24] The sultans of the
'Alawi dynasty, which came to power in Morocco in the seventeenth
century, claimed to have sovereignty in the Ziz-Guir-Zousfana region
and in Touat, but they never achieved enduring political control anywhere
south of the Atlas. Some of them on rare occasions led or sent military
expeditions across the mountains to collect taxes by coercion, but they
never stayed long enough to transform themselves into provincial governments. The only *maknzan* forces which ventured east of the Wad Ziz in the

nineteenth century were Sultan Mawlay Sulayman's expeditions to Figuig
in 1806 and to Touat in 1808.

The failure of the Moroccan government to extend its authority into
the trans-Atlas regions did not, however, undermine the sultan's claim to
sovereignty there. The sultan was *imam*, the spiritual head of the Muslim
community, and *amir al-mu 'minin*, the Commander of the Faithful, the
defender of that community. Theoretically, the limits of his sovereignty
were the limits of the Muslim world. Indeed, the 'Alawi sultans asserted
that because they were *shurfa*, descendants of the Prophet Mubammad,
they, rather than the Turkish sultans of the Ottoman Empire, were the
true caliphs of all Muslims. They never made this claim a public issue,
but they carefully avoided entering into diplomatic relations with the
Ottoman ruler (who had nominal suzerainty over the Turkish Regency of
Algiers), and they never recognized any *de jure* limits to the territorial
extent of their domains. By the religious criteria, therefore, they had as
much sovereignty over Mauritania, Touat, and Timbuktu as they had over
Fez and Marrakech.[25]

Though the sultan's claims to dominion over Morocco's Saharan periphery rested more on Islamic political theory than on the exercise of
power, the gap between pretensions and reality was not quite as wide as
most European observers of the nineteenth century tended to think. The
northwestern Sahara had vital links with the heartland of Morocco through
trade. Since the strength of the 'Alawi sultans depended in part on the
stability of trans-Atlas and trans-Saharan trade, they could not ignore the
internal affairs of the tribes and oasis communities at whose pleasure the
caravans passed. They also had a special political interest in the affairs of
Tafilalt, since it was the birthplace of the dynasty and therefore its ideological headquarters. Whatever influence the sultans could exert over these
distant populations grew out of the prestige and moral force of their
spiritual office. If they could not rule, they could exhort, advise, and
mediate. The tribes and *qsar* communities of the South for their part
recognized the value of cultivating relations with the sultan since the
spiritual and moral authority of his position could provide a stabilizing
force in their political life. As *amir al-mu'minin*, the sultan was the highest
source of political legitimacy and judicial authority. Therefore, tribal
leaders sought investitures from him in order to enhance their own legitimacy and prestige locally. Tribes, villages, and individuals involved in disputes sometimes took their cases to Fez or one of the other imperial capi-
tals to seek arbitration from the sultan or from one of his appointed judges.
The passage of letters, envoys, and delegations between the royal palace
and the desert was a matter of frequent occurrence. The sultans maintained

resident governors in Touat between 1692 and 1792, in Figuig after 1882, and in Tafilalt throughout the 'Alawi period. These representatives did not actually govern, but they served an important function as liaisons between the capital and these three centers. In short, the territories beyond the Atlas could reasonably be called *bilad al-siba*, the 'land of dissidence,' but even so imperial politics reached deep into the desert. Therefore, the political life of the Southeast, though fashioned largely by the local interplay of tribes and communities, each possessing its distinctive institutions and historical experience, nonetheless makes complete sense only within the wider context of *makhzan* influence and action.[26]

Notes

1. The word 'Tafilalt' has several variant spellings, including 'Tafilalet,' 'Tafilet,' 'Tafilelt,' and 'Tafilala.' I have adopted 'Tafilalt' because this spelling is not only one of the common variations, but because it seems to conform most closely to Moroccan pronunciation. An inhabitant of Tafilalt was often referred to as a 'Filali.' The famous product of the region was *'filali'* leather.

2. Jean Despois and René Raynal, *Géographie de l'Afrique du Nord-Ouest* (Paris, 1967), p. 443.

3. E.–F. Gautier, *Structure de l'Algérie* (Paris, 1922), pp. 13, 14.

4. Despois and Raynal, *Géographie*, pp. 123-9, 389-98.

5. Jean Despois, *L'Afrique du Nord* (Paris, 1958), pp. 15-21 and back insert map. On the problem of determining the northern limits of the Sahara, see Robert Capot-Rey, *Le Sahara français* (Paris, 1953), pp. 16-19.

6. Augustin Bernard, *Les Confins algéro-marocains* (Paris, 1911), pp. 50, 69; Despois, *L'Afrique du Nord*, pp. 106, 107; Capot-Rey, *Le Sahara français*, pp. 18-20.

7. Capot-Rey, *Le Sahara français*, pp. 274, 275.

8. Bernard, *Confins*, p. 37; Despois, *L'Afrique du Nord*, pp. 94, 95; Despois and Raynal, *Géographie*, p. 40.

9. French ethnographers and historians often classify the Ait 'Atta and Ait Izdig, together with other tribes of the central and eastern Atlas, as belonging to a Berber subfamily known as the Beraber. They suggest that the Beraber were one of the major branches of the ancient Sanhaja confederation of the western Sahara. (See F. de la Chapelle, 'Esquisse d'une histoire du Sahara occidental,' *Hespéris*, 11, facs. 1 [1930], pp. 82-90.) This term, which is merely a variant of 'Barbar' or 'Berber', certainly did not refer to any organized, self-conscious group in the nineteenth century, though some tribes proudly referred to themselves as 'Beraber' to stress the distinction between them and Arabs or oasis-dwellers.

10. Canavy, 'Les Régions du Haut-Guir et de l'oued Haiber,' *Ren. Col.* (May 1908), pp. 125-35; Bernard, *Confins*, p. 61; Despois and Raynal, *Géographie*, pp. 386, 387.

11. Canavy, 'Les Aït Tserrouchen,' *Ren. Col.* (Oct. 1907), pp. 270-72; Edmond Destaing, *Etude sur le dialecte des Aït Seghrouchen* (Paris, 1920); J. Barrère, 'L'Odysée des Aït Hammou,' *Revue Historique de l'Armée*, 8 (Sept. 1952), pp. 115-38; Bernard, *Confins*, pp. 62-64; Despois and Raynal, *Géographie*, pp. 383, 388, 470.

12. AGGA, 22H. 27, Tommy Martin (Chef de Poste at Bouanane), 'Notes sur la tribu des Oulad en Naceur,' Jan. 31, 1910; 'Notes sur les ksour de la basse vallée de l'Oued Aït Aïssa,' Jan. 19, 1910. M & L, II, 378, 379. Bernard, *Confins*, p. 62.
13. Pierre Albert, 'Notice économique sur la région de Talzaza,' *BSGA*, 4th trimestre (1906), pp. 406-415; Lt. Bauger, 'La Confédération des Beni-Guil,' *BSGAO*, 27 (March 1907), pp. 19-38; R. Paskoff, 'Les Hautes Plaines du Maroc oriental: la région de Berguent,' *Les Cahiers d'Outre-Mer*, 10 (1957), pp. 34-64; M & L, II, 353-373; Despois, *L'Afrique du Nord*, pp. 233, 234.
14. A small section of the Dawi Mani' also lived on the Saïs plain between Fez and Meknès. They may have migrated there before the nineteenth century. J. de Segonzac, *Voyages au Maroc (1899-1901)* (Paris, 1903), pp. 96, 97.
15. de Fraguier, 'Le Sahara Sud-Oranais,' CHEAM, no. 2835, 1957, pp. 23, 24; Despois and Raynal, *Géographie*, pp. 138-141; M & L, II, 250-349.
16. On the nature and evolution of North African tribes, see Jacque Berque, 'Qu'est-ce qu'une 'tribu' nord-africaine,' in *Evantail de l'histoire vivante: hommage à Lucien Febvre* (Paris, 1953), pp. 261-271.
17. See for example John Middleton and David Tait, *Tribes without Rulers* (London, 1958); Marshall D. Sahlins, 'The Segmentary Lineage: An Organization of Predatory Expansion,' *American Anthropologist*, 63 (1961), pp. 322-345; M.G. Smith, 'Segmentary Lineage Systems,' *The Journal of the Royal Anthropological Institute*, 86, part 2 (1956), pp. 39-80.
18. See E. Laoust, 'L'Habitation chez les transhumants du Maroc central,' *Hespéris*, 18, fasc. 1 (1934), pp. 123-43; R.A. Donkin, 'The Ksar: A Completely Nucleated Settlement,' in Durham University Exploration Society, *Report of the Expedition to French Morocco,* 1952 (Durham, 1956), pp. 25-33; E. Menneson, 'Ksour du Tafilalt,' *Revue de Géographie du Maroc*, no. 8 (1965), pp. 87-92.
19. See D. Jacques-Meunié, 'Hiérarchie sociale au Maroc présaharien,' *Hespéris*, 45 (1958), pp. 238-269; Laoust, 'L'Habitation,' pp. 153-58.
20. On the various manifestations of *baraka* in Moroccan society, see Edward Westermarck, *Ritual and Belief in Morocco* (London, 1926), I, 35-261.
21. For a recent discussion see Gabriel Camps, 'Recherches sur les origines des cultivateurs noirs du Sahara,' *ROMM*, no. 7 (1970), pp. 35-45.
22. They made up 60 percent of the population in the Beni Goumi district in the Zousfana valley, according to a recent census. P. Passager and S. Barbançon, 'Taghit (Sahara oranais): Etude historique, géographique et médicale,' *Archives de l'Institut Pasteur d'Algérie*, 34 (Sept. 1956), pp. 423, 424.
23. Jacques-Meunié ('Hiérarchie sociale,' pp. 243-54) gives a thorough classification of the numerous names used to denote social class in southern Morocco.
24. M & L, III, 369, 370. Bernard, *Confins*, pp. 117, 126, 127.
25. Edmund Burke, 'Pan-Islam and Moroccan Resistance to French Colonial Penetration, 1900-1912,' *Journal of African History*, 13, no. 1 (1972), p. 101.
26. A history of relations between the sultans of Morocco and the people of Touat and the Southeast is narrated with reference to Arabic documents collected in Touat and translated into French by A.G.P. Martin, *Quatre siècles d'histoire marocaine* (Paris, 1923), pp. 1-366. Martin served as a Native Affairs interpreter in Touat. Both the civil and military authorities in Algeria strongly opposed his efforts to publish his documents, believing that they gave too much credence to Morocco's diplomatic claims to the central Sahara.

After achieving independence in 1956 Morocco once again pressed its claims to Saharan territory which the French incorporated into Algeria. For an exposition of these claims see Allal El Fassi, *La Vérité sur les frontières marocaines* (Tangier, 1961). The history of Moroccan border questions has been studied in extraordinary detail by Frank E. Trout, *Morocco's Saharan Frontiers* (Geneva, 1969).

2 NOMADS: THE DAWI MANI' AND THE AIT 'ATTA

Among the pastoral tribes of southeastern Morocco and Dawi Mani' and the Ait 'Atta played the most prominent parts in the events of 1881-1912. Taken together, they controlled as grazing land the greater part of the territory the French army penetrated and occupied. Their responses to the colonial crisis, whether peaceful or violent, had a deep impact on the fate of the entire region. Therefore, their places in the social framework and history of the Southeast merit special attention.

The Dawi Mani' spoke Arabic; the Ait 'Atta spoke Berber. Yet their ways of life were similar in many respects, more similar to one another than to those of either the Arabs or Berbers who inhabited the oases. Both tribes herded sheep and camels, followed regular transhumance patterns, exploited date palms and other crops, and engaged in caravan trade. Both were predominantely tent-dwellers and lived in the tough, mobile, belli- cose style of the nomad. Although the political and social institutions of the two tribes differed in significant ways, their internal structural organizations had common characteristics that were lacking in any of the other tribes in the region.

Yet despite these cultural similarities, the political dynamics of the two groups contrasted markedly in the later nineteenth century. The Dawi Mani' had, after some centuries of nomadic drift and military conquest, settled firmly into a territorial and ecological niche. A major portion of their economic interests were centered on particular crop-producing localities, and the possibilities of further expansion were remote. There- fore, they took, generally speaking, a defensive posture in relations with outsiders. The Ait 'Atta, by contrast, were in a state of aggressive, preda- tory movement in the nineteenth century in an effort to accumulate a greater share of the region's resources, particularly those of the oases. Whereas the Dawi Mani' looked inward upon their tribal lands, the Ait 'Atta pushed outward, attacking, coercing, confiscating, wherever the opposition proved weak. Thus the European penetration was to catch these two tribes in decidedly contrasting stages of history.

The Five Fifths of the Dawi Mani'

In the late nineteenth century the Dawi Mani' occupied a wide band of pre-Saharan territory stretching from the Wad Zousfana to Tafilalt. Their ancestors were the Ma'qil Arabs, who migrated from Egypt to the Maghrib in the eleventh century along with the Bani Hilal and the Bani Sulaym. The Dawi Mani' probably coalesced from diverse Ma'qil groups in the vicinity of Tafilalt sometime between the fourteenth and sixteenth centuries. According to legend, 'Addi al-Mani', the eponymous ancestor, came there from Arabia in the thirteenth century in the company of Sharif Mawlay Hasan, the first forebear of the 'Alawi dynasty to arrive in Morocco.[1]

In the seventeenth century the tribe, probably growing larger and in need of broader pastures, began expanding eastward toward the Wad Guir and the Wad Zousfana. This expansion was more a military offensive than a process of nomadic drift. Like the Ma'qil tribes which were advancing northward over the Atlas in the same era, the Dawi Mani' moved deliberately, assimilating, evicting, or sometimes bypassing other nomadic groups which they encountered. They claim their formula for military success to be their special organizational system known as *khams khmas*, or 'five fifths.'[2] *Khams khmas* meant that the tribe was segmented into five collateral subtribes, each of which fielded a military corps under the leadership of a *qa'id*. The five sections were the Awlad abu 'Anan (Oulad bou Anan), the Awlad bil Giz (Oulad bel Giz), the Awlad Yusif (Oulad Youssef), the Awlad Jallul (Oulad Djelloul) and the Idarasa (Idersa). The eponymous ancestor of each was held to be a descendant of al-Mani'.

The choice of the number five was not purely arbitrary. Certain other Moroccan tribes were organized in five primary segments as well. In some groups, such as the Dukkala and the Zimmur of the Atlantic coastal plains, *khams khmas* probably had no structural importance internally but was simply imposed by the *makhzan* as a conventional way of administering tax levies. Among the Dawi Mani', the Ait 'Atta, the Ait Waryaghar of the Rif, and perhaps other tribes as well, the five segments had important corporate functions. These tribes, furthermore, regarded their possession of *khams khmas* as a special virtue, believing it conferred of itself extraordinary military might. According to them, tribes with *khams khmas* were more powerful and better unified than tribes without it. In other words, this five way division, or rather the whole conceived in five parts, had ideological as well as social meaning. Although the cultural origins of the concept of *khams khmas* are not at all clear, Moroccans commonly believed (and still do) that the number five, represented in various ways, was lucky and had the power to ward off the sickness and ill fortune produced by the 'evil eye.'[3] Five fifths, as opposed to four fourths or six sixths, was not, of course, an intrinsically more efficient kind of military or political organization, but confidence in its magic could be a stimulus to aggressive action. If the tribe was consistently successful in battle, then faith in *khams khmas* was only reinforced.[4]

The Dawi Mani' apparently believed that such success depended upon all five segments operating together. That is, the mobilization of only three fifths or four fifths meant not only that fewer men would fight but that luck in battle would be forfeited. Therefore, public opinion demanded the participation of each fifth in full force when the tribe went to war. The *qa'id* of each fifth, who was a permanent leader, was responsible for calling up every able-bodied man, excepting those left to care for the women, children, and livestock. The warriors first held an assembly to decide by consensus whether or not the circumstances called for war. If they decided in favor of action, they elected an *ad hoc* war leader (*shaykh*), who had absolute authority during the duration of the crisis. Each fifth fought as a single corps under the leadership of its *qa'id*, at least ideally. Any group or individual failing to appear was subject to a fine or punitive raid by a special tribal police force, known as the *ait arba'in* (people of the forty), made up of the *shaykh* and a contingent of warriors from each fifth. Following a victory, the booty in camels, sheep, firearms, or other goods were divided among the *khmas* proportionably to the number of men contributed by each. On some occasions when a member of the tribe killed or wounded an outsider, the fifths in assembly opted for the payment of bloodwealth to the family of the victim, rather than go to war in adverse circumstances. In such cases each fifth was responsible for paying an equal share.[5]

The fifths represented the highest level of segmentation in the tribe's kinship structure. Each fifth was divided into a varying number of clans, which together constituted the second level of segmentation. Each clan, or almost every one, was further segmented into lineages. The segmentary structure, as shown in Table 1 for the fifth and clan levels, represents the tribe in the late nineteenth century or later.[6] In the seventeenth century the model would not have looked the same since, as the tribe grew and expanded territorially, new segments formed as the result of subdivision or the assimilation of outsiders, while others disappeared owing to fusion, emigration, or natural extinction.

The tribe undoubtedly grew more by accretion than by natural increase. That is, disparate groups of people, whose tribes were defeated by the Dawi Mani' or who migrated into their territory, found refuge with a family and eventually made a place for themselves on the genealogical tree by forming a new segment or by assimilating themselves into an existing lineage. Many Dawi Mani' clans claim a 'foreign' origin, most often in a nearby pastoral tribe or sedentary community.[7] At the same time, however, every segment at all three levels would insist that its founding ancestor

Table 1: Fifths and Clans of the Dawi Mani'

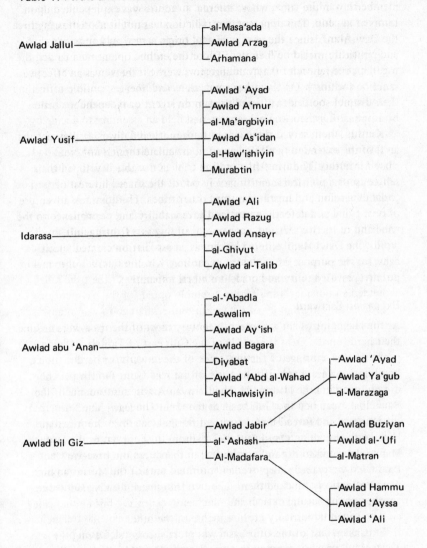

Awlad Jallul
- al-Masa'ada
- Awlad Arzag
- Arhamana

Awlad Yusif
- Awlad 'Ayad
- Awlad A'mur
- al-Ma'argbiyin
- Awlad As'idan
- al-Haw'ishiyin
- Murabtin

Idarasa
- Awlad 'Ali
- Awlad Razug
- Awlad Ansayr
- al-Ghiyut
- Awlad al-Talib

Awlad abu 'Anan
- al-'Abadla
- Aswalim
- Awlad Ay'ish
- Awlad Bagara
- Diyabat
- Awlad 'Abd al-Wahad
- al-Khawisiyin

Awlad bil Giz
- Awlad Jabir
- al-'Ashash
- Al-Madafara

- Awlad 'Ayad
- Awlad Ya'gub
- al-Marazaga

- Awlad Buziyan
- Awlad al-'Ufi
- al-Matran

- Awlad Hammu
- Awlad 'Ayssa
- Awlad 'Ali

was a descendant of al-Mani'. Indeed it had to do so in order to ratify its membership in the tribe, whose internal structure was expressible only in terms of kinship. This apparent contradiction was not at all distressing to the Dawi Mani', since the notion of dual origin served an important social and political function. When the fifth or the entire tribe needed to act together, the reminder that 'our ancestors were brothers' was an effective sanction for unity. On the other hand, clans and lineages could reaffirm their distinct social identity and explain divergent or independent action by emphasizing their original separateness.[8]

Kinship, then, served the needs of both unity and diversity. Beyond the level of the extended family it served to articulate though not create shared interests. The five fifths and the tribe as a whole developed their self-conscious political identity largely out of the shared interest of territorial expansion and hostility toward other tribes. The common adventure of occupying and defending new land gave viability and permanence to the tribe and to its five sections, each one operating as a fighting unit. In other words, the Dawi Mani' entered history as an association created specifically for the purpose of predatory expansion. Kinship ties, whether real or putative, ratified unity and made it a moral imperative.

Expansion Eastward

At the beginning of the seventeenth century most of the tribe were grazing their herds on the great Hammada of the Guir east of Tafilalt.[9] Owing probably to a shortage of pasture, some of the *duwar-s*, or herding units, began moving eastward into the basin of the Wad Guir, though the tribe did not abandon the Hammada. The Hamyan Arabs, descendants of the Bani Hilal, occupied the Guir basin at the time. The Dawi Mani' defeated the Hamyan and forced them to retreat northeastward to the Algerian High Plateaus, where they live today.[10] From the Guir basin, the Dawi Mani' attempted to expand northward. In this direction, however, the Bani Gil, who grazed sheep over an enormous area of the Moroccan high plains, effectively blocked them. The two tribes periodically raided one another during the eighteenth and nineteenth centuries, but neither side ever extended its territory at the expense of the other.[11]

Expansion east of the Guir basin was more successful. During the late eighteenth and early nineteenth centuries, the Dawi Mani' replaced the Ghananma, a much smaller Arab tribe, as political overlords of the villages, known collectively as the Beni Goumi, along the valley of the Wad Zousfana. The two tribes made war on and off throughout most of the nineteenth century. In fact, a Ghananma attack in 1885 on a *qsar* controlled by the Dawi Mani' prompted the last general rallying of the five fifths.[12]

The most distant extension of Dawi Mani' power was in the two northern districts of Touat, where various small groups of warriors joined
with similar bands of Ghananma and Ait 'Atta in terrorizing the *qsar*-
dwellers. By the terms of special pacts of 'brotherhood' with the villagers
the nomads offered 'protection' in return for periodic payment of tribute.
Sometimes agreements were made between a *qsar* and a group representing an entire Dawi Mani' clan (with the obligation to leave the village in
peace binding on the entire tribe) and sometimes between individuals. In
some cases the protectors designated a representative in the *qsar* to collect
the tribute in advance and turn it over to them when they found it convenient to appear.[13] Extorting money or goods from sedentary communities in Touat was clearly a specialized activity of only certain members
of the tribe. Few tribesmen traveled that far south except for extortion
or trade.

The migration and expansion of the Dawi Mani' ended in the early
decades of the nineteenth century. By that time they controlled an
immense area of grazing land bounded on the north by the Bani Gil, on
the west by the Ait 'Atta, and on the east and south by the Ghananma or
by desert unsuitable for herding most of the year. They also exerted political suzerainty over sedentary communities in Tafilalt, Beni Goumi, the
Wad Saoura region, and Touat. They might have expanded further were it
not for the opposition of their neighbors, though the land and resources
they possessed in the nineteenth century were sufficient to support their
population of about 15,000.

Grain, Dates, Livestock, and Booty

Sometime in the eighteenth century the Dawi Mani' began to cultivate
barley and wheat on a broad alluvial plain along the lower Wad Guir near
the present day Algerian town of Abadla. The river bed this far south of
the Atlas was dry part of the year. But periodically, sometimes two or
even three times in one year, the Guir flowed as far as the Abadla plain.
When it did, the watercourse spread out into numerous, meandering
channels, dumping rich sediment over a wide area. Because of the great
force and volume of water in some years, the Dawi Mani' called the area
al-bahariat, 'the lake.' The plain was about forty miles long and as much as
thirteen miles wide. At its southern end the riverbed narrowed into a single
channel again and continued south into the desert.

The autumn flood came in November or December. As soon as the
water level went down the Dawi Mani' planted their grain in the moist, silt-
enriched soil. The arable land was extended by the construction of a net-

work of canals and small diversionary dams that disseminated the water beyond the natural channels. Perhaps six thousand hectares (about fifteen thousand acres) could be irrigated, though probably a good deal less than that number were cultivated in any given year.[14] The crop was usually ready for harvest between April and June. If a flood came in the spring, the grain developed more fully and yielded a superior harvest. Because the wealth of the soil was continually renewed by the deposition of fresh sediment, the yield could be extremely high, possibly as much as thirty quintals (around 140 bushels) per hectare when conditions were most favorable.[15] Consequently, cereal production became a crucial sector of the tribe's economy, not merely a sideline to sheep and camel herding.

In fact the annual calls to sow and to harvest probably acted as a kind of centripetal force against more distant territorial expansion. When the autumn flood came, the word quickly spread, and almost the entire tribe congregated for the planting. Everyone returned again in the spring to cut the grain with sickles, thresh it, and store it in underground silos.[16] The tribe could not, however, rely exclusively on agriculture because the amount of annual yield was as uncertain as it could be plentiful. The rains and floods were capricious and might not come at all for years at a time. Conversely, too much water, especially during the spring flood, could carry away the crop altogether. In 1895, for example, a flood destroyed the crop, but in 1902 and again in 1904 no water arrived at all.[17]

The location of the Abadla plain in practically the dead center of Dawi Mani' territory bespoke its extreme importance to the tribe's economy. But because of the great uncertainty of the crop yield from one year to the next, the exploitation of other resources was essential. The most important of these were date cultivation and herding.

By the later nineteenth century the Dawi Mani' owned thousands of date palms in two major locations: the district of Ghorfa on the southeastern side of Tafilalt and in the Beni Goumi district along the Wad Zousfana. In Ghorfa members of the tribe may have acquired palm groves as far back as the seventeenth century. Since that time, their holdings gradually accumulated through either purchase or outright confiscation. In 1865, for example, violence broke out between men of the Awlad Yusif *khums* and the inhabitants of the *qsar* of Saghrin, allegedly over an attack on a Dawi Mani' woman. Since the date harvest was at hand, contingents from all five fifths arrived in force and laid seige to the *qsar*. The conflict was settled only at the price of Saghrin seeing most of its palms divided up among the fifths.[18]

Palms and the land on which they stood were privately owned. *Haratin* laborers living permanently in the oasis maintained the trees in return for one seventh to one tenth of the dates, and a larger share of produce from gardens planted around the trees. Members of the Awlad abu 'Anan and the Awlad bil Giz fifths had by far the largest investment in the groves of Ghorfa, though the tribe as a whole may have owned only about one fifth of the total number of trees there. The local *qsar*-dwellers or the *makhzan* owned the rest.[19]

The Dawi Mani' began to acquire palms in Beni Goumi around 1825, when the inhabitants of Taghit, the largest *qsar* in the district, called upon them to expel a party of Ghananma, which had seized the village. The Dawi Mani' gradually established political suzerainty over the entire district, accumulating palm groves mainly by intimidation or bald confiscation. Members of the Idarasa, Awlad Yusif, and Awlad Jallul *khmas* owned the most trees.[20]

The palm groves at Ghorfa and Beni Goumi marked the western and eastern poles of Dawi Mani' territory. Between Tafilalt and the Zousfana the tribe herded camels and sheep over an immense area.[21] In November or December most of the tents assembled on the Guir for the barley and wheat planting, remaining in the general area until spring, probably because of the abundance of water. When spring pasturage sprouted on the steppes, the tribe dispersed in *duwar-s* of usually six or seven tents. The *duwar-s* fanned out in all directions from the Guir, though most moved either eastward toward the Zousfana or westward onto the Hammada of the Guir. In May or June they converged on the Abadla plain again for the grain harvest. In August the *duwar-s* began moving toward either Ghorfa or Beni Goumi, expecting to arrive in September or October for the date harvest. Once the dates were packed on camels or stored locally, the tents began trekking back toward the Guir, and the cycle was renewed (see Map 3).[22]

Before the twentieth century the entire tribe lived in tents. They maintained a distinctly nomadic style of living, even though their grain fields largely dictated their seasonal movements. During the grazing seasons, the *duwar-s* usually remained in one location for a week or so while the stock fed in a radius around the camp. Pastureland was the collective property of the tribe. No boundaries were demarcated between the pastures of one segment and another. In fact, kin segments were not strictly localized but tended to mix together quite freely. Close kin generally traveled in the same *duwar*, but kinship was not the major criterion for determining the social composition of a herding unit. Factors such as the reputed good fortune of certain leaders, the availability of labor in relation to the size of the herd, and friendships or antagonisms were more often determinant.

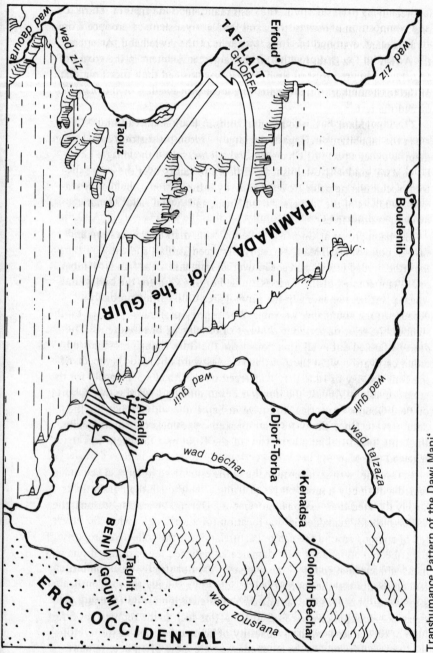

Transhumance Pattern of the Dawi Mani[4]

Even families from different fifths sometimes herded together. The size and composition of *duwar-s* changed frequently as tents moved from one to another or even herded alone for a time. The only general pattern in the movement of kin groups is that the Awlad abu 'Anan and the Awlad bil Giz tended to herd west of the Guir because most of their palms were in Ghorfa. The bulk of the other fifths went east in the direction of Beni Goumi.[23]

Staging raids against other groups in the Sahara was a third kind of economic activity. The Dawi Mani' conducted raids the year round, but they launched more of them when harvests were poor or their own livestock were less plentiful. In other words, raiding provided a contingency source of wealth, a possible safeguard against economic calamity. Sometimes small bands of men staged raids, or razzias (Arabic singular, *ghazwa*), against neighbors in close proximity, such as the Bani Gil or the Ait Izdig. The Dawi Mani' were likewise raided by their neighbors. Indeed, assorted bands from all the tribes in the area played never-ending rounds of tit for tat against one another's flocks and herds. The participants in a raid assembled in advance to plan the operation and choose a leader. A band might be very heterogeneous, representing several different clans, fifths, or even tribes. They planned the raid in secret and traveled to their objective as inconspicuously as possible. The tactic of surprise was always the most effective because the band, slowed down by the livestock it stole, would almost always be pursued by its victims. Once in safety, the group divided the plunder into equal shares, then dissolved.

For many Dawi Mani' raiding was a form of economic specialization. Some individuals were known to make their living almost exclusively from stealing sheep and camels and then selling some of them or trading them for rifles or other goods. The same men tended to show up repeatedly when a raid was announced, and certain warriors, who displayed bravery and consistent good luck, were chosen over and over to serve as leader. The Idarasa had a reputation for providing the best leaders. Men of the Awlad bil Giz and the Awlad Yusif, on the other hand, were considered notoriously unlucky.[24]

The Sixth Fifth

The Dawi Mani' sometimes say that they are organized into six rather than five *khmas*, the additional one being formed by the Awlad Jarir, an Arabic-speaking tribe numbering about 5,000 in the late nineteenth century. The Awlad Jarir developed a close military and political alliance with the Dawi Mani', which may have been formed originally out of the need for mutual defense against neighboring tribes. The Awlad Jarir did not become dependents of their allies, but rather participated in their external wars and shared equally in the plunder. Although the Awlad Jarir became involved in the internal politics of the Dawi Mani', they were in no way incorporated into the kinship structure. Nor did they cultivate grain on the Abadla plain. They were a sixth fifth only in the sense that *khums* means military corps. Their special status, however, symbolized and legitimated the alliance which amounted to a permanent political association.[25]

The Awlad Jarir were segmented into two subtribes, the Mufalha, which included seven lineages, and the 'Asasa, which included three clans further segmented into a total of ten lineages.[26]

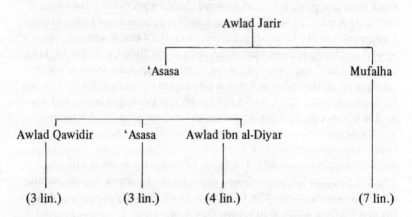

Their pasture lands covered generally the area between Figuig and Béchar. They owned palms scattered in small oases along the Zousfana north of Beni Goumi, but most of their trees were in Béchar and its vicinity. They grew some barley and wheat along the Zousfana. They owned many more camels than sheep and were renowned as professional raiders, especially the warriors of the 'Asasa branch.[27]

Tribal Leadership

The Dawi Mani' had three institutions through which men exercised power and leadership. These were the *jama'a*, or assembly, and the positions of *shaykh* and *qa'id*. The *jama'a* was a representative council of the fifth. Each lineage in the *khums* customarily sent one delegate, but any adult male presumably was qualified to speak at the meetings. Having delegates simply prevented the assembly from being unmanageably large. The *jama'a* was not a formally organized constituent body with governing rules, credentials, and a system of record keeping, but rather an informal gathering-together of the wisest and most influential men. It discussed all matters affecting the welfare of the fifth as a whole, but its major function was judicial. It judged both civil (inheritance disputes, altercations over boundaries between grain fields) and criminal (theft, personal injury) cases brought before it and levied fines against miscreants. It based its decisions on a combination of Muslim law (*shari'a*) and custom. Through their *jama'a-s* the fifths took primary responsibility for regulating the social behavior of the individual members of the tribe. The Dawi Mani' as a whole had no regular *jama'a* but met in assembly only when war with another tribe threatened. The *jama'a-s* of the fifths, which met fairly regularly and had permanent functions, symbolized and gave expression to the greater sense of solidarity and day-to-day corporate responsibility among fifth brothers than was found among the collective descendants of al-Mani'.[28]

The *shaykh* of the tribe was a military commander, elected by the men of all five fifths only when war was imminent. His term of office lasted only as long as the crisis, though no rule prevented the same man from being chosen more than once. Any able-bodied member of the tribe was eligible for election, provided he had the requisite qualities of intelligence and courage.

Whereas the *shaykh* was a temporary office holder with a single responsibility, the *qa'id* of the fifth could hold his title for a lifetime, and he served the *khums* in a number of ways. He was elected by the *jama'a* and in a loose sense was responsible to it. His most crucial duty was to mobilize and lead the warriors of his fifth when the entire tribe went to war. He also acted as spokesman for the fifth in its relations with outsiders, and he arbitrated or mediated minor disputes among its members. He brought more serious cases before the *jama'a* and helped to execute its judgments. Deposition of a *qa'id* for incompetence or any other reason was rare, but his tenure in office was nonetheless at the discretion of the *khums*.[29]

The *shaykh* and the *qa'id-s* were always respected and influential men, but not because of any permanent authority inherent in their office. They were chosen to be spokesmen, mediators, and military standard-bearers, but not governors or administrators. The tribe gave the *shaykh* arbitrary powers during the wartime but then abolished his office when peace returned. His authority was contingent upon the need for quick, unified action. He was the crucial symbol of tribal unanimity, but unanimity was neither necessary nor desirable all the time. Like the *shaykh*, the *qa'id* had real authority only when the fifth mobilized for war. At other times he was a mediator, concensus-builder, and spokesman for the *jama'a*. He had no tools of coercion other than the force of his personality and the public opinion made explicit by the *jama'a*. He held office permanently in order to serve the *jama'a*, to settle some of the minor squabbles within the *khums* that erupted every day, and to stand as a symbol of the fifth's latent capacity to unite for action in a moment.

The *shaykh* and the *qa'id-s* were of course not the only men who exercised leadership. Whenever people joined together, however temporarily, to pursue some shared interest, leaders emerged to offer ideas, generate agreement, and make tactical decisions. Informal leadership was especially important in the functioning of the *duwar*, an impermanent aggregate of families which had to make almost daily decisions on the movements of its herds. If the Dawi Mani' were like other nomadic tribes of the Sahara and the Middle East, the size of a *duwar* reflected in part the effectiveness of its leader. The man who made decisions harmful to the well-being of the group or allowed divisiveness to fester would see the *duwar* dwindle away before his eyes or find another man taking his place. The exercise of power or influence even at the local level was a precarious undertaking, since the supply of qualified *duwar* leaders must have far exceeded the demand for them. Leaders faced constant pressures to do an effective job or make way for a better man.[30]

The influence men were able to exert over others depended upon their display of wisdom, discretion, and courage and upon the strength of the personal ties they developed through kinship, friendship, and probably in many cases, marriage.[31] Though a man first built his reputation among his close kin, the boundaries of tribal segments were not necessarily the boundaries of influence. Since groups coming together for collective action, notably the *duwar* and the raiding party, were not necessarily or even primarily kinship units, then men in the role of leaders could not be strictly identified with one kinship segment or another. The *qa'id* was ideally the leader of an entire fifth, but in practice he did not necessarily have the support of all of its members. In the late nineteenth century the *qa'id-s* of the Awlad Jallul, the Idarasa, and the Awlad bil Giz all enjoyed the backing of only a portion of the *khums*. On the other hand, Ay'ish wuld Musa, *qa'id* of the Awlad abu 'Anan, had great prestige throughout the tribe and probably would have been chosen *shaykh* in the case of a general mobilization.[32]

Alliance and Opposition

Tribal leaders had to be skillful at mediating disputes, but when neither they nor other third parties could arrange a settlement, feuding might break out. Homicide was the most common cause for the eruption of a feud. When one man killed another, he was expected to flee from the tribe's territory in the company of a small group of his close kin. When he had gone, the *jama'a*, a saint, or perhaps a tribal leader could intervene in order to attempt to arrange exchange of blood wealth (*dya*) in camels or money between the family of the murderer and that of the victim. If the exchange was accomplished, both parties ordinarily considered the affair settled, though the perpetrator of the crime was expected to remain in exile for an indefinite period of time. In some instances the kinsmen of the accused would agree to swear an oath to his innocence at the shrine of a saint. If neither blood wealth nor oath-taking could settle the issue, then the kinsmen of the victim might take vengeance by killing a member of the murderer's family. An act of *quid pro quo*, however, might only be the beginning of a series of killings and counterkillings, involving larger and larger numbers of people on each side. The likelihood of a single homicide turning into a feud increased in direct proportion to the social distance between the two families involved. That is, feuding was not feasible within families or sublineages, where blood ties were close or daily cooperation was essential. A feud was most probable when the homicide involved families belonging to two different fifths, though shared interests, marriage ties, or friendships could even then serve to prevent an outbreak of hostilities. Once a feud erupted, it could continue off and on for many years, since any retaliation only further lessened the chances for a definitive reconciliation.

About 1894 fighting broke out between men of the Awlad abu 'Anan and the Awlad bil Giz. This feud appears to have overshadowed all other internal disruptions for many years. Bad relations between the two fifths, or at least between some groups in each, dated back to at least 1881.[33] The two *khmas* remained in a state of either active or latent feud throughout the period of French conquest and even until quite recently. An account of this conflict as recounted by an elderly informant, sheds some light on the nature of feuding and alliance-making within the tribe.[34]

Seven brothers of the Awlad bil Giz used to steal from the Awlad abu 'Anan. At the same time four brothers of the Awlad abu 'Anan would steal from the Awlad bil Giz. One day one of the seven men of the Awlad bil Giz was killed during a raid. His six brothers accused the four of the Awlad abu 'Anan of committing the crime. These four refused to submit to a collective oath. So when both fifths gathered at Tafilalt for the date harvest, the Awlad bil Giz retaliated by killing eleven young men of the Awlad abu 'Anan. A battle then took place in which five more of the Awlad bil Giz fell. The *murabtin* of the Awlad Sidi al-Ghazi of Tafilalt then managed to intervene and achieve a truce.

The Awlad abu 'Anan then decamped and went off toward the

Abadla plain. The Awlad bil Giz went to Boudenib, where they succeeded in rallying to their cause the warriors of the Awlad Yusif, another
of the fifths, and also the Awlad Hamida, a lineage of the Awlad Jarir.
These men joined because of the prospects for booty.

Some time later, eighteen men of the Matran, a clan of the Awlad
bil Giz, left Tafilalt for Béchar with a load of *filali* leather. The Awlad
abu 'Anan, who were on the Abadla plain, heard they were approaching
and so attacked them four hundred strong. They killed all but one of
the caravaners and made off with all the goods and camels. The *jama'a*
of the Awlad abu 'Anan, however, thinking the warriors had done a
foolish thing, took all the booty to Kenadsa and asked the saints there
to attempt to restore peace. It so happened that Si Tayyib, son of the
famous *murabit* Abu 'Amama, was at Kenadsa at the time and agreed to
mediate between the two fifths. The Awlad abu 'Anan gave him blood
wealth payments of ten young camels for each of eleven killings,
claiming that compensation for this number of victims would settle the
score once and for all. Si Tayyib met with the Awlad bil Giz, but they
refused the blood wealth. Because of their intransigence, Si Tayyib,
supported by the *murabtin* of Kenadsa, cursed them, declaring that
they would forever be as weak as ewes.

The Awlad bil Giz, however, continued to prepare for war. They
began to pay every man of the Awlad Yusif and the Awlad Hamida one
half duro per day to remain in alliance with them. The Awlad abu
'Anan, on the other hand, enlisted the support of twenty-five men of
the Idarasa, mostly of the Awlad 'Ali clan. The Awlad abu 'Anan still
hoped to avoid a showdown and encouraged the saints of Kenadsa to
continue their efforts at mediation. But the Awlad bil Giz were already
deciding how they would divide up the sheep of the Awlad abu 'Anan.

Finally both forces met at Tafilalt. The Awlad abu 'Anan managed
to draw their adversaries out of the palm groves and proceeded to cut
them down. When the battle was over, the Awlad bil Giz had lost
twelve hundred warriors, but the Awlad abu 'Anan only eleven
warriors and one *hartani*! Later, the market of Tafilalt literally moved
to Ghorfa for a sale of all the captured property of the Awlad bil Giz
and their allies. Many of the Awlad abu 'Anan wanted to pursue and
kill all the Awlad bil Giz, but the elders stopped them, saying that
enough was enough.

In this account a single case of homicide mushroomed into a feud between
two of the fifths. According to segmentary theory, this is precisely what
should have happened, since the families of the killer and the victim were

genealogically differentiated from one another through the *khums* level of segmentation. The only common ancestor they shared was al-Mani' himself, so they would be expected to unite only against an adversary outside the tribe altogether. In the case at hand the Awlad abu 'Anan were expected to coalesce in support of one adversary because the Awlad bil Giz were about to coalesce in support of the other. In other words, the corporate unity of one fifth was defined by its active opposition to the other. In theory the mobilization of both fifths would produce a state of 'balanced opposition' between the two groups, thus restraining hostility and facilitating peaceful settlement.

As the account shows, however, genealogical relationships did not by themselves determine the lines of alliance and opposition. Groups of warriors from outside the two opposed fifths joined one side or the other for the sake of the booty or simply for the chance of a good fight. Personal ties of one sort or another may have motivated some of them as well. According to a French report, both the Awlad bil Giz and the Awlad abu 'Anan had allies from among the Awlad Jarir. The Awlad bil Giz, moreover, sought support from the Awlad Sidi Shaykh and the Bani Gil, their neighbors to the north.[35] Internal alliances, then, did not only cut across the kinship structure but could extend outside the tribe altogether. Shared interests in resources, personal and affinal links, and perhaps longstanding ties with members of other tribes could all contradict the neat model of segmental opposition.

If opposed fifths or clans achieved a state of balanced opposition, then they must have reached something close to numerical equality. Kin groups, however, varied greatly in size at all levels. The number of tents in each clan, for example, may have ranged from less than twenty to more than one hundred fifty. The fifths were also numerically disproportionate.[36] When a feud broke out, each faction attempted to put together a large alliance. The result was often a precarious balance of power as some men rallied to the weaker side to prevent the stronger from gaining too much. But each side sought allies wherever they might be found, not by following 'rules' of segmentary opposition.

The Awlad abu 'Anan — Awlad bil Giz feud also suggests that alliances were fluid and unstable. No permanent, rigid system of alliances existed either paralleling or crosscutting the lines of segmentation. Some Moroccan tribes did have an internal system of opposed leagues, called *liff-s*, which were permanent or semipermanent and which did cut across the hierarchy of descent groups. The Dawi Mani' had no such system, though they may have used the term *liff* simply as a synonym for 'alliance.'[37]

The process of alliance making, in fact, was probably a good deal more haphazard, fluid, and 'unsegmentary' than the account of the feud reveals. Members of the tribe, and consequently French intelligence gatherers too, tended to describe the groups constituting alliances in terms of kinship. They spoke of opposition between *the* Awlad bil Giz and *the* Awlad abu 'Anan, even though some groups within these fifths might have remained neutral, and bands from other fifths or other tribes might have participated in the fighting on one side or the other. The kinship model served as a kind of 'constitution' of tribal politics, an idealization of the way men ought to line up in political or social relations with one another. Kinship carried with it moral obligations of mutual support, the closer the kin relationship, the greater the obligation. The segmentary 'constitution' permitted the individual to assign everyone in the tribe a kinship category in relation to himself and therefore to determine whom he should be able to count on for assistance, whom he should be wary of, whom he should avoid or attack. In short, the kinship model provided an essential measure of sense, order, and continuity to a network of alliances that was in reality complex, plastic, and tentative.[38]

The transhumant population inhabiting the desert land between the Wad Ziz and the Wad Zousfana reckoned themselves descendants of the venerable warrior 'Addi al-Mani'. That this assertion was in the case of most members of the tribe a spurious one mattered little, since its purpose was to sum up a common historical experience — territorial expansion — and to symbolize shared interest in the defense of the conquered land. In the nineteenth century the solidarity of the Sons of al-Mani' as a corporate body manifested itself only on those occasions when the warriors of all five fifths fought together under a single leader against a neighboring tribe. In the absence of such a crisis the Dawi Mani' as a whole had no active corporate existence, only a potential one. They had no permanent supreme chief or assembly, and the territory they controlled had no precise boundaries. The family tree linking all to al-Mani' and the memories of tribal genesis or past wars against outsiders served to sanction and legitimate unity. However, only the need to safeguard land and resources, or the desire to extend them, could move the tribe to collective action. When the weight of opinion favored a general mobilization (though an attack or raid by another tribe did not necessarily mean that it would), the tribe could pressure recalcitrants to conform by raiding their stock. Even then, there is little doubt that some groups and individuals managed to defy the call to arms, finding it more in their interest on that particular occasion to maintain a discreet neutrality or even to join the other side.

The mobilization of every able-bodied man in the tribe was almost certainly unattainable, even for a short period of time.

When members of the tribe were not fighting or having other dealings with outsiders, they tended to disregard their common parentage and to identify, depending on the context, with a variety of temporary cooperative groupings and alliances which might in some cases include members of other tribes. These groups — *duwar-s*, raiding parties, caravans, associations for sharing resources, feud alliances — formed up and fell apart in response to changing economic or political opportunities and conditions. Again, named segments within the genealogical model (that is, fifths, clans, and lineages), as well as legends of special origins, provided a framework of social identification and a way of articulating both cooperation and conflict. They did not, however, lock the individual into a particular pattern of action. Loyalties and commitments were invariably founded on shared interests, not on either the fictions or realities of descent and origin.

The individual normally took part in a number of cooperative enterprises at the same time, but his participation in any of them was always highly tentative. For one thing, his circles of shared interest often intersected one another, and situations might arise where he would have to support one at the expense of another. But more important, the pre-Saharan environment continually played havoc in the most unpredictable ways with the fortunes of every cooperating group, forcing the individual to be prepared to rearrange his commitments and loyalties at a moment's notice. The patterns of cooperation and alliance could be no more certain nor regular than the volume of rainfall and flood waters or the size of herds from one season to the next.

Indeed, the tribe's internal political life may have been more fluid and more fissiparous in the late nineteenth century than in previous times. Aggressive military expansion had largely played itself out. Desert wastes to the south and east and strong neighbors to the north and west either discouraged or prevented further adventures afield. At the same time the rich agricultural land of the Guir flood plain lured the tribesmen back into their heartland twice a year. This territorial stabilization undermined the usefulness of the *khams khmas* and almost certainly produced an incipient erosion of the bonds of tribal unity. It seems likely, therefore, that toward the end of the century internal matters of power and interest largely absorbed political energies, complicating and proliferating the patterns of alliance and opposition. By contrast, the Ait 'Atta, the Dawi Mani''s neighbors to the west, exhibited more cohesiveness and less internal turbulence. The Ait 'Atta, however, were still very much outward bound on the eve of the colonial crisis.

Khams Khmas: A Berber Version

In the late nineteenth century the land of the Ait 'Atta extended from the Hammada of the Guir westward to the Wad Dra and from the slopes of the Atlas southward to the desert. The tribe's heartland was the Jebel Saghro, a low, barren range running parallel to and a few dozen miles south of the central High Atlas. Most of the Ait 'Atta were sheep and goat herders. Like other pre-Saharan transhumants they drove their flocks northward toward the mountains in summer and deeper into the desert in winter. Some men also owned camels, as well as date palms in the oases of the Dra, the Ziz, and other river valleys of the region. The tribe's total population was probably in the neighborhood of 50,000.[39]

The sections of the Ait 'Atta inhabiting the lower Ziz valley region and sharing the Hammada with the Dawi Mani' belonged almost exclusively to the Ait Unibgi, one of the five primary sections of the tribe. The Ait Unibgi were in turn divided into two subtribes, or *taqbilt-s*. The Ait Khabbash, the larger of them, circulated with their sheep and camels over an extensive area east, west, and south of Tafilalt. Whereas other Ait 'Atta often lived in *qsar-s* during the winter months, most of the Ait Khabbash lived in tents the year-round. A few Ait Khabbash groups mingled with the Ait Umnasf, the other Unigbi *taqbilt*, in the Rteb region of the Ziz valley some miles north of Tafilalt. The Rteb sections conformed more closely to the general Ait 'Atta pattern of residence in houses all or part of the year. Those who left their villages in the spring and summer moved westward from the Ziz in the direction of the middle Ghéris valley and the Jebel Saghro. In the late nineteenth century the Ait Khabbash probably numered between three and four thousand, the Ait Umnasf about four thousand.[40]

Like the Dawi Mani', the Ait 'Atta had *khams khmas*, and since they were neighbors, it is possible that one tribe borrowed the structural principal from the other. In both cases it was believed that possession of *khams khmas* was of itself a source of tribal power and cohesion. The difference lay in the specific purpose it served. Although the Ait 'Atta fifths, like those of the Dawi Mani', may have represented five military corps at some earlier time in the tribe's history, their principal corporate function in the nineteenth century was the annual election of a supreme chief, the *amghar n-ufilla*. His functions were to serve as liaison among the various sections of the tribe, to act as spokesman in relations with outsiders, to coordinate transhumance patterns among the *duwar-s*, to mediate or arbitrate minor disputes, and to coordinate and perhaps lead in time of war.

Each year representatives of the five fifths gathered at a special location in the Jebel Saghro to elect the *amghar*. Two procedural principles governed the election. First, the office passed every year from one *khums* to another according to a fixed system of rotation. That is, each fifth ideally provided the chief once every five years. In practice, an exceptionally effective leader might hold office for a longer period, and, conversely, a poor or unlucky one might be removed from office at any time. Second, the men of the *khums* which was to provide the candidates did not participate in the election but sat in a circle while the members of the other four fifths made the decision by a general vote. It was as if the President of the United States were chosen from among the citizens of California with the citizens of the other forty-nine states doing the voting. These two devices, rotation and cross-election, were used primarily to prevent the emergence of dominant power factions or tyrants. In the Dawi Mani' system, by contrast, each fifth chose its own leader, who might remain in office indefinitely, and rotation and cross-election were not used in the selection of the supreme but temporary *shaykh*. The Dawi Mani', however, appear to have been no more susceptible to petty tyrannies than were the Ait 'Atta. In both tribes factional fluidity and strong egalitarian traditions were probably instrumental in preventing autocratic leadership. The electoral procedures of the Ait 'Atta, therefore, may have amounted to an additional but unessential safeguard.

Since the only corporate function of the Ait 'Atta fifth was participation in the annual election, the sense of unity and brotherhood within it was weaker than within its Dawi Mani' counterpart. The 'Atta fifth did not elect its own chief as the Dawi Mani' *khums* did, it did not stress genealogical ties, and it did not fight as a military unit, at least not in the nineteenth century. Furthermore, kin groups within the fifth inhabited widely separated parts of the tribe's territory, exhibiting a remarkable degree of spatial discontinuity. For example, clans and lineages of the Ait Unibgi (either Ait Khabbash or Ait Umnasf) lived not only around Tafilalt and in the Rteb but also near the lower Dra and in the Dadès valley far up the slopes of the High Atlas.

The sentiment of corporate identity was stronger among members of the *taqbilt* than the fifth. Whereas the only corporate acts of the fifth were to offer up candidates and refrain from voting once every five years or so, the *taqbilt* had its own chief (*amghar n-tmazirt*) and an exclusive annual meeting to elect him. The clans (*ighs amqqran*) comprising the *taqbilt* performed the electoral functipn by rotation and cross-election, just as the fifths did for choosing the chief of the entire tribe. In the case of the Ait Khabbash four clans (Ait 'Amr, Irjdal, Hahyan, and Izulayen), whose founders were reputedly the sons of Khabbash, selected the chief annually,

with each clan offering the candidates every four years. A fifth clan, the
Ait Burk, were *murabtin* and did not participate in the election, though
they may have served as spiritual 'masters of ceremonies' for it. The clans,
like the fifths, had no chiefs themselves. The top chief of the Ait 'Atta
ratified the election of the *taqbilt* leader, who, in turn, was responsible for
appointing local sublineage chiefs. Lineages (*ighs ahzzan*) had no chiefs
and no part in the electoral process. Table 2 indicates the structural and
electoral relationship between the Ait Khabbash and other named, segmented kin groups within the tribe.[41]

Table 2: Segmentary Model of the Ait Khabbash

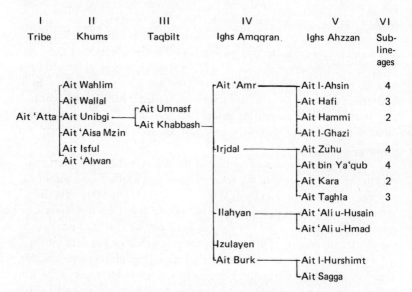

I	II	III	IV	V	VI
Tribe	Khums	Taqbilt	Ighs Amqqran	Ighs Ahzzan	Sub-lineages

The Ait Khabbash and the Ait Umnasf were the only *taqbilt-s* of the Ait
'Atta heavily represented in the Ziz valley region. Most of the tribe inhabited
areas west of what has been defined as southeastern Morocco. In the political life of the Southeast the Ait Khabbash and the Ait Umnasf tended to
behave as though they were two separate and distinct tribes in their
relations with other groups, such as the Dawi Mani' or the people of Tafilalt.
Yet they always regarded themselves as part of the wider Ait 'Atta system
and never failed to play their part in the election of its chief.

Ait 'Atta Imperialism
The immense territory which the Ait 'Atta occupied in the late nineteenth

century was the result of more than three centuries of almost continual
political expansion. The tribe's birthplace was the Jebel Sahgro. In the
thirteenth century the Ma'qil Arabs arrived in southern Morocco and
forced a dispersal of the indigenous Berber tribes. In the sixteenth century,
according to one French account, some of these Berber groups joined into
a political federation under the leadership of the warrior Dadda 'Atta in
order to resist Arab domination. The Ma'qil tribes, however, were beginning
to leave the Saghro region by the late fourteenth century, some of them
moving northward across the Atlas, some pushing southwestward into the
Seguiet el-Hamra and Mauritania, others, including the ancestors of both
the Dawi Mani' and the Arabs of Tafilalt, moving toward the Ziz and
beyond. The new Berber federation, therefore, may have been more an
offensive league aimed at occupying and controlling abandoned territory
than a defensive alliance against Arab oppression. Moreover, it may have
come into being somewhat before 1500.[42]

The brotherhood of the Saghro Berbers was articulated in terms of their
real or putative descent from Dadda 'Atta and his forty warrior grandsons.
Thus, the federation became a tribe, the Ait 'Atta, or 'people of 'Atta.'
Corporate action, at first probably concerned with defense of the Saghro
pastures, was soon directed toward aggressive expansion into the steppe
lands surrounding the mountains. By the seventeenth century the tribe was
outgrowing the Saghro, probably owing to gradual desiccation coupled
with the steady increase of both human and animal populations. This
expansion strengthened tribal cohesion as against outsiders and encouraged
the development of institutions serving political and military unity, notably the election of a supreme chief by rotation and cross-election and the
distribution of pasture rights to specific kin groups over widely separated
portions of the territory.

From the seventeenth century to the end of the nineteenth, 'Atta
aggression dominated the history of much of pre-Saharan Morocco. The
sedentary and pastoral populations inhabiting an immense, irregular circle
of territory around the Jebel Saghro felt the weight of 'Atta power in one
way or another. From the beginning, the tribe expanded primarily by conquest and forceful occupation, secondarily by the peaceful transhumant
migration of sheep and camel herds. On some occasions 'Atta warriors
operated in armies of a few thousand men. Large forces, however, came
together only for specific campaigns and disbanded as soon as the major
battle was over. More often, small, spontaneously organized war parties
operated beyond the home territory, commandeering livestock from other
pastoral groups, raiding for dates and other booty in the pre-Saharan oases,
and in general preparing the way for later occupation or political overlord-

ship.

The initial thrust may have been toward the Atlas slopes since the greenest pasture lands lay in that direction. A small number of deep, narrow river valleys gave access to the mountains. By these routes, however, the expansion achieved only limited success owing to the resistance of other Berber-speaking tribes which had preceded them during the fifteenth or sixteenth centuries. To stand fast against 'Atta pressure, which was applied along a front of more than one hundred miles from the Ziz valley in the east to the Dadès in the west, these tribes banded together in a defensive alliance known as the Ait Yafalman, the 'people who seek the peace.'[43] Raids, skirmishes, and pitched battles between the 'Atta and Yafalman forces went on incessantly from the seventeenth century into the twentieth. During his passage along the southern fringe of the High Atlas in 1884, Charles de Foucauld, the French explorer, received fresh reports, perhaps somewhat exaggerated, of a bloody battle between 8,600 Ait 'Atta and 12,700 of the Ait Mirghad, one of the Yafalman tribes. Losses were estimated at 1,600 for the 'Atta and 400 for the Mirghad. While de Foucauld was there, the two sides were preparing to fight again. The causus belli was the 'Atta's seizure of a number of qsar-s belonging to the Mirghad in the Wad Ghéris valley.[44]

The Yafalman successfully thwarted 'Atta penetration into the High Atlas everywhere except in the Dadès valley region directly north of the Saghro. Here 'Atta groups representing four of the khmas established settlements deep in the mountains. [45] If the Yafalman tribes had been less successful in blockading them, it is likely the 'Atta would have infiltrated the Atlas in much greater numbers or even migrated out of the pre-Sahara altogether.

At any rate, the way was clearer for expansion to the south and east. Southwest of the Saghro they pushed as far as the lower valley of the Wad Dra. In the date growing oases along the river, several subtribal groups established protection agreements (ra'aya) with sedentary communities. The terms of these pacts centered upon 'Atta guardianship of palm groves in return for a percentage of the harvest and rights to grazing land in and around the oasis.[46] Penetration directly south of the Saghro was limited to the part-time occupation of winter pastures in the northern desert, although 'Atta warriors frequently joined the Dawi Mani' and other nomads in raiding for camels deep into the Sahara.[47]

The Ait Khabbash and the Ait Umnasf probably began moving their herds and flocks eastward into the Ziz valley region in the eighteenth century. They must have lost little time in muscling their way into the affairs of the oases and taking a share of the date crops by one means or another.

Aït 'Atta Expansion

The earliest report of their involvement in Tafilalt tells of an 'Atta alliance in 1783-84 with the *makhzan* governor (*khalifa*), who was feuding with a faction of *shurfa*. Sultan Sidi Muhammad led a military expedition which succeeded in expelling the 'Atta warriors from the oasis, though they probably returned soon after he left.[48] In 1816 another *makhzan* expedition routed them again, but two years later they were involved in a war with the Ait Izdig which resulted in the destruction of the *kasba* of Sijilmasa and the total abandonment of the town.[49] Throughout the nineteenth century the Ait Khabbash, and, to a lesser degree, the Ait Umnasf, exerted a violent and heavy-handed influence on the sedentary populations of the valley. The 'Atta offensive was not, however, simply a matter of nomadic blood and thunder. Of greater significance than the violence was the resultant political and social impact on the *qsar*-dwellers.

The most obtrusive manifestation of Ait Khabbash power over other groups was the outright appropriation of land and property. Occupation of the steppe lands around the Ziz valley actually generated little conflict. During the eighteenth and nineteenth centuries, the Ait Khabbash had the land west of the Ziz largely to themselves. East of the valley they shared the Hammada with the Dawi Mani'. The pasturage was sparse but so extensive that intertribal boundary demarcations did not exist and conflicts over grazing rights were isolated and infrequent. Furthermore, reciprocal pacts of aid and hospitality, called *tata* (Arabic) or *tada* (Berber), facilitated peaceful relations between the two tribes. These agreements, which were common in Moroccan tribal society, were made between the members of whole clans, with each individual having a special *tata* partner in the clan of the other tribe. *Tata* was formalized in a special ritual ceremony that varied somewhat from one group to another. Usually, the members of each clan placed their right shoe in a pile. Then each individual chose his *tata* partner by drawing a shoe from the pile of the other clan. A local saint was sometimes present to sanctify the pact. *Tata* brothers (and symbolic blood brotherhood was at least vaguely implied) agreed to give refuge to one another and to perform other acts of assistance. Failure to meet these obligations could have the consequence of tribal dishonor. This institution was a kind of diplomatic bridge between tribes especially useful when herds mingled in the same area, local disputes broke out between families, or safe passage was needed while traveling. *Tata* implied a recognition that numerous points of tension existed between the two tribes and provided one effective method of easing them. *Tata* between the Ait Khabbash and the Dawi Mani' was especially remarkable in that one tribe was Berber-speaking, the other Arab.[50]

In the Ziz valley no such *modus vivendi* was worked out. In Tafilalt the

Ait Khabbash seized permanent control of three *qsar-s* in the Tanijiout district and two more on the outskirts of Sefalat. On many occasions they attacked and attempted to seize or plunder other *qsar-s*, especially in Sefalat.[51] In the Rteb the Ait Khabbash and Ait Umnasf (plus a small group of Ait Isful, another *taqbilt*) occupied about sixteen villages by the end of the nineteenth century.[52] Both groups would probably have commandeered ever more *qsar-s* up and down the valley were it not for the resistance of the Ait Yafalman alliance. In the north the Ait Mirghad and the Ait Izdig, another Yafalman tribe, prevented the 'Atta from advancing further up the valley, but only at the price of fighting that was, according to one Ait Khabbash informant, as frequent as 'the rising of the sun.' The 'Arab Sabbah and the *qsar*-dwellers of Sefalat also joined the Ait Yafalman alliance and called upon the support of the Ait Izdig and Ait Mirghad to check Ait Khabbash aggression in Tafilalt and the districts just north of it.[53]

The way in which the 'Atta invaders treated the sedentary inhabitants after seizing a *qsar* varied widely from one place to the next, depending in part on the kind of resistance they encountered. The previously dominant group in the village was sometimes either killed or evicted. In the Rteb the 'Atta expelled all or most of the Ait Izdig and *shurfa* families and simply confiscated their property, leaving them to seek refuge with their kin elsewhere. In one *qsar* in Tanijiout, according to Ait Khabbash informants, only those people who resisted were forced to leave. Many, including a few *shurfa* families, were allowed to stay and to retain their property.[54] It is likely that in all the *qsar-s* many of the *haratin* remained, since they were still needed for agricultural labor.

Assault and seizure were not the only tactics the Ait 'Atta used in extending their power on their eastern frontier. They also exercised less blatant domination over other groups through special alliances, toll collection, and extortion. Sometime in the late eighteenth or early nineteenth century the Ait Khabbash launched a campaign against the Bani Mhammad and eventually brought them to heel. Perhaps because the Bani Mhammad still preserved a strong tribal structure and may have been partially nomadic, the Ait Khabbash did not subordinate them, but rather united with them in a pact known in the region as *tafargant*, meaning 'interdiction.' The initiating ritual involved the exchange of milk from lactating mothers. *Tafargant* stipulated not only peaceful relations and mutual aid but also strict prohibition on marriage between the two tribes. This taboo implied symbolic brotherhood between them, but it may also have had the practical function of eliminating one source of possible tension.[55]

The bonds of alliance were so strong that the Bani Mhammad became partially integrated into the greater Ait 'Atta political organization. Though never providing the *amghar n-ufilla*, they did participate in his yearly election as part of the Ait Unigbi fifth. They also used rotation and cross-election in choosing their own *shaykh al-'am*, or chief of the year.[56] But even though in a political sense the Bani Mhammad became part of the *khams khmas, tafargant* itself prevented them from becoming assimilated to the Ait 'Atta through either real or putative ties of kinship. Moreover, in spite of the apparently reciprocal nature of their alliance, the Bani Mhammad were never more than junior partners of the Ait Khabbash.

The alliance also developed an economic dimension. Many of the Bani Mhammad were professional caravan merchants, especially active on the routes between Tafilalt and Touat. In their commercial enterprises they joined forces with the Ait Khabbash, who could supply them with guards, drivers, and camels. Other merchants living in Touat or Tafilalt did not enjoy the same protection and privileges as did the Bani Mhammad. Sometimes these merchants 'hitchhiked' with Bani Mhammad caravans. Those who set out on their own usually found themselves paying a toll to cross Ait Khabbash territory or even serving up their merchandise at the point of a gun. Since the Ait Khabbash came to control much of the main Tafilalt-Touat route, they could undoubtedly have plundered caravans at will.[57] But even though French observers usually portrayed them as incorrigible *'coupeurs de route,'* they were generally much more interested in expanding commerce in league with the Bani Mhammad than in hindering or destroying it through brigandage. In short, their commercial activities represented a positive and not insignificant aspect of their penetration east of the Ziz.

The northeastern limit of Ait Khabbash power was the *qsar* of Boudenib, a date-producing center on the Wad Guir inhabited by several *shurfa* families and *haratin*. Here, three hundred Ait Khabbash settled about 1893 in the aftermath of a skirmish with neighboring Ait Izdig.[58] The *qsar*-dwellers of Touat felt the most distant though not the weakest reverberations of the Ait 'Atta expansion. Here, the Ait Khabbash, the Bani Mhammad, and at times other 'Atta groups joined with the Dawi Mani' in tyrannizing the populations of the northern and central districts.[59] As early as 1808 'Atta bands or even individuals were making treaties (*khawa*, meaning literally 'brotherhood') with various villages. Early in the century these relations appear to have been genuinely based on parity and mutual interest. But in the 1830s, as the Ait Khabbash came into the area in greater numbers, their position hardened. They began launching raids against *qsar-s* and following them up with demands for protection money.' To avoid being pillaged or having their palm trees cut down, most of the qsar-dwellers who were subject to this extortion resigned themselves to paying a regular tribute. This state of affairs continued until the arrival of the French.[60]

Ait 'Atta aggression was the dominant theme in the history of southeastern Morocco from the eighteenth to the twentieth centuries. Only in 1900 did the French begin to steal the 'Atta's thunder. The causes of the expansion and the reasons for its long endurance are far from entirely clear. The early phases of it, like other tribal movements out of the Sahara, resulted from a chronic imbalance between population and resources, probably related to long periods of drought.[61] The natural course of 'Atta expansion, or what could have been migration, was toward the greener Atlas pastures. The Ait Yafalman alliance, however, proved to be a highly effective if not decisive barrier against it. With the northern route blocked, therefore, the only alternative for the tribe was to abandon migration and simply to fan out, that is, to take possession of enough pre-Saharan and mountain territory to bring population and resources back into equilibrium. The enduring success of this program west, south, and east of the Saghro permitted the tribe to continue to grow.

The movement of the Ait Khabbash and the Ait Umnasf into the pasture lands on both sides of the lower Ziz was probably accomplished more by peaceful nomadic drift than by purposeful conquest. Indeed, there is no direct evidence that any other pastoralists, other than the Dawi Mani', inhabited that area when the 'Atta first arrived, though the Ait Izdig and the Ait Mirghad might well have circulated much closer to the desert at one time. Most conflict involving the Ait Khabbash and the Ait Umnasf occurred in the oases, which shows that their aggression was directed much more toward the control of agricultural resources than toward the occupation of territory for herding. The staples of their diet were dates, grain, and milk. Indeed they came to depend on dates almost as much as did the qsar-dwellers. Since the extent of arable land, unlike pasture, was strictly limited, nomads and sedentaries either had to share the harvests or else battle for them. More often than not, mutual dependence, involving regular, peaceful exchange of goods, characterized their relations. The 'Atta purchased land and used haratin labor to work it; they traded their meat and wool in the market place for dates, grain, and garden produce; and they guarded palm groves in return for a share of the harvest.

In spite of this essential symbiosis between desert and sown, however, the 'Atta never regarded cultivators, Berber or Arab, white or black, as their social or political equals. To them, with their military prowess, their tribal esprit de corps, and their acute sense of social superiority over sedentary Arabs no less than haratin, all men of the soil were to be despised and coerced. The 'Atta did not hesitate to use force in one form or another when they wanted a larger share of the resources than they could conveniently secure through reciprocity. Were it not for the French intervention, the pattern of aggression against individual *qsar-s* in the Ziz valley and Touat might have continued long after 1900 and even spread to centers further east. One Ait Khabbash informant, looking back on more glorious days, boasted that, except for the French 'counter-offensive,' the Ait 'Atta would have swept all the way across Algeria!

In the long run, however, acts of violence, though almost continuous in the region during the nineteenth century, were always selective and usually restrained. The Ait 'Atta followed no general policy of aimless rapine and pillage, since they aimed to exploit and control the resources of the *qsar* communities, not obliterate them. The knowledge that the region's precarious economic balance depended far more upon the gardens and markets of the oases than upon the meager grasses of the steppe served to temper the application of brute force.

Notes

1. M&L, II, 584-7; George S. Colin,'Origine arabe des grands mouvements des populations berbères dans le Moyen-Atlas,' *Hespéris*, 25 (1938), pp. 265-8; Robert Montagne, *La Civilisation du désert* (Paris, 1947), pp. 243-52; F. de la Chapelle, 'La Sultan Moulay Isma'il et les Berbères Sanhaja au Maroc central,' *Archives Marocaines*, 28 (1931), pp. 18, 19.
2. In French this term is usually transliterated as *'khoums khmas.'* The precise Arabic transliteration is *'khams akhmas,'* but I have dropped the initial alif in this case to conform more closely to local pronunciation and European spelling.
3. The use of the number five as a protective device is discussed in Edward Westermarck, *Ritual and Belief in Morocco* (London, 1926), I, 421, 445-62, 467-71.
4. David M. Hart, 'Segmentary Systems and the Role of "Five Fifths" in tribal Morocco,' *ROMM*, no. 3 (1967), pp. 65-95. Hart compares the function of *khams khmas* among the Ait Waryaghar, the Ait 'Atta, and the Dukkala. He must be credited with having discovered the high incidence of this structure among Moroccan tribes. See also Marcel Lesne, 'Les Zemmour: essai d'histoire tribale,' *ROMM*, no. 4 (1967), p. 55.
5. M & L, II, 589-92; AGGA, 30H. 3, Enquête sur les rapports qui existent entre les indigènes algériens et les tribus du territoire marocain, Lt. Brenot, 'Notice historique de la confédération des Doui Menia,' pp. 5-8, 10, 11.
6. Table 1 is based on M & L, II, 599-610; and interview no. 4.
7. Clans and lineages of the Dawi Mani' claim to have originated among such tribes and localities as the Hamyan Arabs, the Amur, the 'Arib of the Wad Dra region, the Angad of Oranie, the Awlad abu Tayyib of the Marrakech region. Aïn Chaïr (an oasis on the north edge of the tribe's territory), and Figuig. Brenot, 'Notice historique,' pp. 17-22.
8. On the notion of dual origins among the Zimmur see Lesne 'Les Zemmour,' no. 2 (1966), p. 141.

9. Interview no. 4.
10. Capt. Noël, 'Documents pour servir à l'histoire des Hamyan et de la région qu'ils occupent,' *BSGAO*, 35 (1915), pp. 146-8; M & L, II, 584-86.
11. Lt. Bauger, 'La Confédération des Beni Guil,' *BSGAO*, 27 (March 1907), pp. 19, 20. See also Jean Despois, *L'Afrique du Nord* (Paris, 1958), p. 233.
12. Calderaro, 'Beni-Goumi,' *BSGA*, 9 (1904), pp. 307-52; P. Passager and S. Barbançon, 'Taghit (Sud-oranais): étude historique, géographique et médicale,' *Archives de l'Institute Pasteur d'Algérie*, 34 (Sept. 1956), p. 407; Brenot, 'Notice historique,' pp. 10, 11; M & L, II, 593-5.
13. A.G.P. Martin, *Quatre siècles d'histoire marocaine* (Paris, 1923), pp. 159-264 *passim*.
14. Etienne Bovet and François Lamotte d'Incamps, 'Les Conditions socio-économiques de la mise en valeur du perimetre irrigué d'Abadla,' République Algérienne Démocratique et Populaire, 1968. This study was compiled for the Ministère de l'Agriculture et de la Reforme Agraire and other agencies of the Algerian government in connection with the construction of a dam on the Wad Guir at Djorf Torba upriver from the Abadla plain. I am indebted to Mr Lamotte d'Incamps for a copy of the study. Quenard, 'Secteur d'amélioration rurale de la vallée du Guir,' *Documents Algériens*, Jan. 1, 1947, p. 112; Capt. Guoin d'Ambrières, 'Le S.A.R. du Guir,' CHEAM, no. 2.101, Nov. 1952.
15. Quenard, 'Secteur d'amélioration,' p. 112; Bovet and Lamotte d'Incamps, 'Conditions socio-économiques,' pp. 8-10.
16. Lt. Ballot, 'La Vallée inférieure de l'Oued Guir et la coopëration,' *BSGAO*, 66-7 (1945-6), p. 52; R. Capot-Rey, 'Transformations récentes dans une tribu du Sud-Oranais,' *Annales de Géographie*, 16 (March-April 1952), p. 138; M & L, II, 561.
17. AGGA, 30H. 23, Documents établis depuis 14 Mars 1893, Lt. Regnault, 'Doui-Menia,' June 9, 1895; AMG, Alg. 16, Sit. pol. 1904, Jonnart to Min. of War, June 1, 1904, no. 1218. Capt. Jigue, 'Evolution d'une tribu nomade: les Doui Menia,' CHEAM, no. 1553, 1950, p. 27.
18. M & L, II, 593; Brenot, 'Notice historique,' pp. 8, 9; Interview no. 8.
19. Interview no. 7.
20. Calderaro, 'Beni Goumi,' pp. 3-6, 323.
21. M & L, (II, 614) estimated in 1895 that the tribe, not including the Awlad abu 'Anan, possessed about 56,000 sheep and goats and 6,000 camels.
22. M & L, II, 599-612; Capot-Rey, 'Transformations récentes,' p. 140; Interview no. 3.
23. Interviews no. 3 and 5. Studies of other nomadic tribes of the Middle East and Africa were suggestive on the question of the social composition of herding units. Fredrik Barth, *Nomads of South Persia* (Oslo, 1961), pp. 22, 23, 28; J. Bisson, 'Nomadisation chez les Reguibat L'Gouacem,' in UNESCO, *Nomades et nomadisme au Sahara* (Paris, 1963), pp. 55, 56; Ian Cunnison, *Baggara Arabs* (Oxford, 1966), pp. 59-85; I.M. Lewis, *A Pastoral Democracy* (Oxford, 1961), pp. 56-89.
24. Institut de France; Fonds Auguste Terrier, LXI (5951), 'Notes sur les rezzou marocains;' Mercier, 'Une Harka des Doui Menia et Ouled-Djerir vers le Sahel (Août 1904 à Février 1905),' *Ren. Col.* (July 1905), pp. 265-7; Capt. Doury, 'Du Guir à la Mauritanie,' *Ren. Col.* (Nov. 1910), pp. 353-70.
25. Lt. Cavard, 'Les Oulad Djerir,' *Ren. Col.* (Nov. 1904), pp. 279, 280. Calderaro, 'Beni Goumi,' pp. 336-8; M & L, II, 576, 587.
26. The chart of Awlad Jarir segmentation is from Cavard, 'Les Oulad Djerir,' p. 280.
27. AGGA, 22H. 26, Lt. Huot, 'Historique du Cercle de Colomb-Béchar,' 1908; Albert, 'Les Ouled Djerir,' p. 384; Cavard, 'Les Oulad Djerir,' pp. 279-81;

M & L, II, 582, 583.

28. Data on the *jama'a-s* and on the legal system is extremely sparse. Huot, 'Historique'; Brenot, 'Notice historique,' p. 5; M & L, II, 577-9, 581, 589; Interviews no. 5 and no. 7.

29. M & L, II, 577-9, 588; Brenot, 'Notice historique,' pp. 3, 4; Interviews no. 3, 4, and 5.

30. 'No authority was recognized by the confederation. At the head of each tribe (fifth), there was a djemaa, but the notables constituting it rarely agreed with one another; they were most often trying to rival one another, and in practice, each one sought to gather around him a certain number of tents, to develop a clientele for himself, to have a douar on which his influence would shine.' Huot, 'Historique'. The written sources offer scant data on tribal leadership before the conquest. On the exercise of informal leadership among nomadic tribes I have referred to Lloyd Cabot Briggs, *Tribes of the Sahara* (Cambridge, Mass., 1960), pp. 196, 197; E.E. Evans-Pritchard, *The Sanusi of Cyrenaica* (Oxford, 1949), pp. 59-62; Barth, *Nomads of South Persia*, pp. 26-9, 71-90; Cunnison, *Baggara Arabs*, pp. 85, 114, 115; Lewis, *A Pastoral Democracy*, pp. 196-213.

31. The written sources say nothing about Dawi Mani' marriage patterns, but informants (interviews no. 1 and 3) insisted that the exchange of women outside the lineage and even between one fifth and other was not uncommon. Affinal ties between kinship segments would of course have a considerable bearing on the political and social relations between them and between their leaders.

32. M & L, II, 603, 606, 608, 611.

33. AGGA, 30H, 40, Lutte entre deux fractions de Doui Menia, Boitard (Com. Div. Oran) to Gov. Gen., Dec. 30, 1894, no. 638; Brenot, 'Notice historique,' p. 12.

34. Interview no. 6. The informant was an elderly member of the Awlad abu 'Anan, so his account of the feud may have been weighted in favor of his own *khums*. His recollections agree in substance, however, with a briefer summary of the same events reported by Brenot ('Notice historique,' pp. 12, 13) and M & L, (II, 692-4). The account given here is a paraphrased version of the informant's relation in Arabic, which is in my possession on tape.

35. AGGA, 30H, 40, Lutte entre deux fractions de Doui Menia, Metzinger (Com. Div. Oran) to Gov. Gen., Nov. 8, 1894, no. 528; M & L, II, 693, 694.

36. M & L, II, 599-613. According to them, the number of tents in each fifth was: Awlad Yusif, 670; Awlad ibn al-Giz, 400; Awlad Jallul, 312; Idarasa, 424; Awlad abu 'Anan, 470.

37. On *liff* alliances the classic exposition is Robert Montagne, *Les Berbères et le Makhzen*, pp. 182-216. It has been criticized and revised by David M. Hart, 'Clan, Lineage, Local Community and the Feud in a Rifian Tribe,' in Louise E. Sweet, (ed), *Peoples and Cultures of the Middle East* (Garden City, New York, 1970), II, pp. 39-45; and by Ernest Gellner, *Saints of the Atlas* (Chicago, 1969), pp. 64-8.

38. The discrepancy between the vision and the reality in the politics of nomadic societies has been stressed in E.L. Peters, 'Some Structural Aspects of the Feud among Camel-Herding Bedouin of Cyrenaica,' *Africa*, 37 (July 1967), pp. 261-82; Cunnison, *Baggara Arabs*, pp. 187-94; Lesne, 'Les Zemmour,' no. 2 (1966), pp. 142-54.

39. Personal communication from David Hart.

40. AGGA, 30H, 12, Pourparlers avec les Beni Mhamed et Ait Khebbach à Beni Abbès, Regnault (Com. of the Annex of Beni Abbès), 'Notice sur les Ait Khebbach,' Feb. 29, 1904 (hereafter cited as Regnault, 'Notice sur les Ait Khebbach'); AGGA, 31H. 9, Capt. Charpentier (Bureau of Native Affairs Erfoud), 'Etude sur la tribu des Ait Khebbach,' Sept. 20, 1930; Georges Spillmann, *Les Ait Atta du Sahara et la pacification du Haut Dra* (Rabat, 1936),

pp. 93, 94; F. Joly, 'Les Ait Khebbach,' *Travaux de l'Institut de Récherches Sahariennes*, 7 (1951), pp. 133, 134. The population figures are based on estimates by Charpentier, Spillmann, and Joly.

41. The electoral system is described in David M. Hart, 'Segmentary Systems and the Role of 'Five Fifths' in Tribal Morocco,' *ROMM*, no. 3 (1967), pp. 82-92; and in Gellner, *Saints* pp. 81-104. Gellner first brought to light the devices of rotation and cross-election, or as he and Hart call it, 'rotation and complementarity,' found among a number of central Atlas tribes besides the Ait 'Atta.

42. AGGA, 22H. 27, Denoun (Officier-Interprète, Colomb-Béchar), 'Essai de monographie de la tribu berbère des Ait Atta,' April 7, 1913, p. 1; Spillmann, *Ait Atta*, pp. 32, 33, 40, 41.
    This section of the chapter is derived largely from my article 'Berber Imperialism: The Ait Atta Expansion in Southeast Morocco,' in Ernest Gellner and Charles Micaud, *Arabs and Berbers: From Tribe to Nation in North Africa* (Lexington, Mass., and London, 1972), pp. 85-107.

43. F. de la Chapelle, 'Le Sultan Moulay Isma'il et les Berbères Sanhaja au Maroc central,' *Archives Marocaines*, 28 (1931), pp. 23, 24.

44. Charles de Foucauld, *Reconnaissance au Maroc* (Paris, 1939), p. 381.

45. One clan is represented at Ahansal in the heart of the mountains, and, in fact, the entire tribe has long had close relations with the saints of Ahansal (Gellner, *Saints*, pp. 172-8). A conglomerate 'Atta group also inhabits a limited area around Ouaouizarht on the northern side of the High Atlas (Spillmann, *Ait Atta*, p. 36).

46. See F. de la Chapelle, 'Une Cité de l'Oued Dra' sous le protectorat des nomades,' *Hespéris*, 29 (1929), pp. 29-42; D. Jacques-Meunié, 'Les Oases des Lektaoua et des Mehamid,' *Hespéris*, 54 (1947), pp. 397-429; also Niclausse, 'Rapports entre nomades et sédentaires dans le coude du Draa: la raia,' CHEAM, no. 2306, 1954.

47. See note 24.

48. Eugène Fumey (trans), 'Chronique de la dynastie alaouite du Maroc' (Kitab al-Istiqsa), by Ahmed Ennasiri Esslaoui, *Archives Marocaines*, 9 (1906), pp. 336-9; Aboulqâsem ben Ahmed Ezzïani, *Le Maroc de 1631 à 1812*, extracted from the work entitled *al-turjuman mu'arib 'an duwal al-mashriq wa al-maghrib*, trans. O. Houdas (Paris 1886), p. 153.

49. Georges Spillmann, *Districts et tribus de la haute vallée du Draa'* (Paris, 1931), pp. 66, 67; H. Dastugue, 'Quelques mots au sujet de Tafilet et de Sidjilmassa,' *BSGP*, 5th ser., 13 (April 1867), pp. 364, 365, 371, 372; Fumey, 'Chronique,' 10 (1907), pp. 45-9.

50. *Tata* between the Ait Khabbash and the Dawi Mani' is noted in Regnault, 'Notice sur les Ait Khebbach;' F. Albert ('les Ouled Djerir,' *BSGAO*, 25 (Oct. Dec. 1905), pp. 393, 394) gives a list of *tata* links between clans of the Ait Khabbash and Awlad Jarir. Informants of both the Ait Khabbash and the Dawi Mani' confirmed that *tata* existed between them, though not every clan in each tribe had such a relationship. The basic discussion of the institution is G. Marcy, 'L'Alliance par colactation (tâd'a) chez les berbères du Maroc central,' *Revue Africaine*, 2, no. 2 (1936), pp. 957-73. See also, H. Bruno and G.H. Bousquet, 'Contribution à l'étude des pactes de protection et l'alliance chez les Berbères du Maroc central,' *Hespéris*, 33 (1946), pp. 353-70; Spillmann, *Ait Atta*, pp. 50-2; Gellner, *Saints*, p. 137; Lesne, 'Les Zemmour,' no. 2 (1966), pp. 144, 145.

51. Denoun, 'Ait Atta,' pp. 14, 15; Bernard, 'Le Tafilala,' p. 391; Interviews no. 12 and 21. The *qsar-s* in Tanijiout were Mesguida, Sidi bou Bekeur ou Amar, and El Haroun. Those near Sefalat were Megta Sfa and Ottara.

52. Denoun, 'Ait Atta,' pp. 14, 15. These included Zrigat, Amelkir, and Jramna.

53. The most useful contemporary European accounts of the 'Atta offensive in the

Ziz valley are Dr Linarès, 'Voyage au Tafilalet avec S.M. le Sultan Moulay Hassan en 1893,' extracted from *Bullétin de l'Institut d'Hygiène du Maroc*, nos. 3 and 4 (1932), pp. 48, 49; 'Le Tafilelt d'après Gerhard Rohlfs,' pp. 248, 249, 253, 254; and Harris, *Tafilet*, pp. 208, 209, 288. Linarès, Rohlfs, and Harris were all visitors to Tafilalt in the nineteenth century. Also Gendre, 'Tafilalt,' p. 49; and Spillmann, *Ait Atta*, p. 42.

54.   Interviews no. 10, 12, and 21.
55.   Spillmann, *Ait Atta*, pp. 50-52; Interview no. 9.
56.   Spillmann, *Ait Atta*, p. 96; Denoun, 'Ait Atta,' pp. 1, 25.
57.   AGGA, 30H. 3, Enquête sur les rapports qui existent entre les indigènes algériens et les tribus du territoire marocain, Lt. Huot, 'Notice succinct sur les Beraber,' Oct. 18, 1902, pp. 10-13; A.G.P. Martin, *Quatre siècles d'histoire marocaine* (Paris, 1923), pp. 147, 148.
58.   Capt. Canavy, 'Les Régions du Haut-Guir et l'Oued Haiber,' *Ren. Col.* (May 1905), p. 127; Augustin Bernard, *Les Confins algéro-marocains* (Paris, 1911), p. 86; Interview no. 9.
59.   The most distant settlement of Ait 'Atta on the eastern frontier was in the oasis of Tabelbala, a caravan stopover about midway between Tafilalt and Touat. Francine Dominique Champault, *Une Oasis du Sahara Nord-occidental: Tabelbala* (Paris, 1969), pp. 32, 43.
60.   Martin, *Quatre siècles*, pp. 124, 125, 130, 147, 153-60, 287, 288.
61.   See Lesne, 'Les Zemmour,' no. 3 (1967), pp. 100-8.

3 OASIS-DWELLERS: TAFILALT, FIGUIG, AND KENADSA

The oases of pre-Saharan Morocco, scattered out across the desert or running in fragmented ribbons along the river valleys, were the vital centers of all agriculture and trade. They supported remarkably dense populations, which all together comprised a large majority of the region's total. They also sheltered institutions of education, jurisprudence, craftsmanship, and religion, however primitive these might have appeared to the urbane citizens of the imperial cities. The pastoral people of the surrounding steppes, moreover, made the palm groves the headquarters of much of their tribal life. They came primarily to manage agricultural properties and to trade, but also to meet kinsmen, gather news, hold tribal assemblies, organize raids, settle disputes, seek the spiritual or political services of saints, and in some cases even to live part of the year. The oases were the meeting grounds where numerous tribes, clans, and *qsar* communities, otherwise dispersed and fragmented, gathered in order to enlarge, strengthen, and take stock of their social relations. A combination of antagonism and indispensable symbiosis characterized relations between nomads and oasis-dwellers. This fact, however, does not mean that the edge of the palm grove was a distinct frontier between two cultural worlds which merely impinged upon one another from time to time. On the contrary, the oases, like the towns north of the Atlas, were central to the social lives of pastoralists as well as sedentaries because oases and towns alike possessed resources which neither element of the population could do without.

Because the oases were the centers of inter-group life, they were also the focal points of political or military action in the Southeast. The political dynamics of these communities in the late nineteenth century had a substantial bearing on the region's response to the colonial offensive. Indeed, no one was more aware of this than the French army, which conceived the conquest largely as a series of advances from one key oasis to another. Three oases played particularly prominent roles in the events of 1881-1912. Tafilalt, the largest fertile district in the region, was also the most lively center of inter-tribal and *makhzan* politics and the principal staging ground for resistance to the French. Figuig, the second largest center, was much closer to Algeria and therefore under the shadow of the

French army from 1881 onwards. Kenadsa, which lay midway between
Tafilalt and Figuig, was a much smaller oasis, but it was also the head-
quarters of the region's most renowned lineage of politically active saints.
The political aspect of these three communities, together with that of the
Dawi Mani' and the Ait 'Atta, adds up to a fairly comprehensive picture of
the state of southeastern Morocco on the eve of the colonial crisis.

Tafilalt

If southeastern Morocco had a capital, it was Tafilalt: the largest center
of sedentary population in the region; the principal crossroads of both
long-distance and local trade; the cradle and homeland of the 'Alawi
shurfa, and the residence of one of the three *khalifa-s*, or viceroys, of the
sultan. Tafilalt was a kind of Arab island in a Berber sea. Most of its
inhabitants, excepting the *haratin* and Jews, were descendants of Arabic-
speaking Ma'qil nomads, who entered the region from the East in the
thirteenth century and gradually took up agriculture. Other Ma'qil groups
migrated east or north, leaving most of the lower Ziz valley and steppe
lands surrounding Tafilalt to the Ait 'Atta and Ait Izdig Berbers.

Tafilalt was comprised of seven clusters of *qsar-s*, or districts: Sifa,
Tanijiout, Wad Ifli, Ghorfa, Zoua, Sefalat, and Bani Mhammad. Not far to
the north and northwest along the banks of the Ziz and the Ghéris were
four other large oases: Tizimi, Maadid, Jorf, and Fezna. In 1960 the
settled population of this entire region numbered 67,000 living in about
164 *qsar-s*. In the late nineteenth century the population may have been
more in the neighborhood of 100,000, and the number of villages somewhat greater as well.[1]

Each *qsar* was an economic unit whose members cooperated closely
and shared resources, though almost all arable land was privately owned.
The palm groves, gardens, and grain fields around the villages depended
upon water from two main sources, ground water and seasonal floods. The
level of ground water varied from year to year as its replenishment depended upon the volume of both the rain and snowfall in the High Atlas and
the recurrent floods in the Ziz and Ghéris rivers. Ground water was extracted by wells, of which there were a great many in the region, and by
slightly inclined, underground galleries, called *khuttara-s*, which accumulated water and channeled it to the surface. Wells were usually privately
owned and *khuttara-s* were owned collectively by those who built and
maintained them. Flood waters flowed down the Ziz and Ghéris from the
mountains in the spring and fall months, but their volume and timing fluc-
tuated greatly and could never be predicted. When they came they were
channeled into a complex network of irrigation canals, or *saqiya-s* (French,

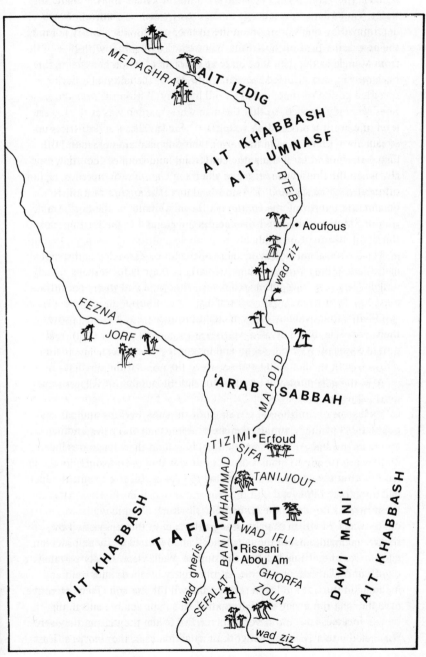

Tafilalt and the Ziz Valley

seguia). The *qsar-s* owned collectively both the canals and the rights to water. The order of precedence in the use of water was almost always determined by one's position on the river or canal, with priority going to the proprietor furthest upstream. When more than one *qsar* used water from a single canal, then the village at the head of it was the first in line. Each *qsar* in turn diverted the water into its own canal system during a specified period of time, usually a full half day. Within the *qsar* the same rules generally applied, so that the man whose garden was at the lowest level of elevation received his water last.[2] Since villages and districts up-stream always had an advantage over their downstream neighbors, the distribution of water was a source of tension and frequent conflict, especially when the flood was meager or when some group attempted to siphon off more than its share. In 1894, for instance, the *khalifa* of Tafilalt organized a punitive foray to prevent the inhabitants of the northern district of Sifa from building a dam across the Ziz and thus diverting most of the flood into their own ditches.

The six social categories of the pre-Saharan oases were all represented in Tafilalt. 'Alawi *shurfa* were particularly numerous for reasons already noted. They may have numbered several thousand and were concentrated most heavily in Wad Ifli, the central district and burial place of Mawlay 'Ali Sharif. Relativel few of them could produce genealogies to prove their bloodline, but they all nevertheless took great pride in their real or putative kinship with the sultan and his royal predecessors. The Idrisi *shurfa* were a smaller group and scattered throughout the districts.

At least eight *murabtin* lineages, the descendants of local saints, maintained *zawiya-s*, or lodges, in Tafilalt. Some of them were active as political mediators or arbitrators, serving both the *qsar*-dwelling and pastoral populations of the region. In the late nineteenth century the leading family in this line were the Awlad Sidi al-Ghazi, whose lodge was located on the eastern side of Sefalat district.[3] It was they who restored peace in Ghorfa after the Awlad abu 'Anan and the Awlad bil Giz fought the first battle of their 1894 feud.

Both the *shurfa* and the saints normally made their living from commerce, ownership of palms and gardens, and collection of *ziyara*, or religious offerings, from the faithful. By no means all of them, however, had sufficient spiritual prestige to inspire a regular flow of donations. The *murabtin* of Tafilalt, as a whole, appear to have reaped much greater income in return for political services than did the *shurfa*. To be effective over the long run a mediating group had to be politically neutral, discretely located, and few in numbers relative to the population they served. Whereas the saintly lineages met these qualifications, the *shurfa*, at least the 'Alawi group, were comprised of a large, sprawling population, whose families fought among themselves and made alliances among the tribes and communities of the region. Indeed they may have hired mediators more often than they supplied them.[4]

The great majority of the inhabitants of Tafilalt were property-owning cultivators who identified socially with a *qsar* and, beyond that, with a cluster of *qsar-s*, or district. Most of them did not reckon kinship above the level of the lineage, which was usually not more than four or five generations deep. A few lineages generally shared a single *qsar*, each one occupying its own quarter. Two groups in the area, however, did have a more ramified kinship organization which cut across village lines. The Bani Mhammad, who occupied the district of the same name, claimed descent from a common ancestor and comprised three clans, each of which was segmented into about four lineages.[5] The 'Arab Sabbah, who lived just north of Tafilalt in the oases of Jorf, Fezna, Tizimi, and Maadid, had a similar 'tribal' organization.[6]

Haratin families were dispersed throughout the region and usually worked as *khammas* laborers for the sedentary groups of higher social status and for the Dawi Mani' and Ait 'Atta who owned palm trees in the area. *Haratin* were not, however, prevented from owning property, and some were independent farmers. Several *qsar-s* in Tafilalt had only *haratin* inhabitants.[7]

The oasis had a Jewish population of about six thousand in the late nineteenth century. Their largest quarter, or *mallah*, was in the *qsar* of Rissani in the Wad Ifli district. Most of them were either merchants, jewelry smiths, or shoemakers.[8]

The *qsar* in Tafilalt, as everywhere else in the Southeast, was an autonomous political unit, a law unto itself. Beyond its high, thick walls political life took on the cast of international relations. The fundamental institution of government throughout the oasis was the *jama'a*, or assembly, of the *qsar*. Normally it was composed of one or more representatives from each lineage. *Haratin* might have participated in some *qsar-s* if their numbers were significant, but Jews never did. The *jama'a* was the supreme executive and judicial body of the village. In addition to deliberating on all political and administrative matters of concern to the residents, it managed the distribution of irrigation water and dispensed penal justice on the basis of either Muslim law (*shari'a*) or custom.

The tightly integrated social life of the *qsar* was vividly manifested in the distinctive electoral procedures practiced widely throughout the oasis. Many *qsar-s* elected a *shaykh* either annually or semiannually to serve as coordinator and spokesman for the assembly. The adult males of the village chose him using essentially the same system of rotation and cross-election that the Ait 'Atta did. That is, the office passed from one lineage to another according to a fixed system of turns, although an exceptional leader could be retained in office for more than one year if no one objected. The electors included only those men belonging to the lineages not providing the candidates. In some *qsar-s* each lineage elected its own delegation to the *jama'a*. In others, however, the entire membership was chosen by cross-election. For example, if a lineage sent four men to the council, then these four were elected by the men of all the other lineages combined. As in the case of the Ait 'Atta these procedures prevented leaders from developing excessive personal influence or from advancing the interests of their lineage over those of the entire village. Under the shadow of perpetual uncertainty over the availability of water, no *qsar* could afford the luxury of chronic internal dissension. The electoral system provided an added guarantee that the community would function as a cooperating economic unit and never deteriorate into a collection of feuding families and lineages.[9]

Since the *qsar-s* themselves were autonomous and largely self-sufficient relations between them were always tense and guarded. Sometimes competition for limited resources, especially water, escalated into open feuding, which could only be settled by the intervention of third party mediators. Yet it would be wrong to imagine that every *qsar* was at all times a closed fortress bristling with guns. Under normal circumstances circulation throughout Tafilalt presented no difficulties, and *qsar-s* frequently worked together to defend themselves against attack (notably from the Ait Khabbash) or to deal with natural emergencies. From time to time the *qsar-s* in each of the seven districts met together in a large *ad hoc* assembly. This body, to which every village in the district could send representatives, functioned and made decisions only under unusual circumstances, such as the outbreak of warfare. It amounted to a kind of league of *qsar-s* which most of the time had only a latent existence. Nonetheless, it gave each of the districts a distinct political identity which localization alone did not generate. The Bani Mhammad, unlike the people of the other six districts, were united by kinship as well as by localized residence. They elected a tribal *shaykh* each year who coordinated the affairs of all the villages, served as their spokesmen, and mediated their minor disputes. Similarly, the 'Arab Sabbah united the four oases just north of Tafilalt by choosing annually a top chief.[10]

Tafilalt would have been devoid of overarching government were it not for the presence of the *khalifa*, or viceroy of the sultan. According to Moroccan political theory in the nineteenth century, the sultan delegated special authority to three *khalifa-s*, who governed in his name and in his absence the three great provinces or 'realms,' which centered on Fez, Marrakech, and Tafilalt. The *khalifa-s* were responsible for overseeing and harmonizing the work of local officials and judges appointed by the central government, for presiding at Friday prayer and religious holidays, and in general for exerting a kind of moral authority over the population under their jurisdiction. They were usually close relatives of the sultan and were assisted by a detachment of royal troops and an administration having the hierarchical structure of a miniature *makhzan*.[11]

In reality, the authority of the *khalifa-s* was subject to the same military limitations and compromises with local power as was that of the sultan. The viceroys of Fez and Marrakech could indeed govern within the gates of their city, though their influence in the rural sectors of their province depended upon the prevailing military balance between the *makhzan* and the tribes. The *khalifa* of Tafilalt, by contrast, was never really a governor at all, since his realm was far beyond the reach of the royal army except on some rare occasions. Tafilalt boasted the status of 'provincial capital,' not because it was any longer a bastion of 'Alawi power in the desert, but because of its religious and ideological significance. The *khalifa* was a living assertion that the roots of the dynasty were still firmly planted in the homeland and resting place of its founder.

The *khalifa* lived in the *qsar* of Rissani in the central Wad Ifli district, which was heavily populated by 'Alawi *shurfa*. His administration consisted of a small number of *shurfa* subalterns and a *qadi*, or judge, who was appointed by the central government. The assemblies of the *qsar-s*, as well as local students of Muslim law (*talib-s*) who developed their own legal clientele, handled most penal and civil litigation in the first instance. The *qadi* adjudicated appeals and exceptionally critical disputes all on the basis of the *shari'a*.

More often than not the *khalifa* had only a few dozen *makhzan* soldiers directly under his authority. Therefore, he could exercise force only on those occasions when a body of *qsar*-dwellers or, more likely, a company of armed nomads would offer their support. He collected *zakah* and *ashur*, the two koranic taxes, as well as *ziyara* for the sultan, from those wishing to offer them voluntarily. But since he had no regular armed force of any significance, he could never collect taxes forcibly — and naturally few paid anything at all. Despite these severe restrictions on his authority, he did perform a number of practical services for both the *makhzan* and the local population. He policed the central market place at Abou Am, mediated quarrels and feuds between *qsar-s* and tribes, administered a considerable amount of land and treasure belonging to the royal family, kept an eye on

and mollified troublesome *shurfa* or members of the palace elite who had
been banished to Tafilalt, and served as a liaison between the sultan and
the *shurfa* or other groups in the region. In short, he stood outside the web
of tribal and village relationships and a cut above the other 'Alawi *shurfa*.
Therefore, he was in an advantageous position to play a prominent mediational role in the political and social life of the region.[12]

The presence of the *khalifa* and the complex *makhzan* interests revol-
ving around him, together with the size of the population and the level of
trade and agricultural production, made Tafilalt the hub of southeastern
Morocco. By comparison most of the other *qsar* communities of the region
receded into parochial obscurity, having no noticeable impact on the
region in the nineteenth century. The principal exception to this rule was
Figuig, which stood at the eastern door of the Southeast and paralleled
Tafilalt in a diminutive way as a center of population, agriculture, and
trade.

Figuig

The oasis of Figuig, a great, green expanse of palm trees, lies in a broad
depression enclosed on three sides by craggy, treeless mountains which
form some of the western links in the Saharan Atlas chain. The Wad
Zousfana, which is born not far north of Figuig, skirts the exposed side of
the depression to the east, then continues southward into the Sahara. The
palm groves occupy an area of about seven and a half square miles. A
steep, irregular cliff running from east to west cuts through the middle of
the oasis, dividing it into upper and lower sections. Six of Figuig's seven
qsar-s lie on the plateau above the escarpment. These were al-Oudaghir,
Oulad Sliman, al-Maïz. al-Hammam Foukani, al-Hammam Tahtani, and
al-Abidat. Zenaga, whose population was almost as great as that of the
other six *qsar-s* combined, lay alone on the plain below the cliff. At the
turn of the century the entire agglomeration of Figuig numbered probably
not more than sixteen thousand people.[13]

In the nineteenth century the population of each *qsar* was composed of
a number of extended kin groups, plus *haratin* laborers. All of the permanent residents of Figuig were Berber-speaking and, in addition, most adult
men spoke Moroccan Arabic. The key unit of social organization was the
clan, called *filqa*, or sometimes *fakhda*. Zenaga had eight or nine of them,
the other villages from three to five. The members of each clan claimed
descent from a distant common ancestor, though no one could name in
sequence all the generations back to him. The families comprising a clan
resided together in a quarter of the *qsar* (with some exceptions), sometimes maintained their own mosque, and sent representatives to a clan

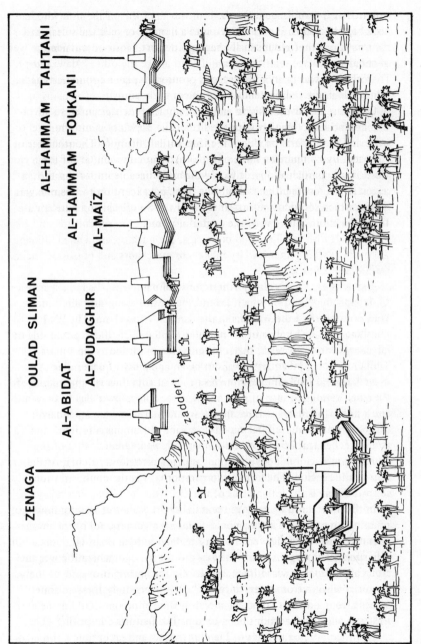

ZENAGA

OULAD SLIMAN

AL-ABIDAT

AL-OUDAGHIR

AL-HAMMAM TAHTANI

AL-HAMMAM FOUKANI

AL-MAÏZ

zaddert

Figuig

council, or *jama'a*. In general, the clan was the focus of the individual's social relationships. It was divided into a number of politically less important patrilineages (*ighs*), usually having a depth of four or five named generations.

With the exception of al-Oudaghir, none of the *qsar* populations as a whole claimed to be descended from a common ancestor. The clans of al-Oudaghir, however, insisted emphatically that their genealogies all extended back to Mawlay Ahmad al-Udaghiri, an Idrisi *sharif* who migrated to Figuig from Fez in the thirteenth century.[14] The residents of the other *qsar-s* tended to discredit this assertion, though, at the same time, many families in Figuig would probably have professed a sharifian ancestry if questioned on the subject. *Soi-disant* Idrisi *shurfa* were in great abundance in Morocco, although relatively few were able to substantiate their allegations with valid genealogical documents.

A few Jewish families lived in Zenaga, al-Oudaghir, and Oulad Sliman. All of them were either jewelry makers or merchants and possessed their own quarters in the *qsar*.[15]

Figuig is practically the northernmost palm grove in the long succession of date-producing oases which extend southward along the valley of the Wad Zousfana and the Wad Saoura to Touat. A count made in 1911 numbered Figuig's palms in the neighborhood of 125,000, making this the largest cluster of groves in the frontier region, with the exception of Tafilalt.[16] Some inhabitants of Zenaga, and possibly of other *qsar-s* as well, owned land and palm groves in the surrounding region, notably in the small spring fed *qsar* of Beni Ounif, which lay a few miles to the south and was inhabited by *haratin* and a few Arab families. A narrow pass carpeted with palms led between two barren mountains, the Jebel Zenaga and the Jebel Tarbla, to connect Figuig with Beni Ounif.[17]

Figuig was a more consistently prospering community than most other *qsar-s* in the region. The key to this prosperity was the constant water supply. Whereas the inhabitants of the Ziz, Guir, and Zousfana valleys owed their food supply in large measure to the whims of fitfully flowing rivers, the residents of Figuig could count on a year-round, if not always abundant, flow of water from twenty underground springs. Horizontal galleries, called *fuggara-s*, led the water to the surface, where it continued along open canals toward the palm groves. The springs provided the only appreciable source of water, since rainfall averaged only three to four inches a year, and the Zousfana, which flowed above ground only part of the year, was too far from the oasis to permit irrigation from it.[18]

As in Tafilalt, farmers owned land privately, and all of them who made use of the water of a single canal had a share in its ownership and maintenance. Figuig differed from Tafilalt, however, in that water rights were not the collective property of the *qsar* to be divided proportionally among the constituent families. Rather they were privately owned and, like land, could be bought, sold, rented, or exchanged.

Figuig had one of the most sophisticated systems of irrigation organization and management in North Africa.[19] Water use was measured in time rather than volume. The unit of measure was the *kharruba*, which represented the flow of water into a garden or reservoir for exactly forty-five minutes. The proprietors who used the water of one major canal took turns according to a fifteen day cycle. In general, 32 *kharruba-s* filled one 24 hour period, that is, 480 in each cycle. If a man owned one unit, he could irrigate his gardens for 45 minutes every 15 days. Some men owned many units and were entitled to use them all during the cycle. Since a proprietor had rights to all the water flowing into the main canal during his turn, only one property could be irrigated at a time. Indeed, a management specialist, called the *sayrafi*, memorized the names of each *kharruba* owner in his order of turn, saw to it that the proper sequence was followed, and supervised purchases, sales, and exchanges of *kharruba-s*, which took place at six month intervals. Moreover, Figuig's legal system, which drew upon custom more than upon the *shari'a*, included an extensive body of laws relating to the use and misuse of water.[20]

Since relatively few inhabitants of Figuig had alternate sources of wealth besides their palms and gardens, the acquisition and protection of water rights were imperative. A man's economic well-being in relation to his neighbors was invariably founded on his possession of more or fewer *kharruba-s*. Prices rose and fell depending on the current volume of water flowing from the spring, the place of the *kharruba* (hour and day) in the order of turn, and the number of gardens and groves to be watered. Yet the supply of *kharruba* 'time slots' were strictly limited, so the demand for them was consistently high.

The problem of the proportional distribution of water tended to pervade all relations between men, clans, and *qsar-s* and had a preponderant impact on political relations in the oasis, perhaps more intensively so than in Tafilalt. The political unity of each of the seven *qsar-s* probably evolved out of the need to defend one or more springs and the network of canals leading from them. Everyone in the village had a common stake in the maintenance and protection of its springs. Two of the largest of them were each shared by residents in more than one *qsar*. The problem in these situations was to defend the galleries leading from the spring and to prevent anyone from tampering with them with the illicit intention of diverting water into another canal system.

Because the realm of common interest seldom extended beyond the boundaries of the *qsar* and its surrounding palm groves, Figuig never developed an oasis-wide system of law or government. The *jama'a-s* of the seven *qsar-s* were each in their own territorial sphere the supreme executive and judicial body. In addition to deliberating on all political and administrative matters of concern to the residents, they had sole competence to dispense penal justice on the basis of written statutes, or *qanun-s*. Local judges handled most civil litigation, but the *jama'a* could intervene in any case (of which there were many) involving water rights on the pretext that the public good was compromised. All the adult males in the village elected the members of the *jama'a* by a majority vote, each clan being alloted a certain number of positions. The term of office was for life.

The *qsar-s* of Figuig were autonomous, cohesive social units, yet somewhat less so than in Tafilalt. They never used rotation and cross-election in choosing the *jama'a* and, although highly respected individuals sometimes came to dominate the proceedings, they never elected *shaykhs*. Moreover, the localized clans within the *qsar-s* had their own assemblies, composed of the heads of all the component families. These bodies had the positive task of supervising the welfare of the clan members, but they also served to sharpen the lines of self-interest between groups within a single village. Perhaps because the water supply, and therefore the agricultural yield, was a good deal more constant in Figuig than in Tafilalt, the *qsar* communities could tolerate internal fissiparousness to a degree. At any rate, the political mechanisms they used do not appear to have aimed so deliberately at ensuring *qsar*-wide cooperation and solidarity as did those of Tafilalt.[21]

Although the citizens of one *qsar* could normally visit or even own property in the territory of another, the civic life of Figuig was indeed meager. The seven villages were continually in a state of either latent or active hostility to one another, more often than not involving the water supply upon which each depended for survival. Open conflict was all the more likely when springs and *fuggara-s* were shared by the inhabitants of more than one village. Then, the temptation to alter or divert the flow of water was sometimes too great to suppress. Along the valleys of the Ziz or the Guir, upsteam villages had the advantage over their downstream neighbors in the appropriation of water for irrigation. In fact, upstream priority was throughout Morocco the most common basis for determining the distribution order of surface water. In Figuig the situation was in a sense reversed. All of the springs in the oasis lay on the plateau above the cliff. The water seeped downward through the ground, sometimes running in little streams down the escarpment. The spring called Zaddert, the largest in the oasis, was located on the upper edge of the cliff just west of al-Oudaghir. Zenaga had to obtain its water supply by tunneling into the spring from below. In order to increase the flow of water into Zenaga, the inhabitants had only to lower the level of the spring by deepening the cavern and underground *fuggara-s*. They could do so by burrowing in or by setting off an explosive charge. As the water level fell, less flowed into the *fuggara-s* on the plateau, namely those belonging to al-Oudaghir, al-Abidat, and, at one time, the village of al-Djouabeur (a ghost *qsar* since the later eighteenth century). Increasing the flow into Zenaga also had the effect of lowering the water table all over the plateau and thus decreasing the supply in the springs used by al-Maïz and Oulad Sliman as well.[22]

The struggle for control of the water of Zaddert appears to have dominated inter-*qsar* relations throughout the nineteenth century. According to de Castries, the French officer whose description of Figuig published in 1882 has been the basis of several subsequent commentaries, al-Oudaghir was, in the fourteenth century, allied with its neighbor al-Djouabeur in a successful struggle to prevent Zenaga from appropriating any water from Zaddert. In the late eighteenth century Zenaga made a pact with al-Oudaghir, and together they destroyed al-Djouabeur. Subsequently, most of the water went to al-Oudaghir, but Zenaga continued its efforts to appropriate a greater share. The spring was the object of regular feuding among Zenaga, al-Oudaghir, and al-Abidat during most of the nineteenth century, with al-Abidat bowing out early in the struggle and falling under the domination of Zenaga. About 1877, Zenaga carried off the final victory by mining the spring and blowing a hole large enough to deprive al-Oudaghir of much of its water. Zenaga then built a small fort in the area of Zaddert to prevent any further manipulation of the water level. Al-Oudaghir, whose population was something less than half that of Zenaga, was no doubt worn down over a long period of protracted and often bloody fighting.[23]

Altercations over water, however, were not the exclusive cause of inter-*qsar* feuding. In 1885, for example, a homicide was blamed for a feud in which Zenaga, al-Maïs, Oulad Sliman, al-Hammam Tahtani, and al-Hammam Foukani took part. In 1886, families in Zenaga and al-Maïs reportedly came to blows over the theft of some goats.[24] About 1892, an inheritance dispute between a young man of al-Maïs and his paternal aunt led to an assassination and a short but bloody fight involving both al-Maïs and Zenaga.[25]

The patterns of alliance and opposition in these struggles were extremely fluid. Within one *qsar* two different clans might be on opposing sides, each in alliance with clans in other *qsar-s*. In the al-Maïs inheritance dispute the clans of Zenaga were reported to be divided into two opposing camps, each in support of one of the contesting parties, although the reasons for their involvement are not made clear. In 1885 and 1886, Zenaga was also divided into two groups, but then the alignment of the clans was somewhat different. In all of these conflicts some *qsar-s* or clans remained neutral.[26] Within the clan overt conflict was probably rare since most of the families resided together in one section of the *qsar* and they married into one another frequently.[27] Marriages across clan lines within the *qsar* were also common and must have served as a deterrent to feuding at that level as well. On the other hand, marriage ties between *qsar-s* were rare.[28]

French writings on politics in the oases of the Sahara tended to explain feuding in terms of struggles between binary leagues, or *saf-s*. The term *saf* (or *sof*), which the French initially employed in reference to leagues of alliance and mutual assistance in the Kabylie Mountains of eastern Algeria, was later extended, sometimes in a presumptive fashion, to denote political factions or parties in the desert communities.[29] Although a kind of 'two party system' did indeed exist in such oases as Ouargla, Laghouat, and Touat, Figuig clearly did not have two *saf-s* nor, for that matter, any definite number of permanent alliance structures. Rather alliance and opposition shifted continually and appears to have been founded, as it was among the Dawi Mani' nomads, mainly on prevailing economic interests and commitments. The opposition between Zenaga and al-Oudaghir was constant during at least part of the nineteenth century, but in this case the specific cause of conflict, the inequitable distribution of water, was constant as well. In all the feuds which were recorded, some *qsar-s* stayed out of the fray altogether. The most likely bifurcation leading to a condition of balanced opposition would have been a cleavage between Zenaga on the plain and all the other *qsar-s* on the plateau. Al-Oudaghir, however, was never consistently aided by any other village on the plateau and remained the decided loser throughout the later nineteenth century.[30]

To state that inter-*qsar* conflict in Figuig was not normally checked by a balanced alignment of families does not mean that no procedures existed for preventing open feuding or bringing it to an end. Feuding on some occasions reached devastating proportions, resulting in wanton destruction of palm trees and gardens. The dependance of the *qsar* on its groves and irrigation works, however, made it unwise to allow intense fighting to continue unchecked for long. Parties on both sides, with personal interests in halting the feud, would sometimes successfully arrange a truce. On other occasions the *jama'a* of a neutral *qsar* might intervene as a mediator.[31] As in Tafilalt, *murabtin* lineages specializing in mediational services were frequently called in to prevent or halt serious outbreaks of violence.[32]

In southeastern Morocco and indeed throughout the Sahara nomads often became embroiled in oasis feuds, sometimes exploiting internal cleavages to assert their own domination over the entire sedentary community. In Figuig, by contrast, interference of nomads in internal affairs or extortion of privileges and tribute was extremely rare, at least in the nineteenth century. In this respect Figuig stands in marked contrast to Tafilalt, where the Ait 'Atta put increasingly heavy strains on the *qsar*-dwellers during the decades before the French occupation. Perhaps Figuig's geographical position in a depression surrounded by mountains provided an exceptionally effective defense against nomad forays. On the positive side, the tribes who pastured in the area benefited considerably from peaceful relations with Figuig. The Bani Gil, Amur, Dawi Mani', and Awlad Jarir all came into the oasis regularly to trade sheep, wool, and grain for dates and imported merchandise. All of them also maintained grain storage silos in one *qsar* or another.[33] Some individuals of the Bani Gil and Amur owned a few palms and *kharruba-s* there.[34] Of course nomads traded and stored grain in many other oases in the region as well. Nevertheless, the people of Figuig did not submit to the sort of intimidation that often characterized nomad-sedentary relations elsewhere in the Southeast.

Tafilalt was an Arab island in a Berber sea, Figuig the exact reverse. The steep mountains which hemmed in the oasis and concealed it from the surrounding region served to accent its linguistic and cultural particularism. It is striking, therefore, that the population exhibited no strong political consciousness in relation to outsiders. No oasis-wide political, judicial, or economic institutions existed, and the notables of the seven *qsar-s* were known to have met together only on the rarest occasions. Indeed, the villages displayed a bitter and endemic hostility toward one another not evident in Tafilalt or other oases of the region. The earliest French description of Figuig noted:

> ... their wars are the most cruel that the inhabitants of the Sahara
> engage in; because they even ravage the palm trees, despite the tacit
> convention, respected everywhere else, to attack only men and to
> spare the life-sustaining tree of both the victor and the vanquished.[35]

This divisiveness was very likely in part a consequence of the oasis' unusual topography and hydrological system. The existence of several springs and the relative steadiness of the flow of water from them (in contrast to the seasonal floods upon which riverain oases heavily depended) diminished

the need for cooperation between the *qsar-s* in the management of irrigation water and therefore in other affairs as well. Indeed, cooperation
was hardly encouraged as long as one village could permanently confiscate water from another by manipulating the water table. Zenaga and
al-Oudaghir quarreled so persistently because the one could not resist the
temptation to acquire an ever larger share of spring water, while the other
faced the possibility of economic extinction. If nomad-sedentary conflict,
that is, Ait 'Atta aggression, was the commanding aspect of history in
Tafilalt on the eve of the French conquest, internal dissension and cleavage
was the pervading circumstance in Figuig. In both cases it was these distinct and contrasting local issues, more than any generic characteristics of
oasis communities, that would shape the populations' response to the
colonial crisis.

Kenadsa

Between Figuig and Tafilalt lay a number of much smaller agricultural
communities scattered out across the desert fringe. Most of them possessed
only one *qsar* and a population of anywhere from a few hundred to a few
thousand. Some of them served as local market centers or as stopovers on
the regional trade routes. Others sheltered the tombs of saints and in some
cases sufi *zawiya-s*, which attracted pilgrims, travelers, pupils of the koran,
sick and downtrodden folk, and litigants seeking saintly arbitration.
Among these minor oases, Kenadsa, located in the territory of the Dawi
Mani' about midway between Figuig and Tafilalt, was one of the very few
whose *zawiya* and holy lineage brought it more than purely local notoriety.
In fact, Kenadsa enjoyed a renown throughout Morocco and western
Algeria out of all proportion to its small size and population.

   The founder of the lodge of Kenadsa was al-Hajj Muhammad ibn Abu
Ziyan, an Idrisi *sharif* of the early eighteenth century who, while traveling
between Morocco and Mecca, developed a reputation for asceticism,
religious knowledge, and miracle working – all the hallmarks of a sufi
saint. He gradually gathered around himself a body of disciples who sought
beneficence, understanding of the faith, and mystical union with the God-
head through association with him and contact with his *baraka*. Under his
leadership Kenadsa became the headquarters of a new sufi brotherhood
(*tariqa*) with its distinctive set of litanies and devotions and its hierarchy of
saintly officers. After his death, his *baraka*, together with the administrative leadership of the order, passed through a line of his direct descendants,
all of them men of piety. Other members of the Awlad abu Ziyan lineage
became noted holy men as well. Following the common pattern of the
North African saint cult, the tomb of Abu Ziyan became the spiritual well-

spring of the *zawiya*. Disciples gathered around it, pilgrims made supplications on it, and tribesmen swore collective oaths before it, all believing in the dead saint's continuing spiritual presence and ability to intercede between them and God.[36]

Kenadsa became famous not only as a shrine, refuge, and headquarters of the Ziyaniya, but also as a commercial entrepôt on one of the trans-Saharan routes between Turkish Algeria and the Sudan. The saints themselves engaged in commerce, and, more important, they specialized in guiding caravans and protecting them from desert marauders. As sufi lodges in North Africa were sanctuaries for refugees and outlaws, so caravans under the protection of a saint were immune from molestation. In both cases anyone who dared incur upon the supernatural authority of the saint risked divine retribution of undetermined severity. The *murabtin* received *ziyara* in return for their commercial services and indeed accumulated considerable wealth. After the French occupied Algeria, however, the route through Kenadsa rapidly declined in importance. The oasis deteriorated into nothing more than a local market place, and by the late nineteenth century the saints had largely given up the mercantile branch of their profession.[37]

The *zawiya* remained prosperous, however, owing to its continuing spiritual and political activities. In a sense the saints had two distinct clienteles. Their spiritual following comprised those who were actual affiliates of the brotherhood or participated in its ritual exercises. Very few of the Dawi Mani' or other tribesmen of the Southeast belonged in this category. The Ziyaniya was like other North African confraternities in that the great majority of its active members were sedentary, often urban people who had the time and inclination to join mystical societies. Most of them lived in the towns and cities of Oran Province in Algeria, though there were some in Morocco, notably the northeastern region. These devotees attended religious and social meetings organized by *muqaddam-s*, or local supervisors of the order. With the permission of French authorities, holy men from Kenadsa, often the head (*shaykh*) of the brotherhood himself, made regular tours into Algeria to visit the various congregations. During these trips they held mystical devotions and dispensed *baraka* in return for offerings, part of which the *muqaddam-s* collected in advance of their arrival.[38]

Among the tribes and *qsar* communities of the Southeast the Ziyani saints had a second, political clientele, for which they performed services of mediation and arbitration that were quite distinct from their spiritual activities as sufi mystics. Good tribal leaders were invariably good mediators as well, but when a major internal or inter-tribal conflict needed settling, they were seldom equal to the task. Every leader was himself entangled in a web of alliances and associations which in all sorts of ways could undermine his function as neutral third party. The wider the conflict the greater the difficulty in finding a leader who did not have some partiality to the cause of one side or the other. In a conflict between two tribes, or two *qsar-s*, mediation by a member of either one of them was out of the question. The settlement of hostilities, therefore, often required the intervention of agents who were readily available but outside the tribal system altogether. The saints of Kenadsa, like other holy lineages of North Africa having exceptionally good reputations for political brokerage, maintained a strict neutrality in inter-tribal affairs and generally agreed to take on only the most serious or intractable cases, often after tribal leaders, or perhaps lesser saints, had failed to find a solution. It was probably no accident that the *zawiya* was situated near the conjunction of the territory of three major tribes: the Dawi Mani', the Awlad Jarir, and the Bani Gil. Throughout North Africa saints having political services to offer commonly settled in locations near where conflict was most likely to occur. In the later nineteenth century the Awlad abu Ziyan mediated (though not always with definitive success) in feuds or wars involving these three tribes, as well as the Ghananma of the Saoura valley and the *qsar*-dwellers of Figuig. Their interventions of course always involved the supernatural in the sense that they based their decisions on divine authority. To contravene the judgment or guarantee of a *murabit* was to contravene God. The tribes and communities who used their services gave them donations, usually in kind and often on a regular basis. Families of the Dawi Mani' and the Awlad Jarir traditionally gave them one sheep a year, in addition to other gifts.[39]

Whereas Tafilalt and Figuig were important in the late nineteenth century for their population, agriculture, and trade, Kenadsa was important only for its saints. Its population was about 2,000, including about twenty families of the Awlad abu Ziyan, plus a few non-holy Arab lineages and some *haratin*. These 'lay' families cultivated the agricultural land of the oasis, all of which belonged to the *zawiya*. The saints also owned considerable land in other oases of the region, including Tafilalt. A *jama'a* composed of the saints plus a few representatives from the Arab families governed the *qsar*.[40]

It should be pointed out that while the Awlad abu Ziyan were among the most highly reputed mediators in the region, they by no means had a monopoly on their trade. The other holy families commanding widespread influence and reverence in the late nineteenth century were the *murabtin* of Kerzaz, a *zawiya* located on the northern edge of Touat; the saints of

Medaghra in the Ziz valley, a lodge affiliated to the huge Darqawa brotherhood; the Awlad Sidi al-Hanafi of the Rteb district of the Ziz valley; the
Awlad Sidi al-Ghazi of Tafilalt; and, lastly, Sidi Abu 'Amama and his son
of Figuig and Touat. (Of all these groups, excepting the saints of Kerzaz,
much more will be said later.) The tribes and *qsar* communities of the
region needed to be able to choose between one group of holy men and
another, since an incompetent mediator was no mediator at all. The effective service a saint rendered was in large measure the result of his having
literally to compete with other saints for business. The history of North
Africa is littered with would-be sufi peacemakers who failed to meet the
exacting standards of their profession. If the holy men mentioned here
were the region's leading lights in the late nineteenth century, other saints,
in other oases, were merely waiting in the wings, ready to seize whatever
opportunities came their way.[41]

In North Africa and the Middle East cities and towns lacked the sort of
social and political unity found in the urban centers of premodern Europe.
Rather they were usually divided into a number of village-like quarters,
each one a distinct, autonomous social entity. Institutions linking one
quarter with another tended to be weak and intermittent. The largest oases
of southeastern Morocco manifested this characteristic to an extreme
degree. Although their populations lived tightly together within the
strictly limited frontiers of arable land, the *qsar*, rather than the oasis as
a whole, was the prime and almost exclusive unit of corporate life. North
African cities at least had a single outer wall, which enhanced their physical unity. The large oases of the Southeast were subdivided by many sets
of walls, which jarringly contradicted the distinct natural unity of the
palm grove.

Small oases with only one *qsar*, such as Boudenib or Béchar, had a
highly integrated social life, fostered and regulated by a single assembly
and in some cases by an elected *shaykh*. Social solidarity was exceptionally strong in *zawiya*-villages like Kenadsa, where all public life revolved
around the special activities and interests of the saints. Oases with more
than one *qsar*, however, almost always had more than one government –
and therefore a high level of internal divisiveness and conflict. Indeed,
antagonistic relations between *qsar*-dwellers and nomads over the exploitation of agricultural resources were not necessarily any more severe or
protracted than between one *qsar* population and another. In Tafilalt the
khalifa and *qadi* of the *makhzan* intervened in political life to some extent
and mediated or arbitrated disputes. But they had no regular administrative apparatus nor any stable means of enforcing their decisions through

coercion. They represented the symbols rather than the substance of central government.

On the eve of the French conquest the dense oasis populations were, as a result of their deep social divisions, ill-prepared to organize and undertake any program of common political or military action. The pastoral tribes in the region, though themselves subject to internal cleavages, at least possessed the integrating ideology of kinship and in the case of the Ait 'Atta a long history of aggressive expansion. Ironically, Tafilalt and Figuig, the two oases having the greatest concentration of population and food resources, were the least capable of mobilizing them for unified action. Tafilalt was an enormous, totally acephalous agglomeration of social modules, which in the face of many years of Ait 'Atta aggression had never put up anything approaching a united front. Figuig was comparatively free of nomadic encroachments and perhaps for that very reason was even more preoccupied with internal rivalries. As the colonial crisis drew near, there was little evidence in political life that some latent community spirit would suddenly spring forth to unite these fractured populations against the new external threat.

Yet at the same time the social isolation of one *qsar* from another was far from total. If village walls succeeded in containing almost all sense of community, people did take part in activities which extended their social horizons and modified to a degree parochial suspicions and hostilities. Of the several ways in which individuals developed lasting contacts beyond the borders of their *qsar* — and these included membership in sufi brotherhoods, common devotion to saints, and *ad hoc* political alliances — the most important as a deterrent to the effects of social fragmentation was trade and the market place.

Notes

1. Daniel Noin, *La Population rurale du Maroc* (Paris, 1970), pp. 183-90; Augustin Bernard, *Les Confins algéro-marocains* (Paris, 1911), p. 358; E. Menneson, 'Ksour du Tafilalt,' *Revue de Géographie du Maroc*, no. 8 (1965), p. 89; F. Gendre, 'Tafilalt,' *Revue de Géographie Marocaine*, 26, nos. 3-4 (1942), p. 52.
2. Morocco, Office National des Irrigation, 'Amenagement de la région du Tafilalt: rapport général preliminaire' (no date). I am indebted to Mr E. Menneson of the Moroccan Ministry of Agriculture for the use of this study. L. Clariond, 'Le Problème de l'eau au Tizimi et au Tafilalet,' *Bullétin Economique du Maroc,* 4 (July 1937), pp. 237-40; Paul Roché, *L'Irrigation et le statut juridique des eaux au Maroc* (Paris, 1965), p. 259; E. Menneson, 'Ksour du Tafilalt,' p. 91.
3. Maurice Bernard, 'Le Tafilala,' *Ren. Col.* (Oct. 1927), pp. 390, 391; Georges Spillmann, *Les Aît Atta du Sahara et la pacification du Haut Dra* (Rabat, 1936), p. 70; Interview no. 16.

4. See Ernest Gellner, *Saints of the Atlas* (Chicago, 1969), pp. 140-59.
5. AGGA, 22H. 27, Denoun (Officer-Interprète, Colomb-Béchar), 'Essai de monographie de la tribu berbère des Ait Atta,' April 7, 1913, p. 8; Spillmann, *Aït Atta*, pp. 95, 96; Interview no. 18.
6. Henriet, ' un Problème de l'Extrême-Sud marocain: répercussions de sa situation politique et sociale sur son relèvement économique,' CHEAM, no. 6, 1937; Interview no. 19.
7. D. Jacques-Meunié, 'Abbar, cité royale du Tafilalt,' *Hespéris*, 46 (1959), pp. 11, 12; Bernard, 'Le Tafilala,' pp. 393-9. Bernard, whose data dates from 1910, lists several *qsar-s* as having only *haratin* inhabitants.
8. Walter B. Harris, *Tafilet* (London, 1895), p. 296. The population estimate is from Gerhardt Rohlfs, the German explorer who visited Tafilalt in both 1862 and 1864. Quoted in Oskar Lenz, *Timbouctou* (Paris, 1886), p. 302.
9. My informant (interview no. 21) described the use of rotation and cross-election in choosing the *shaykh* of his *qsar*, Tabouasamt in Sefalat. He insisted that this system was widely applied throughout Tafilalt, but he denied that the entire *jama'a* was elected by cross-election in Tabouasamt. E. Menneson ('Ksour du Tafilalt,' p. 90) has described the latter procedure. He may only have observed villages where it applied, though he says nothing about election of *shaykh-s*. Rotation of the office of *shaykh* is noted by Bernard, 'Le Tafilala,' p. 391.
10. Interview no. 18, 19, and 21.
11. See Mohamed Lahbabi, *Le Gouvernement marocain à l'aube du XXe siècle* (Rabat, 1958), pp. 74, 75.
12. AMG, Alg. 19, Sit. pol. 1911, Berriau (Com. of the Annex of Beni Abbès), 'Contribution à l'étude de la région du Sud Ouest,' 1911, pp. 16, 30; Gabriel Delbrel, 'Notes sur le Tafilelt,' BSGP, 7th ser., 15 (1894), p. 209; 'Le Tafilelt d'après Gerhard Rohlfs,' *Ren. Col.* (Aug. 1910), p. 251; A. Le Chatelier, *Notes sur les villes et tribus du Maroc: Tafilelet, Tizimmi, Er-Reteb, Medghara* (Paris, 1903), p. 12; Bernard, 'Le Tafilala,' p. 391.
13. An estimate made in 1921 and based in part on a local tax census suggests a population of 16,000. P. Russo, 'Au Pays de Figuig,' *Bullétin de la Société de Géographie du Maroc*, 1st trimester (1923), p. 471. The Moroccan census of 1960 lists 12,185 native inhabitants, but the population almost certainly declined during the Protectorate period owing to emigration to northern cities.
14. R. Gromand, 'Le Particularisme de Figuig,' *Ren. Col.* (April 1939), p. 91; Interview no. 28.
15. Edmond Doutté, 'Figuig: notes et impressions,' *La Géographie*, 7 (March 1903), p. 188; Interview no. 28.
16. Victor Bérard, 'Le Leçon de Figuig,' *Revue de Paris*, 18 (July-Aug. 1911), p. 440.
17. Capt. Cavard, 'Le Ksar de Beni-Ounif,' *BSGAO*, 30 (Oct.-Dec. 1905), pp. 413, 414; J. Bouchat, 'Beni-Ounif (Sahara oranais): étude géographique, historique et médicale,' *Archives de l'Institut Pasteur d'Algérie* 34 (Dec. 1956), pp. 581-3, 594, 595.
18. Charles Delafosse, 'Contribution à l'étude du régime juridique de l'eau au Maroc: essai sur le régime juridique de l'eau à Figuig,' 1932. Mr Delafosse produced this lengthy study of Figuig's legal system as applied to the use of water while serving as a *contrôleur civil* there for eighteen months. He generously provided me with a typed copy of the work, which he had in his possession in Paris. My description of Figuig's irrigation system is based mainly on this study.

  One factor which militated against Figuig's economic prosperity from about the turn of the century was the spread of *ba'ïoudh* (Arabic, *bayud*), a fungus disease which attacks palm trees. It reached Figuig from Tafilalt in 1898, then spread southward into Touat. Neither the extent of the disease nor its economic effects are at all clear, but it may well have had a significant social impact on the populations throughout southeastern Morocco during the late nineteenth and early twentieth centuries. See Edmond Sergent and Louis Parrot, *Contribution de l'Institut Pasteur d'Algérie à la connaissance humaine du Sahara, 1900-1960* (Algiers, 1961), pp. 227-9, 246.

19. Roché, *L'Irrigation et le statut juridique*, p. 270.

20. E. Margot, 'Organisation actuelle de la justice à Figuig,' *BSGAO*, 29 (Dec. 1909), pp. 495-505; Delafosse, 'Régime juridique'.

21. M & L, II, p. 486; R. Gromand, 'La Coutume de la "Bezra" dans les Ksour de Figuig,' *Revue des Etudes Islamiques*, cahier 3 (1931), pp. 277-312; Gromand, 'Particularisme,' p. 155; Doutté, 'Figuig,' pp. 189, 190; Margot, 'Organisation actuelle,' p. 502; Interview no. 28.

22. E.F. Gautier, 'La Source de Thaddert à Figuig,' *Annales de Géographie*, 26 (Nov. 15, 1917), p. 464.

23. de Castries,'Notes sur Figuig,' 7th ser., 3 (1882), pp. 405, 406; Gautier, 'Source de Thaddert,' pp. 459-65.

24. AMG, Maroc C17, Maroc-Frontière-Figuig 1886, Reuillon (Director of Arab Affairs, Aïn Sefra) to Gov. Gen., Aug. 22, 1886, no. 640.

25. M & L, II, 477.

26. M & L, II, 481, 482.

27. M & L, II, 503. They note that 'it is not rare to see members of the same family fight in opposing ranks.' This may be an exaggeration since neither families nor clans could long survive internal feuding. Marriage and residence patterns in the *qsar-s* are described by Pariel, 'La Maison à Figuig,' *Revue d'Ethnographie et de Sociologie*, 3 (1912), pp. 259-80.

28. Interviews no. 28 and 29.

29. A. Hanoteau and A. Letourneux, *La Kabylie et les coutumes kabyles*, 3 vols., 2nd ed. (Paris, 1893); Huguet, 'Les Soffs du Tell, du Sud et du Sahara,' *Revue de l'Ecole d'Anthropologie*, 17 (1907), pp. 369-87; Zannettacci, 'Influence de la politique de l'eau dans la lutte de deux çofs à Laghouat,' *CHEAM*, no. 411, 1935; M & L, III, 188-98; Robert Montagne (*Les Berbères et le Makhzen dans le sud du Maroc*, Paris, 1930) has written the fullest and best-known treatment of binary leagues, whether *safs* or *leffs*. See also Lloyd Cabot Briggs, *Tribes of the Sahara* (Cambridge, Mass., 1960), p. 79.

30. Interview no. 28.

31. Interview no. 28.

32. M & L, II, 477. Doutté, 'Figuig,' p. 189; Interviews no. 28 and 29.

33. Lt. Col. Daumas, *Le Sahara algérien* (Algiers, 1845), p. 269; M & L, II, 472, 481, 484, 489, 494.

34. Interview no. 28.

35. Daumas, *Le Sahara algérien*, p. 264.

36. A. Cour, 'Le Cheikh El Hadj Mhammed Ben Bou Ziyan,' *Revue du Monde Musulman*, 11 (1910), pp. 359-79; 12 (1911), pp. 571-90; L. Voinot, 'Confréries et zaouias au Maroc,' *BSGAO*, 58 (March 1937), pp. 39-45; O Depont and X. Coppolani, *Les Confréries religieuses musulmanes* (Algiers, 1897), pp. 497-9; Louis Rinn, *Marabouts et Khouans* (Algiers, 1884), pp. 497-500.

37. AGGA, 30H. 13, Commission Franco-Marocaine, N. Lacroix to Gov. Gen., August 20, 1901; Général de Wimpffen, 'L'Expédition de l'Oued-Guir,' *BSGP*, 6th ser., 3 (1872), pp. 34-60; M & L, II, 625, 626.

38. AGGA, 16H. 13, M. Colas (Interprète Titulaire à Tlemcen), 'Notice sur les ordres religieux,' 1883; 16H. 4, Dept. d'Oran, 'Personnages religieux étranger à la Commune Mixte,' Feb. 15, 1904; Charles-Robert Ageron, *Les Algériens musulmans et la France* (Paris, 1968), I, 309; Depont and Coppolani, *Confréries religieuses*, pp. 252-5.

39. F. Albert, 'Les Oulad Djerir,' *BSGAO*, 25 (Oct.-Dec. 1905), pp. 386-8; M & L, II, 580, 623.

40. M & L, II, 623-5.
41. Ernest Gellner's book, *Saints of the Atlas*, was especially useful for under-
    standing the political role of saints in Morocco. His study focused on the
    zawiya of Ahansal in the central High Atlas. On the saint cult see also Alfred
    Bel, *La Réligion musulmane en Berbérie* (Paris, 1938), 2 vols; Edmond
    Doutté, *Notes sur l'Islam maghribin: les marabouts* (Paris, 1900); Georges
    Drague, *Esquisse d'histoire religieuse du Maroc: confréries et zaouias* (Paris,
    1951); Edward Westermarck, *Ritual and Belief in Morocco* (London, 1926),
    2 vols.

4 THE COMMERCIAL NETWORK

Commercial caravans approaching Tafilalt from the north in the late nine-teenth century passed by an extensive cluster of ruins just before reaching their final destination at Abou Am in the Wad Ifli district. These ruins had once been the city of Sijilmasa, one of the greatest emporiums of the trans-Saharan camel trade. Sijilmasa, along with the trade route to Timbuktu which sustained it, had known an erratic but persistent decline since the collapse of the Songhay empire in the sixteenth century. Its final abandonment is believed to have taken place in 1818, following the destruction of its *qasba* in a tribal war. In 1893 Walter Harris, the English traveler, could report only 'acres, almost miles of shapeless ruins' where the great city once stood.[1]

Yet the end of Sijilmasa was not the end of trade in Tafilalt. Barely a mile southeast of the crumbling walls the market of Abou Am arose to take its place. Abou Am inherited from its predecessor a dissipating trans-Saharan trade, but it served nonetheless as the commercial nerve center of southeastern Morocco, linked by trade route with other markets in the region and joining all of them to the cities and ports north of the Atlas. The animated scenes at Abou Am on market day symbolized the fact that Sijilmasa's demise and the languishment of the Sudan trade did not bring in its train the atrophy of commercial life in this part of North Africa.

The lines of trade crisscrossing southeastern Morocco in the late nine-teenth century can be divided into four general categories: trans-Saharan trade, trans-Atlas trade with Moroccan and Algerian cities, inter-oasis regional trade, and finally local trade between desert and oasis. The first two categories pertain to long-distance trade extending outside the region. The last two concern the trade serving directly the tribes and *qsar*-dwellers within it.[2] If a bird's-eye view of the region could reveal all these types of commercial activity operating at once, the routes, personnel, and commo-dities would overlap at many points. This division merely differentiates trading operations in terms of their territorial scope, starting with the widest (trans-Saharan trade) and ending with the narrowest (local trade). In fact, all four levels of trade meshed together, forming a single commer-cial subsystem operating within the wider commercial world of North and West Africa. The description pertains generally to the last two decades of the nineteenth century. Commercial developments after 1900 belong to the history of the colonial crisis

Trans-Saharan Trade

All the major trade routes of the Sahara passed through entrepôts located on the northern fringe of the desert. In these markets goods were often transferred from one caravan and group of merchants to another before being shipped north toward the coast or south to the desert oases and the Sudan. In southeastern Morocco trans-Saharan transit trade passed through Figuig and Abou Am. The other notable desert ports of the Moroccan Sahara were, from east to west, Ktaoua and other oases of the lower Dra valley, Tata, Akka, Tindouf, and Goulimine.

Figuig was an important trans-Saharan entrepôt only until the French conquest of Algeria. During the first half of the nineteenth century, caravans originating in Touat, or sometimes coming all the way from the Sudan, brought West African goods to Figuig by way of the well-watered Zousfana-Saoura valley. From Figuig the northbound routes diverged. One of them went to Fez, passing through Debdou and Taza. Another went directly north through Ras el-Aïn to Oujda. A third reached Tlemcen and other towns of the Algerian Tell by way of Aïn Sefra. Imports from the Sudan included ivory, gold dust, gum, ostrich feathers, and, most important, black slaves. Southbound commodities arriving from Moroccan and Algerian towns for transshipment included an array of North African and European manufactures. Carette and Renou, who based their 1844 description of the central Sahara on data collected from informants, wrote that Figuig had more than three hundred shops and that 'when the inhabitants of the western regions see an extraordinary product, they manifest their astonishment by crying: You wouldn't see that, even in Figuig.' Lieutenant Daumas noted in 1845 that the volume of Figuig's commerce gave it the title of 'Fas Ser'ir,' or Little Fez.[3]

From the 1840s Figuig's role in the trans-Saharan system rapidly diminished. French military conquests in the Tell and in the northern fringes of the desert, beginning with the occupation of the entrepôt of Laghouat in 1852, diverted most of Algeria's Saharan trade into either Morocco or Tunisia and Tripolitania. Since Figuig was more important as a commercial gateway to Algeria than to Morocco, its trade suffered to the benefit of markets further west. After 1845 the French authorities began trying to coax the caravans back again. Governor-General Randon made especially energetic efforts in the 1850s and 1860s to rebuild bridges between Algeria and the Sudan. The ordinance of 1843 prohibiting importation of goods from Morocco, Tunisia, and the Sahara was rescinded for the neighboring countries in 1853 and for the Sahara in

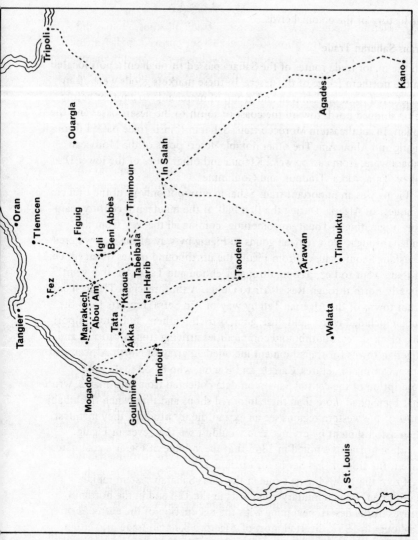

Trans-Saharan Routes

1860.[4] Neither the new law nor a series of trade missions, such as the Colonieu and Burin expedition to Touat in 1860, proved at all fruitful. Failure resulted not so much from the unwillingness of Muslim merchants to trade with the French as from the dissolution of the market for slaves, which had been the backbone of the trans-Saharan trade into Algeria. The institution of slavery was abolished in all French territories in 1848, just when the Algerian authorities were initiating their efforts to revitalize Saharan commerce. A small number of slaves continued to enter the southern borders of the colony for some years after 1848, but merchants had no compelling reason to lead caravans there since the demand for slaves in Morocco remained consistently high throughout the remainder of the century.[5] Though the French posed no military threat to Figuig until the 1880s, it lost its importance as a trans-Saharan entrepôt by about 1850. It continued to serve only as a regional market center and as a stopover on a secondary route between Touat and Fez.

Abou Am, though located only about 150 miles southwest of Figuig, took over most of its slave trade and continued to transship black Africans, as well as small quantities of other West African goods, until the end of the century. At least four main routes linked Abou Am with the Sudan in the nineteenth century. The first went southwestward through the lower Dra valley to Tata or Akka. From there it turned directly south to Tindouf and on across the desert to Taodeni (the location of the great salt mines), Arawan, and Timbuktu. The second route also went from Tafilalt to the Dra valley, but then headed south across the Erg Iguidi to Taodeni. The third track ran southeastward from Tafilalt through Tabelbala to Gourara, the northern district of Touat. From Touat routes led to Timbuktu, Kano, and other points in the Sudan. The fourth route was a slight alternative to the third, following a more easterly course from Tafilalt to the Saoura valley at Igli. There it joined the Figuig-Touat road, passing through Beni Abbès and Kerzaz to Gourara. Caravans sometimes diverged slightly from these main trails if a special itinerary promised greater security or convenience. The crucial criterion for the use of any of them was the availability of water at tolerable intervals.[6] The number of days a caravan spent on the road between Tafilalt and Timbuktu could vary greatly depending upon the route, the size of the caravan, the length of intermediate stops, and the time spent fighting or evading nomadic raiders. The usual time for the trip was something between forty and sixty days.[7]

The theory that trans-Saharan trade was in a state of decline throughout the nineteenth century has been challenged by recent scholarship, which cites export data from Morocco and Tripoli to show that from the 1840s to about 1875 the trade saw something of a boom.[8] Abou Am, how-

ever, was not a significant beneficiary of this growth, owing mainly to a
shift in the flow of the Moroccan trade westward to the Atlantic coast.
The southwestern route through Tindouf and Taodeni served not only the
caravans of Tafilalt but also those of the Sous and the Atlantic littoral.
From about 1840 the port of Mogador attracted a greater and greater
share of northbound trade on this route to the detriment of Abou Am.
Sultan Sidi Muhammad founded Mogador (Essaouira) in the 1760s to
serve as the exclusive entrepôt for external trade on the southern coast.
By installing successful Jewish merchants in the town and lowering the
import duty rates, he soon attracted growing numbers of European merchant ships and commercial agents. By the 1830s Mogador was handling
more trade than any other Moroccan port. The important export commodities were gum and ostrich feathers from the Sahara and Sudan, while
gold and slaves, the more traditional staples of the trade, sold internally
for the most part. One or two caravans of as many as a few thousand
camels, in addition to several smaller ones, arrived at Mogador each year.
In return, European firms imported sugar, tea, textiles, and various manufactures, which went south with a variety of Moroccan goods. Tindouf,
which was reconstructed in 1852, prospered as the key northern desert
port, while Goulimine, lying further to the northwest, developed to the
disadvantage of Akka and Tata, the two major centers on the road to
Tafilalt.[9]

With the export business so brisk at Mogador merchants operating in
the western Sahara had little reason to direct northbound caravans to Abou
Am. Moreover, the price of European goods to be sent south was undoubtedly
lower at Mogador than at Abou Am, owing to the absence of overland
transit across the High and Middle Atlas. Walter Harris bore witness to the
commercial shift when he visited Tafilalt in 1893:

> . . . of the roads to the south of Tafilet but little need be said, as
> proportionately only a very small amount of the Sudan trade comes
> into Morocco by this route, the greater portion being taken via Tenduf
> and the Sus to Mogador.[10]

Harris's observation best applied to the 1860s and 1870s since by 1893
even the route to Mogador had all but dried up. Commercial recession in
Europe, the competition of European outlets in West Africa, political
insecurity in southwestern Morocco, and other factors precipitated a
general and rapid decline after 1875. The French expansion into the
western Sudan and the occupation of Timbuktu in 1894 dealt the final
blow, reducing northbound traffic into Morocco to insignificance.[11]

The prosperity of Mogador and Tindouf before 1875 weakened but did not entirely ruin trade relations between Tafilalt and the Sudan. Slaves, plus small quantities of trade goods, continued to arrive at Abou Am along the southeastern route from Touat until the turn of the century. Touat, and more specifically the town of In Salah in the southern district of Tidikelt, was one of the most active commercial crossroads in the Sahara. Routes converging on In Salah linked the western and central Sudan not only with Morocco and Algeria but with Tunisia and Tripolitania as well. In Gourara, Touat's northernmost district, several oases, notably Timimoun, were secondary relay centers for trade with the western Maghrib.[12] Slaves usually changed hands in Touat from one merchant to another. Filali traders (that is, of Tafilalt) regularly acquired slaves there in return for Moroccan and European goods, although they also accompanied caravans all the way to the Sudan. A few Filali merchants lived in Timbuktu as commercial agents for Moroccan colleagues.[13]

The diversion of caravans away from Figuig and other entrepôts south of Algeria almost certainly benefited Abou Am, since the demand for slaves in Morocco was insatiable until after the turn of the century. It seems likely, in fact, that just when Tafilalt's southwestern routes were going into decline because of Mogador, trade with Touat was on a slight upswing, though the most profitable commodity was slaves rather than feathers and gum. Gerhardt Rohlfs, who was in Tafilalt for the second time in 1864, noted that relations between Abou Am and the Sudan were carried on almost exclusively through Touat.[14]

Tafilalt was only a rest stop for most slaves. Local men of wealth certainly bought a few every year, though no one owned very many — perhaps two dozen was the upper limit.[15] Most of the slaves were sent on to Fez, Marrakech, and other trans-Atlas towns. Females predominated since they were in great demand among the affluent to serve as concubines and domestic servants. Buyers and merchants, like New World plantation owners, also believed a relationship existed between the quality of a slave and his specific place of origin in West Africa. Harris noted that 'the girls of the Hausa country fetched the best prices, being considered more cheerful and neater than those from farther west.'[16]

Even with the probable increase in the slave trade after 1850, Abou Am was hardly the great slave emporium that Sijilmasa had once been. By comparison with the Atlantic trade or with the trans-Saharan trade of previous centuries, imports to any of the pre-Saharan markets were of small dimension. Miège suggests that the trade into all of Morocco reached its nineteenth-century zenith between 1840 and 1855, with 3,500 to 4,000 slaves arriving annually. He estimated that between 1875 and 1885, 500 to

1,000 arrived every year at Tindouf. His estimates are based solely on consular and travel reports pertaining to the Southwest, and he makes no guess for the trade through Touat.[17] For the Southeast the only available figure comes from Rohlfs, who suggests that in the early 1860s 500 to 1,000 slaves arrived in Touat annually for transshipment to Morocco and that probably only a few hundred were sold in Tafilalt and Fez.[18] During the 1880 to 1900 period, the imports to Abou Am certainly did not exceed those into Tindouf and so probably amounted to no more than two or three hundred a year. At any rate, in the late nineteenth century the immigration of West Africans had no appreciable demographic impact on any region of Morocco. Moreover, the economic value of the trade for the merchants of Abou Am was no longer very significant in relation to the total value of regional and trans-Atlas commerce. On the other hand, a trickle of slaves was still entering the country in the 1890s, and attitudes about slavery and slave trading had not yet changed very much despite continuing pressure from European powers to bring both institutions to an end.[19]

The French occupation of Timbuktu in 1894 and Touat in 1900 put an end to all but clandestine slave commerce. Certainly a few slaves entered Morocco after 1900, since the French army took several years to achieve effective surveillance of caravan traffic in the desert. The inadequacy of French control also enabled the Dawi Maniʿ and Ait Khabbash to conduct a few trans-Saharan raiding operations which brought back slaves for sale at Abou Am. Even after importation was no longer possible, slaves were still sold at Abou Am, perhaps until the final occupation of Tafilalt in 1932. The Protectorate government outlawed slavery in 1912, but the ruling could hardly be enforced in areas not yet subjugated.[20]

Trans-Atlas Trade

Trade between southeastern Morocco and the urban centers north of the Atlas was more regular and of much greater volume than the trans-Saharan trade in the late nineteenth century. Caravans departing from Fez and Marrakech, and to a lesser extent from Meknès, Oujda, and Tlemcen, brought the populations of the Southeast most of their manufactures and some foodstuffs. Abou Am and Figuig were the principal centers for the distribution of these goods to the tribes and qsar-dwellers of the region, including Touat. In exchange, the northbound caravans carried, in addition to West African commodities and slaves in transit, dates in large quantities and some regional specialities.

Before 1900 the Fez route was the most active channel for the importation of European and Moroccan products. The Southeast was not an insig-

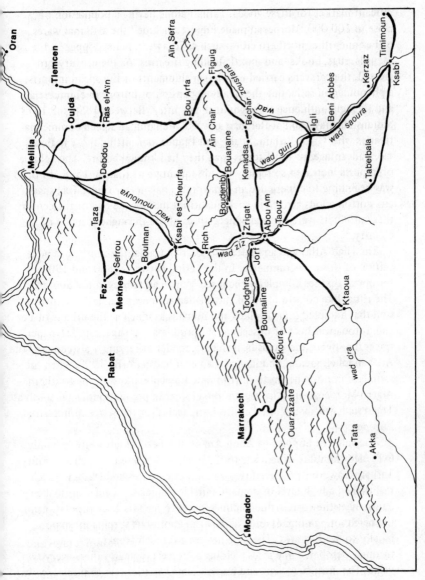

Major Trans-Atlas and Regional Routes

nificant market for these goods, Tafilalt alone having a population of close to 100,000. Moroccan-made imports included the artisanal wares of Fez and other northern cities, such as footwear, belts, copper and brass utensils, rugs, books, and muzzle-loading firearms. As the century progressed, the caravans carried ever larger shipments of European imports, a phenomenon reflecting the steady expansion of European commercial and financial influence throughout the country. Between 1856 and 1873 Sultans Mawlay 'Abd al-Rahman and Sidi Muhammad signed commercial treaties with Great Britain, Spain, and France, permitting those nations more advantageous tariff terms than they had known before. The volume of imports increased so rapidly in subsequent years that by 1878 Morocco was beginning to experience an unfavorable balance of trade. Tea, sugar, and cotton goods arrived in such quantities that by the end of the century these products were becoming necessities of life throughout much of the country.[21]

The High Atlas was an ineffectual barrier against the southward penetration of this new commerce. In the period between 1880 and 1900 European textiles completely eclipsed Moroccan fabrics in the Southeast. The ritual-like consumption of sugar-laden tea became a national institution that addicted qsar-dwellers and nomads as much as the urbane of Fez and Tetouan. A host of miscellaneous products — coffee, candles, paper, spices, hardware and utensils, iron bars, modern firearms — also crossed the Atlas in much greater abundance than ever before.[22] By 1900, when the source of imports began to shift to new French markets in the southern Algero-Moroccan frontier region, the Moroccan populations as far south as Touat had already acquired enthusiastic tastes for the wares of industrial Europe.

The value of imports to Abou Am on the Fez-Tafilalt route certainly exceeded the value of exports to the north in the late nineteenth century. Tafilalt, however, produced two commodities, dates and leather, which maintained a high level of demand outside the region. Under normal circumstances the oasis yielded enough dates to feed its own population and the neighboring nomads and still have an enormous surplus for export, mostly to the Fez area. The date harvest extended from late August through October, some trees yielding a crop every year, others every two years. The most succulent and imperishable varieties (for example, majhul, faqqus, and busakri) were exported north in great sacks of braided palm leaves or wool, or were consumed locally. The less appetizing types were usually fed to animals. Merchants in Fez purchased a substantial portion of the large, sweet majhul crop for transshipment on consignment to England by way of Tangier. These 'Tafilalt dates,' as they were known on the London market, always commanded good prices in Britain, especially just before the Christmas season. The volume of exports from Tafilalt of course varied considerably from one year to the next depending on the size and quality of the harvest and on the relative success of the crop in other districts (notably the Dra valley) which supplied the urban markets.[23]

Filali leather, which the tanners of Tafilalt had been producing for centuries, was known and admired throughout North Africa and the Sahara. The main step in tanning the goat or sheep hides was their maceration in a mixture of water and a special substance called *takawat* (French, *takaouet*), a growth found on branches of the tamarisk tree. The *takawat* grains, which were shaken off the trees and ground up, contained the tannin necessary to convert the hides into soft leather. Sometimes merchants exported raw hides or undyed leather, as well as *takawat*, to tanners in Fez, Tetouan, Figuig, and elsewhere. The Filali tanners, however, dyed much of it either red or yellow, the two colors giving it the distinguishing *filali* mark. Tanneries were found in all the districts of Tafilalt, though the greatest concentration was in Wad Ifli. The tanning industry was so extensive that caravans of as many as one hundred animals left for Fez carrying nothing but *filali*. Ironically, Tafilalt's leather-working industry was minor. A few Jewish craftsmen fashioned belts, shoes, and pouches for local consumption.[24]

An important feature of Tafilalt's commercial relations was the specialization of particular social groups or tribes in the trade of one long-distance route or another. The Fez-Tafilalt trade was predominantly in the hands of Fasis (natives of Fez) and Filali Jews, though merchants of other groups, notably 'Alawi *shurfa*, participated as well. Traders operated from both ends of the route. Fasis often accompanied caravans to Abou Am to sell tea, sugar, and textiles to retailers, then return with dates, leather, and money. Some were known to visit Tafilalt in order to purchase date crops while still on the trees and then to have them shipped north upon maturity.[25] Perhaps a few dozen Fasi merchants lived more or less permanently in Tafilalt, most of them in Abou Am, and traveled north only to make purchases. They owned small warehouses from which they distributed goods to retailers.[26]

The movement of goods, however, did not necessarily involve the movement of traders. Some merchants, both Muslim and Jewish, had correspondents in Fez who received written orders for merchandise and shipped it south with trustworthy muleteers.[27] At least a few Fasi commercial houses maintained agents and warehouses in Tafilalt. At the turn of the century Muhammad ibn Idris Tazi was perhaps the best known Fasi with a commercial operation straddling the Atlas. He belonged to one of the most

successful trading families in Fez, the wealthiest members of which
specialized in European textile imports. Ibn Idris resided permanently
at Abou Am, leaving the direction of the Fez house in the hands of his
relatives. He imported European goods and apparently did not deal to any
extent in date or leather export. His consignments from Fez were sold to
retailers or other bulk traders for European or Moroccan currency, which
he transported back to Fez only at infrequent intervals.

The financial scope of enterprises like that of Ibn Idris is shown in the
informal banking services they performed. Filali traders, after selling a
shipment of dates or leather in Fez, sometimes deposited their money with
one of these firms. They received in return a draft which could later be
drawn on the firm's agency in Tafilalt. This procedure, for which the firm
charged about 10 percent, relieved traders (or Filalis who worked in the
north temporarily) of the often dangerous task of carrying large sums of
money back across the mountains. Because of insecurity on the Atlas
route, the *makhzan* also used the banking facilities of the big firms in order
to pay its officials and its garrison in Tafilalt. In 1907, for example,
Mawlay 'Abd al-'Aziz paid Mawlay Rashid, the *khalifa* in Tafilalt, his monthly
salary of 1500 duros through the intermediary of Ibn Idris.[28]

The journey to Fez, a distance of about four hundred miles, took eleven
or twelve days under normal conditions. Owing to the treacherous mountain passages, mules and burros were used much more frequently than
camels. The larger caravans generally comprised fifty to one hundred
beasts.[29] Often a number of merchants joined together to form a single
caravan for the sake of convenience and security. Each trader either owned
his own pack animals or rented them from other Filali residents or from
Ait Izdig or Ait Mirghad Berbers living north of Tafilalt.[30]

In order to avoid attack or harassment the caravans paid *zattata*, a kind
of toll, to every tribe through whose territory they passed along the way.
In return, the tribe provided guarantors (*zattat*), usually a small body of
armed men, who escorted the caravan to the edge of its territory. At that
point the next tribe in line made its levy. The amount of *zattata*, caclu-
lated on the number of loaded animals in the caravan and always paid in
currency, varied with the value of the goods being transported and with
the conditions of security on the route. It was often exorbitantly high,
especially for Jews, who paid for their persons as well as for their beasts.
But it was something more than bald extortion. The payment carried with
it a shame-compulsion which committed the guarantors to the safety of
their clients at the risk of divine displeasure and therefore tribal dishonor.
Furthermore, the Atlas tribes ultimately derived more benefit from the
passage of caravans than from their indiscriminate pillage. Therefore, the

obligations of *zattata* were taken seriously, and the amount was never so high, at least in normal times, as to discourage trade altogether.[31]

Another major trans-Atlas route linked Tafilalt with Marrakech. Trade in that direction, though, was usually much lighter than with Fez because of the somewhat greater distance and, probably more important, because the Dra valley rather than the Ziz was Marrakech's principal date basket. On the other hand, Filali caravans went there regularly, if not frequently, with leather and dates and returned with the usual array of European and Moroccan goods. The route to Marrakech could also be a satisfactory alternative whenever the Fez trail was too hazardous.[32]

In the days of Sijilmasa the route from Tafilalt to Tlemcen was a trunk line of the trans-Saharan network. The French conquest of Algeria terminated its importance, though prohibition of the slave trade was not the only cause. Merchants of Tafilalt and other centers of southeastern Morocco were quite willing to do business with French Algeria, and after 1867 they could legally export goods of Moroccan origin across the border duty free. The trade potential, however, lay not so much in exports as in the importation of European goods. But high import duties and port taxes in Oran inflated the price of tea, sugar, and textiles far above what merchants were paying in Fez or Marrakech. Moreover, in 1884 the Spanish Presidio of Melilla began admitting duty free many commodities of British, Belgian, and German origin, which traders of the Southeast went north to buy. In 1896 the Algerian authorities, disturbed by their failure to penetrate the Moroccan market, removed tariffs on goods specifically earmarked for Morocco or the Sahara. But by then, Filali traders who wished to take advantage of the new lower prices could go to the railhead at Aïn Sefra, which was a good deal closer to home than Tlemcen.[33]

Aside from Abou Am, the only market center in the Southeast with direct trade ties to the northern cities was Figuig. The westward shift of trans-Saharan trade brought recession to Figuig after the 1840s, but in the late nineteenth century it still had a population of as many as sixteen thousand and was the principal market for the nomads and *qsar*-dwellers living in the surrounding area. Figuig paralleled Abou Am, though on a smaller scale, as a distribution center for goods arriving from the north and from Europe.

Because of the high prices in Algeria, Figuig's merchants transacted most of their business in Moroccan markets until after 1896. A caravan route through Debdou and the Taza pass linked Figuig directly with Fez. This trade was largely in the hands of natives of the oasis, including a few Jewish families, though at least one Fasi merchant reportedly spent a few months every year in Figuig during the 1880s.[34] The Dawi Mani', Awlad

Jarir, and Bani Gil supplied camel, mule, or burro transport and drivers. Figuig's principal export to Fez was various types of locally made woolen garments. These *ha'ik-s* and *burnus* had something of a reputation for quality, not only in Fez but throughout the western Maghrib.[35]

Other routes went north to Oujda by way of Ras el-Aïn and to Melilla by way of Debdou. Trade with both these towns picked up considerably after 1884, when Melilla opened its doors to foreign goods duty free. Merchants of Figuig could probably buy these commodities, especially tea and sugar, cheaper at Melilla or Oujda than at Fez owing, in the case of Oujda, to shorter distance and, in the case of Melilla, to purchase at the port of entry rather than through middle men. This situation did not change appreciably with the extension of the Algerian railroad to Ain Sefra in 1887, since prices were still lower on the Moroccan side despite the much longer caravan transport involved. Only after the turn of the century did a major reorientation of Figuig's trade begin to take place.[36]

Regional Trade

In rural Morocco north of the Atlas the population living within a geographic region traded among themselves through a network of weekly markets, or *suq-s*. The size of *suq-s* ranged from minor ones serving the residents of a few villages to great inter-tribal markets to which several thousand persons traveled each week. Each market within a region was held on a specified day of the week, and all of them were staggered so that a person could do business on any day without traveling an excessive distance. Itinerant traders with their bases in the towns or cities supplied the markets in the surrounding countryside with the products of Moroccan and European industry.

Southeastern Morocco also had a regional trading network, linking the important centers with one another and with the lesser oases scattered here and there across the steppe and desert. The Sahara's wide open spaces, however, gave regional trade in the south a somewhat different character from that in the more densely populated north. Although the larger markets were regularly held on fixed days of the week, they were much too far apart to permit a rotational system. Both villagers and nomads in a given area went habitually to the single nearest market. Furthermore, itinerant traders, found so commonly in the north, could hardly peregrinate back and forth across the northern Sahara on their own. Camel caravans of varying sizes carried most of the regional trade.

The network of regional lines served the populations of the Southeast in two ways. First, they were the branch routes along which goods imported to Abou Am or Figuig from the north reached Touat and other, smaller centers. Second, they carried the products of local industry and agriculture from one oasis and tribe to another. The most active routes in the regional system joined Abou Am, Figuig, and Gourara, forming together a rough triangle. A web of secondary trails linked these three major routes to even the smallest and most isolated oases and *qsar-s* in the region.

Caravans ranging in size from a few burros to two hundred camels departed from Abou Am in a number of directions. The largest camel caravans went south to Timimoun and other centers in Gourara, usually by way of Tabelbala. Before 1900 the *qsar*-dwellers of Touat depended heavily on these caravans to supply them with Moroccan and European goods, though imports arrived by way of Tripoli and Ghadamès as well. Tea and sugar were reaching Touat in the 1890s, though tea drinking was only just then becoming popular in the northern Sahara. The caravans also carried grain, sheep, and wool, since Touat's sedentary population was too large to permit self-sufficiency in agriculture and livestock production. Most imported food and wool, however, came from the Arab tribes of Oranie rather than from Tafilalt.[37] Touat had little of its own to offer the merchants returning north. Commercial activity there had always rested largely on the trans-Saharan transit trade. Aside from the trickle of slaves and West African goods still passing through in the late nineteenth century, Touat exported limited quantities of dates, henna, tobacco, woolen garments, saltpeter, and French silver or gold currency obtained from trade with the Oranie tribes. Date exports soared some years, since Touat's palm groves served as a kind of reserve for tribes to the north when the Ziz valley harvest was especially poor.[38]

The merchants and drivers who handled regional trade in the Southeast were by and large different from those who operated on the trans-Atlas routes. The traders par excellence on the Tafilalt-Touat road were men of the Bani Mhammad, one of the sedentary groups of Tafilalt. Earlier in the century the Bani Mhammad had regularly organized and accompanied caravans bound for Timbuktu and were especially distinguished as slave dealers.[39] Although the decline of trans-Saharan trade may have forced some traders back to work in the palm groves, the tribe still predominated in supplying Touat with tea, sugar, cloth, and manufactures. Most likely they purchased large lots of these commodities from Fasi or Jewish merchants in Abou Am. None of the Bani Mhammad lived permanently in Touat, but each trader had his local 'friends' who served as hosts and intermediaries. Some of them owned or rented storehouses where goods were deposed upon arrival.[40] The Ait Khabbash, the section of the Ait 'Atta which controlled most of the territory between Tafilalt and Touat, supplied the Bani Mhammad traders with most of their camels and drivers.

Since the two groups had a close political association, the Ait Khabbash also provided armed escorts but did not charge *zattata*. The two most frequently used routes between Abou Am and Gourara were those passing through Taouz and Tabelbala and through Taouz, Igli, and the Saoura valley.

Another set of routes joined Abou Am with the tribes and *qsar-s* east of the great Hammada of the Guir. The principal terminus of these routes was Figuig, though caravans passed through or sometimes terminated at lesser centers along the way, such as Kenadsa, Béchar, Boudenib, Bouanane, and Aïn Chaïr. Secondary trails branched off to the upper Wad Guir and Wad Aissa-Haïber regions and to the Beni Goumi district along the Wad Zousfana. The eastbound trade included European and Moroccan goods as well as Tafilalt's hides, leather, grain, and certain varieties of dates not grown in Figuig. The westbound caravans carried Figuig's dates and woolen garments.[41] Figuig's merchants handled most of the direct trade between there and Abou Am.[42] Filali traders crossed the Hammada from time to time, but Figuig received most of its European and trans-Atlas imports directly from Fez, Melilla, or Oujda. Almost all of the transporting across the Hammada was in the hands of the Dawi Mani' and the Awlad Jarir. Both tribes owned extensive camel herds, and together they pastured over much of the territory between the Ziz and the Zousfana. Some sections of the Dawi Mani' owned palm groves in Ghorfa, Tafilalt's southeastern district, and so supplied some of their own dates to the tribes and villages east of the Hammada.[43]

In comparison with Abou Am, Figuig played a minor role in long-distance regional trade. In addition to their relations with Tafilalt and the intervening *qsar-s*, Figuig's merchants shipped European merchandise, grain, wool, and woolen garments to Touat, though on a much smaller scale than did the Bani Mhammad. The Dawi Mani' and the Awlad Jarir did most of the carrying on the Figuig-Touat route.[44]

Local Trade and the Market Place

The important distribution centers in the trans-Atlas and regional networks — Abou Am, Figuig, Timimoun — were also local markets, where the nomads and *qsar*-dwellers of the surrounding area sold or exchanged surplus produce and livestock when it was available. In a narrow sense they marketed rather than traded their goods in that they sold them to meet their need for other commodities. This practice amounted to a kind of extension of the subsistence economy and was distinguished from trading in the strict sense of buying for resale as a specialized activity.

At least some regular exchange of locally produced goods was carried on in probably every oasis where a permanent population existed. In the smaller oases the *suq* generally consisted of a flat, open space in or near the *qsar* and had no permanent installations to speak of. In these places trading between nomads and cultivators might go on at any time rather than on specified days of the week as in the larger centers. Minor markets in the region would include those at Zrigat, Boudenib, Bouanane, Aïn Chaïr, Kenadsa, Béchar, and Beni Abbès. In Tafilalt several small, daily satellite markets existed in addition to Abou Am.[45]

Abou Am was of course a local market as well as an entrepôt. A population of perhaps 150,000, including both the sedentary inhabitants of the Ziz and Ghéris valleys and the nomads of the surrounding steppes, went there regularly to exchange local goods as well as to buy imports. It comprised a large open space in front of the *qsar* of Abou Am where the beasts of burden were tethered and, just south of that, a complex of small, domed earthen structures or huts (which Harris likened to beehives) where sellers offered their wares. Other vendors displayed their goods in small tents.[46] Some trading went on in other locations. Some of the Fasi and Jewish merchants maintained bazaars inside Abou Am *qsar* where they displayed their imports. Tanners who sold leather in large lots for export did business in their own storerooms.[47]

The greatest volume of local trade was in livestock (sheep, goats, camels, and horses), fleece, and agricultural produce. Some products of local industry and mining were sold in the market, though not exported to any degree. These included jewelry, saddlery, shoes (inferior to those imported from Fez), iron tools, and muskets. Jewelry and blacksmithing were almost exclusively in the hands of Jews. Lead (for bullets) and antimony (used as a medicine) were mined in the area in small quantities.[48] A short distance southeast of Tafilalt a large depression yielded salt, whose extraction and sale were the monopoly of the Filali *shurfa*.[49]

Abou Am, like any other market, could function only if law and order prevailed. Everywhere in Morocco two basic rules governed the operation of markets to ensure peace and therefore a free flow of trade. First, the market place had to be neutral territory, sheltered from the violent eruptions which characterized intertribal relations. Men could not be permitted to 'break the market' without incurring heavy penalties. Second, an authority acceptable to all groups who used the market had to enforce the peace by imposing sanctions of one kind or another. In some markets, especially the smallest ones, the council of notables of the group who 'owned' the market place could keep order and impose fines on miscreants. But the essential qualification for a market authority was the capacity to act impartially against all malefactors and peace breakers no matter their tribal or family affiliations. In other words, the market authority could not govern effectively while representing the political interests of one faction or another or attempting to apply local jurisdiction to outsiders who did not recognize it. In areas under central government control the *qa'id*, or governor, usually appointed a *qa'id al-suq* who, with the aid of a contingent of market policemen known as *mukhazini-s*, apprehended law-breakers, heard disputes, collected market taxes, and imposed fines based on koranic or customary law. In areas beyond the reach of *makhzan* administration, law and order depended on the presence of an authority who would not be compromised by intertribal conflict. The most common and most effective solution was to award jurisdiction to a reputable saint and locate the market near his tomb. The *baraka* of the saint cast a protective mantle over the market place, restraining potential 'market breakers' with the threat of divine wrath. When disputes arose, oaths were sworn before the tomb to determine the innocence or guilt of the accused.[50]

Since the crowd at Abou Am on market day represented a congeries of tribes and villages, preserving peace among them was a precarious task. In the late nineteenth century Mawlay Rashid, the *khalifa*, conferred the job upon a local 'Alawi *sharif*.[51] This *qa'id al-suq* had at his disposal a garrison of perhaps fifty to one hundred *makhzan* troops, who were billeted in the *qsar* of Rissani located a short distance north of Abou Am.[52] In most years these *mukhazani-s* represented the sum of sultanic military power in Tafilalt, so they could exercise no more real force in the market place than they could in any other situation. They may have patrolled the market to restrain passions and prevent violence or aided the *qa'id al-suq* in apprehending thieves or other violators. They could do little to contain violence once a tribal confrontation took place. Mawlay 'Ali Sharif, the founder of the 'Alawi dynasty and most *baraka*-laden of all saints in Tafilalt, was probably a more potent check on crime or violence than the *qa'id* and his men. Mawlay 'Ali's tomb was located not far from the market, and oaths associated with market altercations were sworn there.[53] No system of restraints and sanctions, however, worked to perfection. The market could be 'broken.' In 1896 a killing at Abou Am erupted into a major feud that lasted on and off for four years and forced the market to close for a period of several months.

Figuig paralleled Abou Am as an important local center for trade between nomads and *qsar*-dwellers. The Dawi Mani', Awlad Jarir, Bani Gil, Amur, and to a lesser extent the Oranie tribes went there to exchange their grain, sheep, and wool for dates, woolen garments, and a variety of fruits and vegetables. The inhabitants of Zenaga, the largest of the seven *qsar-s* of Figuig, cultivated their own barley along the banks of the

Zousfana. The other villages, however, were largely dependent on the nomads for grain. The Dawi Mani' supplied much of it when their harvests on the Abadla flood plain were good, the rest came from Oranie. The Bani Gil marketed meat and wool almost exclusively.[54]

Market organization in Figuig contrasted in certain ways from that in Tafilalt. Figuig had no central, politically neutral market place, rather each of the seven qsar-s had its own suq. The most important ones were in Zenaga (Monday and Friday) and al-Oudaghir (Tuesday and Saturday).[55] This uncentralized and duplicative market arrangement would probably best be explained by the perennial antagonisms that divided the qsar-s, although there is no doubt that under peaceful conditions the population at large mixed freely in any of the market places. Al-Oudaghir was the most active market center in the late nineteenth century. A large proportion of Figuig's professional merchants lived there, and most of the regional and trans-Atlas trade was handled in its market place.[56] Zenaga, and most likely the other five villages, handled mainly local trade in foodstuffs and woolens. Whereas al-Oudaghir was reputed for its commercial activities and merchant population, Zenaga was known for its exceptional grain and date production and for its weaving industry.[57] The jama'a, or assembly, of each qsar governed and policed its own market.

Monetary Instability and Inflation

Throughout the second half of the nineteenth century Morocco was experiencing chronic monetary ills, and there is no doubt that they had a detrimental effect on economic life in the Southeast. Money as both a form of payment and a standard of value was widely used in the desert periphery. Barter was common only in petty local trade and in the exchange of dates for grain and livestock in Touat. At Abou Am, Moroccan as well as European coins were used in almost all trade. The system of values was the same in the Southeast as throughout the rest of the country. The basic unit of account was the mitqal. A gold coin bearing this name had once circulated in Morocco, but it had all but disappeared by the middle of the nineteenth century.[58] The mitqal was divided into the following units:

    1 mitqal = 10 dirham-s or wuqiya-s (French, oukia) or ounces
    1 dirham= 4 mawzuna-s
    1 mawzuna = 6 flus (singular, fals; French plural, flous)

Dirham and mawzuna referred to Moroccan silver coins which rarely circulated in the later nineteenth century.[59] The fals, a bronze piece, was then the principal coin used for local trade throughout the country. Also in circulation were silver Moroccan coins minted by Mawlay Hasan (and later by Mawlay ʿAbd al-ʿAziz), a few older pieces, and French and Spanish silver. Moroccans generally converted the face value of whatever currencies they were using into *mitqal-s, dirham-s*, and *flus*.

Monetary conditions in the Southeast reflected the deepening crisis into which the currency system of the entire country was falling. This crisis was one of the baneful consequences of European commercial penetration, which resulted in an increasingly unfavorable balance of trade, the flight of good silver currency out of the country, and a steady rise in the volume of bad silver and bronze coins, which rapidly depreciated in value. In 1881 Mawlay Hasan tried to reform the system by striking a new silver currency, called *hasani*, having a par value with the Spanish duro (five peseta piece, called also piaster or dollar). But since the *hasani* duro had a somewhat higher silver content than its Spanish equivalent, the reform proved ineffective. The new coins were hoarded or exported illegally by speculators. In 1891 and subsequent years the government struck more *hasani* money. But by that time the world price of silver was falling sharply, causing these coins to lose much of their value relative to the stronger, gold-based French and British currencies. The *makhzan*, in order to meet internal demand and its own ever-growing fiscal requirements, minted greater and greater quantities of bronze *flus*. A great deal of counterfeit bronze also came into circulation. Furthermore, devalued Spanish silver struck prior to 1868, as well as Philippine pesetas, were introduced massively into the Moroccan countryside by speculators. As a result, the value of currencies in circulation steadily depreciated, whereas gold-based European coins were scarce. The growing volume of bad money over good sent prices on all commodities moving upward. Everyone but the more fortunate merchants and speculators suffered from this trend, especially the rural populations, who expended whatever silver reserves they had (including coin jewelry) and became increasingly dependent on ever-depreciating *flus*.[60]

The lack of quantitative data prevents any useful comparison of monetary conditions in the Southeast with those in the ports or the large cities, where the crisis was felt first. Because of the long distance from the coast, the southern periphery experienced monetary instability and inflation later and probably more gradually than did the rest of the country. On the other hand, Tafilalt's direct commercial ties with Fez and Marrakech may have meant that the crisis reverberated there sooner than in the High Atlas or in other parts of the pre-Sahara. The volume of bronze in circulation in the Southeast was doubtless multiplying toward the end of the century.

Depreciated *hasani* duros were also common.[61] Spanish silver was not used much before the 1890s, but it must have become more plentiful from then on owing to the importation of so many depreciated duros and Philippine coins.[62] Some quantities of French francs, which because of their stability had a greater value in trade than any other currency, entered the Southeast by way of the trade routes from Algeria and Touat. But unless they were hoarded, they probably flowed quickly to Fez or Marrakech and then out of the country.[63]

The spread of inflation to the Southeast would certainly have hit hardest at the *qsar*-dwelling cultivators, whose *flus* were buying less and less, but whose tastes were also beginning to include tea, sugar, and other European imports. Since date production was in the hands of many small producers, there is no reason to suppose that as inflation set in they were able to command appreciably higher prices from the traders who shipped them north. The professional merchants of the region probably stayed afloat by speculative maneuverings and by passing the burden of inflation on to the consumer population. They also faced, however, a trans-Atlas trade that was increasingly risky and expensive owing to other consequences of economic instability — unrest among tribes who were forced to pay taxes, toll increases on the trade routes, and greater incidence of banditry.

Since the Southeast, and especially Tafilalt, was integrated into Morocco's commercial and monetary system, it clearly felt the tremors of economic upheaval emanating from the coastal ports. It should be noted, however, that these difficulties did not arise because European commercial penetration into the Sahara was sudden and unprecedented. The merchants of the Southeast had for centuries moved trade goods both north and south along a network of routes ultimately linking West Africa with Europe. Tafilalt was even an exporter to Europe in its own right in the nineteenth century since part of its date crop was sent through Fez to England. In short, commerce between the Southeast and Europe was reciprocal, and it was well established long before the great commercial crisis began.

A Special Commodity: Firearms

One consequence of French military expansion into southern Oranie in 1881 was a greatly enlarged demand throughout the Southeast for modern European firearms. This commodity bears special consideration because of its importance in the history of Moroccan resistance to the French and because it reached the southeastern market by a number of channels other than the regular caravan trade.

When the French offensive began, the inhabitants of the Southeast already possessed an ample supply of muzzle-loading guns, or muskets, of various models. Some of these were originally imported from Europe, some were manufactured locally or in the trans-Atlas cities, notably Tetouan. Gunsmithing, usually a speciality of Jews, was an active industry in Tafilalt and to a lesser extent in Figuig. Craftsmen were capable of producing beautifully embellished flintlock muskets and pistols, using iron imported from the north. These guns were probably used for hunting and sport as much as for military purposes.

By the 1880s the tribes of the Southeast were more interested in obtaining European breech-loading rifles than in patronizing the local gunsmiths. They did not have to meet the French in battle to realize the total inadequacy of flintlocks when matched against modern rifles. Indeed, the tribes throughout Morocco as well as the central government were reaching the same conclusion. A notable symptom of European informal penetration and the gradual deterioration of internal order was an almost frenetic traffic in guns throughout the country. Mawlay Hasan and his successors purchased thousands of rifles from European dealers in order to strengthen the *makhzan* army. A large proportion of these weapons eventually found their way to the tribes. The sultan often armed the tribal contingents which served in the army as auxiliaries. These men frequently kept the rifles or sold them at private profit. In addition, European dealers, notably British and Spanish, conducted a flourishing contraband trade along the remote coasts, especially the Rif and the Sous, or through the Spanish Presidios. Coastal gunrunning, which the *makhzan* was powerless to control, remained the principal stimulant to internal arms trade until the establishment of the Protectorate.[64]

Despite the great distance from the coast to the Saharan fringe, arms trade accelerated so rapidly in the Southeast after 1880 that by the end of the century no warrior was obliged to carry a flintlock. The main line of arms trade was the set of routes across the high plains from Melilla and the Rif. Guns also arrived from Fez, Marrakech, and perhaps to some extent from the Sous. Because of the great risks in transporting such a coveted commodity the regular commercial caravans did not often carry large shipments. Rather, individuals traveled north to purchase their own rifles, or else they waited for them to filter into the region in small lots through a series of exchanges from one tribe to another. In other words, many rifles reached the Southeast by a kind of percolation process. This meant that at a given time the quantity of rifles in the hands of a tribe tended to vary inversely with the distance between that tribe and the coast.[65]

The French authorities in Algeria prohibited the sale of anything but muskets to populations in Morocco or the Sahara. Still, Muslim contraband traders and Moroccans who visited Algeria temporarily to trade or work introduced some rifles into the Southeast. To cite one example, in 1894 the French intercepted a letter from the rebel leader Abu 'Amama, who was in Gourara at the time, to a Muslim living in the Géryville area concerning shipment of an order of Chassepôt breech-loaders.[66]

The arms trade involved a confusing array of models and firing systems. Flintlock muskets of varying construction, known commonly and collectively as *bushfar* (French, *bouchefer*), abounded, though by the late nineteenth century very few were imported to Morocco from Europe. Percussion rifles, which predominated in Europe between about 1830 and 1860, were also in circulation, but the difficulty of obtaining percussion caps limited their use considerably.[67] In general, the introduction of a particular firing system to Morocco followed upon the invention of a better system in Europe. When European armies made the change from one type of rifle to an improved one, obsolete models were released for sale in the non-Western world. The remarkably rapid succession of advances in gun making during the second half of the nineteenth century meant that firearms technology improved in Africa and Asia but still lagged one or two steps behind European capability.[68] In southeastern Morocco the introduction of large numbers of single shot breech-loading rifles followed the adoption of magazine repeating rifles in Europe during the 1880s and 1890s. The single shot models used in greatest numbers in the region were the American Remington of 1860 (*mashuka* or *qalata*); the French 1866 Chassepôt (*sasbu*); the Martini-Henry (*bu hafra*), used by the British army from 1871 to 1888; and the French Gras rifle and carbine, used by the French military from 1874 to 1885. Mausers, Spencers, Lefaucheux, and other models were traded in smaller numbers.[69]

Toward the end of the century magazine repeaters began to appear in greater quantities. The American 1873 Winchester (*sitta'shiya*), a lever action rifle firing sixteen shots in rapid succession, was quite common in the Southeast in the 1890s. European traders introduced it to Morocco, and it entered the Southeast along the trade routes.[70] The other repeater well-known in the region was the French nine shot Lebel (*tsa'iya*), which was issued to the army in 1886, replacing the Gras. A carbine model was produced in 1892 and an improved infantry model in 1893. This rifle most often came into the hands of Moroccans as a result of raids, ambushes, and thefts committed against French posts and convoys in the frontier region after 1886.

The rifle introduced in perhaps larger quantities than all the other modern models combined was the famous Remington single shot breechloader, which was first produced in 1860. From 1867 to World War I it probably sold more widely outside the Western world than any other model. It had an exceptionally simple yet durable rolling-block mechanism, lending it special suitability in remote areas. Contraband sale of Remingtons in Morocco was so extensive that by the end of the century it had become the 'basic' rifle for tribes throughout much of the country. It was commonly used in parts of the Southeast by the 1890s.[71] A survey made by the French army in 1894 of Moroccan firearms capability in the frontier region concluded that the Remington was more easily obtainable and more widely distributed than any other model. According to the estimate, the Bani Gil possessed 4,000 Remingtons, but only 200 Gras, and 20 Lebels; the population of Figuig 350 Remingtons, 20 Gras, and 5 Lebels; the Awlad Jarir 150 Remingtons, 30 Gras, and 3 Lebels.[72] A report on Figuig made six years later estimated the number of rifles in Zenaga alone at 800 Remingtons, 35 Martini-Henrys, 18 Chassepôts, 47 Lebels, and 75 repeaters of other models.[73] Commerce in Remingtons and the other models may have developed a bit more slowly in and around Tafilalt than in the Figuig area, owing to the somewhat greater distance between Tafilalt and the Mediterranean coast. By the closing years of the century, however, Tafilalt was, according to a French Military Mission report, well supplied with rapid-fire arms, especially Remingtons.[74]

Amunition was of course imported with the rifles, but it was doubtless in chronic short supply. The deficiency was relieved to some extent by the local manufacture of ammunition. Black gun powder was imported from the north, but it was also produced locally. Saltpeter, charcoal from the oleander, and lead were all found locally. The trans-Atlas caravans brought sulphur. To make bullets for breech-loading rifles specialists in Tafilalt, and perhaps elsewhere in the region, learned how to recharge the spent cartridges of imported ammunition with powder and fulminate. In the Sous, and perhaps in Tafilalt as well, fulminate was made from a mixture of imported gasoline and the substance from match heads.[75] These refilled cartridges were almost certainly of inferior quality, but they may have been used widely when European ammunition was scarce. The Lebel and subsequent magazine-loaders used cartridges containing the much more effective and powerful 'smokeless' powder, so manufacturing ammunition for these rifles was not possible. Since most Lebels were stolen or taken in raids rather than imported, ammunition for them must always have been at a premium.

In sum, the firearms trade in the late nineteenth century was active enough to supply any warrior with a Remington or other single shot, some with repeaters. A variety of pistols and revolvers circulated as well. A study in 1905 asserted that nomads in the Tafilalt area were armed 'exclusively' with modern weapons, though many *qsar*-dwellers were still willing to settle for muskets.[76] During the period of heavy resistance between 1900 and 1912, arms trade expanded further as a result of continuing contraband trade, the escalation of raiding into the French controlled zone, and the transfer of weapons from *makhzan* garrison troops in Tafilalt and Figuig to the local population. But even though Moroccan warriors were more often armed with breech-loaders than with flintlocks, the technological gap between them and the French was not significantly narrowed. For the Moroccans had comparatively few repeating rifles and none at all of the machine guns and portable cannons which would win every major battle for the French imperial cause.

Trade and the Approaching Crisis

During the second half of the nineteenth century, the patterns of commerce in southeastern Morocco were undergoing important changes, owing largely to European military and economic penetration of North and West Africa. The first of these changes was the rapid deterioration of trade between the markets of the Southeast and those of western Algeria following upon the French conquests of 1830-1850. The diversion of trans-Saharan traffic away from Algeria almost certainly brought new prosperity to Abou Am's slave market, though Mogador and the desert ports of the southwest attracted the lion's share of the trade in ostrich feathers, gum, and other West African products. A second change was the decline and dissipation of trans-Saharan trade into both the southwestern and southeastern entrepôts during the 1880s and 1890s. Abou Am may have consistently transshipped a few hundred slaves a year throughout most of this period, but the French occupation of Timbuktu in 1894 and Touat six years later reduced importation to insignificance. 1900 effectively marked the end of the trans-Saharan trade through Tafilalt. A third transformation was the gradual acceleration of trans-Atlas trade in European imports. As the trans-Saharan trade atrophied, the southbound trade in tea, sugar, textiles, and manufactures expanded. By 1900 the inhabitants of the Southeast were acquiring tastes for these products, and more and more merchants were profiting from their sale. A fourth change, closely related to the third, was Morocco's growing economic crisis — increasingly unfavorable balance of trade, flight of hard currency, inflation. The people of the Southeast, especially those in and around Tafilalt, were probably feeling the adverse effects of this crisis on trade and buying power some years before the turn of the century.

These four changes taken together produced economic distress and un-

certainty in the Southeast but may also have helped prepare the population for the more drastic shifts in trade that would accompany French
military advances after 1900. By that time the population was in some
measure already attuned to the economic repercussions of European
imperialism in both North and West Africa. The crisis of military and
commercial conquest did not catch them fully by surprise.

If gradual transformations in commercial life made the population
broadly sensitive to European activity outside the region, the trading network itself enabled them to have concrete knowledge of how the European offensive was developing and how Africans both north and south of
the Sahara were responding to it. No desert oasis, however lonely and
unimportant, was isolated from the lines of trade. To describe the commercial system, as has been done here, in terms of particular routes and
specializing groups is certainly to oversimplify it, for caravans, large and
small, went everywhere that people lived. Traders carried not only
merchandise but also news, ideas, and opinions. Market places were hubs
of communication, which linked the *qsar-s* and herding groups with one
another and with the wider world. If great distances divided villages and
tribes within the region, trade drew them together and obliged them to
create links of mutual interest and cooperation across social boundaries.
Trade also kept them in touch with events occurring outside the region
and created strong social and economic ties between them and the populations of the north. In this respect the routes from Tafilalt to Fez and to
Marrakech were most important during the late nineteenth century, since
they linked the Southeast with the sultan's palace and with the political
and intellectual life of the trans-Atlas cities. In times of crisis these routes
could become political 'hot lines,' carrying envoys, delegations, armed contingents, and conspirators urgently in either direction. In short, trade and
the trade route system were powerful counteracting forces against the
parochialism and ignorance which social divisions, natural barriers, and
the climate persistently encouraged. Thus, when the French army marched
into southeastern Morocco, the inhabitants were in varying degrees already
aware and comprehending of the nature of the European challenge.

Notes

1. Walter B. Harris, *Tafilet* (London, 1895), p. 264.
2. A fifth category, the east-west pilgrimage trade between Saharan Morocco and
   the holy cities of Arabia, had no great impact on the total commerce of the
   region, but it introduced a number of novel luxuries, such as spices, perfumes,
   silks, and Indian fabrics, which would otherwise never have been available. See

my article, 'The Trade of Tafilalt: Commercial Change in Southeast Morocco on the Eve of the Protectorate,' *African Historical Studies*, 6, no. 2 (1971), pp. 283-5.

3. E. Carette and E. Renou, *Recherches sur la géographie et la commerce de l'Algérie méridionale* (Paris, 1844), pp. 92-4; E. Daumas, *Le Sahara Algérien* (Paris, 1845), pp. 266-9. These two works contain the only European descriptions of Figuig for the earlier nineteenth century.

4. Jean-Louis Miège, *Le Maroc et l'Europe* (Paris, 1961-63), III, 76-9; Edouard Déchaud, *Le Commerce algéro-marocain* (Algiers, 1906), pp. 14, 15; A. Adu Boahen, *Britain, the Sahara, and the Western Sudan* (Oxford, 1964), pp. 222, 223.

5. Marcel Emerit, 'L'Abolition de l'esclavage,' in Emerit, *La Révolution de 1848 en Algérie* (Paris, 1949), pp. 29-42; August Beaumier, 'Premier établissement de Israélites à Timbouctou,' *BSGP*, 5th ser., 19 (1870), p. 367; Déchaud, *Commerce*, pp. 14, 15.

6. I.D. de la Porte, 'Itinéraire de Constantine à Tafilet,' *Bullétin de la Société Royale de Géographie d'Egypte*, 13 (1925), pp. 205-49; James Grey Jackson, *An Account of the Empire of Morocco* (London, 1814), pp. 285, 286; René Caillié, *Journal d'un voyage a Temboctou et a Jenné dans l'Afrique centrale* (Paris, 1830), II and III, *passim*; Marcel Emerit, 'Les Liaisons terrestre entre le Soudan et l'Afrique du Nord au XVIIIe et au debut du XIXe siècle,' *Travaux de l'Institut de Recherches Sahariennes*, II no. 1 (1954), pp. 34, 35; D. Jacques-Meunié, 'Abbar, cité royale du Tafilalt,' *Hespéris*, 46 (1959), p. 15; L. Mercier, 'Notice économique sur le Tafilalet,' *Ren. Col.* (June, 1905), p. 220; Carette and Renou, *Recherches*, pp. 299-305; Harris, *Tafilet*, pp. 305, 306.

7. de la Porte, 'Itinéraire de Constantine,' p. 206; Carette and Renou, *Recherches*, pp. 299, 302; Caillié, *Journal d'un voyage*, II and III, *passim*.

8. Miège, *Le Maroc et l'Europe*, II, 146-54; III, 74-95, 358-66; IV, 381-5. C.W. Newbury, 'North African and Western Sudan Trade in the Nineteenth Century: A Re-evaluation,' *Journal of African History*, 7, no. 2 (1966), pp. 233-46.

9. Miège, *Le Maroc et l'Europe*, II, 142-54; III, 74-95.

10. Harris, *Tafilet*, p. 305. Also Henri Schirmer, *Le Sahara* (Paris, 1893), p. 358.

11. Miège, *Le Maroc et l'Europe*, III, 358-66; IV, 381-5.

12. M & L, III, 382, 385.

13. René Caillié, (*Journal d'un voyage*, II, 366), speaking of the late 1820s, reported that '[gold, ivory, and ostrich feathers] are ordinarily addressed to the merchants of Tafilet by their correspondents in Temboctou, in return for merchandise sent by the former and which [the merchants in Temboctou] sell in their behalf.' Also (III, 86) 'the Maures of distinction of Tafilet go for the most part to Temboctou to establish themselves, as we would leave Europe to go to the New World to make our fortune: These Maures, after having spent five or six years in commerce, buy gold and slaves and return to their homeland to live at ease.' It seems likely that Filali traders were doing this sort of thing until late in the century. Beaumier ('Premier établissement,' p. 369) estimated in 1870 that twenty to twenty-five merchants from Fez and Tafilalt and about six hundred from Touat were living in Timbuktu.

14. 'Le Tafilelt d'après Gerhard Rohlfs,' *Ren. Col.* (Aug. 1910), p. 251.

15. A typical well-to-do member of the Ait 'Atta tribe might have owned six slaves. AGGA, 22H. 27, Denoun (Officier-Interprète, Colomb-Béchar), 'Essai de monographie de la tribu berbère des Ait Atta,' April 7, 1913, p. 30. A few notables in Touat owned as many as twenty. M & L, III, 389.

16. Harris, *Tafilet*, p. 297. Also Ed. Michaux-Bellaire, 'L'Esclavage au Maroc,' *Revue du Monde Musulman*, II, nos. 7-8 (1910), p. 424.

17. Miège, *Le Maroc et l'Europe*, III, 92, 363.

18. Quoted in M & L, III, 389.
19. See Adu Boahen, *Britain*, pp. 141-5.
20. A former Native Affairs officer who served in Erfoud in 1925 stated that at that time the slave market at Abou Am was still in operation. Interview no. 32.
21. The development of Euro-Moroccan trade relations in the nineteenth century is treated at length in the four volumes of Miège, *Le Maroc et l'Europe*.
22. 'Le Tafilelt d'après Gerhard Rohlfs,' p. 251; Harris, *Tafilet*, p. 297; Delbrel, 'Notes sur le Tafilelt,' p. 220.
23. FO 174/262, James MacLeod (British Vice-consul at Fez), *Memorandum: Tafilet Date Trade, Manner of Export and Method of Cultivation*, April 17, 1901; 174/267, MacLeod to Lowther, May 16, 1906. Charles René-Leclerc, 'Le Commerce et l'industrie à Fez,' *Ren. Col.* (July 1905), pp. 244, 247; Harris, *Tafilet*, p. 297; Mercier, 'Notice économique,' pp. 212, 213, 217.
24. Mercier, 'Notice économique,' pp. 213, 217. Also Roger Le Tourneau, *Fès avant le Protectorat* (Casablanca, 1949), p. 425; A Joly, 'L'Industrie à Tetouan,' *Archives Marocaines*, 8 (1906), pp. 215, 216.
25. Mercier, 'Notice économique,' p. 219.
26. Mercier ('Notice économique,' pp. 214, 215) states that 'un grand nombre' of Fasi merchants lived in Tafilalt, but my suggestion of a few dozen is only a guess. Also Delbrel, 'Notes sur Tafilelt,' p. 220.
27. AMG, Alg. 19, Sit. pol. 1911, Capt. Berriau (Com. Annex of Beni Abbès), 'Contribution à l'étude de la région du Sud-Ouest,' 1911, p. 15.
28. The trans-Atlas commercial operations of Muhammad ibn Idris are described briefly in two French reports: AMG, Alg. 16, Sit. pol. 1906, report by Lt. Pierron enclosed in Gov. Gen. to Min. War. Dec. 31, 1906, no. 3666; Sit. pol. 1907, 'Renseignements fournis par Si Ahmed Beni Mani, représentant à Béchar du commerçant Filalien Si Mohammed ben Driss.' Also, interview no. 20. The informant was the son of an important Filali trader of the turn of the century.
   On the Tazi family in Fez see 'L'Evolution du Makhzen: la famille Tazi,' *Af. Fr.* (February 1904), pp. 50, 51: and René-Leclerc, 'Le Commerce et l'industrie,' pp. 231, 249. A general note on the banking services performed by Fasi commercial firms with branches in Tafilalt is found in Abdelouahab Lahlou, 'Notes sur la banque et les moyens d'échanges commerciaux à Fès avant le Protectorat,' *Hespéris*, 24 (1937), p. 231.
29. Charles de Foucauld, *Reconnaissance au Maroc* (Paris, 1939), p. 391; René-Leclerc, 'Le Commerce et l'industrie,' p. 231.
30. Mercier, 'Notice économique,' p. 219. Interview no. 20.
31. Foucauld, *Reconnaissance*, pp. 367, 385, 390. Mercier, 'Notice économique,' p. 220. See also Edward Westermarck, *Ritual and Belief in Morocco* (London, 1926), I, 535-537; and H. Bruno and G.-H. Bousquet, 'Les Pactes d'alliance chez les Berbères du Maroc central,' *Hespéris*, 33 (1946), pp. 357-62.
32. Mercier, 'Notice économique,' pp. 215-7, 220. Harris, *Tafilet*, p. 303.
33. L. Demaeght, 'Voyage d'études commerciales sur la frontière marocaine,' *BSGAO*, 17 (1897), p. 39; Déchaud, *Commerce*, pp. 14-26; Miège, *Le Maroc et l'Europe*, III, 71-3.
34. M & L, II, 539.
35. Daumas, *Le Sahara algérien*, pp. 265, 266; M & L, II, 469; Déchaud, *Commerce*, p. 55; Interview no. 28.
36. Edmond Doutté, 'Figuig,' pp. 190, 191; Demaeght, 'Voyage d'études,' p. 39; M & L, II, 539; Déchaud, *Commerce*, pp. 17, 18.
37. Augustin Bernard and N. Lacroix, *L'Evolution du nomadisme en Algérie* (Paris, 1906), pp. 222, 223; M & L, III, 386-9; Mercier, 'Notice économique,' pp. 217, 218. The pastoral tribes of the Southeast as well as those of western

Algeria supplied grain and meat directly to the sedentary populations of Touat in return for dates. The Algerian tribes, who were under French control in the late nineteenth century but still free to trade in Touat, organized large, multi-tribal caravans annually. These caravans did not use the Wad Zousfana-Saoura route as did the Moroccan tribes, but traveled across the Erg Occidental several miles further east. Bernard and Lacroix, *Evolution*, pp. 224-38; M & L, III, 367-433.

38. Bernard and Lacroix, *Evolution*, p. 223; M & L, III, 385.

39. Berriau, 'Région du Sud-Ouest,' p. 19; Mercier, 'Notice économique,' pp. 215-7; Interview no. 18.

40. AGGA, 30H. 3, Enquête sur les rapports qui existent entre les indigènes algériens et les tribus du territoire marocain, Capt. Dineaux, 'Rapport . . . au sujet des relations des indigènes de l'annexe avec les tribus du territoire marocain,' Jan. 20, 1903; Bernard and Lacroix, *Evolution*, p. 225; Interview no. 18.

41. de Castries, 'Notes sur Figuig,' *BSGP*, 7th ser., 3 (1882), p. 407; Interview no. 28.

42. Interview no. 20.

43. Mercier, 'Notice économique,' p. 217.

44. Bernard and Lacroix, *Evolution*, pp. 223, 224; M & L, III, 385-589; Interview no. 28.

45. Berriau, 'Région du Sud-Ouest,' p. 15; Harris, *Tafilet*, p. 278; Mercier, 'Notice économique,' p. 215; M & L, III, 382.

46. Harris, *Tafilet*, p. 281; Delbrel, 'Notes sur Tafilelt,' p. 220.

47. Mercier, 'Notice économique,' p. 215.

48. Harris, *Tafilet*, pp. 271, 290, 295, 296; Mercier, 'Notice économique,' pp. 213, 214.

49. Mercier, 'Notice économique,' p. 214;

50. See Walter Fogg, 'The Organization of a Moroccan Tribal Market,' *American Anthropologist*, 44 (1942), pp. 47-61; and 'A Tribal Market in the Spanish Zone of Morocco,' *Africa*, 11, no. 4 (1938), pp. 428-58. See also Francisco Benet, 'Explosive Markets: The Berber Highlands.' in Karl Polanyi, *Trade and Markets in the Early Empires* (Glencoe, Illinois, 1957), pp. 188-217; and Robert Montagne, *Les Berbères et le Makhzen dans le sud du Maroc* (Paris, 1930), pp. 249-53.

51. Communication from Chahid Bouaalem, Boudenib. He served as my interpreter in 1969. His informants were elderly residents of Tafilalt.

52. Rohlfs ('Le Tafilelt d'après Gerhard Rohlfs,' p. 251) noted in 1864 that the garrison was comprised of about one hundred men. Harris (*Tafilet*, p. 274) suggested fifty.

53. Harris and others refer to the market by the name of Mawlay 'Ali Sharif rather than Abou Am, meaning that he was its patron saint.

54. de Castroes. 'Notes sur Figuig,' p. 407; Daumaṣ, *Le Sahara algérien*, p. 262; Interview no. 28.

55. M & L, II, 489, 496.

56. M & L, II, 489. Interview no. 28.

57. Interviews no. 28 and 31.

58. Miège, *Le Maroc et l'Europe*, III, 97, 100. See also Marion Johnson, 'The Nineteenth Century Gold "Mithqal" in West and North Africa,' *Journal of African History*, 9, no. 4 (1968), pp. 558-9.

59. Miège, *Le Maroc et l'Europe*, III, 97; Mercier, 'Notice économique,' p. 218. The system of relative monetary values changed from time to time during the nineteenth century. The one noted here was current throughout Morocco late in the century. See Le Tourneau, *Fès*, p. 283.

60. On the monetary crisis see Germain Ayache, 'Aspects de la crise financière au Maroc après l'éxpédition espagnole de 1860,' *Revue Historique*, 220 (1958),

pp. 271-310; Ed. Michaux-Bellaire, 'L'Organisation des finances au Maroc,' *Archives Marocaines*, 11, no. 2 (1907), pp. 171-251; and 'Les Crises monétaires au Maroc,' *Revue du Monde Musulman,* 38 (March 1920), pp. 41-57; Miège, *Le Maroc et l'Europe*, III, 97-106, 428-36; IV, 113-23.

61. Harris, *Tafilet*, p. 291; Mercier, 'Notice économique,' p. 218.

62. Rohlfs ('Le Tafilelt d'après Gerhard Rohlfs,' p. 251) claims that Spanish money was rare in Tafilalt in the 1860s. Harris (*Tafilet*, p. 291) states that 'damaged Spanish silver' was in use in Marrakech but not accepted in Tafilalt. On the importation of depreciated duros and Philippine coins see Miège, *Le Maroc et l'Europe*, IV, 116-19.

63. Niéger, 'Le Touat,' *Ren. Col.,* no. 7 (1904), p. 175; M & L, III, 375; Bernard and Lacroix, *Evolution*, pp. 223, 224.

64. Miège, *Le Maroc et l'Europe*, IV, 106.

65. AGGA, 30H. 37, Détrie (Com. Div. Oran) to Gov. Gen., Nov. 2, 1891, no. 906; 30H. 22, Contrabande de poudre et armes, Boitard (Com. Div. Oran) to Gov. Gen., June 23, 1894, no. 170; Metzinger (Com. Div. Oran) to Gov. Gen., Nov. 1, 1894, no. 109. AMG, Maroc C5, MM 1889, Gov. Gen. to Min. War, Sept. 28, 1889, no. 5665; Maroc C10, MM 1897, Schlumberger to Min. War, Feb. 1, 1897, no. 4; Maroc C12, MM 1901, Burckhardt to Min. War, Aug. 30, 1901, no. 224; MM 1902, Burckhardt to Min. War, July 4, 1902, no. 286; M & L, II, 541. Mercier ('Notice économique,' p. 216) noted in 1905 that 'it does not seem that any natives are engaging in arms trade between Tafilalt and Morocco' and that 'everyone procures his own arms and goes where he knows he will find them.' According to M & L (III, 206, 207) the inhabitants of Touat had very few modern rifles before the turn of the century and those they did receive may have come more often from Tripoli by way of Ghadamès than from Morocco.

66. AGGA, 30H. 22, Contrabande, Boitard to Gov. Gen., July 14, 1894, no. 235; 21H. 10, Boitard to Gov. Gen., March 15, 1896, no. 718.

67. Capitaine Delhomme, 'Les Armes dans le Sous occidental,' *Archives Berbères,* 2 (1917), p. 124. Delhomme's observations concern particularly southwestern Morocco, but some percussion rifles were probably in use in the Southeast as well.

68. For discussion of this point in relation to sub-Saharan Africa see Gavin White, 'Firearms in Africa: An Introduction,' *Journal of African History*, 12, no. 2 (1971), pp. 177, 178.

69. The models listed as most important are the ones most often mentioned in French military reports from the frontier region.

70. AGGA, 30H. 22, Contrabande, Boitard to Gov. Gen., June 23, 1894, no. 170; AMG, Maroc C10, MM 1897, Schlumberger to Min. War, Feb. 1, 1897, no. 4; Maroc C11, MM 1900, Burckhardt to Min. War, Aug. 9, 1900, no. 144; M & L, II, 541; Mercier, 'Notice économique,' p. 216; Miège, *Le Maroc et l'Europe*, IV, 106.

71. AMG, Maroc C5, MM 1889, Gov. Gen. to Min. War, Sept. 28, 1889, no. 5665; Miège, *Le Maroc et l'Europe*, IV, 106.

72. AGGA, 30H. 22, Contrabande, Boitard to Gov. Gen., June 23, 1894, no. 170.

73. AMG, Alg. 14, Sud-Oranais 1900, Risbourg (Com. Div. Oran) to Com. 19th Corps, May 29, 1900, no. 447.

74. AMG, Maroc C10, MM 1897.

75. Denoun 'Ait Atta,' p. 27; Mercier, 'Notice économique', p. 214; Harris, *Tafilet*, p. 296; Delhomme, 'Les Armes dans le Sous,' p. 124.

76. Mercier, 'Notice économique,' p. 216.

1 The Ziz River valley in the Medaghra district. Drawing by Jeanne Dunn

3   The oasis of Figuig, looking east. Drawing by Jeanne Dunn

4. The French blockhouse guarding the Rentsita's Bar imitates a Roman stronghouse

5   The French market at Boudenib, c. 1910. Drawing by Jeanne Dunn from a photograph in *Augustin Bernard, Les Confins algéro-marocains*

PART II SOUTHEASTERN MOROCCO AND THE FRENCH CONQUEST

5 THE SOUTHEAST BETWEEN FRANCE AND THE MAKHZAN, 1881-1900

When Sultan Mawlay 'Abd al-Hafid signed the Protectorate treaty with France in March 1912, a significant portion of his empire was already under the sure control of the French military. Over the course of three decades the army had gradually infiltrated Moroccan territory, sometimes acting in ostensible cooperation with the Sharifian government, at other times merely extending the borders of Algeria. These pre-Protectorate conquests involved four major theaters of military and political activity. In July 1907 French forces occupied the Atlantic port of Casablanca and during the next two years conquered the adjacent coastal hinterland known as the Chaouia. Along the northeastern frontier intermittent clashes between Moroccan tribes and Algerian troops throughout the second half of the nineteenth century culminated in March 1907 in the occupation of the important town of Oujda and the subsequent conquest of territory as far west as the Wad Moulouya. This region remained part of Morocco but was administered through a French High Commissioner until after 1912. Between 1900 and 1901 the central Saharan oasis complex of Touat (comprising the three districts of Gourara, Touat proper, and Tidikelt) were incorporated into Algeria. From here the French launched their protracted conquest of the Tuareg and other desert tribes. Finally, the spasmodic penetration of Morocco's southeastern marches from the Mountains of the Ksour to the Wad Ziz began in 1881 and was still proceeding when the Protectorate was declared. When French columns reached the banks of the Ziz in 1911, they were approximately one hundred and eighty miles west of the present-day Algero-Moroccan border.

Origins of the French Offensive

During their first fifteen years as rulers of Algeria, the French took little interest in the mysteries of the Sahara. Only after they defeated the resistance leader 'Abd al-Qadir and completed conquest of the Turkish Regency did they turn a curious eye southward. Until then, European knowledge of the North African interior was abysmally, though perhaps understandably, weak. A clause in the Treaty of Lalla-Marnia of 1845, which defined the Algero-Moroccan border from the coast to a point about sixty-eight miles inland, stated that 'as for the country which is south of the kessours [qsar-s] of the two governments [referring to Figuig and villages in the

137

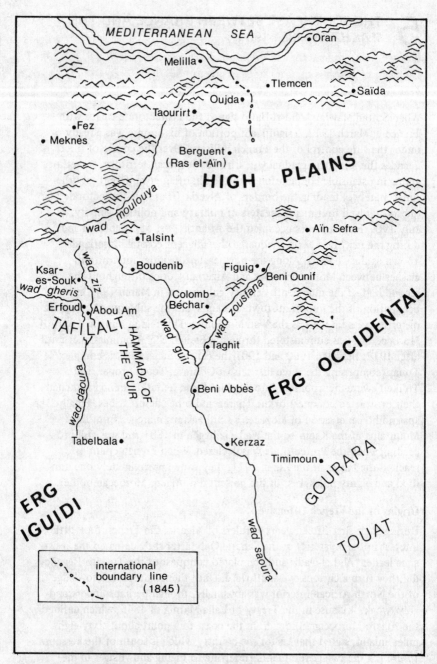

Algero-Moroccan Frontier Region

western Saharan Atlas,] as there is no water, it is uninhabitable and is, properly speaking, the desert; so delimitation there would be superfluous.'[1] This observation was, to say the least, a misjudgment.

Early in the 1850s the French government under Napoleon III began to talk of developing overland commercial relations between Algeria and West Africa and even of uniting Algeria with the colony of Senegal. Governor-General Randon (1851-59), a vigorous advocate of expansion into the Sahara, extended French occupation across the Saharan Atlas in central and eastern Algeria and took steps to attract trans-Saharan trade into the colony. In the west he established the post of Géryville in 1852, whose main purpose was to protect the tribes of the Oranie plains who were then in the process of submitting to French authority.[2] From Géryville a few probing expeditions ventured into the vicinity of Figuig to collect geographical and scientific data. In 1860 two French officers, Colonieu and Burin, led a lightly armed expedition down the Zousfana-Saoura corridor to Touat in an effort to establish commercial relations. But they met with a hostile reception along most of the route, and after traveling as far as Gourara they were forced to turn back.[3] Gerhardt Rohlfs, the German explorer, was the first to publish a detailed description of southeastern Morocco. During the course of two trips across the High Atlas in 1862 and 1864, he visited Tafilalt, Kenadsa, Figuig, and Touat. His travels created considerable sensation in Europe and shed light on territory and people theretofore unknown.[4]

Military expansion southward from the Oranie plains came to a halt in 1864 owing to a major tribal uprising led by the Awlad Sidi Shaykh (Ouled Sidi Cheikh), a politically powerful tribe of *murabtin*-warriors. French forces contained the rebellion within a matter of months, but it continued to flare up periodically until 1883. The Treaty of Lalla-Marnia had given the French the privilege of pursuing dissident tribesmen into Moroccan territory. The government restrained the army from making use of the *droit de suite* very often, fearing diplomatic complications with the *makhzan* and the other European powers. In 1870, however, Awlad Sidi Shaykh insurgents managed to put together an alliance with Moroccan tribesmen of the Dawi Mani', the Awlad Jarir, and the Bani Gil for the purpose of launching raids into Oranie. Consequently, General de Wimpffen, Commander of the Oran Division, was authorized to pursue the raiders into southeastern Morocco. He led his expedition all the way to the banks of the lower Wad Guir and there defeated a large tribal force. He then made a brief assault on the *qsar* of Aïn Chaïr before returning to Algeria. No extension of the military frontier followed this punitive mission, much to the army's displeasure. The most important result of the episode was the establishment of a precedent for army encroachment deep into Moroccan territory.[5]

After the Wimpffen expedition, no further military penetration of the Algero-Moroccan frontier region took place for another eleven years. This inaction was the result of both the continuing agitation of the Awlad Sidi Shaykh in Oranie and the French government's general policy of colonial retrenchment following the Franco-Prussian War in 1870 and the Moqrani revolt in the Kabylie Mountains in 1871. About 1876, however, public interest in colonial expansion began gradually to revive owing mainly to the work of a small group of enthusiasts, among them journalists, explorers, members of geographical societies, and deputies of the National Assembly. Renewed interest in the Sahara derived mainly from the belief that the western Sudan (that is, the savanna country of West Africa) held immense natural wealth and that Franch should be the first power to stake a claim to it. Most French expansionists of the 1870s shared Europe's enthusiasm for the steam engine as a trailblazer of Western civilization. Many of them began urging construction of a rail line from Algeria to the western Sudan where it would link up with an eastward extension of the Senegalese railroad. In 1879 Charles de Freycinet, the French Minister of Public Works and an ardent champion of railroads, dispatched three missions to the Sahara to study possible routes for a line. Captain Pouyanne led one of them south of Oran Province, but because of concern that Moroccan tribes would prove hostile he went only as far as the Mountains of the Ksour. Colonel Flatters was instructed to lead another of the missions all the way to the Sudan, but in February 1881 he and his entire expedition were massacred by Tuareg near In Salah in the central Sahara. The Flatters disaster burst the bubble of '*le transsaharien*,' and convinced the French government that military occupation of the desert would have to precede construction of a railway. Since diplomatic and domestic factors prevented an aggressive Saharan policy for several years, the various railroad schemes were suspended until the end of the century, though they were by no means forgotten.[6]

A brief but sensational uprising in central Oranie in the spring and summer of 1881 was the catalyst for the French army's advance to the Mountains of the Ksour. The leader of the rebellion was Abu 'Amama (Bou Amama, 'man of the turban'), a resident of Figuig and a member of the Awlad Sidi Taj, a tiny pastoral tribe which was politically and genealogically associated with the Awlad Sidi Shaykh. As a young man Abu 'Amama drew upon his purported kinship with the saintly descendants of Sidi Shaykh, who lived in the seventeenth century, to become an active *murabit*. He adhered closely to the standards of his calling, praying incessantly, fasting, and performing thaumaturgical acts. He may also have been an epileptic, an affliction which could easily have enhanced his *baraka*.[7] In 1878 he founded a *zawiya* at Moghar Tahtani, a small oasis on the southern slopes of the Mountains of the Ksour. He developed a set of litanies and mystical exercises patterned after those of the Awlad Sidi Shaykh *murabtin* and began to declare that Sidi Shaykh had chosen him as his spiritual successor. He soon collected a band of disciples and sent some of them to other villages to spread his teaching. In 1880, or perhaps earlier, he began to call for a holy war to expel the French from Algeria.[8]

Exactly why and under what circumstances Abu 'Amama turned from meditation to political activism is not clear, but the tribes of central and southern Oranie were not long in responding. The assassination of the head of the Arab Bureau at Géryville in April 1881 led to a general rising of the tribes of the high plains. In May Abu 'Amama marched northward over the mountains, picking up tribal contingents as he went along. The French were embarrassingly unprepared for a revolt at the time and so were unable to prevent Abu 'Amama's forces from penetrating as far north as the regions of Saïda and Tiaret. The rebels made one major raid in May, during which they killed a number of European agricultural workers, and another in July, after which French forces chased them back into the mountains or into Moroccan territory. Abu 'Amama and a rapidly dwindling following remained in the vicinity of Figuig until sometime in 1882, then headed south to Gourara.

Although the uprising would not have reached the proportions that it did without Abu 'Amama's leadership, conditions among the Oranie tribes favored a sudden outbreak against the French. The gradual extension of land set aside for European colonization had been an underlying cause of the long Awlad Sidi Shaykh rebellion. The 1881 revolt was in a sense the final act of that movement. In 1879 and 1880 the French authorized an acceleration of the transfer of tribal lands to *commune civile* status. The resultant expulsion of pastoral groups from their lands and watering places produced considerable suffering and dislocation. These tribes were forced to move onto the territory of other tribes further south, creating critical land shortage and congestion. The insurrection was probably more than anything else a manifestation of discontent over French land policy. The movement may have lasted as long as it did because garrisons in Oran province were at a minimum level owing to the transfer of troops to the new protectorate in Tunisia. Moreover, both the army and the civil authorities were generally agreed by the late 1870s that tribal resistance was no longer possible.[9]

Indeed, Abou 'Amama's success in fomenting a pan-tribal rising in a

region which the French considered thoroughly pacified was no mean
achievement, especially since he was completely unknown outside his own
village as late as 1879. His sudden rise to prominence is not easily explain-
able since so little is known about his character, his life before 1881, or
the specific nature of his appeal to the tribes. Three factors were clearly
important. First, he was able to draw upon the prestige of the Awlad Sidi
Shaykh even though he was only a distant collateral of the *murabtin* and
had played no previous part in their resistance efforts. Moreover, he
dared to call for an insurrection at a time when the principal Awlad Sidi
Shaykh leaders were either in refuge in Morocco or working with the
French and, in any case, were cautious and divided.[10] Second, the dis-
contented tribes of Oranie needed the leadership of a saint if they were to
attempt to unify. Since *murabtin* were in a distinct social category separate from the 'lay' tribes in a given region, they were ideally suited to
intervene in time of external threat to resolve differences among competing tribes and clans and to shape them into a fighting alliance. Their
baraka legitimized the alliance by giving it divine sanction. Abu 'Amama
followed in the tradition of the warrior-saint whose appearance dated
back to the time of Muslim resistance to Spanish and Portuguese incursions in the fifteenth and sixteenth centuries. Third, Abu 'Amama's
success in leading his forces deep into Algerian territory and his quasi-
victory over a French column in May brought the movement broad support during its initial phase.[11]

The insurrection collapsed almost as suddenly as it erupted. The French
rushed reinforcements into Oranie, took the offensive in July, and quickly
scattered the *murabit*'s forces or forced them to beat a hasty retreat into
Moroccan territory. Abu 'Amama may also have lost support among the
Oranie tribes during the early weeks of the rising when his contingents
from desert tribes south of the mountains began pillaging livestock and
grain stores belonging to Muslims. In that sense the movement never
achieved a unity of purpose. For the tribes of the Oranie plains it was a
final, violent outburst against economic and social conditions created by
colonial rule. For the Saharan contingents it was an opportunity for a last,
grandiose razzia against the tribes of the north. For Abu 'Amama and his
spiritual disciples it appears to have been a holy crusade which attempted,
with fleeting success, to build on the discontent of the northern tribes and
the striking power of the Saharans.[12]

The uprising had two important consequences. The European settlers
in Oran Province and the military immediately demanded the creation of
new posts further south to protect the Tell and the high plains from
further Saharan-born disturbances. Therefore, in December 1881 the army

began construction of a fort at Aïn Sefra close to the northern slopes of the Mountains of the Ksour. During the spring of 1882, columns pursued Abu 'Amama and remnants of his forces as far south as the Wad Zousfana. In 1888 a second post was built at Djenien-Bou-Rezg on the southern side of the mountains and only a day's march from Figuig. This advance set the stage for direct confrontation between the French and the tribes of southeastern Morocco.

The insurrection also had the effect of making Abu 'Amama into a kind of warrior-saint emeritus. His leadership of the last rebellion to occur in Algeria gave him sufficient residual prestige to retain a coterie of followers and to play a significant role in frontier politics for another twenty-seven years. He remained at Deldoul in Gourara until 1896 then moved to Figuig accompanied by a disparate band of religious followers, Saharan adventurers, fugitives from French law, and professional bandits. He never led another attack against the French but on several occasions he entered into abortive negotiations with them for his pardon, sometimes through the intermediation of his son Si Tayyib. Always straddling the political fence, he continued to pose as the standard-bearer of resistance along the frontier but never cut himself off from communication with the French authorities. The Native Affairs officers continually complained of his elusiveness and belittled his influence, though at the same time they made him personally responsible for most of the resistance activity originating in Morocco. Whatever he may have done to encourage resistance after 1882, he clearly provided the French with their most creditable rationale for pushing ever deeper into Moroccan territory.

In spite of the energetic offensive of 1881-2, the French army made no permanent advances south of the Mountains of the Ksour for almost twenty years. During this period, they took control of the villages in a wide area around Aïn Sefra, and they built the satellite post of Djenien-Bou-Rezg, which guarded the southern entrance to the main pass over the mountains. The French foreign ministry, however, worked consistently to prevent them from advancing south or west of Djenien-Bou-Rezg. The Treaty of Lalla-Marnia defined the Algero-Moroccan border only as far south as a point called Teniet el-Sassi, located a few miles northeast of the present Moroccan town of Aïn-Benimathar (Berguent). South of that point the treaty merely designated certain villages and tribes as either Moroccan or Algerian. Figuig and Ich were declared Moroccan, as well as the pastoral Amur, who camped part of the year in the vicinity of Aïn Sefra. Aïn Sefra itself and six other villages in the surrounding area were named as Algerian. The position of the foreign ministry was that as long as the southern frontier remained undefined the army should be restrained from making incursions into territory which the Moroccan government might claim. In general, the ministry was not willing to support an aggressive expansionist policy in Algeria at the price of undermining its commercial and political ties with the *makhzan* or incurring the disfavor of the other European powers which were intent upon preserving Morocco's independence from France.

The Army of Africa, however, was in no mood for another round of retrenchment. Suppression of the Oranie rising gave the officer corps a new head of steam for expansion into the Sahara and a vision of unlimited opportunities for glory and advancement fighting desert marauders. They also had strong support from the Algerian settler community, who wanted the southern frontier of the colony made secure, and from the growing 'colonial party' in France, which, especially after 1890, favored expansion south of Oranie as one campaign in France's bid for African empire.[13] The occupation of Aïn Sefra marked the beginning of three decades of conflict between the army, the *colons*, and the colonial lobby on the one hand, and the foreign ministry on the other over France's political and military objectives in the southern Algero-Moroccan borderlands.

Between 1881 and 1900 the army persistently pressured the government for more freedom of action in pacifying and protecting southern Oranie (as the area around Aïn Sefra came to be known), but the Quai d'Orsay just as persistently refused to condone any operations which might jeopardize relations with the *makhzan*. For example, the army began construction of a redout at Djenien-Bou-Rezg in 1885, but the government made them withdraw after Sultan Mawlay Hasan expressed doubt that the location lay in Algerian territory. Following a meeting between army officers and *makhzan* representatives at Djenien-Bou-Rezg, the sultan agreed to French control. But construction of the post was not resumed until 1888.[14] The army also complained continually that Figuig, which was named a Moroccan oasis by the Treaty of 1845, was the principal staging area for Moroccan raiding parties which harassed the mountain posts and the Muslim populations under French control. The military's call for the occupation of Figuig was echoed by the Algerian civil authorities and the settlers, who regarded the oasis as the nucleus of hostility in the frontier zone. Between 1882 and 1884 Ladislas Ordega, the French Minister at Tangier, made special efforts to get government approval for the occupation on the grounds that the Zousfana-Saoura route for the trans-Saharan railroad was not feasible until Figuig was brought to heel. But despite the clamor for action, the foreign ministry remained adamant about the inviolability of the 1845 Treaty and so continued to resist a military operation against Figuig until 1903.[15]

The army and the Quai d'Orsay also conflicted over the problem of pacifying the Amur, who were Moroccan by the Treaty of 1845 but who pastured in the Mountains of the Ksour and owned property in the French controlled villages. According to Article 7 of the Treaty, Moroccans residing in the vicinity of the Algerian villages had to submit to French jurisdiction. Following the 1881 revolt most of the Amur leaders made formal submission at Aïn Sefra, but between 1884 and 1888 something close to half the tribe (about 240 tents) moved west of the French zone, most of them into the Jebel Beni Smir north of Figuig. From there many of them joined other Moroccan tribesmen in raiding for livestock, attacking convoys, and firing on military personnel. In order to put a stop to the exodus, which became especially acute in 1888, the army sent the remaining sections of the tribe to three years of internment, first in the central Saharan Atlas, then in the Saïda region. The Aïn Sefra command believed, however, that the Amur could be brought to terms once and for all only by sending an expedition to clean out the Jebel Beni Smir. Such an operation was planned on at least two occasions, but the French government, on the recommendations of the foreign ministry, refused to give final approval out of fear that the *makhzan* and the other powers would interpret it as a provocation against Morocco. In the late 1890s the dissident Amur tents began gradually to return to French territory, mainly for economic reasons, but the army did not receive permission to move into the Jebel Beni Smir until the summer of 1903. As far as they were concerned, the only real achievements of the period between 1881 and 1900 were the extension of the railroad from Méchéria to Aïn Sefra and the elevation of the Aïn Sefra military region from the level of *cercle* to subdivision (1894). This change meant that the region was no longer dependent on the subdivision of Mascara but thereafter took orders directly from division headquarters at Oran.[16]

Although the army generally argued for more leeway in southern Oranie in terms of the problems of local pacification and defense of the colony, it never regarded Aïn Sefra as anything but a launch base for the conquest of Touat and, eventually, the entire central Sahara. Public and government interest in Touat and the trans-Saharan railway slackened following the Flatters massacre, but it revived again early in the 1890s, when competition among the powers for African territory was most intense. Following the Anglo-French agreement of 1890, which recognized France's paramount interests in the central Sahara, the army and the civil authorities in Algeria began devising plans for Touat's annexation. Among the most vocal advocates of occupation were Jules Cambon, Governor-General of Algeria from 1891 to 1897, and Eugène Etienne, deputy of the National Assembly

from Oran and leader of the colonial party. Though most army officers
favored a full-scale military operation, Cambon and others were willing to
look for a subtler and less expensive way of persuading the population of
Touat to accept French rule. In 1892 Mawlay 'Abd al-Salam al-Wazzani,
a Moroccan protégé of the French and head of the Tayyibiya (Wazzaniya)
religious brotherhood, was sent to Gourara with an escort of Awlad Sidi
Shaykh and other tribesmen to meet with local leaders and smooth the
way for their peaceable submission to French authority. The sponsors of
the scheme believed that because the Tayyibiya had many affiliates in
Touat, al-Wazzani would be a persuasive spokesman. In fact, he received a
hostile reception in Gourara and had to turn back without completing his
mission.[17] The Algerian authorities also debated the possibility of letting
the loyal Awlad Sidi Shaykh leaders organize a kind of official razzia
which would pacify Touat in the name of France, but this idea was rejected both in 1883 and in 1892 as frought with uncertainties.[18]

The French government rejected Mawlay Hasan's claims that Touat was
in Moroccan territory and agreed that the region ought to be under
Algerian control. But it did not want to risk raising the question of
Morocco's 'national integrity.' Its greatest concern was that Britain would
not regard the agreement of 1890 as sufficient pretext for the absorption
of the central Sahara into Algeria. Only when Britain became preoccupied
with the Boer War in 1899 did the government consent to military action.
Then, the army wasted little time in finding a reason for marching south.
In December 1899 a French geology expedition working near In Salah was
attacked by Tuareg. A column dispatched to rescue the geologists
occupied In Salah, then called for more reinforcements. The conquest of
Touat was underway. During 1900 and 1901, the three districts of
Gourara, Touat proper, and Tidikelt were all occupied without serious diplomatic repercussions.[19]

The *Makhzan* Counteroffensive: Building Bridges to the Dawi Mani'

During the 1880s, Sultan Mawlay Hasan became fully aware of the far-
reaching objectives of France's expansion into southern Oranie. Therefore
he undertook the most vigorous effort since the time of Mawlay Isma'il in
the seventeenth century to fortify *makhzan* influence and prestige in the
Southeast. A military occupation of the region was beyond the capacities
of his army, but he attempted to introduce at least the symbols of
makhzan authority by sending special envoys to make contact with local
leaders, by investing these leaders with government titles, by establishing a
governor at Figuig, and by personally leading a massive expedition to
Tafilalt. He also appealed to the powers of Europe to support his claims to

sovereignty in the Southeast against France's pretensions, though he never received anything more than general assurances in return. Whatever he was able to accomplish in the region was entirely dependent on the strengths and weaknesses of his relations with the local population.

Between 1881 and 1900 the Dawi Mani' Arabs went about their immediate business of planting and herding, raiding and feuding, with a growing awareness of the ominous events unfolding off toward the northeast. Even though the French army was stalled north of Figuig, the tribe certainly suspected by the 1890s that the conquest of Touat, whenever it occurred, would likely involve French occupation of the Zousfana-Saoura valley. This prospect posed a serious threat to the defense of one of the tribe's principal date producing areas. Consequently, they were quite willing to cooperate with Mawlay Hasan in his campaign to strengthen political ties with the frontier tribes. The sultan's diplomatic strategy for countering French claims on part of the region centered on the appointment of a series of local qa'id-s (commanders) and judges as the official representatives of Sharifian authority.[20] In 1890 the sultan awarded the title of qa'id to three Dawi Mani' leaders. In 1892 several of them visited Fez to have their appointments renewed or to receive new ones. Each qa'id received an official letter of investiture and a seal of the makhzan. In 1893 four notables of the Awlad Jarir were given similar honors.[21] The sultan also drew up tentative plans to build a series of forts near the Zousfana to serve as liaison points between the Dawi Mani' and the makhzan. This project raised a stir among the French at Aïn Sefra, but it never came to fruition.[22] Interestingly, the sultan's special emissary to the Southeast in 1891-2 was himself a member of a small Dawi Mani' group which had migrated to the Fez area probably before the nineteenth century. Si al-'Arbi al-Mani'i, a good choice for the job because of his tribal origin, toured through the Southeast as far as Touat to dispense political titles, encourage the dispatch of delegations to Fez, and make assurances of makhzan protection against French aggression.[23]

Advocates of French expansion tended to scoff at Mawlay Hasan's dealings with the Dawi Mani', contending that the sultan could hand out a thousand letters of investiture and still have no real political authority in the Southeast. To state, however, that the Dawi Mani' and the rest of the north Saharan populations did not obey the sultan as citizens of Provençal obeyed Paris amounted to a convenient missing of the point. The 'Alawi sultans could wield political authority, in other words collect taxes, over more than the central portion of Morocco only by continual campaigning and by the astute application of divide and rule tactics among the tribes. In the mountain fastnesses and in the far south, where

only the strongest *makhzan* armies ventured, they could assert their influence by selectively distributing prestigious *qa'id* titles and by giving their
Sharifian blessing to one tribe for pillaging another. If, therefore, the sultans did not have sovereignty in the Southeast by European standards,
they did frequently attempt to translate their spiritual authority into real
political influence in so far as circumstances and their own shrewdness
would allow. If they could not govern the Southeast, they could at least
bring it within the orbit of *makhzan* politics.

Relations between the Dawi Mani' and the 'Alawi sultans, especially
Mawlay Hasan, had more profound political meaning than French observers could perceive or were willing to admit. The Dawi Mani' associate
their founding with the arrival of the first Mawlay al-Hasan in Tafilalt in
the thirteenth century. This connection was a matter of considerable pride
to the tribe, but it also symbolized a long history of alliance making between them and the dynasty. The Dawi Mani' were certainly not permanent allies of every 'Alawi sultan. Nor were they a southern counterpart
to the *makhzan*, or *guish* tribes of central Morocco, which gave the sultan perpetual military service in return for land and tax concessions. From
the evidence at hand, however, the Dawi Mani' were more prone to
alliance and cooperation with the central government than any other tribe
in the Southeast.

To give some examples, contingents of the Dawi Mani' and Awlad Jarir
joined Sultan Mawlay Isma'il in 1679 in making a brief thrust into
Turkish Algeria as far as the Jebel Amour. In 1806 Mawlay Sulayman sent
one of his lieutenants at the head of a Dawi Mani' force to seize Figuig
temporarily and collect taxes.[24] In 1841 Mawlay 'Abd al-Rahman sent
letters to 'Arabs' in the Southeast, almost certainly the Dawi Mani', urging
them to attack the Ait 'Atta as punishment for their raids on villages and
caravans in Touat.[25] In 1894 Ba Ahmad, Sultan Mawlay 'Abd al-Aziz's
regent, dispatched a *makhzan* commander to Tafilalt to lead a large raiding
party of Dawi Mani' and Ait Khabbash against the Ghananma, who had
attacked a caravan taking a *qa'id* from Touat to Fez. This force joined up
with contingents from Touat, then pillaged the Ghananma's date groves
and *qsar-s* in the lower Saoura valley.[26] As for political ties between the
Dawi Mani' and the government, Sultan Sidi Muhammad invested Dawi
Mani' *qa'id-s* in 1864, and Mawlay Hasan did so in 1876.[27] The fact that
these actions took place some decades prior to the beginning of Mawlay
Hasan's political offensive in the Southeast suggests that sultans may have
been investing *qa'id-s* for the Dawi Mani' off and on since the foundation
of the dynasty.

The tribe and the government maintained political contact with one another in three principal ways. In the late nineteenth century at least, the *makhzan* dispatched special envoys, like Si al-ʿArbi al-Maniʿi, to the tribe. More frequently and not only in time of crisis, the tribe sent delegations to the capital, especially during the season of the feast of *ʿid al-kabir* when *qaʾid-s* and tribal leaders from all over Morocco presented themselves before the sultan.[28] On this occasion the Dawi Maniʿ leaders presented personal gifts or offerings, called in this case *ziyara*, to the sultan as spiritual leader. They probably also rendered homage to him as ruler by offering *hadiya*, a contribution in money or in kind which *qaʾid-s* traditionally gave three times a year. The Dawi Maniʿ leaders collected donations from their respective fifths and presented them to the sultan on behalf of the tribe. They did not, however, collect or pay regular taxes, which *qaʾid-s* serving under direct *makhzan* control did do.[29]

The third way in which the tribe and the *makhzan* communicated was through the intermediary of the *khalifa* at Tafilalt. The *khalifa* had at his disposal a miniscule police force, and no one expected him actually to govern. He could, however, wield some political influence by allying himself with local tribes, just as the sultan did. The Dawi Maniʿ, more than any other tribe, were known for aiding him in carrying out commands that would otherwise be ignored. In 1894, for example, Khalifa Mawlay Rashid recruited a contingent of Dawi Maniʿ to help him prevent the people of Sifa, the northernmost district of Tafilalt, from constructing a dam across the Wad Ziz.[30]

French observers repeatedly charged that the sultan's dealings with the Dawi Maniʿ, and with the other populations of the Southeast, amounted to nothing more than a temporary and pretentious expedient to win international support for his claims to sovereignty over the region. It is clear, however, that both the *makhzan* and the Dawi Maniʿ had something to gain by cultivating good relations prior to the time that French expansion became the overriding problem of mutual concern. The central government could exert a vicarious and occasional military influence in the Southeast by enlisting the services of local tribes. The sultans, of course, used this tactic everywhere in Morocco where they did not have permanent political control. Their special objectives in the Southeast, before the French threat, were probably to maintain at least a semblance of authority in Tafilalt, the spiritual wellspring of the dynasty, and to prevent any long-term disruption of trade on the routes through Touat and Abou ʿAm. Before the 1890s they very likely pursued alliances with the Dawi Maniʿ with these aims in mind.

The Dawi Maniʿ, for their part, profited from their special ties with the *makhzan*. For one thing, they got to plunder their neighbors from time to

time with the approval of the sultan. For another, the *qa'id* titles they
received had importance in tribal politics. The Dawi Mani' themselves used
the term *qa'id* to designate the official heads of each of the five fifths.
Therefore, the sultan would normally invest the five men already holding
these positions. The power and influence a man could command of course
depended on his leadership abilities, not on the sultan's appointment. The
qa'id-s were not administrative officials who carried out orders from the
makhzan. Sharifian investiture and possession of the dynastic seal, however, brought respected leaders an added measure of prestige and lent
legitimacy to their political actions. In other words, good leaders could
use the honor of their investiture to good advantage in competing with
other men for influence. The tribe clearly did not take the sultan's choice
lightly. In 1892 a delegation representing part of the Awlad Jallul fifth
traveled all the way to Fez to protest Mawlay Hasan's investing whom they
considered the wrong man. The sultan's refusal to change his mind led two
years later to a brief feud between factions grouped around two rival
qa'id-s, one of whom had Sharifian approval but only minority support
within the fifth.[31]

Mawlay Hasan's efforts to build political bridges to the Dawi Mani',
as well as to other tribes and to the people of Touat, may have had some
consequence in delaying French expansion into the Sahara. The presence
of so many new Moroccan 'officials' in the region magnified the French
foreign ministry's apprehensions about the effects of military expansion
on its political and commercial interests in Morocco proper. Ba Ahmad,
however, who ruled Morocco as regent from 1894 to 1900, was not so
energetic as Mawlay Hasan in naming *qa'id-s* over the Dawi Mani' and
other groups or in drawing the attention of the European powers to these
symbols of Sharifian authority. Although diplomatic developments in
Europe were decisive, Ba Ahmad's failure may have hastened somewhat
France's decision to occupy Touat and the intervening territory.

The *Makhzan* Comes to Figuig

Figuig fell under the shadow of French expansion much earlier than did
the Dawi Mani' owing to its position near the Mountains of the Ksour.
In February 1882 a column from Aïn Sefra pursuing Abu 'Amama's partisans and Amur raiding parties into the mountains passed close enough to
Figuig to get involved in a short skirmish with some of its inhabitants.
From that point on the army, justifiably regarding Figuig as a staging area
for resistance elements, began calling for a military operation against it,
even though the Treaty of Lalla-Marnia specified the oasis as being a
Moroccan locality. The *makhzan*, on the other other hand, recognized

that, treaty or no, the credibility of its claims in the Southeast could not stand before international opinion unless a representative of Sharifian authority were established in Figuig, the second most important population center in the region.

The people of the oasis, until then free of any external control, faced a double but also highly ambiguous threat. The French army was approaching from the northeast, but its actions were highly unpredictable because of the ongoing tug of war between it and the foreign ministry over the direction and limits of expansion. Moreover, the southward extension of the Algerian communications system and the establishment of army posts in the region introduced positive opportunities to the population in the form of increased trade. The question of relations with the *makhzan* were equally as ambiguous, since Figuig, like the Dawi Mani‘, wanted its Moroccan identity reconfirmed as a diplomatic safeguard against the French, yet it was antagonistic to the idea of *makhzan* officials or troops interfering in its several governments or attempting to levy taxes. On top of that, both the French and *makhzan* issues became closely bound up with the shifting internal politics of the seven *qsar-s*. The colonial crisis thus presented the people of Figuig with a complex set of problems and alternatives in some ways quite different from those facing other groups in the Southeast.

After 1881 Figuig became more deeply involved with the sultan and his government than it had ever been before. The *qsar-s* had always recognized the sovereignty of the ‘Alawi rulers, but they had seldom been subjected to their authority. That is, they were rarely constrained to pay taxes to the *makhzan* or contribute contingents to the army. Mawlay Isma‘il, the ‘Alawi sultan most successful in governing south of the Atlas, maintained a garrison of slave troops (*‘abid*) in Figuig between 1679 and 1727, and they presumably collected taxes.[32] In 1806 Sultan Mawlay Sulayman (Moulay Sliman) sent an expedition to Figuig, but this intervention was only transitory.[33] In 1867 Sultan Sidi Muhammad named a governor for Figuig with the title of *khalifa* of the *qa’id* of Oujda. (Here the term *khalifa* means simply deputy and has no parallel relationship to the same term used to designate the viceroys of Fez, Marrakech, and Tafilalt.) The appointee remained in Figuig only long enough to discover that the population had little use for him, then went off to take part in the Awlad Sidi Shaykh uprising in Algeria.[34] It is not unlikely that from time to time the sultans invested notables of Figuig as *qa’id-s*, or commanders, over all or part of the population by simply bestowing on them a letter of investiture and an official seal.[35] But these titles alone carried no real authority.

The central government's long standing laissez faire attitude suddenly changed in 1881, when Mawlay Hasan undertook to provide the oasis with a Sharifian official. The first *makhzan* representative arrived from Oujda in May 1882. One of them, al-Hajj Ahmad ibn Rabah, carried the title of *khalifa* of the *'amil* (governor) of Oujda. After staying in Figuig only several days, both men traveled to Aïn Sefra, presented themselves to the commandant, and made an appeal for peaceful relations and trade across the frontier. They offered their permission for French troops to camp under the walls of Figuig, and they invited officers and traders to visit the *qsar-s*. More than that, they proposed a plan for adjudicating disputes along the frontier whereby Algerians would make their accusations before a *qadi* of Figuig, and Moroccans would go before an Algerian judge.[36] The authorities at Aïn Sefra did not speculate in their report on the motivation behind these amiable proposals, but it seems very likely that the sultan hoped to secure French recognition of *makhzan* authority in Figuig, such that the army would channel all frontier problems through the Sharifian representative rather than through the notables of the *qsar-s* or through leaders of the neighboring tribes. The Aïn Sefra meeting achieved nothing concrete, and the two governments did not follow up on the *khalifa*'s juridical proposals. They did, however, work out a basically similar plan when they appointed the four on-the-spot commissioners under the Protocol of 1901.[37] So, in a sense the *makhzan* was proposing in 1882 the same plan for diplomatic cooperation along the frontier which the two governments would finally agree upon nineteen years later. In 1882, however, neither party was in a position to formalize enduring diplomatic ties between Aïn Sefra and Figuig.

The *khalifa* and his associate remained in Figuig only until August, then returned to Oujda. The next delegation (not counting two *makhzan* officials who resided in the oasis for a month in 1883) appeared in September 1884. This time the sultan's brother, Mawlay 'Arafa, and the *'amil* of Oujda led a delegation to preside over the installation of a new *khalifa*, Muhammad ibn Mubarik (Embarek), as permanent *makhzan* representative. These officials also met with the French authorities at Ich (about mid-way between Figuig and Aïn Sefra), but they made no new proposals and asked that Europeans stay away from Figuig for the time being.[38]

After his escort returned to Oujda, Muhammad ibn Mubarik quickly discovered that the inhabitants of Figuig were no more interested in being governed by 'alien' *makhzan* officials than by the French army. In theory, the *khalifa* did have the authority to collect taxes on behalf of the sultan, to enforce peace and security in the oasis, and to represent the central government's interests in the region. Though the *qsar*-dwellers had been obliged to contribute to the *makhzan* treasury on rare occasions in the past, they had never known an oasis-wide government of any kind, much less a permanent administration from the 'north'. They were therefore suspicious of the *khalifa's* intentions. In fact, they had little to fear, for the *makhzan* had no clear plans to tax Figuig or to interfere in the internal affairs of the *qsar-s*. As far as the government was concerned, the *khalifa's* only obligations were to report on French military activity; to act as spokesman for the sultan in local frontier problems; and, above all, to pose as a symbol of Sharifian authority.

The French soon showed their willingness to work with the sultan's local representative. In the summer of 1885 troops from Aïn Sefra occupied Djenien-Bou-Rezg, which was located on the southern slopes of the mountains and about forty miles northeast of Figuig. They began at once to build a fort, the French foreign ministry having reached an understanding with the *makhzan* that they needed it to protect Aïn Sefra and the Amur from raiding parties operating out of the Jebel Beni Smir. Many in Figuig, however, protested to the *khalifa* that Djenien-Bou-Rezg was in Moroccan territory. Some of them even owned property there. Consequently, the *khalifa* reported the news to Mawlay Hasan, who asked the French not to build the post until the territorial question was decided. The foreign ministry, as sensitive as ever about the boundary question, ordered the troops to stop work and withdraw. In November 1885 the *'amil* of Oujda, the *khalifa*, and several notables from Figuig met with the commandant at Aïn Sefra. After much discussion of the issue in terms of the relevant points in the treaty of Lalla-Marnia, the Moroccan delegation agreed that Djenien-Bou-Rezg was indeed in Algerian territory. More than a year later the sultan conveyed the same conclusion to the French government, and in December 1888 construction of the post was completed.[39] As a result of this affair, the French advanced an entire mountain range closer to Figuig's doorstep, but by setting a precedent for cooperation with the *khalifa*, they accepted the oasis as the center of *makhzan* government along the southern frontier.

Eight *khalifa-s* served in Figuig between 1884 and 1902. In theory they took their orders from the *'amil* of Oujda, but some of them sometimes corresponded directly with the royal palace. The Franco-Moroccan Accords of 1902 gave Figuig an *'amil* of its own. At least five of them resided there between 1902 and 1912 (when, under the Protectorate government, the governor's title was changed to *pasha*). The *khalifa-s* and *'amil-s* of Figuig had diverse backgrounds. Some of them served as minor military or administrative officers in the *makhzan* administration before their arrival in the Southeast. None of them were natives of Figuig.

The high rate of turnover in the governorship reflected the longstanding practice of the sultans to shift provincial officials from one post to another at fairly frequent intervals in order to prevent them from building an independent power base anywhere in the country. For example, Muhammad ibn 'Umar al-Marrakishi (known as Simmu) served as *khalifa* from 1890 to 1897, was governor of Touat from 1897 to 1901, then, fleeing the French, reassumed the post at Figuig, where he died a few months later.[40] Si Muhammad al-Ragragi, the first *'amil*, served a previous thirteen year term as *qa'id* of Essaouira, then was arrested by Ba Ahmad, the regent. After three or four years of imprisonment, he was released and sent to Figuig in 1901 simply to assess the political situation for the sultan. In 1902 he was named *'amil*. He was replaced within a year or so and probably went off to a new post in some other part of the country.[41]

Whatever usefulness the *khalifa-s* and *'amil-s* might have had in keeping the French at bay, most of the inhabitants of Figuig regarded them as instruments of *makhzan* interference and harbingers of taxation. But the residents were also quick to realize that their governors could very well influence the course of inter-*qsar* relations. Though Zenaga and five of the *qsar-s* on the plateau generally treated them with disdain, al-Oudaghir found reason to be more hospitable. In 1884 tensions between Zenaga and al-Oudaghir were running high. Zenaga's manipulation of the spring a few years earlier meant that a disproportionate amount of water was diverted into the lower oasis. Al-Oudaghir soon began to suffer serious shortages, yet lacked the fighting strength necessary to regain control of the spring and lower the bottom of the *fuggara-s* leading into its palm groves.[42] Therefore, the inhabitants were prepared to encourage the governor to try to exercise at least enough authority to get the spring away from Zenaga. Furthermore, they believed that if he should attempt to levy a tax, they would be exempt, as genuine *shurfa* always were everywhere in Morocco. Zenaga, on the other hand, had no intention of relinquishing its inordinate share of water and so rejected the establishment of any authority superseding that of its own *jama'a*. Zenaga also had the most to lose from taxation, since levies would be based on the individual's wealth in palm trees. Zenaga's groves were the biggest and best watered in the oasis.[43]

Finding so little popular support elsewhere, the first *khalifa* established his residence in al-Oudaghir.[44] All the subsequent governors lived there as well and in general became associated with the political interests of its inhabitants. The *qsar*-dwellers apparently took every opportunity to try to use the governor to gain some small advantage over Zenaga, although nothing was ever done about the spring.[45] Since the Zenagans refused to recognize him at all, the sultan made their autonomy official in 1889 by appointing one of their notables as *qa'id*, who would communicate directly with the capital. Zenaga remained outside the governor's jurisdiction until 1902.[46]

When not occupied with affairs relating to the French, the governors holed up in al-Oudaghir or found small ways to irritate the population. Some of them may have been able to command more respect and sympathy than others, but they rarely, if ever, served as mediators in disputes between *qsar-s*. During the feud of 1885-6 involving Zenaga and al-Maïs, informants told the French at Aïn Sefra that the authority of the *khalifa* was 'absolutely unrecognized' and that he remained confined in al-Oudaghir fearing for his safety.[47]

Most of the governors were preoccupied with the problem of ensuring their own maintenance. They had the sultan's authority to levy a palm tax but no means to demand even the revenue for their own living expenses. Before 1902 they had no one but a few *mukhazani-s*, or gendarmes, to back up their rule. All of the *qsar-s* were supposed to contribute a quantity of dates and barley for the governor's support, but they proved niggardly in this respect.[48] Some of the governors, at least, tried to impose a tax of one sort or another but never with much success. In 1888, Khalifa Si 'Umar Susi began collecting a tariff on trade goods both entering and leaving the oasis. He did so partly because the sultan had ordered him to pay an indemnity to the French to atone for having arrested and detained briefly three of their Muslim emissaries. In a letter to Muhammad Torrès, the Moroccan Minister at Tangier, Susi complained: 'I am here in a post without resources, yielding nothing; where do you want me to get the 980 francs for the indemnity I have to pay?' In this case the people of al-Oudaghir protested loudest against the *khalifa*'s actions because Figuig's most active market was in front of their *qsar*. Within a few months the sultan replaced Susi, not because he was attempting to take in revenue, but because the French complained about his hostility and unwillingness to encourage the Amur to remain in Algerian territory.[49] At any rate, none of Susi's successors tried to levy a market tax again until 1909, though all of them found themselves in the same state of insolvency and helplessness.

In the political life of Figuig the governor was more a nuisance than a threat, more a pawn than a commander. It might seem curious that the inhabitants did not manifest their contempt by simply killing him or at least running him out. Before 1903 the French had no desire to ensure his safety, and the *shurfa* of al-Oudaghir could hardly have prevented his being attacked. This tolerance of the governor's presence, in fact, illustrates the nature of the political relationship between Figuig and the cen-

tral government. Throughout the Southeast the sultan was recognized as
the *imam,* the sovereign head of the Muslim community. He retained the
baraka, or divine grace, which brought munificence and good fortune on
that community. As long as he defended the faith against external threats,
his person was sacrosanct. If the government was unjust, rapacious, or
cruel, then the sultan's underlings were responsible. The people of Figuig,
therefore, accepted the governor as the legitimate representative of the sultan. They did not accept him, however, as a stranger come to impose taxes
and meddle in local affairs. On several occasions the inhabitants expressed
their disapproval of him, but they did so by requesting the sultan to re-
move him, not by throwing him out. In 1884, for example, delegates from
all the *qsar-s* traveled to Fez to plead with the sultan to let the seven
jama'a-s govern internal affairs. In 1886 a merchant delegation went north
to ask for the removal of 'Umar Susi. In 1888 representatives from Zenaga
made request for a *qa'id* of their own.[50]

Complaints about the governor did not of course provide the only reason for traffic and correspondence between Figuig and the capital. Some
of the 'Alawi sultans may have ignored Figuig for long periods of time, but
the inhabitants were known to draw upon the moral authority and prestige
of the sovereign to solve local problems. The chief *qadi-s* in Fez and
Tafilalt, both appointees of the sultan, served as courts of appeal for disputes that local judges could not settle. Following the war over the
Zaddert spring in 1877, al-Oudaghir took its case to Fez, although it
received only promises in return.[51] Correspondence between the *makhzan*
and the *jama'a-s* of Figuig was probably quite frequent throughout the
nineteenth century, although volume certainly increased after the French
arrived at Aïn Sefra.[52] Of course, the tribes and the other oasis communities in the Southeast also communicated with the sultan. In 1894 the head
of the French military mission in Morocco reported that a lieutenant of
the *khalifa* of Figuig was returning there from Fez 'carrying numerous
letters from the maghzen for the governor or Amel of Figuig [as he may
have sometimes been called before 1902] Mohammed ben Amar el
Marrakechi, for the Djemaas of Figuig, the Doui Menia, the Ouled Sha of
Touat, Timmimoun, and the Ghenamena.'[53] It is partly in terms of the
exchange of questions and complaints from the trans-Atlas regions in
return for advisories, exhortations, and judgments from the royal palace
that the extent and limits of the Sharifian empire in the nineteenth century must be understood. In his discussion of the *makhzan* bureaucracy
Aubin noted:

This correspondence and responsibility in connection with the tribes is in the hands of the makhzen bureaucracy, which composes the different beniqas [ministerial chambers]. For even in the most distant parts of the blad es-siba, there is no tribe which is not in communication with the makhzen. Although resolved to free themselves from its authority, all of them are careful, nonetheless, to keep up some connection with it, and not to sever themselves completely from a Muslim power which upholds, in the eyes of the infidel foreigners, the standard of imperial unity.[54]

Raiding and Trading

Figuig's response to its French neighbors during the first twenty years after the occupation of Aïn Sefra cannot be categorized in simple terms. What the inhabitants did not do is clear. Neither they nor any of the tribes in the region contributed to any large scale attacks against the French posts north of the Zousfana. The *harka*, or large, pan-tribal military force, would have its day after the turn of the century. Nor is there evidence that any significant number of the *qsar*-dwellers advocated close political ties with the French or the transfer of the oasis to Algeria. Before 1902 only a handful of European civilians and no military personnel had ever set foot in Figuig. Between these two poles, intransigent resistance and surrender, one finds a whole range of attitudes and actions that tended to vary with prevailing economic, political, and military circumstances.

The authorities at Aïn Sefra were correct in blaming Figuig for contributing substantially to the continual opposition they encountered while pacifying the Mountains of the Ksour. The French posts and the Amur groups under their authority were almost continually subjected to raiding and harassment by small bands operating from areas west of the Algerian zone. These resisters were for the most part dissident Amur who left the Aïn Sefra region with their families following the occupation, or nondescript adventurers, some of them fugitives from French justice.[55] Most of them hid out in the Jebel Beni Smir, where military penetration was not authorized. Bani Gil, Dawi Mani', and Awlad Jarir raiding parties, coming from the west and south, also operated in the mountains now and then.

It is unlikely that men from Figuig participated regularly in these raids, since oasis dwellers rarely made a practice of raiding other Muslim groups, though nomads did so as a matter of course. Even so, the French continually complained that men from Zenaga were committing theft, sabotage, and even some assassinations against them. These charges accumulated especially after the French built two posts early in 1900, each only a few

miles distant from Figuig. The post of Duveyrier was created in February
at Zoubia, a point directly east of Figuig. Djenan-ed-Dar, occupied in
March, was directly south. The same year the governor at Figuig was
reportedly encouraging mini-raids on Djenan-ed-Dar and then taking a
cut of the booty.[56] In 1901 the French arrested a few men from Zenaga
for making off with a mule, a plank, forty cow skins, and 140 meters of
telegraph line![57]

Figuig contributed most to the resistance as a sanctuary for nomads
who organized raids in the French zone. These raiding parties by no means
represented a guerrilla army under unified command, but rather ad hoc
collections of individuals who fought the French for a variety of reasons,
not the least of which was the prospect of taking booty. Livestock, rifles,
and other stolen goods were sometimes taken back to Figuig and sold. In
1897 the *makhzan* governor was collecting a percentage on stolen sheep
sold in the market at al-Oudaghir.[58] The single most valuable item on the
market was certainly modern rifles, although they were no doubt offered
in small quantities. In 1900, for example, the French learned that the
governor had procured twenty 1886 Lebels, the model used by the French
forces, in a deal with a successful raiding party.[59] The high demand for
modern firearms suggests that Moroccans may often have ambushed
French military personnel or attacked small convoys expressly to get rifles
and ammunition for later sale.

The French blamed much of the hostility emanating from Figuig on
their old nemesis, Abu 'Amama, who moved there from Gourara in 1896.
During the six years that he and his followers camped near al-Hammam
Tahtani (his birthplace), he spent much of his time laying the groundwork
for a possible jump to the French side. His residual prestige as leader of the
last Algerian uprising was still great among the people of the frontier
region, but he knew very well that by 1896 no refuge, not even Touat, was
safe from the French army. He may even have cast an envious eye on his
Awlad Sidi Shaykh cousins who received tribal commands and generous
subsidies for submitting to the French in the 1880s.[60] While he weighed
the advantages of moving in one direction or another, he used Figuig's
convenient borderland position to maintain contacts with both sides. He
stayed in communication with the *makhzan* and presented himself among
the tribes as the sultan's chief representative in the Southeast, but at the
same time he attempted to negotiate an *aman*, or amnesty, with the
French Native Affairs bureau. The French were anxious enough to come
to terms with him, believing, probably wrongly, that he could make
trouble when they got around to occupying Touat. In 1899, therefore,
they gave him and his family, though not his entourage, the *aman*. During

the following two years, he discreetly supplied the French with bits of intelligence information (which they never fully trusted) and arranged the rental of large numbers of camels to a French entrepreneur who ran supply convoys between the posts. In 1901 he even sent his son, Si Tayyib, to Tlemcen to continue talks at higher levels. But Abu 'Amama himself refused to make a personal visit to Duveyrier, and he apparently put no restraints on his followers who participated in the resistance.[61] This group, which numbered about one hundred 'tents,' was for the most part composed of a heterogeneous assortment of nomads, some of them fugitives and professional cutthroats. A large number were Sha'amba and other bedouin from central Algeria who had fled the French advance there.[62]

Early in 1902 Abu 'Amama left Figuig and moved his camp westward in the direction of Aïn Chaïr. Sultan Mawlay 'Abd al-'Aziz, who regarded the old rebel as a stumbling block in his efforts to stabilize the frontier, ordered him to appear in Fez. Abu 'Amama declined the invitation, probably knowing he would end up in a royal dungeon. Instead, he hovered just beyond the reach of French patrols for another two years, then gradually moved northward toward a rendezvous and alliance with the pretender Abu Himara. By 1906 he was no longer an important political factor in the Southeast.[63]

The growing resistance fever in Figuig put the governors in a dilemma. They were responsible for enforcing the *makhzan*'s policy of avoiding local clashes with the French in order to prevent reprisals and the occupation of more territory. At the same time, the *qsar*-dwellers and their nomad 'guests' put strong pressure on them to take a harder line. The fact that the *'amil* even corresponded with the French made him suspect of collaboration. The first *khalifa*, who was obliged to write condemnatory letters to Aïn Sefra following the occupation of Djenien-Bou-Rezg, later told the French, 'My sentiments . . . haven't changed; but I am literally the prisoner of the Figuig people. I am under the closest surveillance ever since they got the idea that I had sold their oasis to the French.'[64] Although a few of the governors cooperated with the army in small ways to maintain their official image, most of them either condoned or actively supported resistance, revealing their own incapacity to carry out the *makhzan*'s orders.[65]

Even so, Abu 'Amama and the governors were not the only residents of Figuig willing to mitigate their hostility to the French. As resistance activity increased, so did the tempo of peaceful trade between Figuig and the posts. Traffic on the main route to Tlemcen had declined greatly since 1830, but not even the conquest of southern Oranie cut it off altogether. Soon after the French occupied Aïn Sefra, thirty merchants arrived from Figuig seeking permission to continue on to Saïda and Tlemcen.[66] Later, the French received reports that some of the traders of Figuig were even welcoming Algerian expansion as a great boost to commerce in the region.[67] As soon as a market was set up in Aïn Sefra, caravans began arriving not only from Figuig, but from as far away as Tafilalt.[68]

The volume of trade between Figuig and Algeria, however, remained unimpressive until after 1896 owing to the import duties and port taxes which elevated the price of goods arriving through Oran and the other ports. In 1884 Melilla began admitting goods duty free. Despite the extension of the railroad to Aïn Sefra in 1887, products reaching Figuig by caravan from Melilla or even from Fez and Tangier were much cheaper than the same commodities offered at Aïn Sefra. Finally in 1896, the French dropped duties on certain goods entering Algerian ports as long as they were bound for Morocco or the Sahara. After the railroad reached Djenien-Bou-Rezg in 1900, the merchants of Figuig and the surrounding area were able to travel there and get much better bargains than they could waiting for the caravans from Melilla.[69]

The simultaneous pursuit of warfare and commerce reflected a highly individualistic and diverse reaction to the French offensive. The most belligerent elements in Figuig may have opposed the development of trade across the frontier, but no single party had the means to impose a unified course of action, whatever it might be. As long as the Treaty of 1845 protected the population from an invasion, they could enjoy the luxury of raiding the French while at the same time doing business with them. The army was only too aware of the deficiencies in the diplomatic policy which allowed this *double jeu* to go on.

Warning Signals from the Ziz Valley

Although Mawlay Hasan began building diplomatic bulwarks around Figuig soon after the French reached Aïn Sefra, he did not bring his ambitious Saharan policy into full swing until 1888. Before then he was largely occupied subduing and collecting taxes among the tribes of the mountains and the southwestern trans-Atlas regions. Three factors probably moved him to turn his attention to the Southeast. The first was the growing threat of French occupation of Touat and the north central Sahara. The second was the chronic political turmoil in the lower Ziz valley caused by Ait 'Atta aggression, which was making a mockery of *makhzan* influence in the dynasty's homeland. The third was the emergence of a regional power figure, who posed a serious challenge to the authority and prestige of Mawlay Hasan himself.

Tribal insurrections on the outer fringes of government-controlled territory recurred frequently during the nineteenth century, and they followed a fairly uniform pattern. Tribes, discontent over government exactions and interference or fearing that such vexations were on the way, rallied together in revolt under the leadership of a supratribal figure, often a saint or *sharif*. This individual usually did less to organize the movement then he did to inspire it and to justify it in the sight of God by broadcasting charges of oppression, misrule, and injustice against the central government. Much earlier in Morocco's history such stirrings in the rural hinterlands sometimes succeeded to the point of eliminating the dynasty and founding a new one. In the nineteenth century, however, the relatively greater military and administrative capacity of the *makhzan* prevented regional flare-ups from developing beyond the stage of armed protest.

Mawlay Hasan spent the greater part of his reign dealing with active or incipient tribal dissidence. Most of these movements crystallized around local opposition to the government's energetic centralizing campaign. One of them, however, appealed for tribal support by drawing attention to the much wider issue of the *makhzan*'s failure to meet effectively the threat of European penetration in general and French military expansion from Algeria in particular.

Early in the 1880s Si Muhammad al-Hashami ibn al-'Arbi, a *shaykh* of the Darqawa sufi brotherhood, began calling for a *jihad* against the French forces in southern Oranie. He was a member of an 'alawi *shurfa* family which inhabited the Medaghra district of the Ziz valley halfway between Ksar es-Souk and the Rteb. He was a son of the *qadi* of Medaghra and as a young man studied theology and law with Si Ahmad Badawi, *shaykh* of the Darqawa of Fez and disciple of Mawlay al-'Arbi ibn Ahmad al-Darqawi, who founded the brotherhood in the later eighteenth century. Si Muhammad al-'Arbi established such a strong reputation for piety and wisdom that Si Ahmad Badawi made him his spiritual successor, passing on to him his *baraka*. Si al-'Arbi returned to Medaghra to found a new branch of the Darqawa and establish a *zawiya* at Gaouz. By brilliantly exhibiting all the hallmarks of a saint in his teaching, praying, and miracle working, he attracted a large number of followers and students who affiliated with the fraternity and accepted him as their spiritual guide to mystical union with God. More than five hundred pupils, a few of whom were reported to have come from as far away as Baghdad, studied with him at Gaouz. He was the apotheosis of the North African sufi mystic, a *murabit, sharif*, and brotherhood *shaykh* all in one.[70]

He was also rigidly conservative in his ideas about safeguarding the purity of Islam against external influences. During the 1880s, Mawlay Hasan was making modest attempts at military, administrative, and fiscal reform in order to shore up the state in the face of growing European eco-

nomic and political penetration. Morocco's religious leaders vehemently
opposed this program of defensive westernization as foreign to the proper
governing of the Muslim community. The Darqawa emerged as one of the
most strident foes of innovation, and Si al-'Arbi became its leading spokesman. Like so many North African saints before him, he was prepared to
transform his protest against spiritual and moral decadence into a *jihad*.
About 1885 he began to agitate for a rising of Atlas and Saharan tribes in
order to force Mawlay Hasan to give up his flirtations with Europeans and
their blasphemous ideas.[71]

Si al-'Arbi did not declare himself a pretender to the throne nor categorically renounce Mawlay Hasan. Rather, he called on the sultan to lead
a counteroffensive against French expansion in southern Oranie, which,
as far as the *shaykh* was concerned, was the most blatant and disquieting
manifestation of European interference in Morocco. He also declared that
if the sultan refused to spearhead a *jihad*, he had the means to do so himself. Indeed, he was the first leader in the Southeast, aside from Abu
'Amama, to attempt to generate large-scale resistance against the French.
In 1888 he informed a *makhzan* emissary that the Ait 'Atta, Ait Izdig, Ait
Haddidu, Dawi Mani', and other tribes had promised him a total of thirteen thousand warriors, that he had breech-loading rifles, and that an
English company with whom he claimed to have connections would
furnish more of them at his pleasure.[72] There was almost certainly a good
deal of bravado in these assertions, but Si al-'Arbi was indeed serious about
attacking the French. Early in 1885 be wrote to the Darqawa brethren at
Figuig, asking them for information not only on developments on the
frontier but also on the French conquest of Tunisia and on relations between the Ottoman sultan and the European powers.[73] When Mawlay
Hasan's emissary visited Gaouz in 1888, he found the *shaykh* playing host
to none other than Abu 'Amama, who had apparently traveled from
Gourara to Medaghra in response to the call for a second rising in southern
Oranie.[74] Many French observers of the period were convinced that a
grand, pan-Islamic conspiracy united all the leaders of North Africa and
the Middle East and that a stupendous rising against European encroachments on Muslim soil was about to take place. The existence of a mono-
lithic plot can almost certainly be discounted, though leaders such as Si
al-'Arbi or Abu 'Amama were no doubt fully aware of the pressures the
West was exerting throughout the Muslim world. They may have at least
attempted to make contact with religious or political leaders beyond the
confines of Morocco in order to build a broader base of resistance.[75] Si
al-'Arbi's dealings with Abu 'Amama and his intentions to lead Atlas tribes
against an enemy more than two hundred miles away indicate that he was

attempting to generate something more than a regional insurrection against Mawlay Hasan.

In any event, the *jihad* failed to materialize. Because of his saintly reputation Si al-'Arbi was able to attract the interest of several Atlas tribes between Medaghra and Fez. But they were more interested in using his appeal to avoid paying taxes to the sultan than in undertaking a costly expedition against an enemy who posed no immediate threat to them. Mawlay Hasan's successful expedition into the Middle Atlas in June 1888 to pacify and collect taxes from the Ait Mjild prompted the tribes further south to draw away from Si al-'Arbi and make gestures of submission to the *makhzan*.[76] As far as the *qsar*-dwellers of Tafilalt and the lower Ziz were concerned, troubles with the Ait 'Atta commanded far greater attention than developments east of Figuig. The *shaykh* continued to exhort the tribes during the next few years, but he died early in 1892. Immediately his sons and chief lieutenants entered into a debilitating power struggle for leadership of the *zawiya*, resulting in its decline as a center of learning and the dispersal of many of the leading *muqaddam-s* to other areas. When Mawlay Hasan passed through Medaghra the following year, he made sure the *zawiya* would remain quiescent by having the dominant *sharif* there put in chains.[77]

Though Si al-'Arbi's call to arms came to very little either as insurrection or *jihad*, it focused attention for the first time on the threat of French encroachment onto Moroccan territory and helped convince the sultan to take more vigorous measures to prevent it. Furthermore, Si al-'Arbi, like Abu 'Amama before him, set an example of pious militancy which other saints and *shurfa* of the Southeast would try to emulate when the need for pan-tribal unity against the French became much more acute.

The *Makhzan* in Tafilalt, 1893-1900

As early as 1888 Mawlay Hasan considered leading a royal expedition all the way to Tafilalt, ostensibly to pray at the tomb of Mawlay 'Ali Sharif, in fact to make direct contacts with tribal leaders, impose a measure of law and order on the region, and, above all, to demonstrate to his subjects and to Europe that the arm of *makhzan* power reached beyond the High Atlas. The success of such an expedition depended heavily on the behavior of two groups in particular, the 'Alawi *shurfa* and the Ait Khabbash of the Ait 'Atta.

As the homeland of the 'Alawi lineage, Tafilalt stood apart from the rest of southeastern Morocco in its relations with the central government. Since so many *shurfa* lived there, the district could be and often was a hotbed of conspiracy and rebellion against the sultan and his court. Rebellion

was made more likely because the sultan exiled many of the more troublesome or potentially dangerous *shurfa* there and attempted to palliate their
ambitions with special subsidies drawn from the *makhzan* treasury. In
1888, for example, he sent a special envoy to distribute money among
them in order to prevent their supporting Si al-'Arbi's uprising.[78] The
shurfa also undermined the sultan's prestige there by incessantly feuding
among themselves. They were divided into a number of sublineages around
which political factions formed. Despite their credentials for holiness, they
contrasted sharply with the local *murabtin* in their willingness to engage in
protracted blood feuds. By going to Tafilalt Mawlay Hasan aimed both to
restrain their rebelliousness and to try to settle their internal quarrels.

In dealing with the Ait Khabbash, whose offensive against Tafilalt most
embarrassingly revealed the *makhzan*'s weakness in the Southeast, Mawlay
Hasan demonstrated his remarkable ability to turn tribal power to his own
ends. Most of his predecessors appear to have sided with the victims of
Ait 'Atta aggression, at times supporting the Ait Yafalman tribes as a kind
of mountain buffer against 'Atta penetration up the southern slopes.[79]
Indeed, the traditional historical view has been that the intensity of hostility between the royal palace and the tribes increased in direct proportion to their geographical distance from one another. Mawlay Hasan, however, broke with tradition and adopted a genuinely conciliatory position
toward the Ait Khabbash, recognizing that their cooperation would better
serve his interests in the Southeast than a hazardous punitive expedition.
During 1892, a number of 'Atta delegations, mostly Ait Khabbash, as well
as *shurfa* and other groups from Tafilalt, visited the royal court in Fez.
The sultan did not invest any 'Atta leaders with *qa'id* titles, but he obtained assurances of their quiescence when the expedition reached the
lower Ziz. He even considered the idea of going all the way to Touat, using
the Ait Khabbash as his escort.[80]

He made final plans to leave for Tafilalt in the spring of 1893. By then
he had received the pleasing news of Si al-'Arbi's death and knew the
leadership of the *zawiya* was in disarray.[81] Conditions on the lower Ziz,
however, were as tumultuous as ever, and the French were already
stepping up their efforts to lay the groundwork for a bloodless occupation
of Touat.[82] Therefore, with his court, his army, and his harem in tow, he
set out in June along the Fez-Tafilalt caravan route, subduing and
collecting taxes from several of the tribes along the way. He finally arrived
in November in the Wad Ifli district in the center of Tafilalt and there
erected a sprawling camp, numbering about forty thousand people.[83]
He and his ministers spent most of their time meeting with delegations of
notables from the surrounding region, hearing complaints and requests,

distributing and receiving gifts, and arbitrating disputes.[84] The expedition remained there for about three weeks, before returning to the north by way of Ouarzazate and Marrakech.

Although Si al-'Arbi was no longer on the scene to incite the *shurfa*, Mawlay Hasan took care to distribute presents and subsidies among them, awarding certain individuals special options on the purchase of land.[85] He also tried unsuccessfully to arbitrate a feud that had been going on since at least 1892. According to Gabriel Delbrel, a European in the royal party, the contending families were brought before the sultan, but 'they refused to agree to what he demanded of them. Moulaï Hassan, understanding then that a reconciliation was impossible, forbade the other families from getting involved in their quarrel or from giving them any aid whatsoever.'[86]

Although the Ait Khabbash had agreed to make no trouble, they did not let up their pressure on Tafilalt. Dr Linarès reported from the scene: 'The A'it Atta are invading little by little, but in a continuous manner, the region of Tafilalt. The least quarrel, the smallest altercation between a Filali and an Attaoui is the point of departure for an armed struggle in which the A'it Atta clan, more warlike and cohesive than the Filali clan, always has the upper hand.'[87] By the 'Filali clan' Linarès certainly meant the Ait Yafalman allies, including the whole population of the Sefalat district, the 'Arab Sabbah, and assorted bands of Ait Mirghad and Ait Izdig who came into the oasis to join the fray. Mawlay Hasan occupied part of his time trying to arbitrate specific disputes involving the Ait Khabbash in order to restore a measure of calm, but he had little success.[88] Walter Harris observed that warfare between the Ait Khabbash and the 'Arab Sabbah was unceasing and went on to report: '. . . at the time of my stay in the Sultan's camp a skirmish took place between the two in the very presence of Mulai el Hassen, several on both sides being killed, altogether some fifteen it is said. The Sultan promptly imprisoned the ringleaders of each party; but such force was brought to bear upon him by the prisoners' fellow-tribesmen that he was obliged to release them in the course of a few days.'[89]

Mawlay Hasan and his army left Tafilalt without having made any lasting impact on either local politics or French policy. Although he met with delegations from various tribes in the region, he failed to attract more than one important notable of Touat to his camp.[90] The expedition may have given the French foreign ministry slight pause, but it had no deterrent effect on the army and its expansionist allies.[91] Perhaps the sultan's greatest achievement was his preservation of good relations with the Ait 'Atta, which prevented the expedition from ending in the military disaster which some French observers predicted.

Ba Ahmad, who took over the reins of government in 1894, also attempted to exert some influence over the affairs of Tafilalt, drawing on the aid of the so-called grand *qa'id-s* of the High Atlas. Mawlay Hasan had initiated the policy of allying the *makhzan* with Madani al-Glawi (of the Glawa tribe) and other tribal chiefs of the mountain country south of Marrakech. In 1893 on his way back from the Ziz he appointed al-Glawi nominal *qa'id* of Tafilalt, probably with the aim of making him a kind of *makhzan* watchdog on the region. Ba Ahmad strengthened the government's ties with the Atlas chiefs, awarding them special fiscal and political privileges in return for a steady supply of armed contingents to serve as auxiliaries to the regular army. He also must have depended on them to keep open the direct lines of communication between Tafilalt and Marrakech, where he established his capital.

Ba Ahmad did not pay much attention to Tafilalt until 1896, when inter-tribal fighting broke out again and continued in periodic fits of violence during the following four years. The immediate cause of the violence may have been a dispute in the marketplace of Abou Am between two men, one of them of an Ait Yafalman tribe, the other of the Ait Khabbash. The market peace was 'broken,' and the fighting quickly snow-balled until the *suq* itself was pillaged and partially destroyed. According to reports reaching French army officials in southern Oranie and in Marrakech, the underlying cause was once again the aggression of the Ait Khabbash and the efforts of the Ait Yafalman alliance to stop it. Almost every tribe and *qsar* in the region appears to have been involved on one side or the other. Mawlay Rashid, the *khalifa* of Tafilalt, had no means of restraining the Ait Khabbash and so took sides with them. Part of the *shurfa* joined him for reasons of expediency, while others sided with the Ait Yafalman, probably because their own property was threatened.

Ba Ahmad responded to the crisis by sending special envoys on two different occasions to attempt to mediate the conflict. Late in 1896 he sent Si al-'Arbi al-Mani'i, Mawlay Hasan's chief emissary in the Southeast, along with a force of four hundred men, including two hundred contribu-ted by Madani al-Glawi and another of the Atlas *qa'id-s*. This expedition was not large enough to impose a settlement on the population, but al-Mani'i did manage to arrange a cease-fire and took hostages back to Marrakech to ensure that it would be honored until Ba Ahmad arbitrated the various points in dispute. Whatever decisions the regent may have made had no effect since the truce lasted no more than a few months. In 1898 he dispatched another column, this time sixteen hundred men under the leadership of Mawlay Muhammad al-'Amrani, a son of one of the sultan's sisters. Al-Glawi himself and two lesser Atlas chiefs went along as military commanders. The expedition remained in Tafilalt long enough to secure another truce, reconstruct the market, and install a permanent garrison of 225 men. After it left, however, the skirmishing started up once again. The *qa'id* of the permanent garrison later complained to Ba Ahmad that the population would have almost nothing to do with him.[92]

The efforts of Mawlay Hasan and Ba Ahmad to deter French expansion by bringing order to Tafilalt were a failure on both counts. No matter how many special envoys and armed legions they sent to the Southeast, they had neither the military nor the diplomatic resources to achieve anything but a transitory influence over intertribal affairs. Khalifa Mawlay Rashid survived as a symbol of *makhzan* authority not by attempting to govern but by coming to terms with the powers that be. As far as the French were concerned, the 'Atta-Yafalman conflict, which was so deeply rooted in the history of the Southeast, stood only as a glaring example of the *makhzan*'s helplessness and as an invitation to introduce colonial government.

Between 1881 and 1900 the tribes and *qsar*-communities of southeastern Morocco faced two challenges to their traditional autonomy, the advance of the French army to the fringes of the region and the efforts of the *makhzan* to include them, at least marginally, in its program of political centralization. The first challenge was decidedly the more ominous, but at the turn of the century it had not yet grown to critical proportions. The second represented the most energetic government intervention in the far south in a century and a half, but ultimately its impact on local power was small.

If the French forces at Aïn Sefra had been given free rein, they would surely have advanced well south of the Mountains of the Ksour in the aftermath of the Abu 'Amama rising. They would have occupied, or at least bombarded Figuig and penetrated freely into Moroccan territory in pursuit of raiding parties. The army rationalized its aggressive urges by asserting that the north central Sahara was the natural extension of Algeria and that the claims of the sultan on any part of it were of no account. The French government concurred with these sentiments at heart, but it did not want precipitous military adventures to jeopardize its carefully nurtured privileges in Morocco nor its efforts to keep the 'Moroccan Question' on ice. An almost continual tug of war between the foreign ministry and the military over questions of how and when to carry out particular imperial objectives characterized the entire period of French empire-building in Africa. Southern Oranie is a good example of government success in restraining army exuberance over an unusually long period of time. The conquest of Touat took place only after the pros and cons were debated for several years, the occupation of sudanic West Africa was almost completed, and the diplomatic risks were largely removed. Yet the policy of checking military activity in the north central desert was part of the much broader campaign to achieve political and economic ascendancy over all of Morocco. Knowing this, the army never let up pressure for authorization to take more direct action on Morocco's southeastern flank.

After the Abu 'Amama crisis ended and the army settled into its advance posts, the population of the neighboring area, notably Figuig, came gradually to accept the French as a new local power, albeit an especially mighty and unpredictable one. Armed resistance was limited to small, uncoordinated raids in the vicinity of the posts. This activity was not an early phase of purposeful guerrilla warfare but fell largely into the pattern of normal raiding between one tribe and another, the French tribe, in this case, being especially well stocked with booty. Simultaneously, peaceful trade between the posts and Figuig, as well as other market centers, gradually developed, though mostly after 1896. Since Moroccans had long trafficked with French Algeria, there was nothing unusual about this, except that it amounted to a strengthening of commercial ties amid conditions of continued sporadic fighting. It indicated that despite French subjugation of the Amur and the threat of further expansion, no rigid battle lines were about to be drawn. This inconsistency of response, which became more evident as time went on, reflected more than anything else the population's overriding preoccupation with economic survival and the absence of any central authority which could require it to follow a single course of action. In confronting natural crises or tribal conflicts groups with shared interests, whether large or small, invariably put the preservation of resources ahead of standing loyalties or ideologies. This behavior did not change in contacts with the French. Barriers of culture may have stood in the way of trust and goodwill but not in the way of trade, an activity which a growing segment of the population could casually disassociate from the evident imperial aims of the army.

From the vantage point of the Sharifian court Algerian expansionism presented problems of a higher order than the purely local threat of border incursions. Morocco was one of a number of Muslim African countries in the nineteenth century whose ruler attempted to overhaul the mechanisms of state control in order to improve his revenue-gathering capacity and his political credibility in the eyes of the European powers. In a number of cases, notably Egypt, Tunisia, and Zanzibar, the ruler justified his centralizing program with at least general reference to his God-ordained legitimacy, though in reality his success at direct rule over rural populations depended entirely on military coercion and political manipulation. In Morocco, however, the ruler counted heavily on his spiritual and moral prestige as an effective tool in strengthening and extending central authority. By living up to popular expectations concerning the religious obligations of his office, he commanded surer loyalty within the *makhzan* and enhanced his own bargaining position when dealing with urban and rural elites. If he failed to conform to these expectations, he immediately lost popular confidence and invited rebellions.

His most fundamental responsibility was to defend the community of believers (*umma*) against any form of external aggression. The charge was a religious one upon the sultan himself and implied nothing about the temporal power of the *makhzan*. No prescriptions were made as to the territorial limits of the community to be protected nor to the actual military defense requirements of the government. Though Morocco had no fixed boundaries, other than those defined by the Treaty of Lalla-Marnia, the population commonly regarded Touat and all intervening territory as within the sphere of Sharifian responsibility. Mawlay Hasan understood perfectly well that a French attack on Touat or Figuig would immediately bring into question his competence as Commander of the Faithful. Indeed, Si al-'Arbi al-Darqawi regarded even the loss of the Aïn Sefra area to Christians as sufficient excuse for launching an insurrection. If Mawlay Hasan could not take effective steps to repel European encroachments, then he ran the risk of undermining his accumulated store of popular prestige and generating much more severe opposition to his Western-style reforms than he was already experiencing.

He would gladly have pre-empted French expansion by extending direct *makhzan* administration to the desert periphery, but that was not possible. The most he could do was to attempt to throw into relief, for the benefit of both his subjects and the European powers, the political ties which existed, and had existed for centuries, between the royal palace and the people of the far south. If he could not prove through military action that he was 'king' in the Sahara, he could at least try to demonstrate that he was something more than 'pope,' a sobriquet French expansionists liked because it dismissed the political dimensions of his spiritual leadership.

The efforts of Mawlay Hasan and his *de facto* successor Ba Ahmad to stop the French ultimately failed, not so much because of the *makhzan*'s military weakness, but because of European refusal to accept the Moroccan definition of the 'state'. Moreover, if the government had actually attempted to bring the Southeast to tax-paying submission, the population would not have responded nearly so positively as they did under the sultan's diplomatic wooings. The tribes and *qsar*- communities of the region wanted the sultan to protect them from the French, but they were not about to permit the loss of autonomy which a truly effective *makhzan* offensive would have involved. Figuig's relations with its governors probably best illustrates the distinction made in the popular mind between the sultan as Commander of the Faithful and sultan as head of the revenue-hungry government. The French army, of course, found it convenient not to appreciate the distinction at all but to regard the absence of effective administration as tantamount to the absence of sovereignty.

Notes

1. E. Rouard de Card, *Documents diplomatiques pour servir à l'étude de la question marocaine* (Paris, 1911), pp. 22, 23.
2. Augustin Bernard and N. Lacroix, *La Pénétration saharienne, 1830-1906* (Algiers, 1906), pp. 18-57; A. Adu Boahen, *Britain, the Sahara, and the Western Sudan, 1788-1861* (Oxford, 1964), pp. 222-5.
3. Le Commandant Colnieu, 'Voyage au Gourâra et à l'Aouguéroût (1860)', *BSGP*, 7th ser., 13 (1892), pp. 41-97; 14 (1893), pp. 53-97. Bernard and Lacroix, *Pénétration*, pp. 34-6. The first important French study of Saharan geography and society was Lt. Col. Daumas, *Le Sahara algérien* (Paris, 1845).
4. I have relied on two translations of Gerhardt Rohlfs' works: *Adventures in Morocco and Journeys through the Oases of Draa and Tafilalet* (London, 1874); and 'Le Tafilalet d'après Gerhard Rohlfs,' *Ren. Col.* (Aug. 1910), pp. 243-57. For background on Rohlfs and his influence on Germany's Moroccan policy, see Pierre Guillen, *L'Allemagne et le Maroc de 1870 à 1905* (Paris, 1967), pp. 11, 12, 22, 23.
5. Général de Wimpffen, 'L'Expédition de l'Oued-Guir,' *BSGP*, 6th ser., 3 (1872), pp. 34-60; Augustin Bernard, *Les Confins algéro-marocains* (Paris, 1911), pp. 147-9.
6. C.W. Newbury and A.S. Kanya-Forstner, 'French Policy and the Origins of the Scramble for Africa,' *Journal of African History*, 10, no. 2 (1969), pp. 253-65; R.J. Harrison-Church, 'Trans-Saharan Railway Projects: A Study of Their History and of Their Geographical Setting,' in L.D. Stamp and S.W. Wooldridge, *London Essays in Geography* (Cambridge, Mass., 1951), pp. 135-50; Bernard and Lacroix, *Pénétration*, pp. 75-90.
7. Mental disorder as a possible manifestation of *baraka* is discussed in Edward Westermarck, *Ritual and Belief in Morocco* (London, 1926), I, 47-9.
8. The principal works on the uprising are E. Graulle, *Insurrection de Bou-Amama* (Paris, 1905); Général Innocenti, *Insurrection du Sud-Oranais en 1881: Bou-Amema et le Colonel Innocenti* (Paris, 1893); P. Wachi, 'L'Insurrection de Bou Amama,' *Revue Tunisienne*, 8 (July 1901), pp. 336-62; (Oct. 1901), pp. 445-58; 9 (Jan. 1902), pp. 97-104; (July 1902), pp. 289-317. M & L, II, 107-112, 771, and *passim*. A recent discussion focusing on the effects of the rebellion on Algerian colonial policy is found in Charles-Robert Ageron, *Les Algériens musulmans et la France (1871-1919)* (Paris, 1968), I, 62-6, 310, 311.
9. Wachi, 'L'Insurrection de Bou Amama,' 8 (July 1901), pp. 348-50; 9 (July 1902), pp. 311-17. This is the only source I have seen which addressed itself to the question of economic grievances of the Oranie tribes as a cause of the rising.
10. See Ageron, *Algériens musulmans*, I, 63-5.
11. Graulle, *Insurrection de Bou-Amama*, pp. 42-105.

12. It was widely believed in France and Algeria that the Oranie rising was the result of a vast anti-European conspiracy led by Muslim brotherhoods, especially the Sanusiya of Tripolitania, and by pan-Islamic elements, including the Ottoman sultan. No evidence has come to light linking Abu 'Amama to a wider resistance movement, and Ageron (*Algérien musulmans*, I, 65, 66, 310, 311) largely discounts these conspiracy theories. On the other hand, Arabic sources have not been studied in any detail with these questions in mind, and leaders such as Abu 'Amama probably had a much greater awareness of pan-Islamic ideas than Europeans gave them credit for. The chief advocate of the Sanusiya plot theory was Henri Duveyrier, 'La Confrérie musulmane de Sidi Mohammed ben Alî es-Senoûsî et son domaine géographique,' *BSGP*, 7th ser., 5 (1884), pp. 145-226. He links Abu 'Amama directly to the brotherhood (pp. 173, 184).

13. See C.M. Andrew and A.S. Kanya-Forstner, 'The French "Colonial Party": Its Composition, Aims and Influence, 1885-1914,' *The Historical Journal*, 14, no. 1 (1971), pp. 99-128.

14. René Pinon, *L'Empire de la Méditerranée* (Paris, 1904), pp. 203-5.

15. See Jean-Louis Miège, *Le Maroc et l'Europe* (Paris, 1961-63), IV, 37-44.

16. The pacification of the Amur and its diplomatic implications are described in M & L, II, 250-322.

17. Roger Le Tourneau, 'L'Algérie et les chorfa d'Ouezzane à la fin du XIXe siècle,' *ROMM*, numéro spécial (1970), pp. 157-60; Miège, *Le Maroc et l'Europe*, IV, 251-5; M & L, III, 55, 56, 70-4.

18. M & L, III, 49-53, 80, 81.

19. On the Touat question in European diplomacy see Christopher Andrew, *Théophile Delcassé and the Making of the Entente Cordiale* (New York, 1968), pp. 153-6; Guillen, *L'Allemagne et le Maroc*, pp. 230-2, 247, 248, 251-7, 296-9, 359, 360, 565-71; Miège, *Le Maroc et l'Europe*, IV, 249-55; Trout, *Morocco's Saharan Frontiers*, pp. 25-35; M & L, III, 49-123.

20. A.G.P. Martin, *Quatre siècles d'histoire marocaine* (Paris, 1923), pp. 241-64.

21. AMG, Maroc C6, MM 1892, Cauchemez (chief of Military Mission) to Min. War, Report of Feb. 1892, no. 66; Report of May 1892, no. 79. AGGA, 30H. 23, Documents établis depuis 14 mars 1893, Lt. Regnault, 'Oulad Djerir,' Sept. 20, 1893; M & L, II, 685, 686.

22. AMG, Maroc C6, MM 1892, Cauchemez to Min. War, Report of Jan. 1892, no. 58; Report of July 1892, no. 90; Alg. 13, Renseignements sur le Sud-Oranais 1892-93, Détrie (Com. Div. Oran) to Gov. Gen., May 31, 1892; Gov. Gen. to Min. War, June 8, 1892.

23. M & L, II, 685, 686; III, 72; Martin, *Quatre siècles*, p. 249. Si al-'Arbi al-Mani'i, a *makhzan* secretary and *qadi*, was considered for the post of *wazir al-bahr*, or Minister of Foreign Affairs, in 1894. He was passed over for the position, but during the remainder of the century, he played an important role as a special *makhzan* emissary to the Southeast. In 1900 Ba Ahmad sent him to Tangier to protest to the powers France's occupation of Touat. During the mission he died mysteriously of asphyxiation in a turkish bath. AMG, Maroc C8, MM 1894, Schlumberger (chief of Military Mission) to Min. War, July 13, 1894, no. 41; G. Salmon, 'Une Opinion marocaine sur la conquête du Touat,' *Archives Marocaines*, no. 3, 1 (1904), pp. 422, 423.

24. Aboulqâsem ben Ahmed Ezzîani, *Le Maroc de 1631 à 1812*, extracted from the work entitled *al-turjumăn mu'arib 'an duwal al-mashriq wa al-maghrib*, trans. O. Houdas (Paris, 1886), pp. 32, 33, 189.

25. Martin, *Quatre siècles*, pp. 157, 158.

26. AMG, Maroc C9, MM 1895, Schlumberger to Min. War, Report of Aug. 1895, no. 33; Alg. 13, Sit. pol. 1896, Gov. Gen. to Min. War, March 30, 1896, no. 935;

Martin, *Quatre siècles*, pp. 267, 274-8.

27. AGGA, 30H. 23. Documents établis depuis 14 mars 1893, Lt. Niquet (Adjoint Aïn Sefra), 'Renseignements sur les Ouled Djerir, le Doui-Menia, l'Oued Saoura et les Ghenanema,' Nov. 16, 1885. AMG, Alg. 13, Renseignements sur le Sud-Oranais 1892-3, Gov. Gen. Cambon to Min. of Foreign Affairs, May 3, 1892.

28. Interview no. 5.

29. M & L, II, 581, 598; Interviews no. 4 and 5. Other groups in the Southeast probably sent *ziyara* or *hadiya* to the sultan. Some of the villages of Touat, for example, sent 'gifts' to Fez in 1891 (Martin, *Quatre siècles*, pp. 249, 250). On taxation in pre-Protectorate Morocco see Edouard Michaux-Bellaire, 'Les Impôts marocains,' *Archives Marocaines*, 1 (1904), pp. 56-96.

30. Interview no. 22. Mawlay 'Ali, the informant, was a son of Khalifa Mawlay Rashid, who died in 1911. Mawlay 'Ali read from a document he had written entitled 'Ta'rikh min al-sharif Mawlay al-Rashid al-'Alawi,' (History of Sharif Mawlay Rashid al-'Alawi). He informed me that the only other copy was in the hands of the royal family in Rabat.

31. M & L, II, 603; Brenot, 'Notice historique,' p. 22.

32. P. Russo, 'Au Pays de Figuig,' *Bullétin de la Société de Géographie du Maroc*, 1st trimester (1923), p. 452. R. Gromand, 'Le Particularisme de Figuig,' *Ren. Col.* (April 1939), p. 91.

33. Ezzîani, *Le Maroc de 1631 à 1812*, p. 189.

34. AGGA, 30H. 47, Caïds et Amels de Figuig, Gen. Risbourg (Commander of the Division of Oran [hereafter cited as Com. Div. Oran]) to Gov. Gen., June 22, 1901, no. 514; Russo, 'Au Pays de Figuig,' p. 452.

35. Mawlay Isma'il named a resident of Zenaga as commander of Figuig in 1720. Caïds et Amels de Figuig.

36. AMG, Alg. 12, Expédition du Sud-Oranais 1881-83, Marmet (Com. Supérieur of Cercle of Aïn Sefra) to Com. of the Subdivision of Mascara and Mechéria, June 6, 1882, no. 244; Caïds et Amels de Figuig.

37. *Doc. Dip.*, I, 17, 18.

38. AGGA, 30H. 33, Moulay Arafa, Figuig, Etc., Détrie (Com. Div. Oran) to Gov. Gen., Sept. 28, 1884, no. 162; AMG, Alg. 12, Caravansérail defensif de Djenien-Bou-Rezg, Détrie to Gov. Gen., Aug. 15, 1885; Caïds et Amels de Figuig.

39. AMG, Alg. 12, Caravansérail, Marmet to Com. of the Subdivision of Aïn Sefra Nov. 29; 1885, no. 349; M & L, II, 120-2, 537, 538.

40. Caïds et Amels de Figuig; M & L, II, 470; Martin, *Quatre siècles*, pp. 297-9, 315-18, 339-41, 347-9.

41. AGGA, 30H. 13, Commission Franco-Marocaine, 'Résumé historique de la présence de fonctionnaires marocains à Figuig et de leurs relations avec le Gouvernement Français' (Hereafter cited as 'Fonctionnaires marocains à Figuig'). AMG, Alg. 14, Documents trouvés chez Général O'Connor, Capt. Ducloux, 'Rapport hebdomadaire du 14 au 20 sept. 1901,' Sept. 21, 1901; *Doc. Dip.*, I, 25; Caïds et Amels de Figuig.

42. E.F. Gautier, 'La Source de Thaddert à Figuig,' *Annales de Géographie*, 26 (Nov. 15, 1917), p. 464.

43. AGGA, 30H. 33, Moulay Arafa, Figuig, Etc.; Détrie to Gov. Gen., Sept. 28, 1884, no. 162; AMG, Maroc C17, Maroc-Frontière-Figuig, de Négrier (Com. of Southern Posts) to Com. Subdivision of Mechéria, Oct. 7, 1882, no. 1287.

44. AGGA, 30H. 33, Moulay Arafa, Figuig, Etc.; Com. Div. Oran to Gov. Gen., Oct. 25, 1884, no. 199; AMG, Alg. 12, Caravansérail, Détrie to Com. 19th Corps., Aug. 30. 1885, no. 21; AMG, Maroc C17, Maroc-Frontière-Figuig, Reuillon to Gov. Gen., Aug. 22, 1886, no. 640.

45. M & L, II, 486.
46. Caïds et Amels de Figuig. 'Fonctionnaires marocains à Figuig.'
47. AMG, Maroc C17, Maroc-Frontière-Figuig, Reuillon to Gov. Gen., Aug. 22, 1886, no. 640. Many French reports complained about the *khalifa*'s helplessness.
48. M & L, II, 470, 592; Caïds et Amels de Figuig.
49. AMG, Maroc C17, Maroc-Frontière-Figuig, Détrie to Com. 19th Corps, July 17, 1888, no. 259; Nov. 18, 1888, no. 319; Féraud (French Minister at Tangier) to Détrie, Sept. 29, 1888, no. 259; M & L, II, 301-9; Caïds et Amels de Figuig.
50. AGGA, 30H. 33, Moulay Arafa, Figuig, Etc., Détrie to Gov. Gen., Oct. 25, 1884, no. 199; AMG, Maroc C17, Maroc-Frontière-Figuig, Détrie to Com. 19th Corps, Nov. 18, 1888, no. 319; Caïds et Amels de Figuig.
51. M & L, II, 480, 503-5.
52. Between 1881 and 1912 many French army reports note that the governor or the *jama'a-s* of Figuig were sending letters to the sultan or receiving them from him. Concerning a letter from Figuig to Sultan Sidi Muhammad in 1862 complaining about the activities of a Muslim Algerian agent of the French, see Germain Ayache, 'Le Sentiment national dans le Maroc du XIXe siècle,' *Revue Historique*, fasc. 488 (1968), p. 400.
53. AMG, Maroc C8, 1894, Schlumburger to Minister of War May 1, 1894, no. 29.
54. Eugène Aubin (pseud. for Descos), 8th ed., *Le Maroc d'aujourd'hui* (Paris, 1913), p. 241.
55. M & L, II, 298-322.
56. AGGA, 21H. 11, Bou Amama, Risbourg (Com. Div. Oran) to Gov. Gen., Dec. 3, 1900, no. 369.
57. AGGA, 21H. 11, Bou Amama, O'Connor (Com. Div. Oran) to Com. 19th Corps, Aug. 7, 1901, no. 46.
58. AMG, Alg. 13, Sit. pol. 1894-1900, Gov. Gen. to Min. War, Nov. 16, 1897, no. 3110.
59. AGGA, 21H. 11, Bou Amama, Risbourg to Gov. Gen., Dec. 3, 1900, no. 369.
60. AN, F80, 1684, Gov. Gen. to Min. of Interior, Feb. 15, 1888, no. 837; 1695, Gov. Gen. to Min. of Interior, June 11, 1889, no. 3484; Min. of War. to Min. of Interior, Jan. 11, 1890.
61. Dozens of reports on Abu 'Amama's activities during his residence in Figuig are included in the following dossiers: AMG, Alg. 13, Sit. pol. 1894-1900, Mouvements dans le Sud-Oranais (Mars-Août 1900); Alg. 14, Sud-Oranais (1900), Novembre et Décembre 1900, Sit. Pol. 1901, Sit. pol. 1902, Documents Gen. O'Connor. AGGA, 21H. 11 and 21H. 12 (complete boxes). Also Pinon, *Empire*, pp. 205-7.
62. AGGA, 21H. 11, Bou Amama, Risbourg to Gov. Gen., Dec. 5, 1899, no. 1034; Risbourg to Gov. Gen., Oct. 19, 1899, no. 1065.
63. *Doc. Dip.*, I, 24-6, 33, 42, 43.
64. AMG, Alg. 12, Caravansérail, Détrie to Com. 19th Corps, Aug. 30, 1885, no. 21.
65. Caïds et Amels de Figuig; M & L, II, 301-9.
66. AMG, Alg. 12, Expéditions du Sud-Oranais (1881-83), Saussier (Com. 19th Corps) to Min. of War, Aug. 1, 1882, no. 26032.
67. AMG, Alg. 12, Caravansérail, Détrie to Com. 19th Corps, Oct. 1, 1885, no. 35.
68. M & L, II, 540.
69. 'Algérie: les affaires du Touat,' *Af. Fr.* (Sept. 1900), pp. 304-5.
70. P. Odinot, ''Importance politique de la confrérie Derqaoua,' *Ren. Col.* (May 1929), pp. 294, 295.
71. N. Lacroix, 'Les Derkaoua d'hier et d'aujourd'hui,' *Documents sur le Nord-Ouest africain* (Algiers, 1902), pp. 17-20; Miège, *Le Maroc et l'Europe*, IV, 139-41.
72. AGGA, 30H. 34, Si Mohammed bel Arbi du Tafilalet, Féraud (French Min. at Tangier) to Min. of Foreign Affairs, June 14, 1888 (hereafter cited as Féraud to

Min. For. Af., June 14, 1888). Féraud quotes a report from Dr Linarès, one of Mawlay Hasan's European advisors, who was with the sultan's expedition in Ait Njild country and spoke to an emissary who had gone to Gaouz to try to convince the *shaykh* to give up his insurgency.

73. AGGA, 30H. 34, Si Mohammed bel Arbi du Tafilalet Cherif de Medaghra, Si Mohammed bel Arbi to 'all his adepts in the *qsar-s* of Figuig,' Jan. 21, 1885.

74. Féraud to Min. For. Af., June 14, 1888; M & L, II, 150-3. The authors notes that Abu 'Amama had close relations with Si al-'Arbi and theorized that he would attempt to take control of the Darqawa in the Southeast following the *shaykh*'s death.

75. Evidence of the movement of pan-Islamic ideas and agents between the Middle East and North Africa is tantalizingly fragmentary. The Ottoman sultan Abdul Hamid II tried unsuccessfully to establish diplomatic ties with Mawlay Hasan on more than one occasion. (See Guillen, *L'Allemagne et le Maroc*, pp. 181-9.) Miège (*Le Maroc et l'Europe*, IV, 173-9) states that Si al-'Arbi was said to be in contact with emissaries of the Sanusiya. He goes so far as to suggest that the simultaneous occurrence of the Medaghra rising and the efforts of the Ottomans to establish a diplomatic agent in Morocco was no coincidence. Lacroix ('Les Derkaoua,' pp. 18, 19) discredits the possibility of Si al-'Arbi's having pan-Islamic connections.

76. AMG, Maroc C5, MM 1888, de Breuille to Min. War, April 10, 1888, no. 40; May 10, 1888, no. 41; July 10, 1888, no. 42.

77. Dr Linarès, 'Voyage au Tafilalet avec S.M. Sultan Moulay Hassan en 1893,' extracted from *Bullétin de l'Institut d'Hygiène du Maroc*, nos. 3 and 4 (1932), pp. 32, 33; Lacroix, 'Les Derkaoua,' pp. 20-2.

78. AMG, Maroc C5, MM 1888, de Breuille to Min. War, May 10, 1888, no. 41.

79. Georges Spillmann, *Districts et tribus de la haute vallée du Draa'* (Paris, 1931), pp. 59-68; Spillmann, *Ait Atta*, pp. 41, 42; Martin, *Quatre siècles*, pp. 157, 158.

80. AMG, Maroc C6, MM 1892, Cauchemez to Min. War, March 1892, no. 71; May 1892, no. 79; June 1892, no. 83; Maroc C7, MM 1893, Cauchemez to Min. War, April 1893, no. 106; Linarès, 'Voyage au Tafilalet,' p. 48.

81. In June 1892 a dozen *murabtin* from Medaghra, including two sons of Si al-'Arbi, were in Fez to ask the sultan to settle the dispute over the spiritual succession to the directorship of the *zawiya*. Mawlay Hasan may have done nothing, since the dispute served his interests more than a reconciliation. AMG, Maroc C6, MM 1892, Cauchemez to Min. War, June 1892, no. 83.

82. AMG, Maroc C6, MM 1892, Cauchemez to Min. War, March 10, 1892, no. 68; Martin, *Quatre siècles*, p. 268.

83. Walter B. Harris, *Tafilet* (London, 1895), p. 241. Harris joined the royal expedition in Tafilalt after traveling there on his own from Marrakech. Linarès ('Voyage au Tafilalet') accompanied the sultan from Fez. Qa'id Harry MacLean and Gabriel Delbrel were the two other Europeans in the entourage.

84. AMG, Maroc C7, MM 1893, Schlumberger to Min. War, Jan. 1, 1894, no. 8. Schlumberger was in Marrakech during the expedition and received most of his information from Linarès after he returned there. Linarès, 'Voyage au Tafilalet,' pp. 50-2. Harris, *Tafilet*, pp. 243-5.

85. Gabriel Delbrel, 'Notes sur le Tafilelt,' *BSGP*, 7th ser., 15 (1894), pp. 211, 212.

86. Delbrel, 'Notes sur le Tafilelt,' p. 211.

87. Linarès, 'Voyage au Tafilalet,' p. 48.

88. AMG, Maroc C7, MM 1893, Schlumberger to Min. War, Jan. 1, 1894, no. 8; Linarès, 'Voyage au Tafilalet,' p. 48.

89. Harris, *Tafilet*, p. 287.

90. AMG, Maroc C7, MM 1893, Schlumberger to Min. War, Jan. 1, 1894, no. 8; Linarès, 'Voyage au Tafilalet,' p. 52.

91. M & L, III, 98-101.
92. Reports from both the Military Mission in Marrakech and from the French
     Command at Aïn Sefra concerning events in Tafilalt between 1896 and 1900 were
     numerous, though often fragmentary and speculative. These documents are
     scattered in AMG: Maroc C9, Maroc C10, Maroc C11, Maroc C19, Alg. 12, Alg.
     13; and AGGA: 30H. 23 and 30H. 46.

6 THE AFTERMATH OF TOUAT, 1900-1903

The fall of Touat put relations among the French, the *makhzan*, and the population of the Southeast on an entirely new footing. At the international level the whole issue of the extent and limits of the sultan's sovereignty was thrown open, since the Treaty of Lalla-Marnia had nothing relevant to say about territory south of Figuig. For the first time since 1845 demarcation of the Algero-Moroccan frontier became a major issue in diplomatic exchanges between France and the Sharifian court. Within Morocco Mawlay Hasan's Saharan policy of pre-emptive action was now shattered, and Mawlay 'Abd al-'Aziz faced a crisis of confidence at the very outset of his reign. A French diplomatic official who served in Morocco after the turn of the century described popular and government reactions to the seizure of Touat:

> No more was needed to upset the Moroccan conscience, incite it to holy war, and strain to the breaking-point the fragile link between the tribes and the sultan, who showed himself powerless to defend the religious interests of his country against the infidels, and therefore unfit to fulfill the task for which the Sharifian dynasties had been called to the throne.
>
> The shock was so great and the members of the *makhzan* became so painfully convinced of the weakness of the State, that they were unanimously agreed on the necessity of a new system and the urgency of essential reforms which might serve to save the situation.[1]

For the young sultan the choice lay between declaration of a *jihad* and negotiation of a frontier settlement. One road led to military suicide, the other to popular denunciation. For the people of the Southeast the French were no longer simply a local power element and a source of trade but once again an advancing army whose ultimate targets were unknown. A widespread appeal went out to the sultan to take military counteraction, but at the same time the population displayed diverse and inconsistent reactions, only one of which was armed resistance.

The Frontier Accords

In order to secure Touat and tie it directly to Algeria the French army proceeded to occupy several points along the Wad Zousfana and the Wad

Saoura, thus taking control of a long stretch of Moroccan territory extending directly south of Figuig. The initial forces had penetrated Touat by way of El Goléa, an advance post on the southeastern side of the Erg Occidental. It was evident, however, that the Zousfana-Saoura route was the most suitable owing to its abundant watering places and absence of natural barriers. Moreover, the Oranie railroad reached Djenien-Bou-Rezg in February 1900, so troops from the Oran Division could be transported that far south with great speed.[2] In the first six months of the year columns were sent to occupy Zoubia (Duveyrier) just west of Figuig, Djenan ed-Dar a short distance south of Figuig, Taghit in the Beni Goumi district, and Igli at the confluence of the Zousfana and the Guir. Beni Abbès in the Saoura valley was taken in March 1901 and the linkup between Touat and the Zousfana was made the following month.

The Subdivision of Aïn Sefra was responsible for securing the new route to Touat, not only for supply caravans, but also for future railway construction. The forces in the Zousfana-Saoura valley, however, immediately ran into resistance from raiding bands, especially of the Dawi Mani' and the Awlad Jarir, whose territory included the Zousfana. Operating from the Jebel Béchar, Figuig, and the Jebel Beni Smir, these bands harassed the French posts and convoys almost continually during 1900 and 1901. The army garrisons had the fire power to prevent any of their fortifications from being overrun, but they lacked the government's authorization to pursue raiding parties into Moroccan territory. The Oran Division complained that they were in an intolerably defensive position in the valley and once again urged Paris to extend the westward limits of their action.

The government recognized that it could not restrain the army indefinitely and that the occupations of 1900-1 ought to be legitimized by international agreement. Théophile Delcassé, the Minister of Foreign Affairs from 1898 to 1905, built his Moroccan policy around the conviction that the *makhzan* should be treated circumspectly until all the powers explicitly accepted French paramountcy in Morocco. When news of the fall of Touat reached Marrakech early in 1900, Ba Ahmad sent Si al-'Arbi al-Mani'i to Tangier to protest the action before the powers, but got nothing more than sympathetic responses. After the regent's death in May, Mawlay 'Abd al-'Aziz, having no means of his own to force the French to withdraw, decided to accept the territorial loss and work toward a frontier settlement which would leave him with as much of the Southeast as possible. Consequently, both he and Delcassé found it in their interest to negotiate a new agreement, finishing work left undone by the Treaty of 1845.[3]

In July 1901 a Moroccan delegation went to Paris under the leadership of Si 'Abd al-Karim ibn Sulayman (Ben Sliman), the *makhzan*'s Minister of Foreign Affairs. He was accompanied by Si Muhammad Gibbas and Si Ibn Nasr Ghannam, two other government officials. Paul Révoil, who under Delcassé's sponsorship had left his post as Minister at Tangier to become Governor-General of Algeria, was the chief French negotiator. The Moroccans were hopeful of delimiting a precise boundary line much further south than the Treaty of 1845 had done in order to prevent the French army from expanding any further than they had already. Delcassé and Révoil, however, were convinced that marking out the frontier would either prevent the army from dealing effectively with local resistance or else would oblige them to pursue raiding parties into territory declared Moroccan by international treaty. Since the first eventuality was anathema to the army and the second to the foreign ministry, Delcassé favored a policy of joint control of the frontier zone by the two countries, which would give the Aïn Sefra command greater flexibility and at the same time recognize the *makhzan*'s presence in the region.[4]

The Protocol which the two governments signed in July 1901 was on paper a model of Franco-Moroccan cooperation. By its terms both governments were authorized to maintain military posts and customs stations in the southern frontier zone. The Moroccans could do so along a line running approximately through Figuig and Talzaza as far west as the Wad Guir, and anywhere on the west bank of the Guir. The French could locate their posts along the Zousfana (which they had already done) but not west of the Jebel Béchar. Although no new boundary line was defined south of Teniet es-Sassi, these provisions clearly implied that Touat, being southeast of the Zousfana, was to be considered in French territory. The area between the Zousfana and the Guir was left as a kind of diplomatic no-man's-land. The Dawi Mani' and the Awlad Jarir, who inhabited this region and who were responsible for most of the attacks against the Zousfana posts, were given the choice of either submitting to French authority or moving to another part of Morocco with the *makhzan*'s assistance. Since the second alternative was hardly feasible, they were theoretically placed under the jurisdiction of Aïn Sefra, even though no part of their territory was explicitly awarded to France. The three oases in the Guir-Zousfana triangle, Béchar, Kenadsa, and Ouakda, were given the unconditional right to choose either nationality. The Protocol also instructed both governments to name commissioners for both the northern (Marnia-Oujda) and southern frontier zones, who would settle local disputes between Moroccan and Algerian nationals on the spot, rather than allow minor borderland incidents to involve the highest diplomatic levels, as had sometimes happened in the past.

Both sides were reasonably satisfied with the agreement. The French achieved their fundamental aims of legalizing their presence in Touat and the Zousfana-Saoura valley and gaining jurisdiction over the Dawi Mani' and the Awlad Jarir. Yet no territorial limits were made, leaving the way open for future expansion. Mawlay 'Abd al-'Aziz was pleased because his government had not been excluded from the region, yet it would no longer be held responsible for the hostile actions of the Dawi Mani' and the Awlad Jarir. Delcassé and Révoil, of course, saw the diplomatic advantages of continuing to act in collaboration with the *makhzan*. The army, knowing the sultan was too weak to send an effective military force to the frontier, could look forward to extending its range of conquest as part of an ostensibly joint program of pacification.

Implementation of the Protocol proved more difficult than either government anticipated. Between January and March 1902 a special Franco-Moroccan Commission, headed by Si Muhammad Gibbas and General Cauchemez, Commander of the Oran Division, visited the southern frontier to inform the interested populations of the terms of the Protocol, to appoint permanent local commissioners, and to designate locations for the Moroccan guard and customs posts. When the Commission reached Kenadsa, however, they found the Dawi Mani' and the Awlad Jarir in no mood to accept either alternative the Protocol offered them. Si Gibbas was even threatened with his life. The three *qsar-s* named in the Protocol all opted for Moroccan nationality, much to the chagrin of Cauchemez's delegation. The Commission finally returned to Algiers having accomplished nothing but the installation of a Moroccan governor and commissioner in Figuig. The failure of the mission made it abundantly clear to the army and other expansion advocates that protection of the route to Touat would depend on French arms rather than on diplomatic agreement.

Still, the foreign ministry was convinced of the need to build a broad base of cooperation with the *makhzan* — at least on paper. While the army was being restrained from crossing the Jebel Béchar into the Dawi Mani' heartland, Si Gibbas and Cauchemez worked out two supplementary Accords (April 20 and May 7, 1902), this time dealing in great detail with procedures for mutual military, political, and commercial action in both the northern and southern frontier zones. In essence, the Accords rescinded the plan to have Morocco construct a series of military posts along a definite line of territory, and replaced it with a program of joint activity that would in reality be the responsibility of the French. A special clause was written into the April 20 Accord stating that the *makhzan* still had the right to establish customs posts along the line designated in the Protocol, but the boundary question was left as undecided as before.[5]

Even with the Accords as the legal basis for penetration west of the Zousfana, the foreign ministry resisted the army's pressure for another full year. Delcassé insisted on viewing the frontier issue within the wider context of French designs on Morocco and not simply as a matter of Algerian security. Early in 1903 he became convinced that England would recognize French supremacy in Morocco in exchange for settlement of the long-standing Egyptian question. Therefore, he opposed any military initiatives, especially in the direction of Tafilalt, which would drive Mawlay 'Abd al-'Aziz into the arms of Britain or generate further internal instability in Morocco, which might leave it with no sultan at all.[6]

In Search of a Mass Movement – the First Attempt

As soon as Touat and the Zousfana fell to the French, efforts got under way both in the Sahara and other parts of the country to launch counter-resistance. Tafilalt, the principal crossroads of the Southeast and sacred homeland of the 'Alawi *shurfa*, immediately became a kind of headquarters for organizing resistance on a much broader scale than the tribal raiding parties, which over the years had harassed the French in the Mountains of the Ksour. Tafilalt was still a long way west of the occupied area, but there was no doubt considerable fear throughout the country that the army would make straight for the Wad Ziz in order to strike a blow at the roots of Sharifian power and prestige. In the spring of 1900 contingents of volunteer warriors (*mujahidin*) from Fez, Marrakech, and the Atlas began converging on the Ziz in order to take part in a counteroffensive.[7] Ironically, the invasion brought an outbreak of peace to Tafilalt unlike anything the *makhzan* had been able to engineer since the days of Mawlay Hasan's expedition. The warring Ait 'Atta and Ait Yafalman factions called an immediate truce in the fighting that had absorbed them for four years and began making preparations to launch a massive, pan-tribal *harka*, or military force, against the 1,800 French and Algerian troops occupying the oasis of Igli on the confluence of the Zousfana and the Guir.[8] For the first time since the days of Si al-'Arbi al-Darqawi a call to *jihad* went out from the Wad Ziz.

The major task at hand was to find a leader who could transcend tribal divisions and cement together a *harka* capable of marching in unity all the way across the Hammada of the Guir. During the spring and summer of 1900, war plans went ahead, but such confusion and indecision reigned that central coordination of the movement proved impossible. The names of a number of potential leaders emerged: Mawlay Rashid, the *khalifa*; Si al-Hashimi, the *makhzan qadi*; two sons of Si al-'Arbi al-Darqawi; one or two Filali *shurfa*; and at least three well-known Ait 'Atta chieftains. None of them, however, managed or even attempted to put a *harka* in motion, a task only Si al-'Arbi himself might have accomplished had he been alive.[9]

Mawlay 'Abd al-'Aziz was at least partially responsible for the failure of the *harka* to materialize. Convinced that declaration of a *jihad* would only invite French retaliation, perhaps against Tafilalt, he took immediate steps to prevent the resistance forces gathering there from taking matters into their own hands. In June he sent envoys to the Southeast to instruct the population to remain calm, and the following month the appointed Madani al-Glawi as *pasha* of Tafilalt.[10] 'Abd al-'Aziz was in such a tenuous position in 1900 that he needed badly to continue Ba Ahmad's policy of leaning on the Atlas *qa'id-s* for military and political support. If he could not go to Tafilalt himself, he could send al-Glawi with a force large enough to forestall the *harka* and even take command of the oasis under Mawlay Rashid's purely nominal supervision.

Al-Glawi arrived in Tafilalt toward the end of 1900 accompanied by several hundred men of the Glawa and other tribes from the vicinity of Marrakech. His presence, added to the local disaccord, was sufficient to thwart efforts to organize a pan-tribal army. He appears to have convinced a large part of the population that the sultan would take action on the diplomatic level.[11] It is also likely that most of the *qsar*-dwellers, who were tied to their palm groves and seldom had access to horses or camels, were willing to give the sultan more time rather than embark upon an ill-planned march all the way across the Hammada. The Ait Izdig and Ait Mirghad forces assembled in Tafilalt may have agreed to hang back as well, since their pastures and *qsar-s* were far to the north and under no immediate threat from the French. On the other hand, al-Glawi, like other *makhzan* troubleshooters before him, was never anything more than one power among many during his stay in Tafilalt. He remained until sometime in the summer of 1901 but finally returned to Marrakech without having advanced government authority one whit.[12] Contingents from the Rahamna tribe near Marrakech arrived in April to relieve the troops he brought with him, but many of them sold the modern rifles they had been issued and deserted.[13]

If al-Glawi's peace mission fell somewhat short of the sultan's expectations, the Ait Khabbash were almost certainly the cause. For them the fall of Touat had immediate and critical consequences. At the end of the nineteenth century the eastern frontiers of 'Atta-land were still expanding. The incursions of the Ait Khabbash up and down the Ziz valley and in the Saoura valley and Touat had hardly let up since the early 1800s. Their whole way of life was geared to aggressive warfare.[14] Although they fought largely without the help of other 'Atta sections, their participation in the *khams khmas* system, their sense of being part of a grand design of conquest, gave them a self-concept of invincibility. With the exception of the Ait Yafalman alliance, which was defensive and only partially effective, no tribe had been able to check their expansion prior to the arrival of the French.

The occupation of Touat deprived the Ait Khabbash of one of their principal spheres of influence. As soon as the French achieved control in Gourara and Touat proper, they abolished the network of nomad-sedentary 'brotherhood' treaties, which had provided the Ait Khabbash with a substantial income in tribute. All the Ait Khabbash who were in the Touat area withdrew to the northwest, and many of them congregated in Tafilalt to attempt to organize the *harka*. The retreat from Touat marked the first unmistakable and permanent setback in the growth of the 'Atta empire. In a sense, the French army's conquest of the tribe, which was not to come to a climax until 1933, began in Touat in 1900.

The fall of Touat also resulted in an immediate suspension of trade relations between there and Tafilalt. The Ait Khabbash and their Bani Mhammad allies were the principal carriers on this route, and they largely controlled the movements of other caravans. Since they were unwilling to approach the new French posts on friendly terms or allow other traders to do so, no caravans entered Touat from the northwest until late in 1901. A few Bani Mhammad merchants went to the two northern districts during the following months but mainly to settle old accounts, not to rebuild their business.[15] The occupation put an end to all but clandestine slave trade through the central Sahara. Therefore, the Bani Mhammad and the Ait Khabbash lost their share of that as well as the southbound trade in tea, sugar, cloth, and manufactures. Touat quickly became bound to Algeria economically as well as politically. The Oranie tribes began supplying all its grain, wool, and livestock. More important, the European import trade passed from the Filalis into the hands of Algerian Jews, Arabs, and Mozabites, many of whom settled in Touat and began setting up retail shops.[16] The dissolution of the Tafilalt-Touat route probably meant financial ruin for many of the Bani Mhammad merchants. After 1900 French intelligence reports scarcely mentioned their mercantile reputation, though their association with the Ait Khabbash resistance was reported often.

These two factors, the loss of both tribute and trade, impelled most of the Ait Khabbash and Bani Mhammad to ignore al-Glawi's plea for restraint and take unilateral action to drive the French out of Touat. On February 18, 1901, about five hundred warriors, most of them from these two tribes,

made a surprise attack on a French garrison at Timimoun in Gourara. The
one hundred and sixty French and Algerian troops beat back the assault
with rifle and machine gune fire and even used dynamite in the absence of
cannon. The French had nine killed and twenty-three wounded, a loss the
army considered inordinately high. The Moroccans left behind about one
hundred bodies, but the French failed to pursue the raiders, who withdrew
in full order.[17] The battle of Timimoun was widely heralded in Morocco as
a thorough drubbing for the Christians, though the participants learned a
lesson in French firepower.[18] Subsequently, they gave up large scale
assaults and kept to smaller raiding parties of anywhere from a dozen to
one hundred men which operated from safe bases in Tafilalt, Taouz, and
Tabelbala.[19]

Despite the quasi-victory at Timimoun and the resistance spirit of the
Ait Khabbash and the Bani Mhammad, most of the Ziz valley population
continued to procrastinate. Mawlay 'Abd al-'Aziz's diplomatic efforts to
restrain both the French and his own subjects along the frontier partially
accounted for the indecision.[20] The opening of negotiations in July 1901
leading to the Protocol and the Accords may have sustained sanguine
hopes for a border settlement favorable to Morocco. The failure of the
French to carry their offensive west of the Zousfana may also have assu-
aged fears of immediate invasion and some of the enthusiasm for a counter-
attack. The greatest deterrent to a united resistance movement, however,
was the resurgence of internal conflict in Tafilalt. From May 1901 reports
began arriving at the French posts that fighting between the Ait 'Atta and
Ait Yafalman factions had resumed. As during the troubles of 1896-1900,
the Ait Khabbash and Bani Mhammad were generally allied against the Ait
Izdig, Ait Mirghad, 'Arab Sabbah, and the people of Sefalat.[21]

Beneath this troubled surface of dissension and indecision country-wide
discontent over both European encroachments and Sharifian debility continued to fester. The *makhzan*'s increasingly apparent incapacity to prevent
European commercial and political as well as military penetration was
rapidly leading the entire country into a state of turbulence. As Mawlay
'Abd al-'Aziz's shortcomings as a ruler and his predilections for Christian
advice and amusements became known, rural unrest and rebellion against
government authority rapidly mounted. The population responded with
almost universal hostility to the sultan's tax reform program of 1901,
which abolished the sacred Koranic taxes, established a single levy on agriculture, and required everyone in the country to pay, even the *shurfa*,
murabtin, and other privileged groups. There can be little doubt of the
negative reaction in Tafilalt, which had the densest *shurfa* population in
the land.[22] The Franco-Moroccan Protocol and Accords of 1901-2 also

cost the sultan support as soon as their provisions became known, especially the legal transfer of Touat to the French and the relinquishment of sovereignty over the Dawi Mani' and the Awlad Jarir. In Fez the *ulama*, the orthodox religious leaders, published a *fatwa*, or legal opinion, condemning the agreements.[23] The reaction in Tafilalt must have been profound alarm. If the sultan was willing to cast off the Dawi Mani', who were longstanding allies of the dynasty, where would he stop?

From about the time that the Franco-Moroccan Commission visited Béchar and Kenadsa it is clear that 'Abd al-'Aziz no longer had much influence on developments in the Southeast. In June 1902 at least part of the population of Tafilalt reportedly declared their intention to ignore future orders from him and to cease praying in his name in the mosques, an act tantamount to open rebellion.[24] As early as 1898 rumors had spread that certain elements in Tafilalt were attempting to put forth candidates of their own as pretenders to the throne. Since Tafilalt was a place of exile for political figures out of favor with the sultan and a perennial hotbed of dynastic intrigue, it is not surprising that it should become a center of incipient rebellion when 'Abd al-'Aziz assumed the powers of state and the French marched into Touat. Māwlay Rashid, who was a brother of Mawlay Hasan and 'Abd al-'Aziz's uncle, was mentioned as a possible claimant, but he appears to have done nothing to put himself at the head of a rebellion. The name of Mawlay Muhammad, the sultan's older brother, was also hoisted periodically between 1900 and 1903. Though Mawlay Muhammad was a popular candidate in various parts of Morocco, 'Abd al-'Aziz had him safely under lock and key.[25] In the fall of 1902 Abu Himara emerged as a serious pretender in the region east of Fez, and during the subsequent year he sent letters throughout the Southeast soliciting support for a war against both 'Abd al-'Aziz and the French. He did not get any of the tribes in the region to mobilize in his favor, but his challenge did generate a good deal of enthusiasm in Tafilalt and almost certainly contributed to the breakdown in relations between there and the royal palace.[26]

After the departure of al-Glawi, Mawlay Rashid was the only agent the sultan had in the Southeast other than the *'amil* in Figuig. Mawlay Rashid could have played a commanding role in organizing a united resistance movement against the French. He was not only an important member of the royal family and informal head of the Filali *shurfa* community, but he had held his position as *khalifa* since the early 1860s when he was appointed by his farther, Sultan Sidi Muhammad.[27] With that kind of staying power he must have built up a great store of personal prestige, wealth, and influence by the turn of the century. As a *makhzan* official he contrasts sharply with the governors of Figuig, who were all strangers to the South-east and who moved in and out of office in rapid succession. In the after-math of Touat the war advocates in Tafilalt, especially the Ait Khabbash, encouraged Mawlay Rashid to lead a *harka* against Igli. But he opposed attacking the French, probably out of fear of retaliation, and he refused to renounce 'Abd al-'Aziz. Instead, he took an aloof and conciliatory position and remained on the sidelines as much as the population would let him.[28] Indeed, he probably held on to his post as long as he did by being a paragon of caution and restraint. Moreover, he was about seventy-three years old in 1900 and may have lacked the spirit to do anything more than safeguard his own well-being.[29] Still, he remained a key figure in Franco-Moroccan relations on the frontier until his death in 1911.

By the end of 1902 it was clear to the militants in Tafilalt that Mawlay 'Abd al-'Aziz, the most obvious candidate to take charge of resistance against the French, was fully committed to preventing it. In a large sense, the sultans of Morocco had already fought their battles against European penetration and lost. By the time 'Abd al-'Aziz assumed power in 1900, the government had already given in to so many economic and political pressures and had so clearly exposed its military and administrative weak-ness that it had little choice but to go on making whatever compromises it must in order to survive. Remembering only the aggressive politics and spiritual prestige of Mawlay Hasan, the people of Morocco did not realize either the extent of his failure to prevent the germination of a European informal empire or the limitations that this development placed on his successor's capacity to fulfill his traditional duties. Only after the fall of Touat did the population become fully aware that the *makhzan* had degenerated into an effete urban establishment, whose control over the state depended heavily on cooperation with the European powers. From that point on, popular resistance became directed not only against the French but also against the *makhzan* — and eventually against the sultan himself. The people of the Southeast discovered with dismay that what-ever religious, political, financial, or military resources the government could muster would be used to obstruct resistance and to placate the French into foregoing a full-scale invasion. The tribes and *qsar*-communi-ties found themselves as much on their own in facing the colonial crisis as if no central government or army existed. They had either to find their own sources of unity or make their separate terms with the invader.

Dilemmas for the Dawi Mani'

The Dawi Mani' and their allies the Awlad Jarir were the first large pastoral tribes in the Southeast to confront the French army. They controlled most

of the territory between the Ziz and the Zousfana and formed a kind of
buffer between Tafilalt and the area which the army occupied during 1900.
Their behavior in response to the new military offensive had a crucial
impact on efforts to organize pan-tribal resistance.

When French columns moved into the Zousfana valley, all Dawi Mani'
duwar-s pasturing in the vicinity quickly withdrew toward the west and
out of range of patrols. Part of the tribe remained on the Hammada of the
Guir, while the rest congregated in Tafilalt. The sedentary populations
inhabiting the *qsar-s* along the Zousfana put up no resistance to the French
and shortly made peace.[30] Lacking many modern weapons or any means
of surviving for long outside their oases, they had no real choice but to
submit. In fact, they probably expected no worse treatment from their
new overlords than they had received from the Dawi Mani', who had spent
several decades intimidating them, confiscating their palm groves, and
putting them to work as *khammas* laborers. Here was a case of politically
weak and militarily vulnerable *qsar*-dwellers for whom the colonial crisis at
first meant little more than the exchange of one kind of subjugation for
another.

To the Dawi Mani' the crisis appeared a good deal more calamitous. The
French army, possessing vastly superior arms and a military organization
even more efficient than that of the *khams khmas*, had in a single stroke
succeeded in conquering an area over which the Dawi Mani' had spent a
good part of the nineteenth century building up their hegemony. The
possibility of a French column penetrating as far as the Guir flood plain
posed an even greater threat. Under these circumstances the tribe had
three basic options: to resist the conquest through either direct attacks or
guerrilla harassment, to come to some kind of political terms with the
French, or to abandon the eastern half of their homeland altogether. These
alternatives were not very clear, however, because of the uncertainty of
their political and economic consequences. Furthermore, the broad dispersion of political power and influence in the tribe and the considerable
diversity of economic interests from one tent to another prevented the
formulation of any unified plan of action. The French were not like the
Ghananma or the Bani Gil; their military power was much greater and
their intentions much more ambiguous. The invasion did not, therefore,
encourage a simple assembling of the *khams khmas* and a march into battle.

As soon as the French occupied the Zousfana, raiding parties began to
form spontaneously. In considering the option of resistance the tribe was
certainly aware of the potential of French firepower and the price in men
that might be paid in staging frontal attacks on the posts. The garrisons
were armed with Lebel repeating rifles, seventy-five and eighty millimeter

cannons, and machine guns. Firing from inside their blockhouses and forts they could readily stand off an attacking force of much greater numbers. The Dawi Mani', on the other hand, probably had by the turn of the century a fairly abundant supply of breech-loading, single-shot rifles (especially the Remington) and plenty of muzzle-loaders. They had few repeaters, however, and ammunition for all modern models was chronically in short supply. Balanced against French superiority in weaponry were two points in favor of the tribe. One was their capacity to launch sudden raids on French patrols and convoys, using the techniques of surprise and fast retreat that had always served them in desert raids. The French forces were vulnerable because their system of heavily garrisoned posts and large convoys did not permit them to patrol wide areas or pursue raiding parties. The second advantage was the ability of the Dawi Mani' to find refuge and organize resistance west of the 'diplomatic frontier' along the Zousfana, which the army was not yet permitted to cross.

The raiding in the Zousfana-Saoura area during the first two years of the French occupation amounted to a continuation of what had been going on for years around Aïn Sefra, only on a more intensive scale. The biggest and most sensational attack was made against a provisions convoy at El-Moungar (north of Taghit in Beni Goumi) in July 1900. Some four hundred Dawi Mani' and Awlad Jarir took part, killing or wounding about sixteen Legionnaires. The frequency of raids, which involved Ait 'Atta as well as the Dawi Mani', increased during 1901, especially after the French occupied Beni Abbès (March 1st) and subdued the *qsar*-dwelling population of the Saoura valley.[31] Less than a dozen men took part in many of the raids, and their objective was usually the capture of livestock, rifles, or other booty. These forays were sporadic, uncoordinated, and often abortive. They were not part of what could yet be called a resistance movement.

While some of the Dawi Mani' waged war, others weighed the advantages of making peace and returning to the Zousfana. Many tents, especially those of the Idarasa, Awlad Jallul, and Awlad Yusif fifths, relied heavily on their date palm holdings in Beni Goumi. After the French occupied the area, they seized the fall date harvest as a reprisal against the raiding. They did not, however, sequester Dawi Mani' property, but offered to restore it fully in return for successful negotiation of peace terms.[32] Another economic factor was the pasture land along the Zousfana. Dawi Mani' tents could not graze near the river unless they were free from harassment by patrols.

The critical importance of these resources led some leaders to begin parlaying with the French early in 1901. During the course of the year, several groups of tents, usually numbering a few dozen at a time, actually submitted to French authority at Taghit or Igli. Almost all of these tents were of the Idarasa, Awlad Jallul, or Awlad Yusif. By the fall of 1901 a large majority of the Idarasa had made peace agreements. The Awlad abu 'Anan was the only fifth whose leaders made no serious contact with the French during this period. Almost none of the tents of this *khums* had economic interests east of the Guir, and most of them were camping either on the Hammada or in Tafilalt.[33]

The act of submission meant first of all that the tents in question received the *aman*, the official amnesty and promise of protection. In return, the French demanded that they renounce all acts of hostility and keep the Native Affairs officers informed concerning the warlike intensions of the rest of the tribe. The actual political status of these new clients, or *soumis* as the French called them, remained uncertain only until the summer of 1901 when the Protocol gave the French at least theoretical jurisdiction over all the Dawi Mani' and Awlad Jarir. Thereafter, these tents became French subjects and voluntarily gave up the Moroccan identity which Mawlay Hasan had tried so hard to give them. The French appointed *qa'id-s* over the submitted tents, although in practice the incumbent *qa'id-s* were simply given official approval; very little political reorganization of any part of the tribe took place for several years. Furthermore, the *soumis* were not obliged to pasture in the vicinity of the French posts but could practice transhumance according to their usual patterns, approaching the Zousfana mainly at the time of the date harvest. Nothing restrained them from going to the Guir or even to Tafilalt if they so chose. In fact, the first Idarasa tents to submit departed for the Guir as soon as they had arranged peace terms, probably because the grain harvest was forthcoming.[34] The French were obviously aware that their control of the Beni Goumi palms was a sufficiently effective means of curtailing the hostility of at least part of the tribe.

The fact that the Dawi Mani' began submitting to the French in relatively small groups reveals the inherent fissiparousness of tribal politics. Each tent (or even each individual) ultimately had the power to decide whether to submit or not, and each clearly did so primarily on the basis of its economic requirements. The decision was not in the hands of the *qa'id-s* or the members of the *jama'a-s*, who could do no more than persuade the tents under their influence to take one line of action or another. In March 1901, for example, Qa'id al-Kabir wuld Qaddur of the Awlad bil Giz visited Taghit, but he brought only a few tents with him, reporting that most of the *khums* had refused to come. He did not make a formal submission so as to avoid discrediting himself but returned west to try to persuade more of the tribe to make peace terms.[35] Tents which submitted together did tend to belong to the same lineage or even clan within a single *khums*, but this was true mainly because of the general correspondence between genealogical ties and shared interests.

The third and initially the most popular way of responding to the French incursion was withdrawal from the Zousfana-Saoura area altogether, thus putting off any decisions for positive action that might reduce the available options. Since the transhumant axis of much of the tribe extended between the Guir and Tafilalt, their resources in pasture, grain, and dates were for the time being out of reach of the French. The problem, however, could not be solved simply by retreating. Political conditions in Tafilalt also had to be taken into account. There, the Dawi Mani' had been deeply involved in the interplay of political forces for some centuries. Consequently, their response to the French inevitably affected their position in Tafilalt, especially since it was becoming the focal point for resistance. Two developments in the Tafilalt area were especially important in influencing the actions of the Dawi Mani'.

The first concerned the attitude of the Ait Khabbash. During the later nineteenth century, the Dawi Mani' and Awlad Jarir appear to have got along fairly well with their Berber neighbors, aside from the usual camel raiding. The Ait 'Atta expansion was directed mainly northward along the Ziz and southeastward to Touat rather than across the Hammada toward the Wad Guir. The Hammada pasture lands were extensive enough to support the herds and flocks of both tribes without chronic conflict.[36] In 1900, however, these good relations began to deteriorate rapidly. The Ait Khabbash were adamantly opposed to the submission of any Dawi Mani', fearing they would ally themselves militarily with the French and lead them to the banks of the Ziz. As more and more Dawi Mani' tents accepted the *aman* and returned to the Zousfana, the Ait Khabbash, with the support of most of the population of Tafilalt, put increasing pressure on the rest of the tribe to cut themselves off from their pro-French brothers, abandon the eastern portion of their territory, and commit themselves to war.

The second development concerned the new trade opportunities posed by the French expansion. In the nineteenth century Tafilalt was in large measure a commercial dependency of Fez and Marrakech. Most of the important merchants based in Tafilalt made their profits on trans-Atlas caravans. Just before the turn of the century, however, the commercial orientation of all of southeastern Morocco began to shift. After the French dropped tariff barriers on imports to the Sahara and Morocco in 1896, Filali traders started going with increasing frequency to the army

posts in southern Oranie to buy tea, sugar, textiles, and other products at
much lower prices than they could be purchased north of the Atlas. A
radical increase in trade between Tafilalt and the French markets did not
occur until 1903, but the Filalis were certainly seeing the handwriting on
the wall by 1900. While some of them turned eastward with little hesitation, others opposed the shift as a threat to their business with Fez and
Marrakech. The Ait Khabbash and a large part of the population of
Tafilalt supported the opponents, fearing that French commercial penetration west of the Zousfana would only be the prelude to an invasion.

The Dawi Mani' and the Awlad Jarir, however, were in a favored position to benefit from the growth of east-west traffic. During the nineteenth
century, they carried most of the trade on the regional artery between
Tafilalt and Figuig, which went through Béchar and Kenadsa. Therefore,
they were able to capitalize on the growing demand in Tafilalt for French
commodities, although at the same time they risked branding themselves
as collaborators. The objections of the Ait Khabbash restrained many of
them from making contacts with the French between 1900 and 1903.
Many tents, especially those of the Awlad abu 'Anan, committed themselves fully to the resistance cause because they had no economic interests
in the Zousfana area and were willing to forego trade with the French.
Others did not go to the new markets or open peace negotiations only
from fear that the Ait Khabbash and their allies would take reprisals by
raiding their caravans, confiscating their palm groves in Tafilalt or, worse
still, ravaging their grain crop on the Guir flood plain.[37]

In the meantime the Native Affairs officers at the Zousfana posts were
continuing to encourage submissions by making political contacts with the
Dawi Mani' through intermediaries. In some cases they offered official
qa'id positions and, later, subsidies to tribal leaders in return for their
services in persuading the tents over which they had influence to come to
terms.[38] By far the most important go-betweens, though, were the saints
of Kenadsa. The French had, in fact, been cultivating friendly relations
with the Ziyaniya brotherhood for a long time. After the murabtin gave
the General Wimpffen expedition a cordial reception at Kenadsa in 1870,
the Algerian authorities began making contacts with the zawiya. Their aim
was to use it as a friendly religious counterforce to the saintly Awlad Sidi
Shaykh family, which was in revolt off and on from 1864 to 1883.[39]
Nothing came of this plan, but the contacts were maintained, partly
because the murabtin needed French permission to circulate in Oran and
Algiers Provinces to collect ziyara-s from their disciples. As soon as the
Native Affairs men moved into the Zousfana, they enlisted Shaykh Si
Brahim and his kinsmen to provide a liaison between the bureaus and the

Dawi Mani' groups which wished to submit. Conversely, some of the tribesmen sought out the *murabtin* in order to request their mediation.[40]

Following the signing of the Protocol, Governor General Jonnart approved a scheme to recruit Si Brahim in the service of the Franco-Moroccan Commission. The plan was to dispatch him and his fellow saints as advance men to encourage the Dawi Mani' and the Awlad Jarir to accept French nationality and to make sure that the three *qsar-s* of Kenadsa, Béchar, and Ouakda chose the same. At a meeting at Aïn Sefra with General Cauchemez, the French Commissioner, the Shaykh accepted the mission after being offered gifts, a cash subsidy (which may have been up to 50,000 francs), and continued authorization to collect offerings in the north.[41]

When Cauchemez arrived on the frontier, however, he found the *murabtin* in a less cooperative mood. Two of them, both leading members of the Ziyani family, visited Si Gibbas at Duveyrier and purportedly gave him assurance of their loyalty to the sultan. They promised to meet with the French delegation at Figuig but then returned to Kenadsa without doing so. Cauchemez immediately accused the saints of flagrant duplicity and advised his superiors to take reprisals against them.[42] He clearly did not understand the delicate position they were in. Undoubtedly aware of the hostility of many of the nomads toward the Commission, they could do nothing but back down and make a pretense of opposition to the French position in order to maintain their good relations with the Dawi Mani'. Si Brahim appears to have been following a basic rule of *zawiya* politics by attempting to remain in a flexible and ostensibly neutral position between the parties he expected to serve. If he became unambiguously identified with either side, he could no longer serve either the French or the tribes as an effective mediator. Furthermore, he probably knew that the French would eventually move west, but in 1901 his *zawiya* was still in Dawi Mani' territory. More significantly, it was near the prevailing Franco-Dawi Mani' frontier and therefore well located to perform its mediational function. At any rate, Si Brahim's political footwork proved effective. When the Commission visited Kenadsa, he declared for Moroccan sovereignty but at the same time discreetly asked the French for their protection when it might be needed.[43] After the Commission left, he and his kinsmen quickly resumed their comings and goings between the Native Affairs offices and the Dawi Mani' encampments. The tribesmen who were advocating resistance in 1901 probably did not accuse the *murabtin* of collaboration, since the *zawiya* was essentially playing the same role it always had as mediator between one tribe and another. It was expected that the French, as a special sort of neighboring tribe, would recompense the saints for their services as did the Dawi Mani'.

When the French took control of the Zousfana, the Dawi Mani' failed to make what might have seemed the most obvious response. They did not call together the five fifths, elect a war *shaykh*, and launch an attack. Indeed, the military esprit de corps which had served tribal expansion in the eighteenth and nineteenth centuries appeared to disintegrate. Some groups organized small-scale resistance, while others withdrew west to a safe distance and waited, and still others proceeded to make peace with the French.

This inconsistent and fragmented behavior reflected the ambiguities of a situation which confronted many other pastoral transhumant tribes during later stages of the conquest of Morocco. The French would occupy part of a tribe's territory and with it vital resources in agricultural or grazing land. The rest of the territory would remain free, but the resources under French control could not be sacrificed nor could the rhythm of seasonal transhumance be upset without doing severe harm to the economic well-being of many if not all members of the tribe. Furthermore, at the opposite end of the migrational circuit, where other resources were located and where the French were not yet prepared to penetrate, resistance elements congregated and attempted to persuade or coerce others to join them. On top of that, the French would hold out opportunities for trade back and forth across the military frontier in return for submission and cooperation. Under these extremely fluid circumstances some groups made peace with the French and others resisted. But more important, almost all of them avoided as long as they could making commitments which could not be reversed at a moment's notice. Moroccan tribes possessed no central authority systems by which a unified, coherent plan of action could be worked out. The ideology of segmentary lineage cohesion, which was only an ideal model for political action, proved ineffectual when the specific economic interests of numerous groups within a tribe were threatened in such an ambiguous and fluctuating manner. Deciding who were to be friends and who enemies at any given point in time depended not on standards of kinship but on the imperatives of subsistence. The most conspicuous individuals in these uncertain times were mediational agents, especially saints, who facilitated negotiations between Moroccans and French and between one tribe and another.

The Dawi Mani', who prior to 1900 inhabited a stretch of Morocco's indeterminate desert periphery, suddenly found themselves overlapping a military and political frontier which cut through their transhumant ecosystem. The situation was made especially complex because the tribe followed two separate pastoral circuits, one between the Guir and the Zousfana, the other between the Guir and Tafilalt. Factors which affected the essential resources of one group of tents did not affect another at all. Some groups were under pressures from the French, others from the militants in Tafilalt. Moreover, the safety of the grain fields on the Guir flood plain was in doubt after early 1901, when the sultan officially sacrificed the tribe to the French, even though the army remained on the Zousfana many additional months. Under these conditions the spirit of *khams khmas* unity dissolved into a dynamic kaleidoscopic response that defies simple categorization as either resistance or collaboration

The Fall of Figuig

The Treaty of 1845 protected Figuig from occupation when the French advanced into the Zousfana valley. Many of the inhabitants took advantage of this diplomatic shield to continue to take part in small-scale resistance and give refuge to nomad raiding bands, even though the army established two posts only short distances east and south of the oasis. At the same time and in quite a contrary spirit, Mawlay 'Abd al-'Aziz made Figuig the *makhzan*'s political and military headquarters for carrying out its program of cooperation with the French in the southern borderland. Thus, the government pursued its ill-equipped intrusions into Figuig's internal life, while the army watched from afar, chafing to resolve the issue of frontier law and order with direct action of its own.

The Protocol of 1901 committed the Moroccan and French governments to a course of mutual assistance in maintaining security and developing commerce along the undefined frontier. In February 1902 General Cauchemez and Si Gibbas led the Franco-Moroccan Commission into Figuig to inform the inhabitants of the terms of the Protocol, to instruct them to keep the peace on the frontier, and to install a permanent Moroc can commissioner. His job was to settle disputes between Moroccans and Algerians in cooperation with his French counterpart, who would be installed in a nearby army post. Si Muhammad Ragragi, a *makhzan* official whom Mawlay 'Abd al-'Aziz sent to the frontier as a special envoy in 1901, was named *'amil* of Figuig and resident commissioner for the southern region.

Most of the *qsar*-dwellers were disgruntled at these developments. During the previous two years they had witnessed the French occupation of Touat and the entire Zousfana valley, and now Si Gibbas was leading a band of French officers into the oasis. Not only that, the sultan dispatched a letter to the seven *qsar-s* calling upon them to cooperate with Si Gibbas and make peace with the French.[44] Though publicly accepting the Commission's admonitions to evict all malefactors and bandits from the

oasis and adhere to a 'good neighbor' policy, most of the population remained sullen.[45] The most vehement opponents of the Protocol were the
people of Zenaga, the largest *qsar*. Their anxiety stemmed mainly from
the fact that the French were about to build a military post at Beni Ounif,
just south of the oasis, and even to extend the railroad there. Since many
Zenagans owned palm groves around Beni Ounif and also cultivated barley
every year nearby along the banks of the Zousfana, French occupation
posed a serious economic threat.[46] Some Zenagans reportedly tried to
bribe Si Gibbas to prevent the railway from passing near Figuig. The other
qsar-s manifested less concern about the railroad.[47] Certainly many of the
merchants who had been trading at Aïn Sefra and the other posts saw in
its coming the opportunity for greater profits than ever before.

Neither the visit of the Commission nor the signing of more detailed
accords in Algiers a few months later made much of an impression on
Figuig, for attacks against French convoys and personnel only increased
during 1902 and early 1903. The efforts of the *makhzan* to play a more
active role in policing the frontier were singularly unsuccessful. The
governor's promotion to *'amil* and commissioner did little to bolster his
authority. The Zenagans were probably more hostile than ever because the
makhzan rescinded its decision to let them have their own autonomous
qa'id.[48]

The *'amil* could of course do nothing to check resistance activity in
Figuig without an armed force to back up his authority. Until 1901 the
makhzan had no desire to garrison Figuig since the governor's job was to
appease the French, not rule the oasis. The Protocol, however, made
the *makhzan* responsible for keeping the peace on the Moroccan side of
the frontier. Since the new *'amil* would be conspicuously helpless on his
own, he had to be supplied with at least a token force to serve as the
counterpart to the French garrison at Beni Ounif. In March 1902, therefore, the government ordered about 150 soldiers and officers transferred
to Figuig from the garrisons of Oujda and Saïdia (on the Mediterranean
coast). Most of these troops were government levies from the Dukkala
tribe of the Atlantic plains. They were transported to Figuig on the
Algerian railway. Tribal contingents in the Moroccan army were
notoriously undependable, and the Dukkala proved to be no exception.
Almost as soon as they arrived at their quarters in al-Oudaghir, they began
to desert, sometimes after selling the modern rifles they brought with
them. They were of no assistance to Ragragi, who was dismissed (under
pressure from the French) only a few months after taking office because
of his inability to control his own troops. By the summer of 1902 most of
the garrison had vanished.[49] The next substantial contingent did not arrive

until October 1904.[50]

Throughout 1902 and the first half of 1903, the French forces were
hardly more effective than the Moroccan garrison in checking raiding and
violence around Figuig. Although a post was constructed at Beni Ounif in
March 1902, the French government prohibited the military from using it
to pacify Figuig. Patrols were allowed to operate only short distances, and
convoys traveling between one post and another had to be heavily guarded.
In short, the occupation was limited to a number of points rather than to
an extensive zone, a situation which permitted Moroccan raiding parties to
move freely and strike at their convenience.

Under mountaing pressure from the army and the colonial lobby in
Algeria to do something about what they considered an intolerable and
humiliating situation, Jonnart, who became Governor General in the
spring of 1903, proposed a three-pronged counteroffensive along the frontier: the bombardment of Zenaga, and the dispatch of reconnaissance
columns to Béchar and into the Jebel Beni Smir. The French foreign ministry approved the plans, though it specifically disallowed even a temporary
occupation of Figuig.

In order to get a firsthand view of the operations, Jonnart traveled to
Beni Ounif in late May. On the 31st he, the *'amil*, and a small military escort rode to the edge of the oasis for a look around. Suddenly a group of
Zenagans fired on them, and a four hour skirmish ensued in which a number of Legionnaires were wounded. The clash was no more serious than
many which had occurred during the previous three years, but it provided
an added justification for prompt bombardment.[51] On June 8 four sections of cannon were drawn up on the slopes of the two hills to the south
of the oasis, and Zenaga was shelled for about five hours. The mud brick
dwellings of the village were devastated and the minaret of the mosque was
severed, but most of the residents escaped into the surrounding palm
groves. Al-Oudaghir, which flew white flags on its walls during the attack,
was spared along with the other five *qsar-s*.[52]

A few days later, the *jama'a-s* of all seven *qsar-s* met with General
O'Connor, Commander of the Oran Division, and agreed to a set of peace
terms. The notables were instructed to ensure security for both Muslims
and Europeans in Figuig, to expel all elements hostile to the French, to
permit Europeans free access to the oasis, to pay an indemnity of
60,000 francs, and to hand over 150 rifles and fourteen hostages. In return,
O'Connor agreed to protect the residents of Figuig when they visited
French territory and to permit them to retain most of their property
rights in and around Beni Ounif.[53] The indemnity and arms were subsequently delivered and the hostages released.[54] O'Connor and Jonnart left

the 'amil and Si Gibbas (who was still in Algeria) out of these proceedings altogether, thus reverting to a 'tribal policy' of direct negotiations with the people of the region rather than operating exclusively through the makhzan representatives. The foreign ministry, ever careful to avoid offending the sultan or raising criticisms from the other powers, protested that this course of action amounted to an abrogation of the Protocol. Although the army and the Algerian settlers regarded the 'makhzan policy' as an irritating stumblingblock to southern expansion and frontier security, Jonnart deferred to Paris, and in a short time the commandant at Beni Ounif reestablished contact with the 'amil. The sultan did not even protest the bombardment after receiving assurances that it was carried out as a police action within the provisions of the Accords and that his sovereignty over the oasis was secure.[55]

Beaten into submission and effectively abandoned by the sultan, the qsar-dwellers were forced to make a radical recalculation of their relations with the French. Even though the cannons were withdrawn to Beni Ounif and no French troops marched into the oasis, Figuig was indisputably conquered and transformed into a kind of informal protectorate of the Oran Division. The threat of further attacks, which could destroy the palm groves and the intricate irrigation works, was sufficient cause to rule out the alternative of armed resistance. The new problem was how to come to terms with the army, which was clearly in Beni Ounif to stay.

The Battle of Taghit

The army's new offensive of June 1903 extinguished resistance activity in Figuig but only rekindled it in Tafilalt. The advance of a French reconnaissance column to Béchar and Kenadsa produced such a wave of alarm in the Ziz valley that the long-delayed mass harka finally took shape. This time the objective of the mujahidin was not Igli but the army post at Taghit in the Beni Goumi district of the Zousfana valley.

The emergence at long last of two popular and skillful leaders helped to crystallize the harka. Mawlay Mustafa al-Hanafi and his son Mawlay 'Amar, better known as Ba Sidi, were the two most widely known shurfa of the Awlad Sidi al-Hanafi. This 'Alawi family inhabited both the Tizimi district of Tafilalt (qsar Chlalf) and the Rteb oasis (qsar Jramna and possibly others) further up the Ziz. The family had a strong saintly tradition built upon the reputation of Mawlay Mustafa's grandfather, who established zawiya-s in the Ziz valley and developed a large spiritual following. The family also became prominent as political mediators, especially serving the Ait 'Atta of the Rteb in their altercations over pasture and palm groves. At the turn of the century Mawlay Mustafa was the leading mediator in the

district. Although the Awlad Sidi al-Hanafi were of the same descent as the
shurfa of Tafilalt, they, like the Darqawi of Medaghra, were also active
murabtin and did not take part in the internecine quarrels of their cousins
further down the valley.

During most of the nineteenth century, Si Muhammad al-'Arbi al-
Darqawi's *zawiya* in Medaghra eclipsed those of the al-Hanafi. After Si
al-'Arbi's death and the breakdown of his saintly organization, the
al-Hanafi star began to rise under the leadership of both Ba Sidi and
Mawlay Mustafa. In fact, they may well have attempted to rebuild their
prominence by taking over Si al-'Arbi's *jihad*-oriented teachings and
appealing to his former followers. They did not, however, aim to assume
leadership of the Darqawa brotherhood since they were affiliates of the
Qadiriya, another order with a large membership in the Southeast.

The *harka* required a reputable saint to act as either active or nominal
leader. He provided the *baraka* which made the venture good in the sight
of God and served as an extra-tribal figure around which the highly fissiparous population could rally. Together Ba Sidi and Mawlay Mustafa ful-
filled the requirements well. Mawlay Mustafa was widely respected as a
learned ascetic and skilled mediator and had been working to organize a
resistance movement since 1900. In the months following the fall of Touat
he was even mentioned as a possible challenger to Mawlay 'Abd al-'Aziz.[56]
Ba Sidi, on the other hand, had a reputation for being a pugnacious and
fear-inspiring individual who exhibited leadership and fighting skill impres-
sive to the *harka* warriors, especially the Ait Khabbash. The two men
together were a kind of warrior-saint team, the son taking the first role,
and the father the second.[57]

The resistance forces assembled not in Tafilalt but in Boudenib on the
Wad Guir, perhaps in order to attract warriors from the upper Guir and the
Wad Aïssa-Haïber region as well as from the Ziz valley. Military organization and discipline were lacking, other than the over-arching command of
Ba Sidi. Mawlay Mustafa stayed behind, perhaps only because of his
advanced age. (Ironically, Si Braham of Kenadsa also turned up at Boudenib
— but as an emissary of the French to try to persuade the *harka* to dis-
band.)[58] Each warrior, whether he walked or rode, traveled with the contingent from his own tribe or village. The *harka* left Boudenib early in August,
advanced as far as Béchar, and there established a base camp. The backbone
of the army were men of the Ait Khabbash and the Awlad Jarir, many of
whom were probably mounted on mules, camels, or horses. A large contingent of Dawi Mani', mainly Awlad abu 'Anan who had moved near Tafilalt
in 1900, also took part. *Qsar*-dwellers from the Ziz, Guir, and Aïssa-Haïber
valleys, groups from the Ait Yafalman tribes, and bans of Abu 'Amama's

followers joined the ranks as well, swelling the force to four or five thousand men. As many as three thousand women and children also accompanied the contingents as far as Béchar. Although the movement does not appear to have attracted the attention of the High and Middle Atlas tribes as it did in 1900 and 1901, small bands of adventurers from more distant parts of Morocco may well have been represented. The camp at Béchar must have been a scene of incredible tumult, and the problems of food and water supply were undoubtedly considerable.

The *mujahidin* believed themselves well enough armed to attack the French at Taghit and drive them from the Beni Goumi district. Although muzzle-loading guns were still in common use in the Southeast, probably a substantial majority of the warriors carried modern breech-loading rifles, especially single shot Remingtons. These guns were obtained through trade, or from earlier raids against the French. The attackers at Timimoun, for example, carried off an estimated eighty Lebel repeaters.[59] Also during the course of 1901 and 1902, the *makhzan* garrison troops in Tafilalt reportedly sold or lost more than two thousand rifles of various models, almost all they brought in.[60] Many of these guns probably saw service at Taghit. The French field reports on the *harka* made no attempt to assess its firepower, except to note that some of the participants had Lebels and that a great many were 'très bien armés.'[61]

On August 17 the *harka* marched into Beni Goumi and for three days attempted to assault the post at Taghit and the *qsar* of Barrebi. The garrison of 470 Algerian troops beat back every attack, making liberal use of two 80 millimeter cannons. On August 20 most of the Moroccans gave up the battle, disbanded into small groups, and headed back toward the west. During the fighting, the French had nine killed and twenty-one wounded. According to the army's estimate, the *harka* lost close to two hundred. Some of these deaths were avenged on September 2, when about two hundred mounted warriors who had sought refuge in the Erg Occidental after the battle launched a surprise attack on a convoy at El Moungar. The assailants pillaged the convoy and killed twenty-six men, including two French officers, then escaped toward the west.[62]

The *harka* that fought the battle of Taghit was the first of a series of popular, rural coalitions to confront the French army in various parts of the country between 1903 and 1912. It was the first time during the conquest period that Moroccans demonstrated a capability to mobilize mass, pan-tribal resistance. The key to the success of the movement was the emergence of two supra-tribal leaders, saints who possessed an abundance of spiritual prestige and who stood outside the tangle of tribal alliances and animosities. The al-Hanafi father and son team followed in the tradi-

tion of Abu 'Amama, Si al-'Arbi al-Darqawi, and other figures of the North
African past as individuals who applied their reputations as holy men and
their skills as mediators to the task of uniting a number of tribes and social
groups otherwise having no common ties of political organization or
leadership. Indeed, saints and *shurfa*, including the sultan himself, were the
only individuals who, because of their special positions within the acephalous structure of Moroccan rural society, could command even the short-
term allegiance of many tribes at one time. Of course, the mere formal
qualification of being a saint or *sharif* meant nothing without the accompanying attributes of piety, forceful character, and political acuity, as well
as a capacity to be at the right place at the right time. Despite the abundance of both *murabtin* and *shurfa* in the Ziz valley, not one of them
effectively took charge of resistance efforts from 1900 to the early
summer of 1903.

The *harka* of Taghit succeeded as a makeshift pan-tribal league but
failed lamentably as an army. It revealed the limitations and defects of
large-scale coalitions and foreshadowed the fate of every subsequent
attempt at mass warfare both in the Southeast and elsewhere. Large numbers, popular zeal, and God-inspired leadership simply could not make up
for the lack of up-to-date arms and ammunition, efficient logistics, military discipline, and command organization, all of which the French
possessed. The saintly leaders, and here one could also point to Abu
'Amama in his leadership of the 1881 rising, were good standard-bearers
but bad generals. They brought to the battlefield no special military
training or experience. Indeed, the society normally had no need for
specialists of that sort. Consequently, the *harka* in motion was no more
than a throng grouped loosely in numerous tribal contingents and having
no common strategy except frontal assault. When the French beat back
the attack, the magic of pan-tribal unity quickly dissolved in a general
sauve qui peut. At that point the leaders had either to try to lay the
groundwork for a new league or bow out. In short, a mass force could
inflict some casualties, but it could not drive the enemy away. Indeed, the
battles of Taghit and El Moungar had an effect exactly contrary to what
Ba Sidi and his warriors intended. Rather than expelling the French from
the Zousfana, they only gave them the justification they needed to
advance toward the Wad Guir.

At the end of the summer of 1903 resistance in the Southeast appeared to
be in a state of collapse. The al-Hanafi coalition had crumbled, more and
more of the Dawi Mani' were making peace at the Zousfana posts, and
Figuig was reduced to quiescence. On top of that, the sultan had not only

renounced his responsibilities as Defender of the Faith but was actively attempting to subvert resistance and calling upon the population to co-operate with the French army in implementing the Protocol and the Accords. By agreeing to the plan for joint Franco-Moroccan police action in the frontier zone without carrying *makhzan* power and influence beyond what Mawlay Hasan had been able to achieve, 'Abd al-'Aziz was in effect leaving the imposition of central authority in the region, whether Algerian or Moroccan on paper, almost entirely in the hands of the French. He and his ministers appear to have been mainly interested in making a quick settlement of the frontier question by obtaining assurances of Sharifian sovereignty over part of the region, especially Figuig and Tafilalt, without taking further direct responsibility for maintaining law and order. Thus the callous abandonment of the Dawi Mani' and the Awlad Jarir to French jurisdiction. As far as the *makhzan* elite was concerned, the fiscal and commercial crisis, the revolt of Abu Himara, and the power struggles between one courtly faction and another were much more absorbing issues than the waging of a futile *jihad* on the desert frontier.

Notes

1. Eugène Aubin, *Le Maroc d'aujourd'hui*, 8th ed. (Paris, 1913), pp. 220, 221. Also G. Salmon, 'Une Opinion marocaine sur la conquête du Touat,' *Archives Marocaines*, no. 3, 1 (1904), pp. 416-24.
2. 'Le Chemin de fer de Djenien-Bou-Rezg,' *Af. Fr.* (March 1900), pp. 91-4.
3. On Delcassé's Moroccan policy see Christopher Andrew, *Théophile Delcassé and the Making of the Entente Cordiale* (New York, 1968), pp. 255-67.
4. G. Saint-René Taillandier, *Les Origines du Maroc français* (Paris, 1930), pp. 5-11.
5. Frank E. Trout, *Morocco's Saharan Frontiers* (Geneva, 1969), pp. 38-51; Saint-René Taillandier, *Origines*, pp. 11, 66-81.
6. Andrew, *Delcassé*, pp. 180-200; Saint-René Taillandier, *Origines*, pp. 121-4.
7. AMG, Alg. 14, Sud-Oranais 1900, Révoil to Min. of Foreign Affairs, May 17, 1900; 'Notre Action dans le Sud Oranais et les affaires du Maroc,' *Af. Fr.* (June 1900), p. 206. In May and June 1901 the Marquis de Segonzac, traveling in the Middle Atlas, reported that many men of the region had gone off to the Southeast to fight the French. J. De Segonzac, *Voyage au Maroc, 1899-1901* (Paris, 1903), pp. 77, 130, 137, 138.
8. AMG, Alg. 13, Mouvements dans le Sud-Oranais (Mai-Août 1900), Grisot to Min. War, May 21, 1900; Alg. 14, Sud-Oranais 1900, Risbourg to Grisot, June 9, 1900, no. 516.
9. AMG, Alg. 14, Sud-Oranais 1900, Révoil to Min. of Foreign Affairs, May 17, 1900; Risbourg to Com. 19th Corps, May 29, 1900; Alg. 13, Mouvements dans le Sud-Oranais (Mai-Août 1900), Grisot to Min. War, June 3, 1900.
10. AMG, Alg. 14, Sud-Oranais 1900, Risbourg to Com. 19th Corps, June 22, 1900, no. 545; Révoil to Min. of Foreign Affairs, July 17, 1900.
11. AMG, Alg. 14, Sud-Oranais 1900, Jonnart to Min. War, Dec. 4, 1900, no. 2825; Jonnart to Min. War, Dec. 11, 1900, no. 3010; Sit. pol. 1901, Grisot to Min.

War, April 10, 1901, no. 9016; Maroc C11, MM 1900, Burckhardt to Min. War, Dec. 30, 1900, no. 182

12. AMG, Alg. 14, Sit. pol. 1901, Jonnart to Min. War, May 21, 1901, no. 982.

13. AMG, Maroc C12, MM 1902, Burckhardt to Min. War, April 3, 1902, no. 266; May 31, 1902, no. 274; July 4, 1902, no. 286; Alg. 14, Sit. pol. 1901, Capt. Susbielle, 'Rapport hebdomadaire de l'Annexe d'Igli,' April 6-13, 1901.

14. In response to the question, 'What is the secret of Ait 'Atta power?,' an Ait Khabbash informant replied that they were just like the Americans — numerous, powerful, and fearless of death!

15. Capt. Flye-Saint-Marie, 'Le Commerce et l'agriculture au Touat,' *BSGAO*, 24 (Oct.-Dec. 1904), pp. 364, 368; Martin, 'Les Transactions commerciales dans l'annexe de Beni Abbès pendant l'année 1905,' *BSGAO*, 27 (Oct. 1906), pp. 360, 363-9; Augustin Bernard and N. Lacroix, *Evolution du nomadisme en Algérie* (Paris, 1906), p. 225.

16. Bernard and Lacroix, *Evolution*, pp. 225, 227, 236.

17. AGGA, 22H. 33, Premier harka beraber: combat de Timmimoun, Clavery, 'Rapport sur la harka marocaine qui a attaqué Timmimoun le 18 février, 1901,' March 8, 1901; Paul Lenard, 'La Vérité sur Timmimoun,' *Echo d'Oran*, May 5, 1901; Capitaine-Commandant Breveté Tillion, *La Conquête des oasis sahariennes* (Paris, 1903), pp. 126-8; A.G.P. Martin, *Quatre siècles d'histoire marocaine* (Paris, 1923), pp. 357-60.

18. Burckhardt reported from Marrakech that rumors were spreading of a French disaster at Timimoun. AMG, Alg. 14, Sit. pol. 1901, Burckhardt to Min. War, March 17, 1901, no. 196. Several informants spoke of Timimoun as one of the finest hours of the resistance. Interviews no. 9, 10, and 18.

19. Interview no. 9.

20. AMG, Alg. 14, Sit. pol. 1901, Susbielle, 'Rapport hebdomadaire de l'annexe d'Igli,' March 30 — April 5, 1901; Risbourg to Com. 19th Corps, April 8, 1901, no. 708; Grisot, to Min. War, April 10, 1901, no. 9016. J. de Segonzac (*Voyages au Maroc*, pp. 137, 138), writing from the Middle Atlas in June, 1901, noted that the sultan 'had read in the *khotba* [sermon] in all the mosques of Tafilelt a letter forbidding an attack against the French, except if they invade Moroccan territory.'

21. AMG, Alg. 14, Sit. pol. 1901, Grisot to Min. War, May 17, 1901, no. 9349; Jonnart to Min. War, May 21, 1901, no. 982; June 2, 1901, no. 1050; June 16, 1901, no. 1127; Alg. 14, sit. pol. 1902, Révoil to Min. War, Jan. 22, 1902, no. 73.

22. AMG, Alg. 15, Correspondance 1903, A. Le Chatelier, untitled monograph on the al-Hanafi *shurfa* of the Rteb (hereafter cited as Le Chatelier, 'al-Hanafi'). This study mentions the opposition of the *shurfa* of the Ziz valley to the sultan's tax reform.

23. Martin, *Quatre siècles*, p. 397.

24. AMG, Maroc C12, MM 1902, Burckhardt to Min. War, June 30, 1902, no. 283.

25. Reports that elements in Tafilalt were promoting either Mawlay Rashid or Mawlay Muhammad as pretender reached the French from time to time in 1900 and 1901. AMG, Alg. 13, Mouvements dans le Sud-Oranais (Mars-Août 1900), Grisot to Min. War, May 12, 1900, no. 9730; Alg. 14, Sud-Oranais 1900, Laferrière to Grisot, June 2, 1900, no. 482; Sit. pol. 1901, Bertrand, 'Rapport hebdomadaire de l'annexe d'Igli,' April 13-19, 1901; Sit. pol. 1902, Révoil to Min. War, June 7, 1902.

26. AMG, Alg. 15, Correspondence 1903, Jonnart to Min. War, April 1, 1903, no. 530; Jonnart to Min. War, June 8, 1903, no. 9821; Maroc C13, MM 1903-04, 'La Situation au Maroc au Avril 1903.'

27. Martin (*Quatre siècles*, pp. 176, 177) quotes a letter from Sidi Muhammad, who assumed the throne in 1860, to the people of Touat dated 1862. In it he instruc-

ted them to communicate with him through Mawlay Rashid, his *khalifa* in Tafilalt.

28. AMG, Maroc C12, MM 1902, Burckhardt to Min. War, May 31, 1902, no. 274; Martin, *Quatre siècles*, pp. 367, 368.

29. Mawlay Rashid was born in 1827. Interview no. 22.

30. AMG, Alg. 14, Sud-Oranais 1900, Bertrand (Com. of the column to Igli) to Com. Div. Oran, May 10, 1900, no. 13; Calderaro, 'Beni Goumi,' *BSGA*, 9 (1904), pp. 310-12, 316, 317, 333.

31. AMG, Alg. 14, Sud-Oranais 1900, la Martinière (Chargé d'affaires at Tangier) to Min. of Foreign Affairs, Aug. 6, 1900; Capt. Augiéras, 'La Pénétration dans le Sahara occidental,' *Ren. Col.* (July 1923), pp. 229-33; Tillion, *La Conquête des oasis sahariennes*, pp. 95, 96.

32. AMG, Alg. 14, Sud-Oranais 1900, Risbourg to Com. 19th Corps, Oct. 7, 1900, no. 616.

33. AMG, Alg. 14, Opérations du 1st trimestre 1901, Jonnart to Min. War, Jan. 22, 1901, no. 238; Sud-Oranais 1901, Jonnart to Min. War, May 10, 1901, no. 922.

34. AMG, Alg. 14, Sud-Oranais 1901, Jonnart to Min. War, May 10, 1901, no. 922.

35. AMG, Alg. 14, Opérations du 1st trimestre 1901, Risbourg to Com. 19th Corps, March 21, 1901, no. 63aa.

36. Ait Khabbash informants (interview no. 9) affirmed that they and the Dawi Mani' usually pastured in peace on the Hammada, though blood vengeance sometimes occurred.

37. AMG, Alg. 14, Sud-Oranais 1901, Jonnart to Min. War, May 7, 1901, no. 903; Alg. 15, Correspondance 1903, Jonnart to Min. War, Aug. 13, 1903, no. 1531; AGGA, 22H. 22, Tournée de reconnaissance, Pierron (Com. of the Cercle of Colomb) to Lyautey, Jan. 23, 1904, no. 54.

38. AMG, Alg. 14, Opérations du 1st trimestre 1901, Grisot to Min. War, Feb. 25, 1901, no. 9086; AGGA, 30H. 13, Commission 6eme partie, Cauchemez to Gov. Gen., March 15, 1902, no. 138.

39. AGGA, 16H. 13, M. Colas, 'Notice sur les ordres religieux,' 1883; 21H. 11, Bou Amama, Jonnart to Min. of Foreign Affairs, June 14, 1901.

40. AMG, Alg. 13, Mouvements dans le Sud-Oranais (Mars-Août 1900), Gov. Gen. Laferrière to Min. of Foreign Affairs, Jan. 26, 1900; Sud-Oranais 1900, Risbourg to Com. 19th Corps, Oct. 7, 1900, no. 616; Alg. 14, Novembre-Décembre 1900, Jonnart to Min. War, Nov. 17, 1900; Opérations du 1st trimestre 1901, Grisot to Min. War, Feb. 25, 1901, no. 9086; AGGA, 30H. 13, Commission 1er partie, Lacroix to Gov. Gen., Aug. 20, 1901.

41. AMG, Alg. 14, Documents Gen. O'Connor, Gov. Gen. Révoil to O'Connor, Sept. 12, 1901; Com. 19th Corps to O'Connor, Aug. 19, 1901; AGGA, 30H. 13, Commission 8eme partie, Cauchemez to Gov. Gen., Feb. 18, 1902, no. 89.

42. AGGA, 30H. 13, Commission 8eme partie, Cauchemez to Gov. Gen., Feb. 18, 1902, no. 89.

43. *Doc. Dip.*, I, 34.

44. *Doc. Dip.*, I, 23-6.

45. AMG, Alg. 14, Documents Gen. O'Connor, Capt. Fariau (member of Commission) to O'Connor, Feb. 21, 1902.

46. AMG, Alg. 14, Documents Gen. O'Connor, O'Connor, 'Rapport sur la situation au 12 Octobre,' Oct. 12, 1901.

47. AMG, Alg. 14, Documents Gen. O'Connor, Cauchemez to O'Connor, Feb. 23, 1902.

48. AMG, Alg. 15, Correspondance inter-ministerielle 1903, Jonnart to Min. of Foreign Affairs, May 31, 1903, no. 73885; AGGA, 30H. 49, Affaires du Sud-Oranais, O'Connor to Gov. Gen., Feb. 21, 1903, no. 385.

49. AGGA, 30H. 16, Année 1903, Com. Subdiv. of Tlemcen to Com. Div. Oran, Feb. 13, 1902, no. 824; 30H. 49, Affaires du Sud-Oranais, O'Connor to Gov. Gen., Oct. 4, 1903, no. 114; AMG, Alg. 14, Sit. pol. 1902, Gov. Gen. to Min. War, March 4, 1902, no. 328; Gov. Gen. to Min. War, July 4, 1902, no. 716; Gov. Gen. to Min. War, Aug. 5, 1902, no. 850; Saint-René Taillandier, *Origines*, p. 68.

50. In April 1902 the *makhzan* asked the French government to cooperate in dispatching a new three hundred man garrison and a new *'amil* to Oran by sea and from there to Figuig by the railway. In return, the French obtained permission to supply the garrisons at Oujda and Figuig with military instructors. A military mission did go to Oujda but never to Figuig. The Moroccan garrison contingent, reduced to about 140 men, did not leave the port of Larache until May 1903. It arrived in Oran but then was diverted to Oujda to help against the rebellion of Abu Himara. The new *'amil* and perhaps a few dozen troops eventually reached Figuig. AMG, Maroc C12, MM 1902, Burckhardt to Min. War, April 30, 1902, no. 271; *Doc. Dip.*, 1, 31, 44-7, 59, 60, 63, 64, 89-92; Saint-René Taillandier, *Origines*, pp. 70-81, 124, 133, 134, 138.

51. AMG, Alg. 15, Correspondance 1903, Gov. Gen. to Min. of Foreign Affairs, May 31, 1903, nos. 73885 and 73975.

52. 'Algérie: Au Figuig,' *Af. Fr.* (July 1903), pp. 219, 220; René Pinon, *L'Empire de la Mediterranée* (Paris, 1904), p. 252; Interview no. 28.

53. AMG, Alg. 15, Correspondance 1903, Jonnart to Min. War, June 16, 1903, no. 28; 'Algérie: Au Figuig,' pp. 220, 221.

54. AMG, Alg. 16, Sit. pol. 1904, Jonnart to Min. War, March 24, 1904, no. 633.

55. Trout, *Morocco's Saharan Frontiers*, p. 54.

56. AMG, Alg. 14, Sud-Oranais 1900, Risbourg to Com. 19th Corps, June 29, 1900, no. 552; Sit. pol. 1901, Révoil to Min. War, July 3, 1901, no. 1247.

57. A. La Chatelier, 'al-Hanafi'; Interviews no. 10 and 23.

58. AMG, Alg. 15, Correspondance 1903, Jonnart to Min. War, Aug. 16, 1903, no. 1575.

59. AMG, Alg. 14, Sit. pol. 1901, Susbielle, 'Rapport hebdomadaire de l'annexe d'Igli,' March 30 – April 5, 1901.

60. AMG, Maroc C12, MM 1902, Burckhardt to Min. War, May 31, 1902, no. 274.

61. AMG, Alg. 15, Taghit, Susbielle, 'Rapport sur les opérations autour de Taghit,' Aug. 25, 1903.

62. AMG, Alg. 15, Taghit, Susbielle, 'Rapport sur les opérations autour de Taghit,' Aug. 25, 1903; El-Moungar, Jonnart to President of the Council, Sept.11, 1903; Correspondance 1903, Jonnart to Min. War, Sept. 4, 1903, no. 1731; AGGA, 22H. 37, Défense de Taghit, O'Connor to Com. 19th Corps, Sept. 7, 1903, no. 69; Si Brahim to Susbielle, Aug. 26, 1903 (trans. from Arabic); 'L'Attaque de Taghit,' *Revue de Paris*, 10 (Oct. 15, 1903), pp. 699-714; Blaudin de Thé, *Historique des compagnies méharistes* (Algiers, 1955), pp. 21, 22.

7 RESISTANCE AND THE COMMERCIAL SHIFT, 1903-1907

In the fall of 1903 following the battle of Taghit the French army crossed the Jebel Béchar and proceeded to take control of the territory between the Zousfana and the lower Guir. During the ensuing months, the veteran *mujahidin* of the Ziz valley remained immobile, and the level of trade between there and the French posts picked up dramatically, suggesting altogether that the era of resistance in the Southeast was already drawing to a close. The market place and the steam engine appeared to be replacing the rifle and the cannon as the primary instruments of French conquest and control. At the same time, however, the régime of Mawlay 'Abd al-'Aziz continued to totter under the weight of European pressures and internal upheaval. While many in the Southeast wished to take advantage of French trade and to forego further Taghits, the population was by no means isolated from the momentous events occurring on the wider diplomatic front or from the rising tide of opposition throughout Morocco to both French penetration and Sharifian compromise.

'The Lyautey Method'

Following the battles of Taghit and El Moungar, the French army, the Algerian settlers, and the 'colonial party' immediately raised an outcry against the policy of military restraint along the frontier which allowed such banditry and lawlessness to go unchecked. Amid the clamor for action, Governor-General Jonnart secured the appointment of General Louis-Hubert-Gonsalve Lyautey as Commander of the Subdivision of Aïn Sefra. Lyautey had earned something of a reputation as a colonial soldier in both Tonkin and Madagascar, and Jonnart was apparently convinced that he could bring order to the frontier zone once and for all without undertaking an expensive, heavy-handed, diplomatically harrowing campaign. Jonnart went so far as to give him almost complete freedom of action, which meant that Lyautey communicated directly with the Governor-General and the Minister of War, rather than going through the chain of command in the Division of Oran and the Nineteenth Corps.[1]

Lyautey served as Commander of the Subdivision from 1903 to 1906, then as Commander of the Division of Oran until 1910. He arrived at Aïn Sefra having had no firsthand experience dealing with either a Muslim or a desert-dwelling population. During his first months on the frontier, he had to rely heavily on the advice of Native Affairs officers who were veterans to the region.[2] But as little as Lyautey knew about either the land or the people, he lost no time in renouncing the narrow, cautious military objectives of his predecessors. In both Tonkin and Madagascar he had served under General Joseph Galliéni and had become an ardent advocate of his progressive ideas about colonial warfare. Like Galliéni, he regarded the pacification of 'native' populations less as a problem of battle strategy than one of political control leading eventually to economic and social development. By the time he reached Aïn Sefra he was not only a soldier but a colonial theorist as well. The Algero-Moroccan frontier was to be a proving ground for his hypotheses about the nature of 'native' societies and the best methods of bringing them under control with a minimum of force. In other words, when he took over his command, he already had in mind a grand, though vague scheme of political and administrative engineering.

His approach to desert warfare represented a dramatic departure from the methods of the previous commanders. They had limited their effective occupation of the Mountains of the Ksour and the Zousfana-Saoura valley to a small circle of territory around each post. Convoys had to move from one post to another under heavily armed escort. Raiding parties, therefore, were free to organize within a short distance of the occupied areas and to strike at their convenience without fear of being pursued very far. In reorganizing the military system Lyautey had two fundamental objectives. One was to make French military power so evident that hostile groups would come to terms without fighting. The other was to combat them on their own terms. He rejected the 'decisive battle' strategy by which continental wars were fought in favor of unhurried and thorough pacification of one block of territory after another, using political techniques as much as military.[3]

The key component in his pacification force were the Saharan Companies: lightly armed, mounted units equipped to pursue the enemy with lightning speed over long distances. The first Saharan Company, composed entirely of locally recruited tribesmen, was formed in Touat in 1902. Its initial purpose was to solve the problem of transporting large, expensive convoys of troops from Algerian bases to the central Sahara. The men in the unit were responsible for their own mounts and maintenance, cutting down the number of supply caravans as well. Two Companies were formed in the frontier zone in the spring of 1904. One was stationed at Beni Abbès in the Saoura valley and mounted on *meharis*, or riding camels. The other operated from the post of Colomb-Béchar, which was established adjacent to the *qsar* of Béchar in October 1903. This Company used

horses, since the terrain permitted it. Both units were put to work patrol-
ling in a wide radius around their bases.

Backing up the Saharan Companies were the mounted *tirailleurs* and
spahis of the Algerian army. Lyautey streamlined these units for desert
duty, removing cumbersome uniforms used in the north and making the
personnel responsible for their own maintenance. Their increased mobility prepared them to move in quickly in support of the Saharan Companies. The third line in the frontier forces were mounted troops of the
Foreign Legion. They served as reserve mobile units and were also to be
counted on in case of any disloyalty among the all-Muslim units. Finally,
European regulars formed the garrisons of the posts and had charge of
sections of machine guns and 75 and 80 millimeter artillery. Lyautey
reduced somewhat the number of posts in the region but increased the size
of the remaining ones.[4]

Since Lyautey's troops were equipped with rapid firing Lebel rifles,
machine guns, cannons, plenty of ammunition, and a rapid logistical
system, they had a vast technological superiority over their adversaries
whenever a fight broke out. There is no doubt that Lyautey achieved the
conquest of southeastern Morocco as quickly and as efficiently as he did
largely because of his great military advantage. In his reports and writings
he made little of this point but stressed, rather, the nonmilitary methods
he applied to the job of pacification and control. He conceived of his posts
as 'centers of attraction' rather than as 'poles of repulsion,' which meant
that he aimed primarily to attempt to convince hostile groups and their
leaders to come to terms by offering them amnesties, monetary subsidies,
medical care, and, most important of all, new commercial opportunities.
To test his theories of 'pénétration pacifique' he relied on the aid of an
elite corps of young officers of the Service de Renseignements, previously
known as the Bureau des Affaires Indigènes, and before that as the Bureau
Arabe. These men, all devoted disciples of the Lyautey Method, were
specially trained to lead the Muslim army units, to negotiate the submission of tribal leaders, to set up local administrations and markets, and in
general to deal directly with the Muslim population. They either spoke
Arabic themselves or had an interpreter close at hand. They devoted much
of their time to gathering intelligence information concerning resistance
activities and political conditions in the regions west of the occupied zone.
They also collected and organized a great deal of data on social and political institutions among the unsubmitted tribes and oasis communities. Much
of the ethnographic material written during this period was the work of
Lyautey's men.[5]

Jonnart chose Lyautey not only because of his soldierly qualities but also because he had the audacity to put the army on the offensive once again and the shrewdness to get away with it before the eyes of the foreign ministry. The European community in Algeria and some of the officers in the Division of Oran favored a 'tribal policy' along the frontier, whereby the army would ignore the sultan and his local representatives and deal with the tribes and oases as independent political entities. Lyautey upheld Delcassé's '*makhzan* policy' but for different reasons than the Foreign Minister had in mind:

> I believe that one must see in the Franco-Moroccan accord and in the fiction of a mixed police force something very flexible and very broad which will permit us to cover ourselves every time we need to, to take action in places which would be inaccessible to us without this accord, to make use of agents who, without it, would escape us; it is in this spirit that I ask to be authorized to apply it.[6]

Lyautey adhered faithfully to the formalities set forth in the accords by keeping in regular touch with the *makhzan* governor at Figuig (and after 1906 with the Moroccan commissioner at Oujda) concerning French military movements in order to maintain the appearance of joint action. He also agreed to hold military activity within the limits set by the foreign ministry. He kept up constant pressure on the government, however, to authorize probes deeper into territory recognized by the accords as Moroccan. His arguments were not new in the history of colonial warfare: no occupied zone could be made absolutely secure without dispatching patrols and building posts further afield to protect it. Once a point was occupied, retreat was unthinkable since any sign of weakness would be a great encouragement to the forces of resistance. From 1903 to 1912 relations between the army and the foreign ministry amounted to a continual tug of war over the limits of westward expansion. Jonnart invariably sided with the army.

The most notorious incident was Lyautey's unauthorized occupation in June 1904 of Ras el-Aïn, a watering place on the Moroccan high plains used by the Bani Gil. Lyautey intended to establish a post and market there in order to bring about the submission of the Bani Gil, who had been raiding Algerian territory for many years, and to check the influence of Abu 'Amama. Unexpectedly, the foreign ministry countermanded the operation, fearing that such a thrust might prompt Germany's intervention and damage French influence with Mawlay 'Abd al-'Aziz. The sultan did protest the action, even though Lyautey claimed to have the authorization of the Moroccan commissioner at Oujda. Lyautey used dilatory tactics

to keep his troops in position and with the help of Jonnart got the government to approve the occupation in October. The name of the post was
changed to Berguent, since Ras el-Aïn was designated as a Moroccan point
in the 1902 Accords. This affair not only brought to the surface deep-
seated conflict between Lyautey and the Quai d'Orsay over frontier policy,
but set the pattern of conquest for the following eight years. Once the
government recognized the right of the army to use the Accords as an
umbrella to cover occupation of Moroccan territory, justification could
readily be found for absorbing more and more of it.[7]

Lyautey clearly had no precise nor ultimate territorial objective in
penetrating deeper into Morocco. During his first months on the frontier,
he aimed to occupy Tafilalt and extend the railroad there as quickly as
possible. At the time, many French expansionists were talking less of building a railway across the central Sahara and more of pushing it westward
to the Atlantic coast as a way of cutting off Morocco from the south.[8]
By the fall of 1904, however, Lyautey decided that the population of
Tafilalt was too large and too hostile to be brought to terms by any means
other than a massive, costly, logistically hazardous campaign. He determined instead to consolidate French control along the entire length of the
frontier from the Mediterranean to the Wad Saoura and to advance gradually, clearing the way for the construction of both northern and southern
rail lines which would one day facilitate the conquest of all of Morocco.[9]
Therefore, the army continued to press forward because Lyautey wanted
to occupy as much Moroccan territory as possible before France declared
a protectorate and because each modest territorial advance automatically
required a succeeding one in order to safeguard the first.

Lyautey's basic strategy along the southern frontier was to create an
advance line of posts and 'circles of action' to protect the railroad and the
installations in the Mountains of Ksour and the Zousfana-Saoura valley.
In October 1903 he occupied Béchar, calling it Colomb (later, Colomb-
Béchar) to circumvent the provision of the 1902 Accords which made
Béchar a Moroccan village.[10] The other advance posts subsequently established were Forthassa Gharbia west of the Jebel Beni Smir (March 1904),
Berguent on the central high plains (June 1904), and Talzaza about
forty-five miles north of Colomb-Béchar (April 1905). The first two posts
were used mainly to secure the submission of the Bani Gil, a task largely
completed with little fighting by the end of 1904. In October of that year
the railroad was opened between Beni Ounif and Ben Zireg, a point
located in a pass between the Jebel Antar and the northern end of the
Jebel Béchar. From there it was extended southwestward to Colomb-
Béchar, where it arrived in July 1905. Further south, Beni Abbès became

the headquarters from which one of the Saharan Companies ranged over a wide area west of the Wad Saoura. Beginning in 1904 patrols visited the oasis of Tabelbala quite frequently and in conjunction with the Saharan Companies of Touat circulated in the Erg Iguidi.[11]

Once Lyautey's forces were established at Colomb-Béchar, Governor-General Jonnart undertook a major reorganization of the Subdivision of Aïn Sefra. Taghit, previously the center of a *cercle*, was reduced to a simple post, and a new *cercle* was created with headquarters at Colomb-Béchar. Beni Ounif, replacing Djenan ed-Dar, became the center of an annex directly responsible to the Subdivision. Militarily, the changes meant that Colomb-Béchar was to be the new center of action, not a peripheral post dependent on Taghit. Politically, they were tantamount to a declaration that both Beni Ounif and Colomb-Béchar were henceforth part of Algeria, not Morocco. The government in Paris, probably cautious about adverse reaction from the sultan, did not approve the changes until August 1905.[12]

Lyautey and his fellow officers acted under the general assumption of the times that just and benevolent sentiments motivated colonial expansion. His program of 'peaceful penetration' naturally rested on the conviction that the population by and large wanted the progressive changes he was prepared to introduce. Though he denied the existence of any shred of *makhzan* authority in the Southeast, he eagerly endorsed the notion that the *makhzan* spoke for the population of the region when it signed the agreements of 1901-2.

Given these assumptions, the army could only view resistance as anomalous and generally unpopular. Its explanation of it centered on three points: the endemic political anarchy of the tribes, the local misapprehension of French aims, and the influence of intransigent 'agitators.' Most of the incessant raiding against posts, convoys, and pacified tribes was denounced as professional banditry which the absence of any Moroccan authority in the territory permitted to go unchecked. The army attributed most other resistance, including the *harka* of 1903, to ignorant fears of the army's intentions or to the work of conspirators who wished to subvert France's mission for reasons of personal gain or religious fanaticism. The list of agents provocateurs included *makhzan* officials who represented anti-French elements within the government, as well as sufi saints, *shurfa*, and members of Muslim brotherhoods, both local men and outsiders, who were attempting to protect personal power and influence through xenophobia. The army categorically rejected the notion that people of the region who took part in resistance acted out of any sense of loyalty or attachment to the 'Alawi dynasty or to Morocco as a whole.

The army's conception of the Muslim response to its offensive, whether it was resistance or resignation, rested on the assumptions of paternalism and cultural and racial arrogance that dominated European thought in the decades before World War One. The colonialist literature and journalism of the period usually accepted these assumptions as well. As a result, Europeans habitually reported the conquest of southeastern Morocco as an event in their own history, disregarding the personal and collective crises of the conquered.

The Figuig Protectorate

After the shelling of Zenaga, Figuig quickly settled into a new relationship with the French already having the essential characteristics of the protectorate that was to be formalized nine years later. The *makhzan* governorship remained intact, and *'amil-s* appointed in Fez came and went. The seven *qsar-s* continued as before to discharge their own internal affairs, and no oasis-wide administration was erected. Yet Lyautey made it quite clear that the preservation of peace in and around the oasis was to be the responsibility of the Native Affairs bureau and garrison at Beni Ounif. The population was no longer free either to take part in the defense of Morocco or to settle its inter-village conflicts through feuding.

The *makhzan* representatives serving in Figuig had always been impotent to impose central authority, and now they were helpless to prevent the French army from doing it for them. They had no significant influence over either internal politics or the actions of the Native Affairs office in Beni Ounif. They were not actually agents of the French (as their successors would be after 1912), but they had no solid basis of support either in Figuig or in Fez for taking energetic initiatives of their own. Lyautey was willing to pay them the deference prescribed by the formalities of the accords as long as they did not get in the way of pacification or take their position as *makhzan* officials too seriously. The most they could do, beyond tagging along with the French commissioner, was to offer spirited gestures of defiance from time to time. In January 1904, for example, the assistant to the *'amil* served as intermediary in peace talks at Aïn Sefra between the French and the Bani Gil. The man became so assertive in his efforts to represent the Bani Gil (a Moroccan tribe by the Treaty of 1845) and to drive a hard bargain with the French that Lyautey had him put out of the meeting.[13] Later that year *'amil* Si Muhammad ibn Majbud perturbed Lyautey by selling official *makhzan* seals, which he had made locally, to Bani Gil leaders other than the ones the French had been negotiating with. According to the army, he was attempting to undermine their influence among the tribe and also to raise money for himself from the price of the seals.[14]

The Moroccan garrison stationed in Figuig as part of the accords appears to have been of almost no use to either the 'amil or the French. The contingent of 102 troops which arrived in October 1904 was made up mainly of teenage boys and old men recruited in Tangier.[15] Similar replacements may have been sent a few times during succeeding years. The soldiers had little training or discipline and no desire to take regular orders from the 'amil. The inhabitants wanted nothing to do with them, except perhaps to purchase their rifles. Those who did not desert spent most of their time holed up in al-Oudaghir, emerging occasionally to raid gardens or find ways to harass the population. In May 1906, for example, the notables of Zenaga sent a letter of complaint to the sultan after a group of soldiers killed a man in the market place.[16] On more than one occasion members of the garrison went to Beni Ounif to ask the French to feed them or to complain that their pay, which was sent by the railroad, never arrived before they were on the point of starvation.[17] It is clear that during the final years of Morocco's independence the state of chronic up-heaval made the recruitment of well-trained soldiers for an outpost such as Figuig an impossible order. Showing little sympathy for the makhzan's token effort, Lyautey continually ridiculed the garrison, at one point likening it to a group of 'wretched players recruited for a gala evening in a bad provincial theatre.'[18]

When Lyautey arrived on the frontier, the military submission of Figuig was already achieved. Therefore, he and his lieutenants were able to pro-ceed at once to a program of social and economic action designed to ensure army surveillance over political activities within the oasis and to increase the population's dependence on Beni Ounif. In line with this plan an infirmary was constructed there and its services offered to Moroccans. In 1905 French doctors began visiting Figuig to perform vaccinations.[19] Lyautey and his men toured the oasis on occasion and dined with the 'amil.

By far the most important facet of the program was the encouragement of trade across the frontier. The Native Affairs bureau constructed a market at Beni Ounif which became the most active suq in the region after the railroad reached there in the spring of 1903. Agents of French and Algerian trading houses began setting up shops and residences there and selling imported goods to the population of the surrounding area. Bani Gil, Dawi Mani', and Awlad Jarir nomads visited the market in large numbers, buying tea, coffee, sugar, textiles, and various manufactures in return for sheep, wool, grain, and dates. Caravans also began arriving from Tafilalt in much greater numbers than had ever gone to Aïn Sefra. At the end of the

fourth quarter of 1904, twenty-six Algerian firms were operating in Beni
Ounif to the amount of 1,300,000 francs in total trade. During 1904,
10,600 men and 27,047 camels passed through the center, 20,350 sheep
were traded.[20]

All the inhabitants of Figuig, and especially the Zenagans, lost no time
in adjusting to the post-bombardment conditions and flocking into the
market. The trade items they offered included dates, fruits, vegetables,
and locally made woolen garments. These goods were either exported to
Algeria and beyond or consumed by the military and railway personnel at
the various posts in the area. Although no figures are available on the number of people from each qsar who visited the market, the French authorities estimated that about three hundred people a day made the short walk
from the oasis.[21]

The commercial importance of Figuig itself grew along with that of
Beni Ounif. Merchants took loads of imports back to the oasis and sold
them in the qsar shops. Between April and June of 1904 about 170 tons
of grain, foodstuffs, and merchandise arrived at Beni Ounif, consigned
directly to Figuig traders. Al-Oudaghir may well have benefited most from
this exchange, since it had always been Figuig's major entrepôt, and an
exceptionally high percentage of its residents were professional merchants.[22] Figuig also made profits from commerce with Moroccans from
further west, perhaps including Berbers from the upper Guir and Ziz
valley regions, who were unwilling to mingle with the French at Beni
Ounif. Most of the goods they brought in, especially sheep and wool,
eventually reached Beni Ounif anyway. Lyautey pointed out that the
willingness of Moroccan tribes to trade with the French indirectly by way
of Figuig was an excellent reason for not occupying the oasis.[23]

The prosperity of Beni Ounif declined considerably after the railroad
was extended on to Ben Zireg (February 1904) and then to Colomb-
Béchar (July 1905). The greatest volume of trade with Moroccan nomads
and with Tafilalt tended to follow the railhead, so that the creation of the
market at Colomb-Béchar eclipsed the other markets back up the line.
Still, local exchange between Figuig and Beni Ounif continued to be brisk.
In April 1906 the notables and merchants of Zenaga approved without
reserve the project to build a carriage road between Beni Ounif and the
edge of the oasis.[24] The same year European tourists, assured that marauders and bandits were a thing of the past, received an invitation from the
army to visit Figuig while on holiday in the desert![25]

Thus Figuig preceded Oujda and Casablanca as a territorial beachhead
in France's drive to take possession of Morocco. Although the people of
the oasis became only 'informal' subjects of France following the bombard-

ment, they found themselves from that time on falling further and further behind the front lines of conquest and therefore increasingly isolated from the forces of popular resistance.

Peacemaking and Trade in the Dawi Mani' Heartland

In the fall of 1903 Lyautey ordered the establishment of a new post near Béchar to serve as the hub of a wide military zone and the nerve center for political and economic warfare against the unsubmitted Dawi Mani' and Awlad Jarir. From Colomb-Béchar the Saharan Companies began to fan out in all directions in order to track down raiding parties and demonstrate to the two tribes, as well as to the resistance leaders in Tafilalt, that the Army of Africa had come to stay. In January 1904 the first reconnaissance patrol visited the Guir flood plain. Lyautey also ordered construction of a market at Colomb-Béchar and sent out encourgement to Jewish merchants of Tafilalt to set up shop there.[26] In October 1905 the railway between Colomb-Béchar and Beni Ounif went into service. By the fall of 1906 diplomatic reservations were removed, permitting patrols to cross the Guir and circulate on the Hammada. Late in 1907 a small post was established on the Guir plain.[27]

The occupation of the Guir-Zousfana basin obliged every tent of the Dawi Mani' and the Awlad Jarir to recalculate the state of its political relations both with the French and with its neighbors in Tafilalt. The options of resistance or continued isolation in and around Tafilalt must have appeared much less feasible following the defeat of the *harka* at Taghit. Both tribes were undoubtedly still demoralized by that failure when the French began building Colomb-Béchar. After Lyautey's mobile patrols began operating from there, small-scale raids, much less mass *harka-s*, became extremely risky operations.

Changes in the economic prospects for the two tribes weighed heavily on the side of peace. With the creation of Colomb-Béchar the French were in a position to control the Guir flood plain. An interdiction on the planting and harvest of grain there would have severe economic consequences for most of the Dawi Mani'. In 1904 the tribe needed access to its fields more urgently than usual because rain fell there in May after a three-year dry spell.[28] The Awlad Jarir, who had been able to withdraw from the Zousfana valley with relatively little strain on their economy, could ill afford to lose a single harvest from the extensive palm groves they owned in Béchar and the vicinity. On the positive side were the tantalizing new commercial opportunities the French occupation heralded. The arrival of the railroad at Beni Ounif in 1903 led to a great increase in the influx of European goods into the Southeast. By coming to terms with the French the Dawi Mani' could reassume their dominant position as carriers on the Figuig-Tafilalt route, only now they would pick up their loads as far west as the rail cars brought them.

Between 1904 and 1908 almost all the Dawi Mani', as represented by their leaders, received the *aman* from the French and established fairly regular contact with the Native Affairs officers at Colomb-Béchar. The French command there estimated that the first meeting with thirty leaders in January 1904 represented establishing contact with about 1,250 tents, with 300 previously submitted at Taghit, and 450 still in Tafilalt.[29] All of the tents which made peace in 1904 and after were given a special political status enabling them to circulate more freely between the Guir and Tafilalt. Rather than actually submitting to French authority they became *ralliés*, a term meaning 'the rallied ones,' 'allies,' or 'partisans.' That is, their *qa'id-s* were not invested by the French but only approved, maintaining the fiction of independence which would supposedly allow them to go to Tafilalt to tend their palms or to trade without incurring the hostility of the Ait Khabbash and the other resistance elements.[30] The independent Dawi Mani' generally agreed that the scheme would work, since Qa'id Ay'ish wuld Musa, the Awlad abu 'Anan leader who had led most of the *khums* in a close alliance with the Ait Khabbash until 1904, negotiated with the French and accepted *rallié* status for his followers. Actually, he sent one of his nephews to Colomb-Béchar rather than go himself, no doubt seeing the advantages of keeping a foot in both camps until the political situation became more certain.[31] It is very likely that by remaining in Tafilalt he could continue to make protests of loyalty to the Ait Khabbash and even return wholeheartedly to the resistance effort if it managed to turn back the French advance.

The Awlad Jarir, who had been especially active in raids against the French on the Zousfana, were divided in their response to the new offensive. During the expedition to Béchar in June 1903, almost the entire tribe scattered to the west despite the efforts of Si Brahim to arrange talks.[32] When none of the tents came back after Béchar was occupied, the French confiscated the tribe's date crop. Then they informed the leaders by emissary that unless they came to terms all their property there would be sequestered. Within several weeks, tents of the Mafalha, the sub-tribe possessing most of the palms at Béchar, began to turn up at the post. Most of the Mafalha made formal submission during the following few months, in some cases after making contact through Si Brahim. These tents were given *soumis* status and required to remain in the vicinity of Colomb-Béchar, even though some of them possessed palms in Tafilalt.[33]

In contrast, almost all the tents of the 'Asasa, the other major section, remained in the west. Since most of them had no palms at Béchar, the French could not apply economic pressures. In fact, many of the 'Asasa were known to make their regular living by stealing camels, so they were hardly advised to pitch their tents near the French posts. Some of them were long-time followers of Abu 'Amama and went north with him in 1904. Most of them allied with the Ait Khabbash and continued sporadic raids into the French controlled zone.[34]

The Dawi Mani' and Awlad Jarir who did make peace with the French began at once to cash in on the new trade brought by the railroad and Lyautey's markets. As in the past, the Dawi Mani' operated two kinds of trading enterprises. In the one case they traded for their own account, buying directly from the merchants at the French posts and selling at a profit at Abou Am. They also exported goods from Tafilalt in the same way. In the other case they rented their services as carriers to Muslim or Jewish merchants at Abou Am, receiving a negotiated sum for each camel load (estimates run from eighteen to eighty francs, depending on the nature and weight of the load). Caravans ranged in size from ten to several dozen beasts.[35] Sometimes the Dawi Mani' carriers handled the buying and selling at Colomb-Béchar or Beni Ounif on behalf of Filali traders. At other times they worked through agents which a few of the most important Filali merchants sent to reside at Colomb-Béchar.[36]

The most important commodity exported from Tafilalt to the railhead was dates in four or more varieties. Other products included *filali* leather, sheep and goats (mainly for the consumption of the French garrisons), tobacco, babouches (slippers made in Tafilalt), woolen burnous, and silk products (both imported from Fez). The major exports from the French markets were, of course, tea, coffee, sugar, cotton textiles, and various manufactures.[37]

Both the Dawi Mani' and the merchants made substantial profits on sales at both ends of the trade route. In 1905-6, for example, a load of dates purchased at Abou Am for twelve or thirteen francs sold at Colomb-Béchar or Beni Ounif for twenty to thirty francs. Sheep bought in Tafilalt for twelve to fifteen francs sold at the French posts for fifteen to twenty francs. Conversely, sugar purchased at thirty-five francs the quintal (one hundred kilograms) sold in Tafilalt for seventy to ninety francs.[38] Each carrier profited in proportion to the number of transport camels he could put into service. Some men reportedly invested their carrying fees in the expansion of their transport herds from ten to as many as eighty camels.[39]

Throughout 1904 and 1905, then, most of the Dawi Mani' who had not yet made formal submission were nonetheless moving toward political accommodation with the French in order to preserve their resources in the

Guir basin and expand their trade. But they still had to reckon with the militants of Tafilalt, who, despite the defeat at Taghit in 1903, were gaining broad support for a new counteroffensive. Caught between the French army on one side and the Ait Khabbash and their allies on the other, the Dawi Mani' were finally forced in 1906 to decide between the two.

The Abortive Resistance of 1906

The frustrated attack on Taghit produced such discouragement in the Ziz valley that the population watched passively while the French occupied the Guir-Zousfana basin and entered into negotiations with most of the Dawi Mani'. The al-Hanafi family, whose *baraka* proved to be less potent than was believed, quickly faded into the background. In September 1904 Mawlay Mustafa attempted to assemble another *harka*, but he failed to attract much support.[40] The display of French power at Taghit was sufficient to raise doubts in the minds of many about the wisdom of further large-scale resistance. In December 1903 a report reached Beni Abbès that representatives from the Ait Khabbash, other Ait 'Atta *taqbilt-s*, the local Ait Yafalman tribes, the Bani Gil, and a few other groups had held a council in the desert south of Tafilalt to discuss the alternatives to war.[41] Apparently the consensus of opinion was to remain hostile since no white flags were raised in subsequent months. Still, this meeting was an early sign that negotiations were not out of the question even for the bellicose tribes of the west.

In Tafilalt the atmosphere of crisis subsided to one of caution and uneasy tension during 1904 and 1905, while Lyautey consolidated his control over the lands of the Dawi Mani', Awlad Jarir, and Bani Gil and built his markets at Beni Ounif and Colomb-Béchar. Then, early in 1906 the advocates of resistance began to take center stage once again, calling for another mass *harka* and an embargo on trade with the French posts. This resurgence of militancy was the result of both country-wide and local developments.

From 1904 through to 1906 were years of smoldering discontent throughout Morocco. Economic dislocation gripped the country, and people of both town and tribe were becoming more acutely aware of the ultimate aims of France's program of 'peaceful penetration.' The French government's arrangement with Great Britain to exchange Egypt for Morocco, its attempts to impose a highly restrictive reform program on the *makhzan*, and, finally, its diplomatic victory over Germany at the conference of Algeciras convinced much of the population that the country had been sold out by both the other European powers and Mawlay 'Abd al-'Aziz.

During 1905, the people of the Southeast shared the country-wide expectancy over Germany's moves to intervene against France. The Aïn Sefra command even noted a sudden coolness among the groups under its control or surveillance. Following Kaiser Wilhelm's visit to Tangier in March, for example, the army reported that Moroccans in Figuig and vicinity who had previously shown a friendly and cooperative attitude were being evasive and reserved.[42] During the same period, 'amil Si Muhammad ibn Majbud became uncharacteristically hostile, encouraging the inhabitants of Figuig to cut off relations with the French and making public declarations about German intentions to safeguard Moroccan independence. Since anti-French elements in the *makhzan* were becoming increasingly outspoken, it is very likely that Majbud was receiving orders from Fez to agitate for a resurgence of resistance along the frontier.[43]

The news that the conference of Algeciras only opened the way for much greater French influence over the country's affairs produced resignation in Figuig and other submitted areas, but a hardening of resistance sentiment almost everywhere else in the country. During the first half of 1906 pro-German *makhzan* officials tried vainly to persuade the sultan to reject the Act of Algeciras. When he signed it on June 18, he effectively set in motion a vigorous drive to find a candidate who would claim the throne on a platform of *jihad*. In July a son of Mawlay Rashid arrived in Tafilalt from Fez and began at once to call for a massive assault on Colomb-Béchar.[44] In short, the call for a new mass movement was in part a response to events occurring outside the Southeast.

On the local level France's commercial penetration of Tafilalt also aroused resistance spirit, partly because a significant portion of the population was all too willing to tie the Ziz valley economically to the French railroad. The advocates of closer trade relations could cite a number of advantages. Filali merchants could import European merchandise from the French markets much less expensively than from Fez, even though the traveling distance, especially to Beni Ounif, was still great. The absence of duties at the Algerian ports, cheap rail transportation to the south, and the stability of the franc all combined to keep the price of goods at the new markets much lower than they were in Fez or Marrakech. Since the Dawi Mani' themselves carried virtually all the trade between Tafilalt and the railhead, no *zattata* was charged, which on the trans-Atlas routes raised prices still higher. Conversely, Filali dates, leather, livestock, and woolens found a ready market at the French centers, either for export or for local consumption. Moreover, the French paid in francs (though they may have accepted Moroccan currencies), relieving to some extent the chronic shortage of hard currency in Abou Am.[45] Finally, the French *suq-s* were

remarkably peaceful, the Native Affairs officers representing a more
efficient and nonpartisan market authority than Abou Am had probably
ever known. In May 1906 James McLeod, the British Vice-Consul at Fez,
wrote:

> . . . I would observe that dates from Tafilet have, during last autumn,
> for the first time, been exported at Oran, having reached that port by
> the Algeria Sahara railway from Béchar, Beni Ounif and Aïn Sefra.
> Some of these lots are stated to have been sent to the United States
> of America, and some to India, but to which ports in those countries I
> have not been able to learn, — for the reason that the consigners of
> those parcels were either Tafilet or Oran, and not Fez merchants.
> The bulk of the Oran shipment went, however, I am told to London.
> . . . the agent here of the (French) Compagnie Marocaine says that
> their Beni Ounif branch-house bought lots there simultaneously with
> his buying of lots here. Both lots were shipped to London (Beni Ounif
> via Oran, and Fez via Tangier and Gibraltar) and the Fez lots yielded a
> net profit of only three percent, while those of Beni Ounif produced a
> net gain of fifty five percent, — the difference arising mostly from the
> enormous cost of transport from Tafilet to Fez and Fez to Tangier.[46]

In 1904 the number of Filali caravans going east increased considerably
over previous years. A number of Filali Jews moved into Colomb-Béchar
under Lyautey's encouragement and either became commercial agents for
other Jews remaining in Tafilalt or else opened retail shops.[47] As the
trade continued to grow in 1905-6, much of it fell into the hands of a few
prominent Muslim merchants, who had the capital to purchase imports
in much larger volume than the Jews or other modest traders. Muhammad
ibn Idris Tazi, the Fasi who had figured so outstandingly in the Fez-
Tafilalt trade, was the most important of these.[48] He, like every other
trader, was obviously feeling the pinch in his commercial relations with the
north. Early in 1906 he sent a representative to Colomb-Béchar to order
cotton and silk textiles from both English and French firms. It is almost
certain that Ibn Idris had already established credit with European manu-
facturers or exporters when he was buying all his merchandise through Fez.
Some of the Tazi family of Fez had Moroccan agents in England who purchased and shipped cotton goods. At least one member of the family,
Shaykh Si 'Abd al-Salam Tazi (who became Minister of Finance under
'Abd al-'Aziz), resided in Manchester for several years around the turn of
the century and also visited Paris and Lyon.[49] So Ibn Idris's agent at
Colomb-Béchar could order large shipments quickly and without working

through Algerian middlemen. In the summer of 1906, for example, Ibn Idris contracted with a London firm to send him all the blue cotton 'guinea' cloth they produced. In July the Dawi Mani' carried 150,000 francs worth of it to Tafilalt. Because of the low prices and large volume, Ibn Idris very quickly became the most successful merchant in the oasis. His market included not only the Ziz valley but also the Dra area, where the populations could no longer count on being supplied from Marrakech. He had not previously been in the export business, but now part of his capital was used to buy Filali products for shipment to the railhead. He bought wool, not at the *suq*, but directly from the sheepherders, thus undercutting traders and retailers of more modest means.[50]

As the Dawi Mani' carriers and merchants like Ibn Idris became more and more prosperous, other elements in Tafilalt demanded that all trade with the French be prohibited. The Ait Khabbash, and a portion of the sedentary population, opposed the trade on political grounds and accused the Dawi Mani' of conspiring to lead the French to the banks of the Ziz. Other merchants, especially a large number of *shurfa* who had longstanding commercial relations with the northern cities, objected to the trans-Hammada trade because it drastically undercut their own. After 'Abd al-'Aziz came to power, the *makhzan* gradually lost control of more and more of the countryside, including territory through which the major internal trade arteries passed, notably the Fez-Tafilalt route. Consequently, tribes imposed higher *zattata* rates and attacked caravans more frequently. Since the sultan was unable to do anything to remedy the critical fiscal situation, prices continued to fluctuate within a trend of soaring inflation. Under these conditions, there can be little doubt that by 1903 the price of imports at Abou Am was extremely high and that the export of dates and leather to Fez languished. The merchants who preserved their ties with the north were clearly in a plight. However, many of them, especially the *shurfa*, were unwilling politically or unable financially to shift to the trans-Hammada trade, which might have saved their business.[51]

Early in 1906 the anti-trade forces, with the acquiescence of Mawlay Rashid, succeeded in imposing a ban on traffic with Colomb-Béchar. The Filali merchants having dealings there were ordered to return to Tafilalt with all their merchandise, which they did. In July commercial activity at Colomb-Béchar plummeted.[52] Ibn Idris was actually expelled from Abou Am and had to pay a heavy sum to ensure his safe conduct out of the oasis. Perhaps for him it was a blessing in disguise. He proceeded to Colomb-Béchar, settled down, and lived there as a prosperous merchant until his death about 1925.[53]

Many Dawi Mani' caravaners did not escape the crisis so easily. Mawlay

Rashid, who was in this case speaking for the anti-trade group rather than the *makhzan*, informed them that they had to give up all trade with the French and return permanently to Tafilalt or else suffer the confiscation or destruction of their palm groves in Ghorfa district.[54]

The tribesmen owning date palms, especially men of the Awlad abu 'Anan, were placed in an acutely equivocal position by this development, since their date resources were no less important to them than their grain fields on the Guir. On top of that the French command decided in May 1906 to require all the Dawi Mani' in the Guir area to give up their ambiguous *rallié* status and make formal submission. The Commandant of the Cercle of Colomb-Béchar met with a delegation of Dawi Mani' leaders on the Guir plain and offered them six months in which to either submit to French authority or leave the area altogether in accordance with the Protocol of 1901. The French officers knew very well that the latter alternative was an impossible one.[55]

The portion of the tribe caught in this vice spent the remainder of the year sending delegations to both the French at Colomb-Béchar and to Mawlay Rashid and the resistance leaders in Tafilalt, attempting to gain both time and some sort of compromise.[56] In July Lyautey submitted a report on the conduct of the Awlad abu 'Anan leaders which revealed their attempts to keep a foot in both camps until the last possible moment:

> The Oulad Bou Anane have . . . decided to put to death any one of them who has dealings with the French *without having informed the jama'a* [italics mine]. This seems to indicate that they have not abandoned all hope of a settlement. But they would like to avoid giving the appearance that they initiated an act of submission and would rather appear to accept concessions offered by us. This is really a conception of the native mentality. Furthermore, in all their conversations they bring up the deadline which we accorded them. They seem to be undecided people, rejecting any definitive decision until the expiration of this deadline with the secret hope that *something* will happen between now and then.[57]

The trade embargo was but one manifestation of the drive to organize another mass resistance movement. This time the most prominent *mujahidin* were Mawlay Muhammad, a son of Mawlay Rashid; Mawlay Abu, the *khalifa*'s adjunct; and Sidi al-Bukhari, a *sharif* of the Ghorfa district who was selected by a drawing of straws to serve as war leader for a period of three months.[58] Mawlay Rashid himself still favored a policy of restraint, but the militants, especially Mawlay Abu, finally persuaded him to approve both the embargo and a new *harka*.[59] Support was also sought among the Atlas tribes in an effort to build a much greater pan-tribal movement than the leaders of the Taghit force had been able to do.[60] In August a delegation went to Telouèt in the High Atlas to ask Madani al-Glawi to join the cause.[61] The *shurfa* leaders knew that the military power of al-Glawi and the other grand *qa'id-s* was growing rapidly. They probably also knew that al-Glawi had given up on 'Abd al-'Aziz as early as 1903 and was preparing to throw his support to Mawlay 'Abd al-Hafid, the sultan's anti-French brother, as pretender to the throne. Al-Glawi almost certainly gave his blessing to the *harka*, even though he had tried to prevent one in 1901. But he did not go to Tafilalt nor send any contingents, probably because he was preoccupied with the more criticial task of bolstering his forces around Marrakech in anticipation of 'Abd al-Hafid's bid for power.

A massive march on Colomb-Béchar may have come very close to taking place, but some time in November the movement began to crumble. 'Abd al-'Aziz may have been partially responsible. He sent letters from Fez ordering the population to remain calm, and this action gave Mawlay Rashid enough courage to reverse his position and renounce the *harka*.[62] Both the sultan and the *khalifa* knew that if the assault failed and the French hoisted their flag over Tafilalt, a country-wide rising would almost certainly follow. On the other hand, the sultan's prestige had about reached its lowest ebb by 1906, so he could hardly have destroyed the movement with a single command. More likely, the local leaders simply could not solve the immense problems of organizing, supplying, and trans-porting their army before popular enthusiasm began to wane and contin-gents began to drift away.[63] The absence of strong leadership may also have been a factor, as it was in 1900. Though all the prominent leaders were *shurfa*, none of them was a reputed saint. The Filali *shurfa* commun-ity was extremely divisive, and the entire population of the oasis was split on the question of trade with the French. Whatever the combination of internal and external causes may have been, war preparations were aban-doned in December.

When the *harka* movement collapsed, the trade ban was also partially lifted, relieving the Dawi Mani' with economic interests on both sides of the Hammada of having to choose between Tafilalt and France. Tribal leaders negotiated an arrangement with Mawlay Rashid, permitting cara-vaners to import European merchandise as long as they bought and sold it on their own account. They could not trade or carry goods on behalf of professional merchants, nor could they export Filali products to the French markets.[64] About the same time Lyautey decided that he could

ensure good relations with the tribe by letting the *ralliés* retain their
ambiguous political status.[65] Because of these compromises, the Dawi
Mani‘, excepting the submitted tents, were able to remain for several
years ostensibly uncommitted to either Algeria or Morocco, retain their
resources, and engage in some degree in trade on both sides of the
Hammada.

Although part of the tribe survived the occupation of their heartland
without becoming French subjects, none but the most intransigent
warriors were prepared to take part in resistance after 1906. The abundant grain harvest which the Guir plain yielded in the fall of 1907 was a
further argument in favor of peace.[66] When the last mass *harka-s* assembled in 1908, few of the Dawi Mani‘ were on hand.

The defensive compromises of the Dawi Mani‘ contrasted sharply with
the behavior of the Ait Khabbash, who, despite the collapse of the 1906
movement, continued their less pretentious but persistent resistance.
Operating from bases west of the French patrolled zone, raiding parties of
usually less than a dozen men made frequent hit-and-run attacks on targets in the Guir-Zousfana area. Normally a band would lead several camels
loaded with food supplies to a concealed spot near the French zone. Then
they would reconnoiter the area, watching for the Saharan Company
patrols and circling around until they found a vulnerable objective: a convoy, a herd of camels, a lonely sentinel. They struck suddenly, made their
kill or seized their booty, then raced back to where they had hidden their
supply camels and escaped back across the Hammada.[67]

The Ait Khabbash were able to continue this form of resistance with
little risk to the well-being of the tribe. Whereas the Dawi Mani‘ were
obliged to give up when the French occupied their heartland, the Ait
Khabbash still had at their backs the vast expanse of Ait ‘Atta land. The
mobility and the fighting skill of these warriors only partially explains
their dogged determination to thwart the French army. Unlike any other
tribe in the region, they were committed to resistance by the very nature
of their history. The Dawi Mani‘ tended always to pull inward to protect
the grain fields at the core of their territory. All of the other transhumant
groups in the region were also more or less confined to a definite radius
of pasture land. The Ait ‘Atta, on the other hand, were still very much in
a stage of predatory expansion at the end of the nineteenth century. Ait
Khabbash resistance was less a defensive response than the continuing
momentum of tribal aggression, which in the east was beating hard against
the solid wall of French military power.

At the end of 1906 French forces were ranged along the lower Wad
Guir, many miles west of any line that could be construed as necessary to

the defense of Algeria. Only eighty miles of the barren Hammada separated the army from Tafilalt. This advance from the Zousfana to the Guir
was accomplished without any major military confrontations. Moreover,
General Lyautey and his Native Affairs team moved quickly to introduce
to the newly occupied territory the material apparatus of colonialism —
administrative bureaus, infirmaries, markets, and the railroad.

Lyautey promoted Franco-Algerian commercial expansion into southeastern Morocco primarily as a facet of his political and military strategy.
He was convinced that the establishment of markets was the most effective way to coax hostile or suspicious tribesmen into the French posts,
where the Native Affairs men stood ready to glean intelligence, initiate
negotiations, and secure political submissions or peace agreements. Indeed,
in frontier Morocco (and later throughout the country), more than in any
other French African colony, the army consciously developed markets and
commercial transport as an instrument of pacification and control.

In this endeavor Lyautey was in close accord with Algerian business
interests and with various members of the French 'colonial party,' including Eugene Etienne, Deputy from Oran and key figure in the Comité du
Maroc. For these men the top priority objective in Morocco was not armed
conquest for its own sake but rather the expansion of commercial, financial, and diplomatic influence. They praised Lyautey for his successes at
pénétration économique and, by contrast, had severely criticized the
ruinous military excesses of the French marines in the West African Sudan,
whose conquests seemed to stimulate only the slave trade.[68] Oran business-
men and merchants were naturally eager to follow the army into southeastern Morocco, importing European goods and siphoning off the export
trade in dates and leather which normally passed through Fez or
Marrakech.[69] Owing to the extension of the railway south of Aïn Sefra,
they found the Southeast more readily accessible to their enterprises than
any other part of Morocco or the western Sahara. Before the turn of the
century, the Atlas ranges had to some extent shielded the region from the
economic upheavals that were shaking the northern and central parts of
the country. Lyautey's offensive, however, permitted international trade
to skirt the Atlas and penetrate directly into the desert fringe. Conquest
and commerce were introduced simultaneously, and the impact of the
new trade quickly advanced far ahead of the lines of military action. The
coming of the French, therefore, presented the population of the entire
region with a complex and uncertain combination of threats and opportunities.

No one in the Southeast, least of all the caravaners and merchants,
could ignore the commercial promises the French markets and railway

held out, given the troubled state of the existing network. The trans-Saharan trade was moribund. Touat was being supplied exclusively by Algerian tribes. The Trans-Atlas traffic was becoming increasingly hazardous and costly. At the same time, the people of the region were acquiring hardier tastes for tea, sugar, and other European imports, which the railroad could now supply at substantially lower prices than they could be obtained from Fez. Moreover, the larger oasis communities had surplus dates and other local products to sell outside the region. In response, the Native Affairs bureaus made it a policy of their markets to buy at attractive prices whatever goods Moroccans had to sell. Although comparative statistics are lacking, it is clear that between 1903 and 1906 the weight of commercial activity began to shift from the trans-Atlas routes to the trails linking up with the railway. Abou Am, the heir of Sijilmasa, appeared to be transforming itself from the principle entrepôt of southeastern Morocco into a satellite market of the Franco-Algerian trade network. Figuig, in a limited sense, returned to its pre-1845 position as a commercial outpost of Oranie.

Yet France's commercial penetration into regions beyond the sphere of her army's control did not proceed as expected. Trade between Tafilalt and Colomb-Béchar declined drastically in the summer of 1906 and until 1910 remained at levels far below the army's early predictions. Lyautey's conviction that the entire population between the Ziz and the Zousfana would respond with unqualified enthusiasm to the stimulus of the new markets and that resistance would dissolve in direct proportion to the level of commercial prosperity proved to be a far too simplistic view of local realities. The persistence of resistance and of opposition to Franco-Moroccan trade resulted not from the intransigent fanaticism of a few, as Lyautey tended to suggest, but from rational calculations and particular political and economic circumstances. These centered mainly on the continuing predatory expansion of the Ait 'Atta, a nomadic imperialism in competition with the French; on the efforts of trans-Atlas merchants to protect their markets and to resist the enterprises of the likes of Muhammad ibn Idris; and on popular responsiveness to the upsurge of country-wide protest against French imperial designs. Thus, despite military defeats, the failure of *makhzan* leadership, and the lure of profitable trade, the advocates of resistance still held the upper hand in the Ziz valley at the end of 1906.

By this time, however, the populations from the Zousfana to the Guir, notably the inhabitants of Figuig and the Dawi Mani', were obliged to come to terms with the colonial order. Indeed, the process by which every group, or even every individual, struck its bargains with the French army, rather than the modes of armed resistance, reveal most distinctly the dynamics of political action in this region. The crisis of conquest was ultimately less a matter of primary resistance than one of adjustment and accommodation to rapidly changing economic conditions and political relationships.

The behavior of both the Dawi Mani' and the people of Figuig at the height of the crisis was neither obdurate opposition nor fatalistic resignation, but rather cautious, tentative compromise marked by a conspicuous absence of collective unity or consistent action. This behavior followed in part from the unpredictable nature of the French invasion. Beyond that, it related to the very nature of the environment and to the ever-abiding necessity to search out and safeguard economic resources. The French lost no time in demonstrating that they could confiscate or destroy palm groves, irrigation works, grain fields, or livestock, unleashing catastrophe on any tribe or *qsar*-community they chose. At the same time, they established conditions for lasting inter-tribal peace and for expanded trade. In short, their coming added to the extreme caprices of nature a whole new set of economic uncertainties. Consequently, every tribe and *qsar*, indeed every group, large or small, with shared interests in resources, was obliged to weigh its response to the French army against the effects, for better or worse, on its economic well-being. The crisis produced not an adjournment, but an intensification of the struggle to outwit the environment, as cooperating groups and individuals sought simultaneously to protect their vital resources and to avoid unconditional submission to the advancing army.

Since political relationships were, owing to this struggle, fluid and unstable in all times and circumstances, the introduction of new threats and uncertainties tended to make them more so than ever. In effect, the process of coming to terms with the French threw into sharp relief the style of inter-tribal politics, especially the tendency for alliances, within tribes or between them, to expand, contract, and change in response to the economic needs of the hour, and for individuals to avoid making irreversible commitments to one line of action or another. The Dawi Mani' illustrated this behavior strikingly when caught between the Ziz valley *mujahidin* on one side and the French on the other. The ideology of military unity through kinship could, in the absence of central authority, be highly effective in ephemeral raids and wars against neighboring tribes. But it had little value in circumstances where survival depended essentially upon the ability of groups with shared resources to reconcile their politics to their economic interests through a fragmented, contradictory process of attack, compromise, and evasion. Throughout the period of intense change and uncertainty between 1900 and 1906, the Dawi Mani' never once coalesced into a corporate tribal unit but remained only an amorphous and shifting collection of leaders and followers, all engaged in a continuous process of calculating and recalculating the advantages of one course of action or another. In these conditions resistance to the French was not an absolute, but merely one option among several in planning the strategy of survival.

Both the Dawi Mani' and the people of Figuig demonstrated during these seven years that their fundamental interest was not to resist but to face the crisis in such a way that the complex and precarious processes of exploiting the land would not be interrupted. Their vision was not so limited that they failed to recognize the advantages of bargain and compromise and the dire consequences of unyielding resistance. If they had not done so, given the French army's willingness to achieve conquest at whatever cost, loss of life and economic dislocation and misery would likely have been far greater than they were.

Notes

1. Louis-Hubert-Gonsalve Lyautey, *Vers le Maroc: Lettres du Sud-Oranais, 1903-1906* (Paris, 1937), p. 13.
2. *Lyautey devant le Maroc: Lettres in édites du Général Lyautey au Colonel Reibell (1903-1908);* Présentation de Jean Brunon (Marseille: *Vert et Rouge, Revue de la Légion Etrangère*, n.d.), p. 13.
3. A great deal has been written about the Lyautey Method. The most complete — and perhaps most laudatory — expositions are found in Lyautey's own works, especially *Vers le Maroc*. See also Jean Gottman, 'Bugeaud, Gallièni, Lyautey: The Development of French Colonial Warfare,' in Edward M. Earle, *Makers of Modern Strategy* (Princeton, 1943), pp. 238-49; Kim Munholland, 'The Emergence of the Colonial Military in France, 1880-1905,' diss. Princeton University, 1964.
4. E. Arnaud and M. Cortier, *Nos Confins saharien: Etude d'organisation militaire* (Paris, 1908), pp. 77-84, 156-60; Blaudin de Thé, *Historique des compagnies méharistes* (Algiers, 1955); Augustin Bernard, *Les Confins algéro-marocains* (Paris, 1911), pp. 197-200; Lyautey, *Vers le Maroc*, pp. 48-56.
5. The Native Affairs officers regularly gathered intelligence information through Muslim spies and informants. Algerians working for the French sometimes traveled to hostile areas to mingle with the population and pick up useful information. At other times Moroccan informers came secretly to the posts and were paid a sum worthy of the information they offered. Intelligence was also obtained from traders and caravaners. These methods were frequently noted in field reports from the Native Affairs officers. Lyautey's officers also made generous use of bribes in order to secure the submission or cooperation of Muslim leaders. Lyautey considered this tactic extremely important and sometimes complained about the insufficiency of 'secret funds.' In 1904 he wrote to Jonnart, 'No district needs [secret funds] more than my Subdivision. Commander Pierron has, for three months, gotten along on the 600 francs that I sent him

two months ago. He has had to develop intelligence contacts with Tafilalt, organize the best intelligence service, pay emissaries generously, buy when required (let's speak frankly) hesitant loyalties . . . Nothing is more pitiful, in the presence of men who have so generously offered you the *diffa* [hospitality] when visiting them, to be reduced, after having secured an important agent, to paying them back by solemnly offering them a hundred sous.' AMG, Alg. 16, Sit. pol. 1904, Lyautey to Gov. Gen., Jan. 13, 1904, no. 1. Lyautey also received special funds for bribes and subsidies from the Comité du Maroc, an offshoot of the colonial party. Jonnart knew about these funds. See C.M. Andrew and A.S. Kanya-Forstner, 'The French "Colonial Party": Its Composition, Aims and Influence, 1885-1914,' *The Historical Journal*, 10, no. 1 (1971), p. 116.

6. AMG, Alg. 16, Sit. pol. 1904, Lyautey to Gov. Gen., Jan. 13, 1904, no. 1.
7. Kim Munholland, 'Rival Approaches to Morocco: Delcassé, Lyautey, and the Algerian-Moroccan Border, 1903-1905,' *French Historical Studies*, 5, no. 3 (1968), pp. 328-43; Carl V. Confer, 'Divided Counsels in French Imperialism: The Ras el-Aïn Incident in 1904,' *Journal of Modern History*, 18 (March 1946), pp. 48-61; Lyautey, *Vers le Maroc*, pp. 75-120.
8. Bernard, *Confins*, pp. 274-8; Munholland, 'Rival Approaches,' p. 339.
9. Lyautey, *Vers le Maroc*, pp. 56, 58, 110, 111, 213-15.
10. Lyautey, *Vers le Maroc*, p. 14; André Colliez, *Notre Protectorat Marocain* (Paris, 1930), p. 68.
11. On military penetration of the desert west of the Wad Saoura and Touat see Capt. Augiéras, 'La Pénétration dans le Sahara occidental,' *Ren. Col.* (July 1923), pp. 225-9.
12. The first few months of government delay in approving the reorganization may have been related to the negotiations between England and France leading to the Entente Cordiale. The foreign ministry may have wished to avoid any advances on the frontier until England finally agreed to recognize French interests in Morocco in exchange for settlement of the Egyptian question. In August 1905 the government created the Territoires du Sud, which gave the Sahara a separate administration from that of Algeria. The Subdivision of Aïn Sefra was changed to the Territory of Aïn Sefra, separating it from the Division of Oran. After Lyautey became Division Commander late in 1906, he still retained a great deal of control over the Aïn Sefra command. Frank E. Trout, *Morocco's Saharan Frontiers* (Geneva, 1969), pp. 59-62, 94-7.
13. AMG, Alg. 16, Sit. pol. 1904, Lyautey to Gov. Gen., Jan. 13, 1904, no. 1; Gov. Gen., to Min. of Foreign Affairs, Jan. 25, 1904, no. 12226; Lyautey to Gov. Gen., Feb. 1, 1904, no. 6. Lyautey, *Vers le Maroc*, p. 42.
14. AMG, Alg. 16, Sit. pol. 1904, Quiquandon (Provisional Com. Subdiv.) to Com. Div. Oran, Sept. 21, 1904; Lyautey to Min. War, Sept. 27, 1904, no. 17M.
15. AGGA, 30H. 51, Maroc-Figuig, Lyautey to Gov. Gen., Nov. 7, 1904, no. 282.
16. AMG, Alg. 16, Sit. pol. 1906, Gov. Gen. to Min. War, May 19, 1906, no. 1411.
17. AGGA, 30H. 51, Maroc-Figuig, Pariel (Chief of Beni Ounif Annex) to Lyautey, Nov. 26, 1904; AMG, Alg. 16, Sit. pol. 1909, Pariel to Lyautey, Feb. 1, 1909, no. 118. *Doc. Dip.*, I, 158, 177, 187, 188, 195.
18. AGGA, 30H. 51, Maroc-Figuig, Lyautey to Gov. Gen., Nov. 7, 1904, no. 282.
19. AMG, Maroc C17, Maroc-Frontière-Figuig, Jonnart to Min. War, Dec. 27, 1904, no. 2248; Sit. pol. 1908, Jonnart to Min. War, Oct. 15, 1908, no. 3506. 'Dans l'Ouest et le Sud-Oranais,' *Af.Fr.* (March 1905), p. 118.
20. 'Le Mouvement commercial des confins oranais,' *Ren. Col.* (June 1905), pp. 227, 228.
21. 'Algérie: la situation dans le Sud-Oranais,' *Af. Fr.* (Feb. 1904), p. 55; 'Algérie: le marché de Beni-Ounif,' *Af. Fr.* (Aug. 1904), pp. 266, 267.

22.   Interview no. 28.
23.   Louis-Hubert-Gonslave Lyautey, *Paroles d'action* (Paris, 1927), pp. 38, 39.
24.   AMG, Alg. 16, Sit. pol. 1906, Jonnart to Min. War, April 7, 1906, no. 970.
      'Algérie: dans l'Ouest et le Sud-Oranais,' *Af. Fr.* (May 1906), pp. 128, 129.
25.   'Algérie: dans l'Ouest et le Sud-Oranais,' p. 128.
26.   AMG, Alg. 16, Sit. pol. 1904, Lyautey to Gov. Gen., Jan. 13, 1904, no. 1.
27.   AMG, Alg. 16, Sit. pol. 1906, Min. of Foreign Affairs to Gov. Gen., Oct. 11,
      1906, no. 108.
28.   AMG, Alg. 16, Sit. pol. 1904, Jonnart to Min. War, June 1, 1904, no. 1218.
29.   AMG, Alg. 16, Sit. pol. 1904, Jonnart to Min. War, Jan. 9, 1904, no. 42.
30.   AMG, Alg. 16, Sit. pol. 1906, Pierron to Lyautey, May 17, 1906.
31.   AMG, Alg. 16, Sit. pol. 1904, Jonnart to Min. War, Dec. 26, 1903, no. 2507;
      Jan. 9, 1904, no. 42.
32.   AMG, Alg. 15, Opérations dans le Sud-Oranais 1903, Col. d'Eu, 'Rapport sur
      les opérations effectuées par la colonne dite de Béchar du 16 Juin au 3 Juillet
      1903.'
33.   AMG, Alg. 16, Sit. pol. 1904, Lyautey to Gov. Gen., Jan. 13, 1904, no. 1;
      Jonnart to Min. War, June 1, 1904, no. 1218.
34.   AMG, Alg. 16, Sit. pol. 1904, Lyautey to Gov. Gen., Jan. 13, 1904, no. 1;
      Jonnart to Min. War, June 1, 1904, no. 1218; Alg. 19, Sit. pol. 1912-14,
      Gov. Gen. Lutard to Min. War, April 7, 1913, no. 1191. F. Albert, 'Les Ouled
      Djerir,' *BSGAO*, 25 (Oct.-Dec. 1905), pp. 396-8.
35.   Canavy, 'Notes sur le commerce de Colomb-Béchar avec l'Ouest,' *BSGAO*, 26
      (Jan.-March 1906), p. 69 De Clermont-Gallerande, 'Le Mouvement commercial
      entre Beni-Ounif et le Tafilelt,' *BSGA* (1905), p. 547.
36.   AMG, Alg. 16, Sit. pol. 1906, Jonnart to Min. War, Aug. 9, 1906, no. 2209;
      Pierron to Lyautey, May 17, 1906; Canavy, 'Notes sur le commerce,' pp. 69,
      70; De Clermont-Gallerande, 'Le Mouvement commercial,' p. 542.
37.   L. Mercier, Notice économique sur le Tafilalet,' *Ren. Col.* (June 1905), pp. 215-7.
38.   AMG, Alg. 16, Sit. pol. 1906, Pierron to Lyautey, May 17, 1906.
39.   AMG, Alg. 16, Sit. pol. 1906, Jonnart to Min. War, Aug. 9, 1906, no. 2209.
40.   AMG, Alg. 16, Sit. pol. 1904, Lt. Col. Quiquandon (Provisional Com. Subdiv.),
      'Résumé succinct des rapports mensuels,' Sept. 20, 1904.
41.   AMG, Alg. 16, Sit. pol. 1904, Lyautey to Gov. Gen., Jan. 13, 1904, no. 1.
42.   AMG, Alg. 16, Sit. pol. 1905, Pariel to Lyautey, Oct. 27, 1905.
43.   AMG, Alg. 16, Sit. pol. 1905, Pariel to Lyautey, Oct. 27, 1905; Gov. Gen. to
      Min. War, Nov. 17, 1905, no. 1768; Sit. pol. 1906, Gov. Gen. to Min. War,
      Jan. 4, 1906; April 7, 1906; Pariel to Lyautey, Aug. 13, 1906, no. 1073. In
      February, during the Algeciras conference, the Pasha of Tangier wrote the *'amil*
      of Figuig that Germany would help Morocco in forcing France to give up all
      territory occupied since 1900. AMG, Alg. 16, Sit. pol. 1906, Lyautey to Gov.
      Gen., March 2, 1906, no. 35C.
44.   AMG, Alg. 16, Sit. pol. 1906, Jonnart to Min. War, July 27, 1906, no. 2075.
45.   'La Situation au Tafilelt,' *Af. Fr.* (Oct. 1902), pp. 363, 364. The article reports
      that as a result of trade between Tafilalt and the rail terminus at Duveyrier,
      twelve to fifteen thousand francs were flowing into Marrakech from the south
      each week. This figure may be inaccurate, but the movement of francs into the
      Southeast certainly increased steadily from 1902 onward.
46.   FO 174/267, MacLeod to Lowther, May 16, 1906.
47.   AMG, Alg. 16, Sit. pol. 1906, Jonnart to Min. War, July 27, 1906, no. 2075.
      De Clermont-Gallerande, 'Le Mouvement commercial,' pp. 542, 543. During the
      following two decades, a large portion of Tafilalt's Jews migrated east to
      Colomb-Béchar or to other parts of Algeria, seeking not only economic better-
      ment but also greater political and social freedom. This exodus must ultimately

have represented a significant loss to Tafilalt's economy. L. Céard, 'Gens et choses de Colomb-Béchar,' *Archives de l'Institut Pasteur d'Algérie*, 11, no. 1 (1933), pp. 81, 82.

48. AMG, Alg. 16, Sit. pol. 1906, Jonnart to Min. War, Aug. 9, 1906, no. 2209; Interview no. 20.
49. Charles René Leclerc, 'Le Commerce et l'industrie à Fez,' *Ren. Col.* (July 1905), pp. 231, 249, 250; 'L'Evolution du Makhzan: la famille Tazi,' *Af. Fr.* (Feb. 1904), pp. 50, 51.
50. AMG, Alg. 16, Sit. pol. 1906, Jonnart to Min. War, Aug. 9, 1906, no. 2209; Jonnart to Min. War, Dec. 31, 1906. Capt. Canavy, 'Notes sur le commerce de Colomb-Béchar avec l'Ouest,' *BSGAO*, 26 (Jan.-March 1906), pp. 69, 70; Interview no. 20.
51. AMG, Alg. 16, Sit. pol. 1906, Jonnart to Min. War, Aug. 9, 1906, no. 2209; M. Marchand, 'La Situation commerciale à Fez,' *Ren. Col.* (Dec. 1906) pp. 421, 422; Bernard, *Confins*, pp. 298, 299; Lyautey, *Vers le Maroc*, pp. 294, 295.
52. AMG, Alg. 16, Sit. pol, 1906, Pierron to Lyautey, May 17, 1906; Jonnart to Min. War, July 27, 1906, no. 2075; Aug. 9, 1906, no. 2209; Oct. 1, 1906, no. 2690. Lyautey, *Vers le Maroc*, pp. 289, 290, 294, 295.
53. AMG, Alg. 16, Sit. pol. 1906, Pierron to Com. Terr., Dec. 6, 1906; Interviews no. 20 and 27.
54. See note 52.
55. AMG, Alg. 16, Sit. pol. 1906, Jonnart to Min. War, Oct. 1, 1906, no. 2690.
56. AMG, Alg. 16, Sit. pol. 1906, Jonnart to Min. War, Aug. 22, 1906, no. 2327; Pierron to Lyautey, Dec. 23, 1906, no. 731; Sit. pol. 1907, Pierron to Lyautey, Dec. 23, 1907, no. 770.
57. AMG, Alg. 16, Sit. pol. 1906, Jonnart to Min. War, Aug. 1, 1906, no. 2125.
58. AMG, Alg. 16, Sit. pol: 1906, Jonnart to Min. War, Aug. 9, 1906, no. 2206; Sept. 20, 1906, no. 2608; Lt. Bauger (Native Affairs officer at Forthassa) to Lyautey, Nov. 15, 1906, no. 193.
59. AMG, Alg. 16, Sit. pol. 1906, Pierron to Lyautey, Aug. 2, 1906; Bauger to Lyautey, Nov. 15, 1906, no. 193; Doury (Native Affairs chief at Colomb-Béchar), 'Renseignements généraux,' Nov. 20, 1906.
60. AMG, Alg. 16, Sit. pol. 1906, Pierron to Lyautey, Nov. 3, 1906, no. 669.
61. AMG, Alg. 16, Sit. pol. 1906, Bauger to Lyautey, Nov. 15, 1906, no. 193.
62. AMG, Alg. 16, Sit. pol. 1906, Doury, 'Renseignements généraux,' Nov. 20, 1906; Pierron to Lyautey, Dec. 6, 1906; Lyautey to Gov. Gen., Dec. 15, 1906, no. 1235; Jonnart to Min. War, Dec. 15, 1906, no. 3528. Reports reached the French posts late in the summer that the sultan was backing the *harka*. It is possible that he did give vague verbal support to it for a time. Between June and October he made some attempts to mitigate the effects of the Act of Algeciras, which he signed under great pressure from the French, by making gestures in favor of resistance. Edmund Burke, III, *Prelude to Protectorate in Morocco: Precolonial Protest and Resistance, 1860-1912* (Chicago, 1976), pp. 87-90. This book is a revised and enlarged version of 'Moroccan Political Responses to French Penetration, 1900-1912,' diss. Princeton University, 1970.
63. AMG, Alg. 16, Sit. pol. 1906, Pierron to Lyautey, Dec. 11, 1906, no. 731.
64. AMG, Alg. 16, Sit. pol. 1906, Lyautey to Gov. Gen., Dec. 15, 1906; Sit. pol. 1907, Pierron to Lyautey, Dec. 23, 1906, no. 770.
65. Lyautey, *Vers le Maroc*, pp. 334-7.
66. AMG, Alg. 16, Sit. pol. 1907, Lyautey to Gov. Gen., Sept. 21, 1907, no. 661.
67. Interview no. 9.
68. A.S. Kanya-Forstner, *The Conquest of the Western Sudan* (London, 1969),

pp. 207-9.
69. See, for example, Edouard Déchaud, *L'Hinterland commercial de l'Oranie*
    (Oran, 1909). Déchaud was Secretary of the Oran Chamber of Commerce, and
    his study was published by the Comité Oranais du Maroc.

8 THE SOUTHEAST IN THE ERA OF MAWLAY 'ABD AL-HAFID, 1908-1912

With the ratification of the Act of Algeciras France abandoned its re-strained policy of *pénétration pacifique* and in the spring of 1907 made two new military thrusts into Moroccan territory. In March forces under Lyautey occupied Oujda and for the first time established a beachhead for expansion into the northern sector of the frontier zone. In July troops landed at Casablanca on the Atlantic coast and within weeks began advancing into the Chaouia plains. These incursions aroused the population far more than had the conquests of Touat and the Guir-Zousfana. Oujda was an old and important city, indeed the only center of Moroccan urban culture and *makhzan* authority in the Northeast. The boundary east of Oujda was undisputed, so in seizing the city the French unilaterally crossed an internationally recognized frontier. The landings at Casablanca represented an even more blatant intervention, since this town lay in the heart of the country and in easy marching distance from all four imperial cities.

In the aftermath of Touat Mawlay 'Abd al-'Aziz had been moved to undertake a program of internal reforms. By 1907, however, he had com-promised himself beyond the limits of independent reformative or mili-tary action. From the moment he signed the Act popular sentiment turned increasingly in favor of Mawlay 'Abd al-Hafid, who from his power base at Marrakech laid plans for a challenge to the throne in collusion with Madani al-Glawi and other Atlas chieftains. The fall of Casablanca was the catalyst for revolt. On August 16 the *'ulama* of Marrakech proclaimed 'Abd al-Hafid rightful sultan. In the weeks that followed he repudiated his brother's policy of defensive accommodation with the European powers and declared a *jihad* against the French forces on Sharifian soil. Contingents of his tribal partisans set off to join the Chaouia tribes in resistance. By September popular enthusiasm for 'Abd al-Hafid was spreading so rapidly in Fez that 'Abd al-'Aziz found it wise to transfer his court to Rabat. Early in January the *'ulama* of Fez declared for the pretender, clearing the way for his entry into that city the following June. 'Abd al-'Aziz, plagued by a shortage of effective troops and an over-abundance of European advice, attempted a series of halfhearted counter-attacks against his brother's forces. After sustaining a disastrous defeat north of Marrakech in August, he fled to Casablanca and abdicated,

leaving the country in the hands of a régime promising a radical return to
militant Islam.

Out of the Lion's Den

The tribes and *qsar*-dwellers of the Southeast by and large greeted the
Hafidiya with enthusiasm. The fires of mass resistance which had sputtered
out somewhat ingloriously at the end of 1906 flared up once again at the
expectation of 'Abd al-Hafid coming to the defense of the *umma*, thus ful-
filling the traditional sultanic duty which 'Abd al-'Aziz had so consistently
repudiated in his public actions. All those who had taken part in the fruit-
less mass movements of 1900, 1903, and 1906 knew that a *jihad* ordained
and inspired by the sultan was the most potent ideological principle for
mobilizing pan-tribal action — far more so than the appeals of local saints
acting alone.

In the fall of 1907 Mawlay 'Abd Allah, a son of Mawlay Rashid, accompanied a delegation of Filali *shurfa* to Marrakech to profess their allegiance
to 'Abd al-Hafid and urge him to order a mass assault on Colomb-Béchar.
In a spirit of resistance that transcended regional frontiers Mawlay
Muhammad, another son of Mawlay Rashid led an armed contingent of
Ziz valley men north to fight for the Hafidiya. He subsequently took
command of all its forces in the Chaouia. 'Abd al-Hafid may in fact have
chosen him in order to win the support of all the Filali *shurfa*.[1] Many of
them, following the course of a large part of the Moroccan political elite,
undoubtedly preferred to hedge their bets until no doubt remained as to
the outcome of the royal struggle. Mawlay Rashid certainly did. In an act
characteristic of political behavior in Morocco he sent two sons off to
'Abd al-Hafid but at the same time wrote a reassuring letter of support to
'Abd al-'Aziz. The beleagured sultan tried to buttress the *khalifa*'s loyalty
by arranging for him to receive his monthly stipend of fifteen hundred
duros through the financial services of the Tazi family, whose trading
house in Tafilalt was still in operation in 1907. Later, when 'Abd al-'Aziz's
defeat became certain, Mawlay Rashid committed himself fully to the
jihad sultan.[2]

'Abd al-Hafid was of course in no position to assume personal direction
of resistance in the Southeast. He was far more urgently occupied with the
Chaouia fighting and with consolidation of support among the urban elites
and the principal leaders of the central Moroccan tribes. However inspiring
his proclamations and his deeds north of the Atlas, the periphery still
needed men to organize resistance on his behalf. It was under these
circumstances that the center of militancy suddenly shifted from Tafilalt
to the remote reaches of the Wad Ait Aïssa and to the *zawiya* of Douiret

Sbaa (Da'irs Saba'), the Lion's Den.

The saints of Douiret Sbaa were one of a number of holy lineages which served the political and spiritual needs of the tribes and *qsar* communities of the fragmented flanks of the eastern High Atlas. Prior to 1907 the lodge had only local influence, much less, for example, than the *zawiya* of Kenadsa. In that year, however, Mawlay Ahmad Lahsin al-Saba' (French, Moulay Ahmed Lhassen Sbaa), the *shaykh* of the lodge, began to preach the *jihad*. What human or supernatural promptings transformed him into a warrior-saint are not evident, but there is no doubt that in doing so he followed closely in the footsteps of Si Muhammad al-'Arbi al-Darqawi, the famous *shaykh* of Medaghra. Mawlay Lahsin was born in Figuig of an Idrisi *shurfa* family, but he left home at an early age to take up sufi studies with Si al-'Arbi. After his master's death in 1892, he, like other prominent disciples, established a *zawiya* of his own to teach the Darqawa 'way' and to serve the local tribes. In all likelihood he shared Si al-'Arbi's conviction that the Muslim community was in grave moral decline and that intransigent holy war was the only acceptable way to confront the European threat. Whereas the al-Hanafi family of the Rteb had tried to replace the Medaghra *jihad* tradition with their own, Mawlay Lahsin attempted to revive it as the self-proclaimed heir of Si al-'Arbi.[3]

He asserted essentially the same kind of saintly leadership as did Si al-'Arbi, the al-Hanafis, and Abu 'Amama before him, in that he could do little more than temper tribal animosities and ratify in the sight of God their ephemeral joint enterprises. But whereas previous pan-tribal leaders had been obliged to launch their causes in the face of Sharifian indifference or outright opposition, Mawlay Lahsin was able to ride the crest of Hafidiya militancy. The French believed that he and 'Abd al-Hafid were in direct communication with one another. Very likely they were since 'Abd al-Hafid was trying very hard in 1908 to establish contacts with rural resistance leaders throughout the land and to preserve the '*jihad* sultan' image which had earned him countrywide support. He dispatched letters throughout the Southeast, including Figuig, urging the population to defend itself against foreign aggression.[4] There is little doubt that Mawlay Lahsin acted, at least implicitly, in the name of the new sultan and that he linked his cause with the Hafidiya *jihad*.

The Last *Harka-s*

Mawlay Lahsin preached among the populations of the eastern High Atlas in the fall of 1907. The following February warriors of the Ait Izdig, Ait Seghrushin, Ait 'Aysa, and various *qsar*-communities assembled at Douiret Sbaa.[5] The zealous response of these tribes was an indication of the

widening scope of the southeastern battlefront. The French did not yet
menace them directly, nor had they played a leading part in earlier resistance. Nonetheless, three to four thousand men, plus the expected entourage of women and children, responded to Mawlay Lahsin's call for an
assault on Colomb-Béchar. Curiously the Ziz valley populations held back,
despite the growing popularity of 'Abd al-Hafid there. Perhaps Mawlay
Lahsin was unknown in the Ziz valley and Tafilalt and did little or nothing
to recruit support in that direction. For some, the memory of Taghit may
still have been fresh enough to deter commitment to an operation whose
success was far from certain. Others, especially *shurfa*, probably hesitated
while the outcome of the palace struggle still hung in the balance.

In any event, Mawlay Lahsin's *harka* set off in the direction of Colomb-
Béchar. The *shaykh* led the way as spiritual and moral standard-bearer, but
apparently no single field commander was chosen. On April 16 the *harka*
reached Menabha, a point several miles southeast of Aïn Chaïr, and there
ran into a French column which had been sent out from Colomb-Béchar
as part of a general alert. The *mujahidin* succeeded in mounting a surprise,
predawn attack on the column, and although the French drove them off
with cannon and machine gun fire, they suffered 120 casualties, including
nineteen killed. This was the highest loss they had ever sustained in a single
battle on the frontier. The *harka* retreated westward, but a fresh column
from Colomb-Béchar pursued it, marching all the way to Douiret Sbaa,
where it shelled the *zawiya*. The column failed to make contact with the
main body of the *harka*, which managed to regroup in Boudenib during
late April and early May. On the 13th, however, the French advanced on
the oasis and met the *harka* on its outskirts. The battle lasted several
hours, but under artillery fire the *mujahidin* retreated, first into Boudenib,
then on the following day westward into the desert. The French occupied
the oasis and the *harka* disintegrated. The army estimated that the
Moroccans had numbered between five and six thousand at Boudenib and
that during all the fighting of April and May about six hundred of them
were killed.[6]

The fall of Boudenib brought the French to within less than forty miles
of the Wad Ziz. To the people of the region it signaled the end of border
incursions and the beginning of an invasion comparable to that in the
Chaouia. The battles in April and May did not, as in the case of Taghit,
produce discouragement but only fanned the flames of resistance and
brought more tribes into the conflict. Indeed, armed bands from distant
High and Middle Atlas tribes began arriving in the region.[7] Part of the
reason may be that although the battle for the Chaouia was all but lost to
the French, 'Abd al-Hafid was still inspiring popular confidence in the

jihad by his bold advance toward Fez through the territory of the perennially rebellious Middle Atlas tribes. On May 16, two days after the fall of Boudenib, he made a triumphant entry into Meknes.

The Ziz valley Arabs and the Ait Khabbash were shaken by the French advance and during the course of the summer sent several thousand men north to the Guir. They chose no commander in chief, but prominent among the contingent leaders were 'Ali u Idir of the Ait Khabbash and Ba Sidi al-Hanafi of the Rteb.[8] Mawlay Rashid, persevering in his opposition to adventures that might only draw the French into Tafilalt, stayed behind once again.[9] His warnings, however, were lost in the general enthusiasm for what promised to be the final test of strength.

The French estimated that between fifteen and twenty thousand people, armed with everything from Lebel repeaters to knives and clubs, gathered in late August at Touggourt, a *qsar* located about nineteen miles up the Guir from Boudenib. Mawlay Lahsin al-Saba' was there as leading saint, his prestige apparently still intact because he himself had advised against the attack at Menabha. On September 1 the throng moved out, marched down the Guir, and ranged itself in front of a butte west of Boudenib on which the French had constructed a blockhouse. An emissary was sent up to the fort carrying the challenge of the *mujahidin*:

> To the chief of the French 'fraction' at Boudenib. May beneficence be on those who follow the upright life, those who humble themselves before merciful God and seek justice. Know that, since your arrival in the Sahara, you have badly treated weak Muslims. You have gone from conquest to conquest. Your dark soul fools you by making you race to your destruction. You have made our country suffer intense harm, which tastes as galling to us as the bitter apple. The courageous and noble Muslim warriors approach you, armed for your destruction. If you are in force, come out from behind your walls for combat; you will judge which is nobler, the owl or the hawk.[10]

The French did not come out, and the *harka* attacked the blockhouse. The battle lasted sixteen hours. The *mujahidin* charged time and time again, but seventy-five men held them off with the aid of sections of 75 and 80 millimeter cannon firing from both the blockhouse and a small redoubt north of Boudenib. The attackers finally gave up and retreated, leaving about 170 dead on the field. The *harka* reformed during the following days, but on September 5 a French relief column of four thousand men arrived from Colomb-Béchar. Two days later a second battle was joined on the plain west of Boudenib, and once again cannon fire gave the day to the

French. After four hours of fighting, the *mujahidin* scattered and fled, leaving 300 more dead. The *harka* disintegrated, and most of the warriors headed into the mountains or down the Ziz valley.[11]

The Aftermath of Boudenib

The battle of Boudenib was a major event in France's conquest of Morocco. The defeat and dispersion of the *harka* cleared the way for an uninterrupted and largely unchallenged occupation of the upper Wad Guir and the far eastern Atlas. After Boudenib, Mawlay Lahsin joined forces with 'Ali Amhawsh, a widely known saint from the upper Moulouya region. Together they tried off and on for the next few years to raise another *harka* among the populations of the Ziz and the territory west of it. But neither of them ever succeeded in making the slightest challenge to French power east of the valley.[12]

On the countrywide level the disaster at Boudenib served to intensify pressure on 'Abd al-Hafid to accelerate his avowed *jihad*. He had emerged victorious over 'Abd al-'Aziz in August and therefore appeared to be in a position to turn his full attention to the task of expelling the French. Unfortunately, he found his brother's legacy of rebellion and financial ruin more than he could handle with the resources at hand. Once in power he had no choice but to turn first to the reform and reorganization of the administration and the army. Yet he could not hope to begin to task without European acquiescence and support, since the functioning of the country's central political and economic institutions was inextricably bound up with European political, commercial, and financial interests. The price of European recognition was acceptance of a Franco-Spanish note calling on him to agree to the provisions of the Act of Algeciras, to accept the government's international debts, and to proclaim an end to the *jihad*. Under tremendous pressure from the French he agreed in December 1908 to honor the terms of the note. Subsequently, he sent letters throughout the country, including Tafilalt, ordering his subjects to stop fighting. This compromise produced widespread disillusionment and cost him much popular support.[13] The *mujahidin* who had taken part in the battle of Boudenib probably gave up hope of any further Sharifian support of resistance in the Southeast.

Meanwhile, the French army made Boudenib the pivot point for conquest of the upper Wad Guir and Wad Aïssa region. In seizing the oasis the army presented its government with a fait accompli. Paris agreed only to a temporary occupation, as Moroccan sovereignty in this region was not in question. The army, however, lost no time in transforming Boudenib from an advanced post of the French military zone into a strategic center whose protection necessitated further incursions west and north.[14] The Ait Izdig and the Ait Seghrushin, the two principal tribes of the region, were brought to terms following a series of punitive expeditions and minor skirmishes between 1909 and 1911. In the summer of 1911 Native Affairs officers negotiated a peace agreement with Ait Izdig leaders at Gourrama, which was located only about twenty-five miles from the Wad Ziz.[15]

French operations north and west of Boudenib paralleled actions in both the northern frontier region and in the far south. Following the occupation of Oujda in 1907, the army gradually advanced northward toward the Mediterranean coast, southward onto the high plains to link up with forces based at Berguent, and westward to the banks of the Wad Moulouya. In June 1910 a post was established at Taourirt, and patrols began moving as far west as Guercif, which was almost halfway from the Algerian border to Fez. Columns operating from Taourirt, Berguent, and Boudenib brought almost all of Morocco east of the Moulouya under control by the end of 1910.[16] In the far south the Saharan Company of Beni Abbès occupied Tabelbala in June 1910 and continued to push into the western Sahara. By 1912 columns were operating far to the southwest of Tafilalt in the Erg Iguidi.[17]

On the diplomatic front the French sought to ratify the interventions of 1907-8 by working out an accord with Mawlay 'Abd al-Hafid. He desparately needed to strengthen *makhzan* military and administrative control outside the major cities, but he could achieve little without large infusions of money. The French were prepared to grant a loan, but only in return for legal recognition of their 'temporary' occupation and reorganization of Moroccan territory along the frontier and in the Chaouia. The sultan accepted these conditions and signed the Accord of Paris in March 1910. As far as the Southeast was concerned, the agreement committed the army to withdraw from Boudenib and its eastern neighbor Bouanane, but only on condition that the *makhzan* assume responsibility for military control and protection of commerce in the region between the French zone and Tafilalt. Since 'Abd al-Hafid was in no position to take any effective steps to meet this condition, the army in effect legitimized its presence in a wide area around Boudenib despite the fact of Moroccan sovereignty. The accord also authorized indefinite occupation of both Berguent, which was recognized as Moroccan, and the posts between the lower Guir and the Zousfana, which were incorporated into Algeria.[18] The question of extending a fixed boundary further south than the 1845 line, which ran only to a point northeast of Berguent, was not to be opened until after the creation of the Protectorate.

Boudenib was valuable to the French not only as a military base but

also as a strategic market patterned on Colomb-Béchar and Beni Ounif. By
early 1910 a European-style village had sprung up across the river from the
qsar. Fifty-one Europeans, 108 Algerian Muslims, 87 Moroccan Muslims,
and 90 Moroccan Jews were already living there, engaging in commerce
and services to the garrison. Boudenib by no means eclipsed Colomb-
Béchar as a commercial center, because the latter remained not only the
chief administrative and military post in the region but also the terminus
of the rail line. The necessity of camel transport from there to Boudenib
(which the railroad never reached) forced prices up and encouraged many
inhabitants of the Guir-Aïssa region to continue to patronize the Colomb-
Béchar merchants. Nonetheless, caravans came to Boudenib in increasing
numbers from the north and west, from as far away as the upper
Moulouya and even from Fez.[19]

The army was particularly concerned to develop commercial links with
the Ziz valley, especially after the trade between Tafilalt and Colomb-
Béchar failed to reach the levels expected. In negotiations leading to the
1910 accord the French tried to open the way for more successful
commercial penetration of the valley. The accord stipulated that the army
would withdraw from Boudenib and Bouanane only after the *makhzan*
established a system of escorts and guard posts to protect traffic between
Tafilalt and the Guir. In a perfunctory effort to comply 'Abd al-Hafid
sent 'Umar Sharadi, a *makhzan* official, to Tafilalt to implement the terms
of the agreement. He never succeeded, however, if for no other reason
than the hostility of the Ait Khabbash and the trans-Atlas merchants.[20]
Indeed, the Ait Khabbash, the only Ziz valley group to continue resistance after the battles of 1908, managed to block most trade between the
lower Ziz and Boudenib, even though many inhabitants of the valley were
eager to pursue it.[21] European goods continued to reach Tafilalt mainly
by way of Colomb-Béchar, where Dawi Mani' carriers managed to organize
and protect at least occasional caravans despite Ait Khabbash harassment.[22]
This situation probably continued without much change until 1915, when
the army occupied the valley north of Tafilalt.

Despite the intransigence of the Ait Khabbash, a large part of the
sedentary population of the Ziz valley began to recalculate its relations
with the French after Boudenib. The *qsar*-dwellers had gone to war expecting to drive the army back into Algeria. When this effort ended in disaster
and when 'Abd al-Hafid began to behave more and more like his predecessor, many concluded that neither their political nor their economic
interests could any longer be served by armed resistance. Moreover, the
threat of the army marching into the valley was now far more acute than
it had hitherto been. In this respect the cultivators of the Ziz reached the

same conclusion after Boudenib that the people of Figuig had after the bombardment of Zenaga.

Political feelers were cautiously extended. In 1911 the army held talks at Boudenib with representatives of both the 'Arab Sabbah and the Ait Umnasf of the Rteb (collaterals of the Ait Khabbash) through the intermediation of Sidi ibn Muhammad, a *sharif* of Boudenib. The resultant agreements involved promises of peace in return for freedom to pasture and trade in the French controlled zones.[23] The Ait Umnasf, the first 'Atta group to negotiate seriously with the French, probably saw little advantage in taking the obdurate position of their Ait Khabbash cousins. They were a small, almost entirely sedentary section of the tribe and in easy range of Boudenib. In fact, the army made its first reconnaissance of the Ziz valley in May 1911 and received a peaceable welcome from the people of the Rteb.[24]

Mawlay Rashid, who had never been convinced that mass resistance would keep the French out of Tafilalt, put out conciliatory feelers of his own. In the spring of 1909, after Mawlay Lahsin al-Saba' and 'Ali Amhawsh had abandoned attempts to organize another *harka* in Medaghra, he sent a letter to the commandant at Boudenib pleading his desire to oppose further resistance activity in Tafilalt.[25] Early in 1911 he opened secret talks through Si Brahim of Kenadsa and another intermediary to arrange for the French to pay the stipend which he had not received since the abdication of 'Abd al-'Aziz. The army was delighted to oblige, since this gave them an excellent point of leverage in Tafilalt, especially with the 'Alawi *shurfa*.[26] Some payments may have been sent, but Mawlay Rashid died later in the year. His passing brought to a close a truly remarkable career in the politics of both *makhzan* and tribe. His service as *khalifa* lasted about fifty years, which in the musical chairs games of *makhzan* office-holding represented an extraordinary tenure. Over the years he demonstrated exceptional skill at maneuvering among the jarring political forces of the Ziz. Had he lived longer, he might well have continued to play the broker when the French penetrated the valley. But as it was, the Southeast did not lack for go-betweens.

Man of the Future: The Rise of Muhammad Oufkir

During the months following the army's seizure of Béchar in 1903, the commanding officer there made contact with members of the *jama'a* of Aïn Chaïr, a small date-producing and commercial center located midway between Figuig and Boudenib. Its population numbered about 3,500 and, like Figuig, represented a Berber-speaking enclave in the territory of Arab tribes. In fact, Aïn Chaïr lay about where the pastoral frontiers of the Bani

Gil, the Awlad Jarir, and the Awlad al-Nasir conjoined. These tribes, together with the Ait Seghrushin Berbers to the west, visited Aïn Chaïr regularly to exchange sheep for dates and homespun woolen garments. Caravans also passed through the oasis on the way between Figuig and the Ziz valley. The population was divided into two clans. Each one inhabited a *qsar* of its own, though their notables joined to form a single council. The larger clan comprised nine lineages, the largest of these being the Awlad (or Ait) Oufkir (u Faqir). Some time around 1900 one Muhammad ibn Kaddur Oufkir, perhaps the richest man in the oasis, was chosen *shaykh* of the *jama'a*.[27]

The fall of Béchar must have set off an intense debate in the *jama'a* as to the pros and cons of entering into relations with the French. The inhabitants had given the General Wimpffen expedition a fierce reception in 1870, and some of the notables advocated the same policy should the French once again come near. Oufkir, however, favored restraint and quickly established himself as leader of a dominant faction of 'doves.' During 1904 and early 1905, he and other notables met on a number of occasions with French officers either at Colomb-Béchar or at other places distant from Aïn Chaïr. Oufkir very likely convinced most of the *qsar*-dwellers of the soundness of these overtures when, in April 1905, the army constructed an advance post at Talzaza, a point located only about twenty-two miles southeast of the oasis. The following May Oufkir felt confident enough of popular support to journey to Aïn Sefra in the company of the commander of Colomb-Béchar.

Despite initial suspicions, Lyautey quickly accepted Oufkir's protestations of peace and offers to serve as an intermediary between the army and unsubmitted tribes. Aïn Chaïr had gained a considerably exaggerated reputation among French expansionists as a hotbed of fanatical hostility, owing mainly to the skirmish which occurred there in 1870. Lyautey could not get authorization to send a column against the oasis but recognized Oufkir's initiatives as an opportunity to neutralize it through the techniques of *pénétration pacifique*.[28]

Between 1905 and 1908 Oufkir visited Aïn Sefra and Colomb-Béchar a number of times and gave the Native Affairs officers intelligence information on events occurring in the west. In 1906 he began to put them in direct contact with men of the Ait Seghrushin.[29] In the spring of 1908 he contacted leaders among various tribes in an effort to dissuade them from joining up with Mawlay Lahsin al-Saba' and his *harka*. He failed there, of course, but he did manage to retain the advantage over a pro-*harka* faction in Aïn Chaïr and ultimately convinced most of the inhabitants to stay out of the fighting, even though the *mujahidin* passed through the oasis on their way to Menabha.[30]

In the aftermath of the battle Aïn Chaïr was incorporated into the French-controlled zone, and Oufkir was assured of the army's protection. Under these circumstances he could afford to act more boldly. In November 1909 he invited French officers to dine in his house, which represented the first time Europeans entered the oasis. A few months later he publicly shot Mawlay Mubarik ibn Abu, the leader of the last faction to oppose his leadership.[31]

By this time Lyautey regarded Oufkir as perhaps the single most important political figure in the region. Although he was unknown in the *makhzan* and had an almost negligible base of personal power on the eve of the Protectorate (in contrast to al-Glawi and the other chieftains of the High Atlas), he appears to have displayed two qualities that particularly impressed the General. The first was his striking political energy and ruthlessness, coupled with an unwavering loyalty to the French army. Augustin Bernard remarked, 'He is an intelligent and clever man, cruel and rapacious. He has pressed upon the inhabitants of Aïn Chaïr, cowed by his superiority and his audacity, a formidable tyranny.'[32] In 1909 Lyautey was already looking forward to the reorganization of the Southeast, indeed of all of Morocco, utilizing influential local leaders as agents of colonial rule in dealings with the population. Since the Southeast had no 'grand *qaid-s*' and no dominant families and since the exercise of power tended to be highly fluid, the choice of these agents was as in much of rural Morocco later on, far from obvious. Therefore, the army was on the lookout for men with personal force, intelligence, and an appreciation of the inevitability and worth of French rule, whatever their prevailing political status in the region might be.

Oufkir's second qualification was his early success in bringing the army together with the Ait Seghrushin for trade and negotiations, a task he worked at off and on between 1906 and 1911. There is some indirect evidence to suggest that Oufkir had been involved in regular commercial relations with men of the Ait Seghrushin prior to the arrival of the French. Although he may well have exaggerated his 'influence' within the tribe, it seems that whatever previous contacts he had were related to trade.[33] At any rate, trade was used to the mutual advantage of both the army and Oufkir in persuading most of the tribe to make peace. Late in 1909 the *shaykh* asked the army to give him a loan of 10,000 francs with which to purchase sheep from Ait Seghrushin herders. Lyautey asserted that Oufkir was making a 'disguised request for a subsidy,' but then recommended that the funds be supplied to him out of the army budget. (Earlier, Si Brahim of Kenadsa had received a cash loan through an Oran bank.)

Oufkir would purchase a large number of sheep in a single lot, sell them to the army or for export, and reap a profit from the transaction as a reward for his loyalty to France. The Native Affairs men, for their part, would tighten their hold on Oufkir, enhance his prestige and hence their own among the Ait Seghrushin, and entice the tribe into further commercial relations. The government approved the loan early in 1910, and the enterprise was presumably carried out. It is possible that similar loans were made available in subsequent years.

At the same time Oufkir requested the loan, he also asked the army to officially invest him as commander over Aïn Chaïr, as well as over the Bani Gil, the Awlad al-Nasir, and the Ait Seghrushin. He was clearly counting protectorate chickens, since Mawlay 'Abd al-Hafid had no interest in him, nor was there any precedent in *makhzan* administration for such a post. The Bani Gil in fact were officially under the authority of the *'amil* of Figuig. Lyautey was sympathetic to Oufkir's ambitions, but he was obliged to delay giving him an official position owing to the French government's continuing skittishness over unilateral political reorganization in Sharifian territory.[34] The *shaykh* did not, however, have to wait long. When the Protectorate was declared, he was appointed Pasha of Boudenib, which made him the chief Moroccan official in an extensive area that later became the military Territory of Boudenib. The only comparable position in the region was the *pashalik* created at Figuig in 1912. Oufkir was undoubtedly one of the earliest and fastest rising stars in the neo-*makhzan* administration.

He continued to serve the Protectorate faithfully for many years, and when he died in 1936 he bequeathed to the Southeast Oufkir family paramountcy in much of the region's administration. Sons and other kinsmen continued to hold *qa'id*-ships and other posts in the Southeast into the 1970s. Muhammad Oufkir the younger served with distinction in the French army, then went on to tremendous power and world notoriety as Minister of Interior and Defense in the cabinet of King Hassan II. In 1972 he became implicated in a plot on the king's life and died a violent death, bringing to an abrupt end sixty years of political eminence for the Oufkirs of Aïn Chaïr.

Continuity and Change on the Eve of the Protectorate

The passing of Mawlay Lahsin al-Saba' and the advent of Muhammad Oufkir symbolized the turning point from independence to colonialism for much of the Southeast. Between 1909 and 1912 the great battles of resistance were all fought and lost in Morocco's heartland. The people of the pre-Sahara undoubtedly followed events in the north, especially the risings around Fez and the *jihad* of Mawlay Ahmad al-Hiba, with a certain amount of anticipation. But when 'Abd al-Hafid signed the Protectorate treaty in March 1912, most of them had already resigned themselves to the inevitability of French rule.

Only in Tafilalt and in the desert south and west of it did significant fighting continue in subsequent years. The army encountered negligible resistance when they occupied Medaghra, the Rteb, and the territory of the 'Arab Sabbah in 1915. Late the following year a small post was established in Tafilalt itself. But armed clashes, initiated mainly by the Ait Khabbash, continued to occur, and in the fall of 1918 the post was abandoned in favor of a larger and more easily defensible one at Erfoud just north of the oasis. From then until 1932 Tafilalt remained free of French control. Most of that time it was governed by the resistance leader Bil Qasim N'gadi (Belkasem Ngadi) and a following of nomads, mostly Ait 'Atta. The army could doubtless have routed him and occupied the oasis several years earlier than they did. They chose instead to contain the dissidents within Tafilalt and its vicinity and to advance only in concert with the conquest of the Wad Dra and the heartland of the Ait 'Atta, a job not completed until 1933. Therefore, the history of Tafilalt's final two decades of independence belongs more appropriately with that of resistance and conquest in the central and western sectors of the Saharan fringe.

For most of the Ait 'Atta 1912 was no watershed in their war against the French but only the end of the first round of a struggle that was to continue west of the Ziz for many years. The last great battle took place in the Jebel Saghro in 1933. Ironically, the Ait Khabbash, the first 'Atta *taqbilt* to confront the French, were also the last to surrender. Capitalizing on their mobility and their ability to withdraw further and further west of the zone of French action, they continued to launch small-scale raids for more than thirty years after the fall of Touat. The retreat of a stubborn band of warriors toward the Atlantic coast and their final submission south of the Anti Atlas in 1934 reveals the depth and rigidity of the war mentality which had governed these nomads during the long era of Ait 'Atta imperialism.[35]

Excluding these Berber intransigents and the rebels of Tafilalt, 1912 was a year of political transition for most of the people of the Southeast. Before 1912 the French army undertook political reorganization only in areas definitively annexed to Algeria. But armed with the Treaty of Fez it proceeded to impose neo-*makhzan* administration, turn *qa'id-s* and *shaykh-s* into functionaries, write a new rule book for tribal politics, and create a de facto international boundary line which sliced the region in two. Autarky and resistance had of course been brought to an end in different areas at different times. But 1912 marked the beginning of the era of colonial government, an era that was not to reach some parts of rural Morocco, including the lands west of the Ziz, until many years later.

Social and economic changes came more gradually. The three decades of conquest and resistance were times of great political tumult and uncertainty, marked by successive outbursts of violence and destruction. They were not, however, years of general social upheaval and transformation. Despite the recurrent fighting and the movements of army columns, *harka-s*, and raiding bands, the rhythms of agricultural and pastoral life remained largely undisturbed in many parts of the region. The army did not use scorched-earth tactics nor imprison or relocate large numbers of people, as it did in northern Algeria in earlier years. Excepting a small number of Europeans who set up businesses in the vicinity of the army posts, the land-hungry settlers who had displaced and uprooted so many thousands in Algeria were not attracted to the desert fringe. Generally speaking, the first three decades of French involvement in southeastern Morocco had much milder social and economic effects on the population than did the comparable period of conquest in northern Algeria.[36] Drastic shifts and disturbances in the patterns of rural life were to come to the Southeast later with the development of administrative centers and improved communications, the opening of coal mines at Kenadsa, the migration of thousands of young men to the cities of both North Africa and Europe, and, finally, the Algerian war. The new forces of the twentieth century would, in other words, remodel and transform the tribes and *qsar*-communities of the Southeast in ways that Lyautey himself could not have imagined.

Patterns of Resistance and Leadership

The French military advance in southeastern Morocco was largely a response to popular resistance, which went on in one part or another of the region almost continuously between 1881 and 1912. Muslim forces numbering in the hundreds or thousands entered the field hardly more than a half dozen times during the period, but clashes between small raiding parties and French personnel were a matter of almost weekly occurrence. Resistance was indeed tenacious, yet none of it achieved more than very limited objectives, and much of it ended in catastrophe. Whether in raids or large-scale fighting, Moroccan warriors had few military advantages over their adversary. They had the tactical advantages of knowing the terrain and of being able to assemble, stock supplies, and take refuge in territory where the French army did not have its government's permission to tread.

On the other hand, the open pre-Saharan steppe was not conducive to guerrilla-style warfare, especially after the French created the Saharan Companies, which matched Moroccan bands in speed and mobility. The great *harka-s* had superiority in numbers over the garrisons or columns they attacked, but they had to confront disciplined troops, impregnable defensive positions, and vastly superior fire power. In the late nineteenth century Moroccans were acquiring modern breech-loading arms in relatively greater numbers than resistance forces in many other parts of Africa, owing to the intensive contraband trade on the Rifian coast. These weapons, however, varied greatly in quality, and ammunition was always in short supply. Repeating rifles were never available in large numbers. Indeed, at the turn of the century the weapons technology of the Moroccans was still falling behind that of the French, who were acquiring the Lebel repeater models with their 'smokeless' powder, as well as machine guns and portable artillery. In short, popular forces lacked the military capability to overrun French positions or to force the army to retreat from any part of its expanding zone of occupation.

They also lacked region-wide political or military institutions and therefore had no foundations on which to build an army or a centrally-directed guerrilla organization. Resistance was stubborn, but it was also spasmodic and amorphous. Raiding bands effectively harassed the French and their Muslim clients, stealing, committing acts of sabotage, and inflicting minor casualties. But raiding was spontaneous and uncoordinated. There is no evidence that a guerrilla movement with a common strategy and leadership existed at any level. Moreover, the men who took part in small-scale raids were motivated not only by the desire to defend their land against foreign occupation but also by more mundane urges to make off with a share of the livestock, equipment, and arms which the French army brought with it in such immense quantities. In that sense they raided the French for the same reasons they raided one another's *duwar-s*.

The army frequently accused Abu 'Amama of masterminding much, if not all, of the hit-and-run warfare in the region, making him into a *bête noire* to justify offensive actions deeper into Moroccan territory. The old saint's entourage, an uprooted and desperate lot, many of whom came from the north central Sahara, were no doubt responsible for a good share of the fighting. There is little doubt that Abu 'Amama encouraged resistance part of the time in order to preserve his warrior-saint reputation. But after he returned north from Touat in 1896, he had neither the prestige nor the power to direct or control the resistance activities of the Dawi Mani', the Awlad Jarir, or the Berber tribes of the west.

The Ait Khabbash initiated more small-scale resistance than any of the

other nomadic groups in the region. Their exceptional belligerence, however, was closely related to the aggressive expansion of the Ait 'Atta. No
other tribe in the region was in an expansive phase in the late nineteenth
century. Yet despite the Ait 'Atta's conviction of invincibility, they, like
all other pastoral tribes in Morocco and the Sahara, lacked the political
institutions out of which disciplined regiments or guerrilla cells could be
made. The bonds of *khams khmas* enabled them, like the Dawi Mani', to
mobilize and bring together large numbers of men for short-term military
actions. But in confronting the French the issue was not to be decided in
a single battle. Therefore, they fought only as their acephalous politics
permitted them to fight – in dispersed, uncoordinated bands. Their
struggle was energetic and unyielding, but also erratic and fragmented.

Against this background of raiding and skirmishing regional leaders
tried on six different occasions to organize movements of mass resistance,
hoping each time that a combination of large numbers and righteous zeal
would be sufficient to drive the French back into Algeria. Three of these
movements, Si Muhammad al-'Arbi's agitation in the late 1880s and the
stirrings in Tafilalt in 1900 and 1906, were abortive affairs which failed to
give rise to any armed action. The other three culminated in mass assaults
on French positions – Taghit, Menabha, and Boudenib. These *harka-s*,
though unsuccessful, demonstrated that despite the absence of central
military institutions, the people of the region were capable of organizing
pan-tribal coalitions that held together at least long enough to experience
unmitigated defeat. These movements refuted common European notions
of an anarchic Morocco helpless to mount any large-scale resistance at all.
Yet none of the *harka-s* was more than a kind of super-raid, a precarious
and transitory alliance of separate groups responding to a sudden crescendo
in the crisis of European penetration either along the frontier or in the
heartland. None of them possessed the elements of discipline, pyramidal
organization, or coherent strategy that would give evidence of a unified,
region-wide resistance movement enduring from one French advance or
makhzan compromise to another.

Deficiencies in weaponry and military organization, however, do not
fully explain the failure of the population to forge a cohesive movement.
A number of African peoples engaged in struggles against European conquest in the nineteenth and early twentieth centuries faced essentially the
same difficulties and yet found solutions to what T.O. Ranger has called
the 'problem of scale.'[37] That is, they succeeded in creating effective
politico-military organizations which cut across tribal or ethnic barriers
and which mounted far broader and more tenacious resistance than
European conquerors expected. Outstanding examples were the resist-

ance movements of the Ndebele-Shona peoples in Rhodesia, the Maji Maji rebels in Tanganyika, the Samorian army in West Africa, and the Sanusi Bedouin in Cyrenaica.

In several cases of unusually effective resistance either an innovative indigenous religion or a revitalized Islam provided the ideological basis for pan-tribal solidarity. In both its orthodox and popular manifestations Islam embraced a number of ideas and institutions which could be applied to the task of enlarging the scale of resistance. In his study of Tukulor resistance to the French conquest of West Africa A.S. Kanya-Forstner writes:

> Militant Islam presented the greatest challenge and mobilized the sternest resistance to the European occupation of Africa in the nineteenth century. Muslim polities, with their written languages, their heritage of state-making and the cohesive force of a universal religion preaching the brotherhood of all believers, could generally organize resistance on a wider scale than political units whose extent was limited by the ties of common ancestry. Muslims also had a strong incentive to oppose the advance of Christian power. The practice of their religion involved the strict observance of ritual and social obligations, and this made it theoretically imperative for them to live in an Islamic community, governed by a righteous ruler according to the precepts of the law (*Sharia*). Since the realms of politics and religion were supposedly inseparable, it was their duty to establish the political as well as the religious ascendance of Islam and, when necessary, to defend their community by force of arms.[38]

The history of European conquest in Africa and Asia makes it clear, of course, that Islam did not always answer effectively to the need for militant ideology and organization. Nonetheless, if the tribes of southeastern Morocco did not achieve enduring unity, it was not because their religion failed to equip them with some potent tools.

In Islam the fundamental instrument of popular mobilization in the face of foreign threat is the *jihad*. Europeans, including French officers on the Moroccan frontier, have generally held to the rather facile view of *jihad* as frenzied, xenophobic warfare. In fact, in Islamic thought the term embodies far deeper and more complex meaning than the phrase 'holy war' signifies. Pursuit of the *jihad* involved a commitment not only to expand the frontiers of Islam and defend it from external aggression, but also to revive and transform both the individual and the community in line with the dictates of the *shari'a*. According to the classical scholars, the

jihad included three distinct phases: first, the *jihad* of the heart, or purifi-
cation of the carnal soul; second, the *jihad* of the tongue and hands, or
preaching what is righteous and declaiming evil; and third, the *jihad* of the
sword, or the armed struggle against foes and unbelievers. Therefore, holy
war in the path of God was not only an instrument of assault and defense,
but also of revival and reformation for both the individual and the *umma*,
the society of the faithful. Indeed, in the nineteenth century *jihad* gave
impetus to a succession of political and social revolutions among Muslims
or partly Muslim peoples in Arabia, the Nilotic Sudan, and West Africa.[39]

In classical political thought the essential duties of the Muslim ruler
were to govern justly, to enforce the *shari'a*, and, when necessary, to proclaim the *jihad* of the sword. The sultan of Morocco contracted to fulfill
these duties by virtue of his claim to the titles of *imam* and *amir
al-mu'minin*, or Commander of the Faithful. If a *jihad* was to be declared,
the sultan was to do it. The tradition of Sharifian leadership in the *jihad*
had a long history extending back to the Moroccan resistance against
Iberian incursions in the fifteenth and sixteenth centuries. It also had
remarkably widespread acceptance in western Africa, as witnessed in 1894,
for example, when a delegation of citizens of Timbuktū journeyed to
Marrakech to appeal to Mawlay Hasan to protect them from the French.[40]
The *jihad*, ordained and led by the sultan, was the obvious and by far the
most compelling principle around which Moroccans might coalesce in the
face of the European challenge. The population, including the people of
the Southeast, turned instinctively to 'Abd al-'Aziz for action following
the fall of Touat. From then until 1907 militants all over Morocco repeatedly urged him to take up the *jihad* of both resistance and internal
renewal.[41] When 'Abd al-Hafid finally opened the floodgates of *jihad*-ist
sentiment, he touched off the most sweeping and tumultuous anti-European movement that Morocco had ever known.

There is evidence that supporters of the early Hafdiya were urging not
only war against the French but also the revival of Islam and stringent
enforcement of the *shari'a*.[42] Mawlay Lahsin al-Saba' preached *jihad* in
the name of 'Abd al-Hafid, but since almost nothing is known, given the
limited sources available, of what he or other leaders said or wrote publicly, it is difficult to discern the specific ideological content of the 1908
harka-s. It is not evident, for example, whether they preached radical
restoration of the *shari'a* or prophesied the cataclysmic destruction of
unbelievers. The French command reported Mawlay Lahsin as proclaiming
that all the saints of Islam would join his forces and that God would transform French bullets into succulent dates.[43] Yet, notwithstanding this hint
of millenarian expectations, it can only be surmised whether the mass

assaults at Menabha and Boudenib were prompted by *jihad*-ist feeling that went beyond resistance to deeper visions of a society purified and revitalized from within on the model of primitive Islam.[44]

Whatever the revivalist tendencies surfacing in Morocco in 1907-8, the *jihad* played itself out in less than two years. Hardly anyone in the country, least of all 'Abd al-Hafid, was prepared to follow it to its logical conclusions. The pretender and the elite elements supporting him were intent upon gaining control of the *makhzan* and pursuing fiscal and administrative reforms, but not upon unleashing a social-revivalist revolution which, had it occurred, would almost certainly have swept them all away and hastened European intervention. 'Abd al-Hafid rode the crest of popular fervor to victory over his brother, but he could not hope to consolidate his power without abandoning radical Islamic solutions in favor of those which might more realistically fit into the scheme of European commercial, fiscal, and diplomatic requirements.

The rural populations, for their part, wanted *jihad* against the French but not the logical consequences of its fulfillment – the ascendancy of a sultan capable of collecting taxes and imposing law and order throughout the country. In other words, they were caught between a frantic urge to resist foreign aggression and a deep-seated suspicion of the political sultanate, the only Moroccan institution through which a lasting coalition of local and regional forces could even be attempted. Indeed, the 1907-8 movement was in large measure a protest against too much of the wrong kind of government (*makhzan*), though the right kind (*imam* and *umma*) was perceived as a 'golden age' ideal. Since the 1908 pan-tribal movements in the Southeast reflected conditions in the rest of the country, they failed to endure not only because of French victories, but also because the *amir* himself became more preoccupied with the pursuit of worldly government than the 'rightly-guided caliphate.' When he turned his back on the *jihad*, it went sour, temporarily in some areas, permanently in the Southeast. Mawlay Lahsin and other die-hards might continue to appeal for resistance in the language of *jihad*. But without the Sharifian connection, *jihad* lost much of its ideological force.

'Abd al-Hafid was of course not the only figure in the 1900-12 period to claim the *amir*-ship and thus the right to declare *jihad*. Because of the close link in the minds of Moroccans between social justice and Sharifian rectitude, regionally based protests against government oppression or other social ills traditionally coalesced around righteous challenges to the legitimacy of the incumbent sultan. In the crisis atmosphere of the pre-Protectorate years pretenderism was rampant. Abu Himara in the Northeast, Mawlay Ahmad al-Hiba in the Southwest, and Mawlay Zayn al-Abadin

in the Meknes region all made serious challenges. A number of lesser
sharif-s, soi-disant or genuine, also launched rebellions, though with short-
lived and feeble results.

It is remarkable, therefore, that the Southeast did not at some point
during these years generate its own *amir* and its own *jihad*. Incipient
pretender movements did in fact take shape around Si al-'Arbi al-Darqawi,
Mawlay Mustafa al-Hanafi, and, perennially, Mawlay Rashid. Moreover, at
least one local 'dark horse,' a man named Mawlay Za'tar, launched a brief,
inconsequential movement among the Ait Seghrushin and the Awlad
al-Hajj (Upper Moulouya) in the spring of 1910.[45] None of these stirrings
grew into a significant rebellion, but less owing to the lack of popular
motivation and support than to interminable hesitation and indecision and
the inadequacy of effective organization at the optimum moment. Caution
and defensiveness characterized political activity in Morocco during these
years far more often than aggressive, unequivocal action. Whenever a rebellion succeeded in attracting large numbers of people, leaders in other parts
of the country who were harboring conspiracies of their own tended to
pull back and await the outcome, avoiding bold action as long as political
conditions remained fluid. This style of politics applied eminently to the
shurfa leaders of Tafilalt, who were numerous, divided into competing
factions, and deeply entangled in the shifting alliances of the notable families of the northern cities. Rather than put forward a Sharifian candidate
of their own at some critical point, they appear to have maneuvered,
parried, and outwaited one another into a state of chronic inaction. In the
meantime, leadership of resistance passed into the hands of local saints
having the prestige and the mediational talents to engineer, if not a
challenge to the throne, then at least a rising of the tribes.

A succession of mass *harka-s*, however, did not conceal the failure of
Sharifian *jihad* to provide either continuity or cohesiveness to resistance.
Where else, then, could Moroccans, particularly the people of the Southeast, have turned in order to broaden the scale of resistance? In the Islamic
world in the nineteenth and twentieth centuries rural movements to resist
or fend off colonial conquest crystalized in most cases around either of
two distinct principles of integration and unity. These were mahdism and
militant sufism. Both incorporated *jihad* and revivalism to a greater or
lesser degree of doctrinal refinement. Since these principles were so conspicuous in the organization of Muslim resistance, it is worth considering
briefly why neither of them, as it turned out, had any compelling influence on the course of events in the Southeast.[46]

Mahdism, the doctrine of the Redeemer whom God will send to the
world to expel the anti-Christ and establish a millenial reign of justice cul-

minating in the Day of Judgment, had broad currency among rural peoples
in the troubled, doubting atmosphere of nineteenth-century Islam. The
most spectacular and by far the most successful movement of this kind
was the Sudanese Mahdiya (1881-98), which drove out the Turko-Egyp-
tian regime and evolved into a centralized state.[47] Although the people of
Morocco were familiar with Mahdist doctrine and had built the Almohad
empire on its foundations in the twelfth century, messianism in this form
was not a significant ideological force during the pre-Protectorate years
despite the severe social and economic stress. Abu Himara claimed the title
of Mahdi during the first weeks of his rebellion, then cast it off when
popular response proved unenthusiastic. Minor rebels may have tried the
same ploy in other localities, but there is no evidence of Mahdis appearing
in the Southeast in the 1881-1912 period. The most likely explanation for
the near absence of Mahdism in Morocco is that messianism and millen-
arianism to spare were already inherent in the Sharifian principle and were
indeed evident to a degree in both the early Hafidiya and the al-Hiba
movement of 1912. Furthermore, the idea of Sharifian legitimacy was so
deeply engrained in the popular mind that no would-be redeemer could
hope to gain large-scale support for rebellion by any other ideological
route. Even if a Mahdi were to succeed in raising a regional insurrection,
the *'ulama* of Fez, whose opinion on the fitness of a *sharif* to govern
constituted the principal act of legitimation, would have vigorously
opposed any pretender attempting to by-pass their authority by putting
forth a separate principle of rulership. Mahdism in nineteenth century
Islam was likely to strike the most responsive chords in peripheral areas
where a popularly recognized institution of traditional Islamic authority
was either absent or under serious attack. Morocco, including its desert
fringes, does not fit that category.

Muslim brotherhoods (*tariqa-s*), generating and directing forces of
militant sufism, were the vehicles of resistance in several parts of the
Islamic world. Notable African examples were the Qadiriya in Algeria
under the Amir 'Abd al-Qadir, the Tijaniya in West Africa under al-Hajj
'Umar, and the Sanusiya in Libya under the Sanusi family. In undertaking
to widen the scale of resistance brotherhoods combined the ideological
appeal of distinctive, even exclusivist doctrines with a hierarchical
organization of lieutenants and lodges which welded together ethnic or
tribal troups. Religious orders, unlike segmented tribes, were not acephalous units. The *shaykh* was often capable of translating spiritual authority
over his disciples into nearly absolute political control.

Any of several large brotherhoods in Morocco, including the Qadiriya
and the Tijaniya, had potential for organizing pan-tribal resistance, yet

none of them played a major part in the effort. The history of their relations with the *makhzan* in the nineteenth century helps explains their failure. Sultans and sufi *shaykh-s* were by the very nature of their spiritual
authority in a permanent state of either active or latent competition for
the moral and political allegiance of the population. Mawlay Hasan and
his predecessor tried to check the regional temporal power of the orders
through a combination of appeasement, repression, and tactics of divide
and rule. They by no means eradicated the political influence of sufi
leaders in rural areas, but they were quite successful in containing the
development of regional power centers which might disrupt trade and tax-
collecting and even threaten the throne (for many *shaykh-s* were also
'Alawi *shurfa*). When, after 1900, the need for broad-based resistance became acute, none of the orders were found to display the sort of autonomy, discipline, or rigorously militant leadership that made the Sanusiya
so successful in organizing the Cyrenaican tribes to resist the Italian invasion of Libya. In fact, some of the Moroccan brotherhoods, notably the
Tayyibia (Wazzaniya), resisted *makhzan* centralization by adopting a
policy of collaboration with European political and commercial interests
prior to the creation of the Protectorate.

Several brotherhoods were represented in the Southeast. The Darqawa,
which had numerous *zawiya-s* scattered throughout the region and certainly the largest popular affiliation, was the only one which might realistically have provided a framework for pan-tribal resistance, especially
during the lifetime of Si al-'Arbi al-Darqawi. But, as was the case with
many reputed saints in rural areas of Morocco, Si al-'Arbi's power was
manifested primarily in personal mediation and arbitration of tribal dispute. The pastoral tribes of the Ziz and Guir would likely have responded
in force had he been alive after 1900 to spearhead a mass *harka* against the
French. But these tribes were at the same time largely indifferent to
Darqawa organization, doctrines, and mystical devotions. Even though Si
al-'Arbi and, later, Mawlay Lahsin al-Saba' may well have used the network of Darqawa *zawiya-s* to disseminate resistance propaganda, there is
no evidence that the brotherhood was the unifying principle for any of the
pan-tribal movements or that its doctrines emphasized a program of puri-
tanical revival as did, for example, the Sanusiya in Libya or the Tijaniya in
West Africa. In Morocco in general the Darqawa had no special reputation
for militancy.[48] In fact, Muhammad Oufkir, the leading pro-French personality in the Southeast, was a Darqawa brother.[49] The Ziyaniya of
Kenadsa, the only widely-known order with its 'mother' *zawiya* in the
region, never aligned itself with the forces of resistance, but played a conciliatory role from the beginning of the conquest. It had no other alterna-

tive, since most of its spiritual disciples, those seeking the Ziyani 'way' to union with the Divine, lived, not in the Southeast at all, but in the towns and villages of French Algeria.

In his study of Pan-Islam in Morocco Edmund Burke asserts that 'a major drawback of Islam as a focus of political loyalty was the gradual accretion of a host of local beliefs and practices, including saint worship and maraboutism. In order for resistance to be successful, some means had to be found to transcend these particularistic interests.'[50] Neither Mahdism or militant sufism offered transcendent solutions for the people of southeastern Morocco, and large-scale resistance was in the end an unqualified failure. Yet it was only through 'maraboutism' that such resistance was undertaken at all. Though parochial Islam and the saint cult did indeed obscure the primordial unity of all believers in Morocco, resistance at the regional and local levels, where it was always the most stubborn, relied heavily on the leadership of saints. They were the only individuals in rural society, aside from a few extraordinarily charismatic tribal leaders, whose special role as arbitrators and brokers for competing kin groups and factions suited them for the task of orchestrating pan-tribal action. Abu 'Amama led the last major insurrection in French Algeria by forging, however fleetingly, coalitions of both northern and southern tribes. Mawlay Mustafa and Ba Sidi al-Hanafi mobilized and directed the mass assault on Taghit in the face of opposition from the sultan himself. Mawlay 'Abd al-Hafid's *jihad* would never have penetrated the Southeast were it not for the local initiative of Mawlay Lahsin al-Saba'.

Recognizing the heroic struggles of these men does not, on the other hand, erase the fact that their contributions to solving the problem of scale were transitory and of not much consequence. Perhaps they could have done more had they been men of truly extraordinary personal capacities. In the annals of Muslim resistance their deeds seem to pale when matched against those of the Amir 'Abd al-Qadir, al-Hajj 'Umar, the Sudanese Mahdi, or even Mawlay Ahmad al-Hiba in southwestern Morocco. Moreover, none of them appears to have possessed exceptional brilliance in matters of Islamic theology, jurisprudence, or mystical science. This shortcoming placed them in the ranks of the great majority of rural Moroccan saints, but it separated them from leaders such as Muhammad ibn 'Ali al-Sanusi of Libya, Ma al-'Aynayn of the western Sahara, or even Si al-'Arbi al-Darqawi, whose considerable intellectual credentials contributed greatly to their popular prestige. The most that can be said of the warrior-saints of the Southeast is that they applied their spiritual reputations and mediational talents as best they could in the struggle against political fragmentation and economic self-interest.

It was indeed fragmentation and self-interest which called forth the best talents of leaders, though not necessarily in the cause of resistance. While warrior-saints inspired large numbers to war, other men worked less obtrusively at the business of compromise and submission, easing the population's way into the colonial era. These other men would cursorily be identified as the 'collaborators' of the early colonial period. But this term carries with it a strong taint of duplicity and betrayal, and it too easily suggests superficial distinctions between 'good' leaders who fought for the people and 'bad' ones who connived with the invader. In attempting to understand the dynamics of political action in this period type-casting of the prominent personalities leads nowhere. For in a political arena where institutions of central authority were lacking at any level and where the exercise of power was extremely diffuse and fluid, men never attained important positions of leadership unless they were successfully responding to a significant body of popular opinion — unless there was a demand for whatever course of action they were embarked upon.

David Seddon's description of the style of tribal leadership in north-eastern Morocco is apt for the Southeast as well:

> In order to achieve, or to maintain, a position of power and wealth within the lineage, within the tribe, or even within the region as a whole, a man sought to attain a number of goals, most of which were closely related, subject to considerable uncertainty, and could be considered both as ends, in themselves, or as means to further ends. Political and economic success depended on the ability to gather and to keep a large following, and it could be said that the overall aim and final goal of an ambitious man was to attract and maintain such a following.... Ultimate success was related to the ability of an individual to plan and follow an effective 'path.'[51]

Whatever the personal goals of a leader and however he might benefit from his position of power, he could not enlarge or even preserve his following unless his 'path' led in the direction of increased material security for them. The fundamental function of all political action in this capricious environment was to defend resources and, whenever possible, multiply them. Men remained leaders only so long as their decisions served this end. Groups of leaders and followers, whatever their particular aims for joining together, never constituted more than alliances of varying scope and duration. They coalesced and dissolved in response to their leader's success or failure at warding off a host of human and natural threats. It was a quick-witted, versatile, and lucky man indeed who could steer his clientele along a 'path' for very long without veering into some sinkhole of misfortune, thereby damaging or forfeiting his prestige.

The style of leadership did not essentially change when the French first came upon the scene. It has already been pointed out that cooperating groups, as well as individuals, were careful above all else to avoid being edged into positions or commitments where optional courses of action were eliminated. Starting from this axiom, no one ultimately regarded the French army as the unqualified foe, but rather as one of a variety of unpredictable forces with which to try to come to terms in one way or another. The political turbulence throughout the Southeast, the changing course of events in other parts of Morocco, and the bewildering uncertainties over the consequences of submitting to French rule put severe strains on leaders at all levels to make decisions that would keep their alliances intact.

Some leaders, such as Mawlay Lahsin al-Saba' or the al-Hanafi family, became prominent because of their success at organizing coalitions of resistance, even though these were ephemeral. Other men, notably Abu 'Amama in the years after 1882, maintained a clientele by engaging in a continual round of defensive probes and maneuvers which minimized political defeats but never involved decisive action. Still others, like Si Brahim of Kenadsa and Muhammad Oufkir, developed their following by effectively organizing and speaking for groups wishing to negotiate and make accommodations with the French. But whatever the particular routes these men followed, their style and methods were essentially the same. These were to create an alliance through persuasion, to mediate and reconcile differences within it, and to take actions (which might mean no action at all) that would accrue to its benefit. It should be remembered that the Southeast, unlike areas of Morocco where *makhzan* officials or 'grand *qa'id-s*' held sway, was devoid of leaders with either the authority or the coercive power to impose their will arbitrarily on any significant sector of the population.

At least this was so until the consolidation of French rule. For then some fortunate men were rapidly transformed from alliance leaders into permanent functionaries of the neo-*makhzan* administration, wielding powers handed them from above. The most notable of these men was Muhammad Oufkir, but the French also appointed many others to posts as village *shaykh-s* and tribal *qa'id-s*. An example of one of these men shows that the pattern of Oufkir's early career was by no means unique. Al-Kabir wuld Kaddur became *qa'id* of the Awlad bil Giz *khums* of the Dawi Mani' in 1883 and received an official investiture from Mawlay Hasan in 1892. In 1901, during a period of active Dawi Mani' resistance, he visited the French

post at Taghit and entered into preliminary discussions over the terms of
submission for himself and a body of followers. When the Franco-
Moroccan Protocol commission visited Béchar in 1902, the army pro-
visionally confirmed his title. Early in 1904, as more and more of the Dawi
Mani' found it expedient to enter into relations with the French, he went
to Colomb-Béchar and negotiated the specially ambiguous status of
rallié for himself and his clients. In April, after the army had consolidated
its control over the lower Guir, he returned to the post and officially submitted. By this time most of the Awlad bil Giz were prepared to follow
him. In 1914 the French Algerian command named him chief *qa'id* of the
khums and praised him for his dedication to the French cause. He was,
according to members of the tribe, the only Dawi Mani' leader to hold by
French authority a title originally granted to him by Mawlay Hasan.[52]

A common view of early colonial administration in areas of Africa
where institutions of rulership were either weak or nonexistent is that
ambitious men with little or no established power simply ingratiated themselves to the Europeans by their skills, intelligence, or cunning and thus
received appointments as much-needed local agents of authority. Although
this phenomenon did occur not only in the Southeast but throughout
Morocco, the careers of Muhammad Oufkir and al-Kabir wuld Kaddur
show that men who cooperated with the colonialists were not necessarily
acting purely out of selfish opportunism. In rural Morocco the ability of a
leader to persuade his fellows and to reconcile disputes was prized above
all other personal qualities excepting courage. As groups in different parts
of the Southeast came to realize that their vital resources could best be
secured, and even extended, by trading or making political compromises
with the French, they required effective intermediaries and spokesmen
who already had friendly contacts with the army. These groups, in other
words, reached a point where they found it practical to make an alliance
with the invader. But they needed a trusted leader to open the appropriate 'path.' From that standpoint, men such as Oufkir, Kaddur, or Si
Brahim cannot be written off as collaborators or lackeys, for they were
in fact bold and effective leaders in the complex and protracted politics of
submission. Because of their successful interventions, they won the thanks
of both fellow Muslims and the French and therefore proceeded to broaden
their clientele and to perform further political services for both sides.
Suddenly, however, the rules of the game began to change, and mediators
were transformed into servants of the neo-*makhzan*, whose immediate
objective in the conquered areas was not persuasion and brokerage but the
imposition of law and order.

Notes

1. Edmund Burke, III, *Prelude to Protectorate in Morocco: Precolonial Protest
    and Resistance, 1860-1912* (Chicago, 1976), pp. 110, 249; A.G.P. Martin,
    Quatre siècles d'histoire marocaine (Paris, 1923), pp. 450, 464, 465,
    471.
2. AMG, Alg. 16, Sit. pol. 1907, Capt. Doury, 'Renseignements fournis par Si
    Ahmed Beni Mani, représentant à Béchar du commerçant Filalien Si Mohammed
    ben Driss,' Nov. 18, 1907. The informant was described as a longtime resident
    of Marrakech and personal acquaintance of 'Abd al-Hafid.
3. AMG, Alg. 17, Sit. pol. 1908, Bailloud (Com. 19th Corps), 'Notice sur Mouley
    Hamed es Sebai et sur les Derkaoua,' March 31, 1908; N. Lacroix, 'Les
    Derkaoua d'hier et d'aujourd'hui,' *Documents sur le Nord-Ouest africain*
    (Algiers, 1902), p. 22; P. Odinot, 'L'Importance politique de la confrérie
    Derqaoua,' *Ren. Col.* (May 1929), p. 295.
4. AMG, Alg. 17, Sit. pol. 1908, Lyautey to Gov. Gen., Feb. 2, 1908, no. 107;
    Feb. 24, 1908, no. 148; Bailloud, 'Notice sur Mouley Hamed es Sebai et sur les
    Derkaoua,' March 31, 1908. Institut de France, Fonds Auguste Terrier, LVI
    (5946), 'Les Opérations dans le Sud-Oranais en 1908.' (hereafter cited as 'Sud-
    Oranais en 1908.) Martin, *Quatre siècles*, p. 479.
5. AMG, Alg. 17, Sit. pol. 1908, Lt. Husson, 'Renseignements,' April 1, 1908;
    'Sud-Oranais en 1908.'
6. 'Aux Frontières de l'Algérie: le combat de Menabha et les opérations de la
    colonne Vigy,' *Af. Fr.* (May 1908), pp. 179-83; 'Aux Frontières de l'Algérie,'
    Af. Fr. (June 1908), pp. 220, 221; Georges Demanche, 'La Pénétration dans
    le Sud-Oranais,' *Revue Française de l'Etranger et des Colonies*, 33 (1908),
    pp. 275-80; 'Sud-Oranais en 1908;' Martin, *Quatre siècles*, pp. 479, 480.
7. 'Sud-Oranais en 1908;' Martin, *Quatre siècles*, pp. 491, 492. Martin states that
    some uniformed regulars from 'Abd al-Hafid's army fought at Boudenib and
    that after the battle the French took prisoners from as far away as the Zayan
    country near Rabat, the Haouz near Marrakech, and the Sous.
8. 'Sur les confins de l'Algérie,' *Af. Fr.* (Sept. 1908), pp. 312, 313; Interviews no.
    10, 16, and 18.
9. AMG, Alg. 17, Sit. pol. 1908, Gen. Vigy (Com. Terr.) to Gov. Gen., Sept. 17,
    1908, no. 98/B; 'Aux Frontières de l'Algérie,' *Af. Fr.* (July 1908), pp. 248, 249;
    Interview no. 16.
10. AMG, Alg. 17, Sit. pol. 1908, Com. Fesch, 'Lettre du Chef de la harka au
    Commandant d'Armes de Bou Denib,' Aug. 29, 1908. This document is a French
    translation of the letter.
11. Capt. Lechartier, *Colonne du Haut-Guir en Septembre 1908* (Paris, 1908);
    Augustin Bernard, *Les Confins algéro-marocains* (Paris, 1911), pp. 164-9; 'Sur
    les confins de l'Algérie,' pp. 312, 313; Martin, *Quatre siècles*, pp. 491, 492.
12. AMG, Alg. 17, Sit. pol. 1908, Jonnart to Min. War, Oct. 15, 1908, no. 3517;
    Sit. pol. 1909, Gen. Alix (Com. Terr.) to Com. Div. Oran, March 6, 1909, no.
    159; Jonnart to Min. War, March 26, 1909, no. 675; April 25, 1909, no. 898.
    Martin, *Quatre siècles*, pp. 491, 492. Mawlay Lahsin al-Saba' continued to
    preach *jihad* on the fringes of the French-controlled zone until at least as late as
    the fall of 1913. AMG, Alg. 19, Sit. pol. 1911, Lt. Col. Ropert, 'Rapport,' July
    18, 1911; Sit. pol. 1912-1914, Gov. Gen. to Min. War, Sept. 25, 1913, no.
    3344. 'Ali Amhawsh continued to play a leading part in resistance in the east-
    central Atlas for many years. See Saïd Guennoun, *La Montagne berbère* (Paris,
    1929), pp. 148-54.
13. Martin, *Quatre siècles*, pp. 497-500.

14. Louis-Hubert-Gonsalve Lyautey, *Vers le Maroc: lettres du Sud-Oranais, 1903-1906* (Paris, 1937), pp. 299, 302, 307-12.

15. Military operations in the region north and west of Boudenib are reported in AMG, Alg. 17, Sit. pol. 1908 and 1909; Alg. 18, Sit. pol. 1910; Alg. 19, Sit. pol. 1911 and 1912-1914. Also Bernard, *Confins*, pp. 173-9.

16. Bernard, *Confins*, pp. 179-87.

17. Capt. Augiéras, 'La Pénétration dans le Sahara occidental,' *Ren. Col.* (July 1923), pp. 243-6.

18. Frank E. Trout, *Morocco's Saharan Frontiers* (Geneva, 1969), pp. 87-9; Bernard, *Confins*, pp. 188, 189.

19. Lt. d'Herbigny, 'Le Développement de Bou Denib en 1909,' *Af. Fr.* (May 1910), pp. 155, 157; Bernard, *Confins*, pp. 256-60.

20. AMG, Alg. 18, Sit. pol. 1910, 'Lettre chérifienne adressée à Moulay Rechid au Tafilalet' (French trans.); Alg. 19, Sit. pol. 1911, Gen. Toutée (French High Commissioner for the Algero-Moroccan frontier) to Gov. Gen., Jan. 13, 1911, no. 968HC.

21. AMG, Alg. 19, Sit. pol. 1911, Lt. Col. Ropert, 'Rapport,' July 18, 1911; Guespereau, 'Le Haut-Guir en fin décembre 1911,' *Ren. Col.* (May 1912), pp. 202, 203; d'Herbigny, 'Le Développement de Bou Denib,' p. 157; Interviews no. 10 and 23.

22. Guespereau, 'Le Haut-Guir,' p. 200.

23. AMG, Alg. 19, Sit. pol. 1911, Toutée to Gov. Gen., Jan. 13, 1911, no. 967HC.

24. AMG, Alg. 19, Sit. pol. 1911, Toutée to Gov. Gen., June 15, 1911, no. 316M.

25. AMG, Alg. 17, Sit. pol. 1909, Jonnart to Min. War, April 25, 1909, no. 898.

26. AMG, Alg. 19, Sit. pol. 1911, Toutée to Gov. Gen., Jan. 13, 1911, no. 968HC.

27. Oufkir was one of eighty-five notables among Aïn Chaïr's population. He reportedly owned 5,000, or about one twelfth of the total number of palm trees in the oasis. He also owned 4,000 more in a nearby palm grove. AGGA, 22H. 23, Lt. P.T. Albert, 'Notice économique sur les Ksour de la région de Talzaza: Aïn Chaïr, Bou Kaïs, El Ahmar, Mougheul, Sfiçifa,' May 20, 1906. Another report noted that 'each family weaves a certain number [of wollen jellabas] to sell; the family of Mohammed ou Fékir derives a considerable profit from it.' AGGA, 22H. 27, Com. Laquière, 'Rapport sur Aïn-Chaïr,' Nov. 26, 1909. Also, Bernard, *Confins*, pp. 57-8.

28. AMG, Alg. 16; Sit. pol. 1904, Gov. Gen. to Min. War, June 4, 1904, no. 1233; Lyautey, *Vers le Maroc*, pp. 190-2.

29. AMG, Alg. 16, Sit. pol. 1906, Lt. Pierron to Lyautey, Feb. 24, 1906.

30. AMG, Alg. 17, Sit. pol. 1908, Com. 19th Corps to Min. War, March 19, 1908, no. 21215; Sit. pol. 1909, Lyautey to Gov. Gen., Dec. 13, 1909, no. 449K. 'Nos Relations avec le Ksar marocain d'Aïn-Chaïr,' *Af. Fr.* (Feb. 1910), pp. 56-8.

31. AMG, Alg. 17, Sit. pol. 1909, Capt. Doury 'Compte rendu,' Nov. 4, 1909; AGGA, 22H. 27, Com. Laquière, 'Rapport sur Aïn Chaïr,' Nov. 26, 1909; Bernard, *Confins*, pp. 98, 204-6, 216, 217.

32. Bernard, *Confins*, p. 98.

33. AMG, Alg. 16, Sit. pol. 1906, Pierron to Lyautey, Feb. 24, 1906; Alg. 17, Sit. pol. 1909, Capt. Doury, 'Compte rendu,' Nov. 4, 1909; Alg. 18, Sit. pol. 1910, 'Aman des Ait Bouchaouen,' Aug. 2, 1910; Lyautey to Min. of France in Morocco, Oct. 11, 1910, no. 685HC; Alg. 19, Sit. pol. 1911, Toutée to Gov. Gen., April 12, 1911, no. 1160HC. Since Oufkir was a member of the Darqawa sufi brotherhood, he may also have had contacts with people of the Ait Seghrushin through its channels. The Darqawa brethren at Aïn Chaïr were in the orbit of the *zawiya* at Douiret Sbaa, which was in Ait Seghrushin territory. Furthermore, Oufkir was initiated into the order at Sefrou by Si Muhammad ibn

Ahmad, whose son established another *zawiya* among the Ait Seghrushin. AGGA, 22H. 23, Lt. P.T. Albert, 'Notice économique sur les Ksour de la région de Talzaza: Aïn Chaïr, Bou Kaïs, El Ahmar, Mougheul, Sfiçica,' May 29, 1906; Odinot, 'L'importance politique,' p. 295.

34. AMG, Alg. 17, Sit. pol. 1909, Lyautey to Gov. Gen., Dec. 13, 1909, no. 449K; Alg. 18, Action vis-à-vis des Ait Tseghrouchen et des Beni-Guil, Lyautey to Min. of France in Morocco, Jan. 25, 1910; Sit. pol. 1910, Regnault (Min. of France) to Lyautey, Feb. 9, 1910. Bernard, *Confins*, pp. 199, 206, 217.

35. On later resistance and conquest in Tafilalt and in the lands west of the Ziz, see Georges Spillmann, *Les Aït Atta du Sahara et la pacification du Haut Dra* (Rabat, 1936), pp. 99-101, 106-44. Also Pierre Vicard, 'Le Territoire de Bou Denib avant et pendant la guerre: le dernier soulèvement du Tafilalt, 1918-1919,' *BSGA* (1921), pp. 17-33.

36. Because of the near absence of economic data or observations by contemporary authorities on broader consequences of the conquest, it is not possible to do more than speculate on the nature and extent of social or economic change in the Southeast between 1881 and 1912. There is little doubt that central and maritime Morocco experienced far more severe economic and social upheavals during these decades than did the Southeast. World economic forces struck the country much earlier and more intensely in the ports, the major interior cities, and the plains regions than in the mountains or on the Saharan rim. The people of the Southeast experienced no disturbances comparable to the massive social instability and impoverishment that afflicted the tribes and towns north of the Atlas as the result of the infusion of cheap European goods, the decline of exports, monetary inflation, the transfer of vast areas of land to foreign commercial interests, and the rampant profiteering and speculation of a small number of European and Moroccan entrepreneurs. On the other hand, the decline of Saharan and trans-Atlas trade, the growth of European import traffic, and inflation clearly had effects on the Southeast that went beyond the ruin of some merchants and carriers and the prospering of others. What impact, for example, did the atrophy of trans-Atlas trade have on the economic well-being of the date-producing population of Tafilalt, which relied heavily on the annual shipments to Fez? How did the French army's demand for locally-produced livestock and produce to feed its forces affect pastoral and oasis economies? To what extent did French francs circulate in the region and reduce, if at all, the effects of devaluation of Moroccan currency? To what degree were the people of the Southeast, in comparison with central and coastal Morocco, dependent upon European tea, sugar, and textiles by 1912? These and other questions relating to more far-reaching economic and social changes remain unanswered.

37. T.O. Ranger, 'Connexions between "Primary Resistance" Movements and Modern Mass Nationalism in East and Central Africa,' *Journal of African History*, 9, no. 3 (1968), pp. 437-58; no. 4 (1968), pp. 631-41. By the same author, 'African Reactions to the Imposition of Colonial Rule in East and Central Africa,' in L.H. Gann and Peter Duignan, *Colonialism in Africa, 1870-1960*, I, pp. 293-324.

38. A.S. Kanya-Forstner, 'Mali-Tukolor,' in Michael Crowder, *West African Resistance* (New York, 1971), p. 53.

39. See John Ralph Willis, 'Jihad fí Sabíl Allāh – Its Doctrinal Basis in Islam and Some Aspects of Its Evolution in Nineteenth Century West Africa,' *Journal of African History*, 8, no. 3 (1967), pp. 395-415.

40. AMG, Maroc C7, MM 1894, Schlumberger to Min. War, April 1, 1894, no. 25.

41. In 1881 Abu 'Amama turned to the sultan, dispatching a delegation of tribal

leaders to ask Mawlay Hasan to support the Oranie rebellion. See Pierre
Guillen, *L'Allemagne et le Maroc de 1870 à 1905* (Paris, 1967), p. 77.

42. Burke, *Prelude to Protectorate,* pp. 124-27.

43. AMG, Alg. 17, Sit. pol. 1908, Lyautey to Gov. Gen., Feb. 2, 1908, no. 107;
'Sud-Oranais en 1908.'

44. Among the militant risings in Morocco between 1900 and 1912, the *jihad* of
Mawlay Ahmad al-Hiba in 1912 had the most distinct millenarian and revivalist content. People of the Sous and the western Atlas, desperate from prolonged
famine and economic decline, flocked to al-Hiba's banner, proclaiming war
against the Christians and the end of temporal governors and non-Koranic taxes.
While in power in Marrakech during the summer months, al-Hiba proceeded to
impose a series of stringent reforms, including the abolition of all but the
'ushr and *zakah* taxes and obligatory marriage for all women. Al-Hiba clearly
had visions not only of defeating the French but also of building a reformed and
purified Islamic society. The al-Hiba movement is given detailed study in Burke,
*Prelude to Protectorate,*pp. 199-207.

45. AMG, Alg. 18, Sit. pol. 1910, Gov. Gen. to Min. War, April 21, 1910, no. 881;
Actions vis-à-vis des Ait Tseghrouchen et des Beni-Guil, Lt. Berriau, 'Rapport,'
June 5, 1910.

46. A third principle of solidarity, Pan-Islam, had a minor though noteworthy influence on Moroccan resistance. It centered on attempts to strengthen ties between
Morocco and the Ottoman Empire and to introduce into Morocco Ottoman
military advisers and resistance activists. In 1911-12 a Pan-Islamic organization
headed by Egyptian nationalists tried to support and coordinate the mass
resistances which developed around Fez and Marrakech. Although these men
made contact with some resistance leaders, disseminated anti-French propaganda, and supplied some arms to al-Hiba, they failed to establish a pan-tribal
organization or strategy. See Edmund Burke III, 'Pan-Islam and Moroccan
Resistance to French Colonial Penetration, 1900-1912,' *Journal of African
History*, 13, no. 1 (1972), pp. 97-118; and Nikki R. Keddie, 'Pan-Islam as
Proto-Nationalism,' *The Journal of Modern History*, 41 (March-Dec. 1969),
pp. 17-28. Leaders in the Southeast may well have discussed the ideas of Pan-
Islam, but there is only one small piece of evidence of Pan-Islamic activity.
In 1903 Si 'Abd al-Malik, a grandson of the Amir 'Abd al-Qadir and an agent
of both Pan-Islamic interests and the German legation in Tangiers, circulated in
the Figuig area, met with Abu 'Amama, and tried to incite the local population
to resist the French. His mission had no consequence, but it points to the possibility of other efforts by Pan-Islamic activists to make contact with resistance
leaders in the Southeast. See, Guillen, *L'Allemagne et le Maroc*, pp. 679-82.

47. See Peter M. Holt, *The Mahdist State in the Sudan, 1881-1898* (Oxford, 1958);
and L. Carl Brown, 'The Sudanese Mahdiya,' in Robert I. Rotberg and Ali A.
Mazrui, *Protest and Power in Black Africa* (New York, 1970), pp. 145-68.

48. P. Odinot, 'Role politique des confréries religieuses et des zaouias au Maroc,'
BSGAO, 51 (March 1930), pp. 62-4; Lacroix, 'Les Derkaoua,' pp. 3-15.

49. See footnote 33.

50. Burke, 'Pan-Islam and Moroccan Resistance,' p. 99.

51. J. David Seddon, 'Local Politics and State Intervention: Northeast Morocco
from 1870 to 1970,' in Ernest Gellner and Charles Micaud, *Arabs and Berbers:
From Tribe to Nation in North Africa* (London and Lexington, Mass., 1972),
p. 123.

52. AMG, Alg. 14, Opérations du 1st trimestre 1901, Risbourg to Com. 19th Corps,
March 21, 1901, no. 63aa; Alg. 16, Sit. pol. 1904, Jonnart to Min. War, Jan. 9,
1904, no. 42; June 1, 1904, no. 1218. AGGA, 21H. 29, Relevés des notes des

chefs indigénes du Territoire d'Ain Sefra (1914), 'El Kebir ben Kaddour'; 30H. 13, Commission 6ème partie, Cauchemez to Gov. Gen., March 15, 1902, no. 138. M & L, II, 588, 610, 611. Interview no. 5.

9 SOUTHEASTERN MOROCCO AND AFRICA IN THE ERA OF EUROPEAN CONQUEST

The three decades of history traced in this book coincide squarely with the high period of European conquest throughout the African continent. The same year that Abu 'Amama raised tribal rebellion in Oranie, France occupied Tunisia and Britain was on the brink of invading Egypt, two events auguring the 'scramble' for African territory. Thirty-two years later, when Mawlay 'Abd al-Hafid signed the Treaty of Fez, the European conquest of Africa was largely completed and colonial government was taking root.

From a continent-wide perspective the events which occurred in southeastern Morocco between 1881 and 1912 represented but one of dozens of theaters of encounter between Africans and intruding Europeans. As the outlines of African history in the nineteenth and twentieth centuries become sharper, the stereotypical colonial view of these encounters as the triumph of civilization over savagery has given place to a body of new conceptions centering on the continuities in African culture and society and on the rationality of African responses to conquest.

These conceptions are the result of historical research undertaken almost entirely in sub-Saharan Africa. Comparative studies and symposiums on African resistance, innovation, and change during the conquest period have limited their field of enquiry almost exclusively to black Africa or to a major region within it.[1] Whatever the subject, comparative historiography has seldom spanned the thirsty Sahara. Obviously, North African history lends itself more readily to comparison with the Middle East because of the common links and sources of culture. The fact remains, however, that northern Africa from Morocco to Egypt (leaving aside the older French Algerian colony) fell prey to the same sorts of pressures from the same western European powers at generally the same time in history as did sub-Saharan Africa, whereas the partition of the Middle East heartland took place somewhat later under the vastly altered world conditions resulting from the Great War. Moreover, common aspects of social structure (segmentary lineage organization), political history (states attempting to consolidate or expand), and Islam (sufi brotherhoods) found both north and south of the desert invite comparisons between the North and black African experience during the first stage of the colonial era.

The broadest of the new conceptions to come out of the reinterpretation of African responses to European conquest prove applicable to almost all societies, including those north of the Sahara. For example, it was as true for the Maghrib as it was for black Africa that indigenous political behavior under colonial pressure — whether resistance, evasion, or accommodation — was rational and calculated; that colonial conquest was, to use J.F.A. Ajayi's phrase, 'an episode in African history,' which altered but did not actuate processes of development and change; that some societies attempted to repel, limit, or come to terms with the European offensive by creating new institutions and ideologies or by adapting old ones to meet unprecedented challenges; and that among some groups aspects of nineteenth-century organization, leadership, and ideology carried into the twentieth century to nurture modern movements of protest and nationalism. On this last point the impact of Sharifian traditions in Morocco on both early colonial resistance and post World War II nationalism is a striking example.

In setting southeastern Morocco's response to conquest against the broader pan-African experience, it must be noted that most studies of Afro-European encounters have focused upon situations where states and central leadership rather than uncentralized systems (segmentary lineages, age-grades, autonomous villages) or petty chiefdoms existed. Southeastern Morocco was a region where political organization was acephalous and segmentary. It was in general very similar to that found in the rest of rural North Africa and the Sahara and comparable in many ways to systems found among the Somali, Tiv, Nuer, and other societies commonly labeled as segmentary. On the other hand, the people of southeastern Morocco cannot be categorically described as 'stateless' owing to the influence which the 'Alawi sultans and the *makhzan* exerted on political life. Although the local complexion of history, politics, and economy largely shaped the population's response to the French, the impact of the central government cannot be discounted.

The *makhzan* had nothing close to control over events in the Southeast during the period of conquest, but it was nonetheless an important third factor in the politics of the region, much as the government of Zanzibar was on the East African mainland in the nineteenth century. The people of the Southeast, like those of other mountain and desert regions who most of the time escaped administration and taxes, regarded themselves as members of the community of the faithful and therefore eligible to call upon its head, the 'Alawi sultan, to provide services of mediation, judgment, and ratification of locally-based authority.

In the nineteenth century a succession of sultans, paralleling the actions of the Islamic leaders of Tunisia, Egypt, and Zanzibar, attempted to extend the range and depth of central authority, utilizing European military technology and acting partly in response to the spreading manifestations of European informal empire. These efforts, which culminated in the centralizing drive of Mawlay Hasan, largely failed owing to the weakness of governmental and military institutions, the subversive effects of European commercial penetration, and the lack of any sustained superiority in weaponry over the tribes, who trafficked busily with European rifle merchants. The tide of centralization, beaten back by force of arms in some mountain regions, lapped rather gently into the remote Southeast in the 1880s and 90s in the form of a partially fruitful program to strengthen lines of communication with the tribes and *qsar* communities. This centralization by correspondence, as it were, proved attractive to both the *makhzan* and the Saharans, confronted as they were by the lengthening shadow of Algerian expansionism. The *makhzan* hoped to preserve its territorial integrity and hence its prestige, while the Southeasterners were happy to be of the Moroccan state — just so long as they did not have to be in it.

Mainly as a result of Mawlay Hasan's energetic fence-mending, his successors were in an improved position to intervene politically in the Southeast as the crisis of French expansion mounted. Mawlay 'Abd al-'Aziz emphasized his mediational functions, attempting to cool a hot frontier by negotiating with the French and exhorting the tribes. Mawlay 'Abd al-Hafid, by contrast, during the first two years of his reign drew upon the ideological resources of the Sharifian tradition to promote mass resistance. The official agents which the sultans appointed in the region, namely the *khalifa* in Tafilalt and the *'amil-s* in Figuig, entered into local politics as either allies or brokers, sometimes in matters involving the French, but they lacked the means to command obedience. They personified at one and the same time the sultan's incapacity to dominate the political game and his determination to put pieces on the board.

The political game was one in which segmentary patrilineal kinship provided the basic charter of social affiliation and the blueprint for the allocation and sharing of resources but did not determine the configurations and limits of political relations. What Lawrence Rosen says about the Middle Atlas appears to have held true in the Southeast:

> The constant focus in Moroccan society is not . . . on corporate groups but on individuals; not on the sanctions through which behavior can be channelled and limited but on arranging associations wherever they appear most advantageous; not on a widely ramified set of solidarity groupings of which one is a member but on the customary ways in which

personal ties to others can be contracted.[2]

Thus breaking down the segmentary kinship structure of a tribe or oasis community would in itself reveal very little for certain about the ways in which political groupings coalesced and changed in response to particular objective situations. Kinship affiliation set broad norms for behavior, but much room was left for individuals to order and reorder their human ties to keep pace with recurrent shifts and surprises in the natural and political environment.

Under conditions of extreme economic uncertainty, in which no lineage, class, or faction could accumulate sufficient power to control the distribution of resources, competition for them stimulated a profusion of more or less temporary groupings of leaders and followers, which coalesced to pursue specific, short-run objectives. These groups moved into action to defend or to augment shared resources. Since the lasting control of resources was so unpredictable, this action usually involved taking advantage of other groups which appeared weak (Zenaga's excessive expropriation of water in Figuig) or ganging up defensively against those which were gaining too much (formation of the Ait Yafelman coalition to stop the Ait 'Atta), thus producing a politics of probe, retreat, and stalemate. In describing what he sees as general characteristics of politics in segmentary tribal societies John Waterbury states:

> Segmentary systems tend toward an internal equilibrium, which, it cannot be too strongly stated, is seldom achieved nor long maintained. However, neither are gross imbalances in the power of given units within the system long tolerated. Other units will regroup and coalesce to offset or wear down any undue power accumulation on the part of others. This is so well known to participants that units that have gained a slight power advantage will not try to increase it unduly, preferring modest gains to a total reversal of fortunes.[3]

The coming of the French army did not inhibit or discourage this style of behaviour but only exacerbated it. Terrence Ranger, John Hargraves, and other historians of black Africa have shown that European conquests seldom took the form of sudden, massive invasions, but were far more often characterized by slow, uncertain advances, troubled by shortages of money and men, irresolution over objectives, conflicts between armed forces and government, and ignorance of African society and geography.[4] Consequently, Africans often had the time and opportunity to probe and bargain their way into a relationship with the colonial power. Such was

certainly the case in Morocco, where the fitfulness and ambiguity of
French actions produced the same characteristics in indigenous response
and gave wide scope to fragmented, inconsistent politics. Furthermore,
despite the army's liberal use of violence whenever it seemed appropriate,
its fundamental aims were not slaughter, confiscation of land, or the
deliberate destruction of cultural institutions and values, but rather paternal pacification and the establishment of a climate conducive to the introduction of European trade and civilization. So it was in many parts of the
continent, where the first phase of colonialism presented Africans with an
ambiguous combination of threats and opportunities, encouraging neither
fanaticism nor resignation but rather accommodation along whatever lines
would diminish the unpredictability of the situation and preserve vital
resources and values. In societies where central institutions were particularly strong the state and army might be able to dictate the line of response, whether resistance or cooperation. Among populations lacking
central authority response was likely to be most coherent and consistent
in situations where Europeans proceeded early to assault vital resources or
deeply-held values. Thus the great pan-tribal rebellions in Southern
Rhodesia and Tanganyika, where the populations were subjected to extensive expropriation of land and livestock or to forceful mobilization of
labor.

Drawing largely upon research on Moroccan politics in the nineteenth
and twentieth centuries, Amal Vinogradov and John Waterbury have set
forth a model of political behavior in societies, past or present, where
effective central authority is lacking, where the resource base is limited
and uncertain, and where political life is ordered and sustained by competition among autonomous segments, alliances, or in their term 'security
groups.'[5] According to Vinogradov and Waterbury, political competition
in such societies involves a high degree of uncertainty. The function of all
security groups, whose memberships may change, overlap, and vary in
size, is 'to provide their members security, defense, and a modicum of
predictability.' The central characteristics of societies in which security
groups compete for scarce resources are a preoccupation with the defense
of members and their resources and an avoidance of bold initiatives that
might risk too much; a zero-sum game or 'constant-pie' conception of
power, that is, the conviction that resources are so limited that a gain for
one group implies a loss for another; a continuous effort to probe and
take advantage of the weaknesses of other groups but also a determination to join with them to prevent a still stronger group from appropriating an excessive share of resources; an effort to maximize options and to
avoid unalterable commitments; a refusal to regard any other group as

friend or enemy in any absolute sense in order to hedge against the future probabilities of having to switch one's allies. In such systems

> . . . alliances are fragile because the commitment of member groups to them is always tentative and contingent. Alliance leaders try to compensate for this weakness by ideological appeals. Such appeals tend to be messianic, transcendental and hortatory. The appeals have only momentary effect upon alliance cohesion. Political action remains pragmatic, instrumental, and flexible. In general political competition among security groups is characterized by ambiguity and inconsistency in identity, action, and belief.[6]

In the late nineteenth century the tribes and oasis-communities of southeastern Morocco shared with peoples all across Africa the problem of finding ways to thwart European conquest. The need for unifying principles and strategies to cement communities, classes, tribes, and regions to meet the challenge was widely felt. Indeed, examples abound of African peoples achieving unprecedented levels of organization and cohesion to resist the intruder. Yet almost everywhere in Africa were found the pre-industrial conditions where limitation and uncertainty dominated the production and allocation of material resources. And in many parts of the continent central government which would otherwise regulate the distribution of resources was either ineffectual or absent. Such societies might include not only those having segmentary lineage systems, which tribes in North Africa, the Sahara, and certain parts of black Africa did, but also those where the social framework was age-sets, secret societies, petty chiefdoms, or amorphously linked clusters of villages, or even where central government was weak or in upheaval. In such cases one might expect to find in the late nineteenth century a persistent tension between the deeply-rooted pragmatism of segmented politics and the 'messianic, transcendental and hortatory' forces urging men to make common cause against the invader. This tension was the dominant feature of political behaviour in southeastern Morocco, whose example suggests some general observations about the nature of Afro-European encounters in the period of conquest.

In segmentary lineage systems in Africa kinship was the principle of solidarity through which a large number of people might coalesce temporarily to wage war against outsiders. The behaviour of tribes in southeastern Morocco when confronted by the French army confirms the view of Marshall Sahlins that, despite the workability of the 'massing effect' — my fellow tribesmen and I against the world — in inter-tribal warfare,

'limited economic coordination, the relativity of leadership and its absence
of coercive sanctions, the localized, egalitarian character of the polity, the
ephemerality of large groupings, all of these would doom a segmentary
lineage system if brought into conflict with chiefdoms or states.'[7] Many
Moroccan tribes held their own against the *makhzan* without inventing
principles of unity other than kinship because of the *makhzan*'s endemic
weaknesses. But segmentary ideology was ineffectual against France, not
only because of the power and unitary organization of its army but also
because of the politically and economically ambiguous nature of the
crisis, which called forth the skills of security group defense and maneuver,
not a reflexive massing of the segments.

Coordinated mass resistance in segmentary lineage societies depended
on the emergence of extra-tribal leaders, organization, and ideology persuasive and compelling enough to heal over, at least for a time, the natural
fissipariousness of political action. Southeastern Morocco represents a
case where this kind of experimentation, the mass *harka-s* of 1903 and
1908, achieved only the most transitory success. Of far greater import in
African history were the achievements of the Sanusiya brotherhood in
organizing the Bedouin of Cyrenaica against the Italians or the exploits
of the charismatic Sheikh Muhammad Abdille Hassan in leading the
Somalis against the British.[8] In some places, on the other hand, the forces
of *resistance* to unity consistently won out. E.R. Turton's description of
the behavior of the southern Somali confronted by British expansion in
Kenya comes closer to the Moroccan example.

> . . . when the various examples of Somali resistance are examined in
> detail, they turn out to have been much more limited than is generally
> appreciated. The only example of a whole clan being involved in a
> rebellion was that of the Herti in 1893. Yet this unity seems to have
> been achieved by pure chance. . . .On all other occasions, moreover, the
> lack of unity amongst the Somali was extremely conspicuous. When the
> government first sent an armed caravan to the Ogaden Sultan at
> Afmadu, there was a fight not between the government troops and the
> Ogaden, but amongst the Ogaden themselves, who could not agree on
> whether to resist or to capitulate. In 1898, only four out of the seven
> Ogaden sub-clans took part in the hostilities, and in the 1900-1 cam-
> paign this number was not improved on. Even in the Marehan uprising
> of 1913 and the Aulihan rebellion of 1916, there were sections of these
> two clans that remained aloof from the hostilities or actively assisted
> the government.

It is clear that Somali resistance to the extension of British adminis-

tration was undertaken within the traditional framework of their seg-
mentary system, and this made the attainment of widespread coopera-
tion extremely difficult'. . .   The example of Sheik Muhammad Abdille
Hassan in British Somaliland, who united Somali segments through the
Salihiyya *tariqa* (brotherhood), made an impact on the southernmost
Somali. But attempts to emulate him in the south failed. Appeals to
Islamic solidarity did not manage to unite the Marehan in 1914.[9]

Historians of the early phase of colonialism, out of a desire to demolish
colonial myths and to demonstrate the rationality, complexity, and
creativity of popular reactions to conquest, have tended to be enthusiastic about African experiments to create large-scale resistance movements
and military organizations. Conversely, they have, at least by implication,
usually regarded the failure of such experiments to be everything they
might have been as a consequence not only of European power but also
of negative divisions and particularisms within African society. John
Illife, for example, conceives of the widespread Maji Maji rebellion against
the Germans in Tanganyika in 1905 as 'a great crisis of commitment'
which 'finally crumbled as crisis compelled reliance on fundamental loyalties to kind and tribe.'[10] The same could generally be said of mass resistance in southeastern Morocco. A close look at the patterns of political
behavior, however, reveals that neither ethno-linguistic groupings (Arabs
and Berbers), nor tribes, nor discrete oasis communities (at least not the
larger ones) were hard-core units of fundamental loyalty. Rather in an
environment of constant competition among more or less temporary
alliance groups for control of resources, loyalty – at least above the
family level – was conceived as being entirely contingent upon economic
or political advantages. In his East African case, Turton asserts that in
facing the problem of raising a united front against the British, 'the
inherent rivalry between different groups was a crippling disadvantage
that the Kenya Somali were unable to surmount.'[11] But to whom was it
a 'crippling disadvantage,' to all of the Somali or only to some of them,
when it was through 'the inherent rivalry between different groups' that
a degree of political order was maintained in conditions, in this case
severe, of material insecurity? In other words, the failure of Moroccans
and southern Somalis to achieve enduring cooperation to mount resistance cannot be attributed merely structural cleavages among tribes and
segments but to the dynamic urge of alliance groups and individuals to
form and reform their corporate commitments and their fellow feelings
to suit the particular economic or political exigencies of the day.
    The spasmodic and ephemeral character of mass activism in south-

eastern Morocco exposes the tension and conflict between the moral
incitements of saints, pretenders, and other resistance leaders to forge a
common cause and the far more natural inclinations of individuals to avoid
dogmatic commitments which might diminish the range of political
options and propel them into dangerous, intractable situations from
which there might be no escape. In the context of the broad patterns
of political behavior the mass *harka-s* appear as alliances of doubters
and provisional fanatics, who saw mass assault as a feasible option for
repelling the French but who availed themselves of the ideology of
jihad, Sharifianism, and saintly charisma, not as a new-found ethic of
unity, but as a device for legitimizing a scale of cooperation that under
any but the most unusual circumstances would be anathema. When the
assaults failed the mass movements disintegrated, not mainly because of
suspicions, rivalries, and 'fundamental loyalties to kind and tribe,' but
because no one had committed himself to anything but the short-run
objective in the first place. This attitude, a kind of resistance to resistance,
must not be construed as crass amoralism, cowardice, or love of anarchy.
Rather it was the dynamic operation of a diffuse, multicentered system of
politics.

There is no reason to believe that in the context of the colonial crisis
the tension between cohesion and consistency on the one hand and the
centrifugal forces of security group politics on the other hand was limited
to societies with segmentary lineage systems.[12] Some African societies
possessing central institutions may have been politically, economically,
and culturally integrated to the extent that response to conquest took
on a truly national character in which the population was by and large
united to whatever line of action its leaders chose to take. Most societies
in the nineteenth century, even many states, could not be placed in that
category. In reference to East and Central Africa Ranger notes that 'a
historian has indeed a difficult task in deciding whether a specific society
should be described as "resistant" or as "collaborative" over any given
period of time. Many societies began in one camp and ended in the other.'[13]
In fact, the exercise of classifying African societies according to category
of response may in many cases be both unfruitful and misleading if it
produces the implication that state policy backed by effective means of
coercion is to be equated with popular activism or that the existence of a
highly visible resistance movement is to be equated with near universal
commitment to it. For example, to label the Morocco of 'Abd al-'Aziz as
collaborating, and the Morocco of the early Hafidiya as resisting would
merely lead us back to the simplistic conceptions of the colonial literature.
It is perhaps more reasonable to assume that in all but the more thoroughly

integrated societies (Ashanti? Buganda?) the proponents of moblization and unity, whether state officials or religious leaders, had continually to fight against currents of local self-interest, patrimonialism, and power which linked all political action to the ever-abiding problem of individual and security group survival. Therefore, if it is important to examine the institutions, ideologies, and techniques by which a society extended the scale or efficiency of corporate action under the shadow of colonial conquest, it may also be important to understand the institutions and mechanisms by which individuals, local communities, and alliances defended themselves, not only against Europeans, but also against the pressures and importunings of kings, generals, saints, prophets, and other meddlers who would corner them into taking risks and making sacrifices dangerously incompatible with the urgent imperatives of protecting land, water, crops, and herds.

In a recent study of rural rebellion in Algeria one scholar has made the point that some Western scholars have mistakenly probed for roots of nationalism in the nineteenth century Maghrib on the assumption that 'North African history proceeds down a path well marked by European nations which passed that way before it.'[14] In the context of black Africa, Ranger and others have argued convincingly for the existence of substantive connections between nineteenth-century resistance and modern nationalism. However, the slackening and troubled pace of national integration and civic commitment in many modern African states following the ebullient decades of mass nationalism brings into sharper focus the tenacity of individuals and primordial groups in defending interests and resources against the forces of encapsulation. The patterns of indigenous response to the European scramble for Africa must be seen not only in terms of the creative thrusts toward resistance, unity, and hence nationalism, but also in terms of the institutional devices and political strategies by which people grappled with the colonial crisis in their own ways and at their own front gates, despite the efforts of men with broader visions or bigger weapons, European or African, to push them down some dangerously winding road toward millenial bliss or national consciousness.

Notes

1. See, for example, Michael Crowder (ed.), *West African Resistance* (New York, 1971); L.H. Gann and Peter Duignan (eds.), *Colonialism in Africa, 1870-1960,* I (London, 1969); Robert I. Rotberg and Ali A. Mazrui (eds.), *Protest and Power in Black Africa* (New York, 1970).
2. Lawrence Rosen, 'The Social and Conceptual Framework of Arab-Berber Rela-

tions in Central Morocco,' in Ernest Gellner and Charles Micaud (eds.), *Arabs and Berbers: From Tribe to Nation in North Africa* (Lexington, Mass. and London 1972), p. 158.

3. John Waterbury, *The Commander of the Faithful: The Moroccan Political Elite – a Study in Segmented Politics* (New York, 1970), p. 65.
    The bahavior of the Ait 'Atta might seem to contradict this pattern. But the tribe's expansion did not take the form of massive offensives to seize territory and resources but of prudent sallies and tactical retreats in which most of the fighting was carried on by ad hoc war bands.

4. T.O. Ranger, 'African Reactions to the Imposition of Colonial Rule in East and Central Africa,' in L.H. Gann and Peter Duignan, *Colonialism in Africa, 1870-1960*, I (London, 1969), 293-301; John D. Hargreaves, 'West African States and the European Conquest,' in *Colonialism in Africa*, pp. 200-5.

5. Amal Vinogradov and John Waterbury, 'Situations of Contested Legitimacy in Morocco: An Alternative Framework,' *Comparative Studies in Society and History*, 13, no. 1(1971), pp. 32-59.

6. Vinogradov and Waterbury, 'Situations,' p. 36. I would not assert, for lack of detailed ethnographic field work, that the peoples of pre-Saharan Morocco had a 'constant-pie' conception of human relations and that this conception shaped their political behavior. However, the debate among social scientists over the question of 'constant-pie' orientations among peasant societies has been suggestive. See George M. Foster, 'Peasant Society and the Image of Limited Good,' *American Anthropologist*, 67, no. 2 (1965), pp. 293-315; James C. Scott, *Political Ideology in Malaysia* (New Haven, 1968), pp. 91-149.

7. Marshall D. Sahlins, 'The Segmentary Lineage: An Organization of Predatory Expansion,' *American Anthropologist*, 63 (1961), pp. 322-45.

8. E.E. Evans-Pritchard, *The Sanusi of Cyrenaica* (London, 1949); I.M. Lewis, *The Modern History of Somaliland* (New York, 1965). On the resistance leadership of prophets among the Nuer, the archetype of segmentary systems, see E.E. Evans-Pritchard, *The Nuer* (Oxford, 1940), pp. 184-9.

9. E.R. Turton, 'Somali Resistance to Colonial Rule and the Development of Somali Political Activity in Kenya 1893-1960,' *Journal of African History*, 13, no. 1 (1972), pp. 124, 125.

10. John Iliffe, *Tanganyika under German Rule 1905-1912* (Cambridge, 1969), pp. 25, 26; 'The Organization of the Maji Maji Rebellion,' *Journal of African History*, 8, no. 3 (1967), p. 495.

11. Turton, 'Somali Resistance,' p. 124.

12. On the complex and inconsistent nature of Khoisan response to Dutch expansion in South Africa see Shula Marks, 'Khoisan Resistance to the Dutch in the Seventeenth and Eighteenth Centuries,' *Journal of African History*, 13, no. 1 (1972), pp. 55-80.

13. Ranger, 'African Reactions,' p. 304.

14. Peter von Sivers, 'Apocalypse and Autarchy: An Indigenous Revolt in Eastern Algeria, 1879,' unpublished MS, 1973.

GLOSSARY OF SPECIAL TERMS AND TRIBAL NAMES

'amil
: 'āmil; governor; specifically the title held by the top makhzan official in Oujda and Figuig.

baraka
: baraka; quality of divine grace.

duwar
: duwār; herding group.

harrar, pl. ahrar
: ḥarrar, aḥrār; oasis farmer.

hartani, pl. haratin
: hartāni, ḥaratin; oasis laborer, of negroid descent.

jama'a
: jamā'a; tribal or village council.

khalifa
: khalīfa; viceroy of the sultan of Morocco, appointed in Fez, Marrakech, and Tafilalt; deputy to a provincial governor or administrator.

khams khmas
: khams akhmās; five fifths; the division of a tribe into five primary sections.

khums
: khums; a fifth; a primary section of a tribe.

makhzan
: makhzan; central government of Morocco.

mallah
: mallāḥ; Jewish quarter in a village or city.

murabit, pl. murabtin
: murābiṭ, murābiṭīn; a saint.

qadi
: qāḍi; judge.

qa'id
: qā'id; tribal leader; Moroccan government administrator.

qsar
: qṣar; walled village.

shar'a
: sharī'a; Islamic law.

sharia pl. shurfa
: sharīf, shurafā'; descendant of the Prophet.

shaykh
: shaykh; tribal leader; head of a sufi zawiya.

suq
: sūq; market.

taqbilt
: taqbilt; tribe, or segment of a tribe.

tariqa
: ṭariqa; sufi brotherhood.

tata
: ṭaṭa; intertribal pact of protection and hospitality.

'ulama
: 'ulamā; religious scholars.

zattata
: zaṭṭaṭa; toll paid to guarantee safe passage through a tribe's territory.

zawiya
: zawīya; sufi brotherhood; center for a sufi brotherhood or a saintly lineage.

ziyara
: ziyara; religious offering, given to saints, shurfa, or the sultan.

273

Arabic-speaking tribes

Amur	Amūr; Mountains of the Ksour region.
'Arab Sabbah	'Arab Ṣabbāh; lower Wad Ziz valley.
Awlad al-Nasir	Awlād al-Naṣīr; Wad Ait Aissa.
Awlad Jarir ('Asasa, Mulfalha)	Awlād Jarīr, 'Asasa, Mufalha; lower Wad Guir to Wad Zousfana.
Awlad Sidi Shaykh	Awlād Sidi Shaykh; plains of Oranie (Western Algeria).
Awlad Sidi Taj	Awlād Sidi Tāj; Mountains of the Ksour region.
Bani Gil	Bani Gīl; Moroccan high plains.
Bani Mhammad	Bani Muḥammad; Tafilalt.
Dawi Mani' Awlad abu 'Anan Awlad bil Giz Awlad Yusif Awlad Jallul Idarasa	Dawi Manī', Awlād abu 'Anān, Awlād bil Gīz, Awlād Yūsif, Awlād Jallūl, Idārasa; Tafilalt to Wad Zousfana.
Ghananma	Ghananma; Wad Saoura valley.
Regibat	Regibāt; western Sahara.
Sha'amba	Sha'āmba; north central Sahara.
Shurfa	Shurafā'; Mountains of the Ksour region (not to be confused with shurfa as collective term for descendants of the Prophet).

Berber-speaking tribes

Ait 'Atta Ait Unibgi Ait Khabbash Ait Umnasf	Ait 'Atta, Ait Unibgi, Ait Khabbash, Ait Umnasf; Wad Ziz to Wad Dra.
Ait 'Aysa	Ait 'Aysa; Wad Ait Aïssa, Wad Haïber.
Ait Izdig	Ait Izdig; Wad Ziz to upper Wad Guir; member of Ait Yafalman confederation.
Ait Mirghad	Ait Mirghad; eastern High Atlas; member of Ait Yafalman confederation.
Ait Seghrushin	Ait Seghrushin; far eastern High Atlas
Ait Yafalman	Ait Yafalman; tribal confederation of central and eastern High Atlas.

Saintly lineages

Awlad abu Ziyan	Awlād abu Ziyān; Kenadsa.
Awlad Sidi al-Ghazi	Awlād Sidi al-Ghāzi; Tafilalt, Ghorfa district.

Awlad Sidi al-Hanafi	Awlād Sidi al-Hanafi; Rteb, Ziz valley
Awlad Sidi Mawlay Karzaz	Awlād Sidi Mawlay Karzāz; Wad Saoura valley.
Darqawa zawiya of Douiret Sbaa	Dā'ira Saba'; upper Wad Ait Aïssa
Darqawa zawiya of Medaghra	Medaghra district, qsar Gaouz, Ziz valley.

SOURCES

Europeans rather than North Africans furnished most of the documentation for this study. In addition to material published in books and periodi-
cals, I have relied heavily on two documents collections, the archives of
the French Ministry of War (Vincennes) and the Algeria series of the
Archives d'Outre-Mer (Aix-en-Provence). The bulk of the material in both
collections represents the views of French army officers serving in the
Algero-Moroccan frontier zone or in Morocco with the Military Mission.
Many of the letters and reports contained in some dozens of boxes are
irrelevant to questions of Moroccan history. Almost all of them are per-
vaded by biases, prejudices, or distortions of one sort or another. It is
certain, for example, that the army consistently reported events in such a
way as to secure the government's permission for further territorial expansion. Nonetheless, these documents are important because the army collected and analyzed, often with thoroughness and perceptivity, a great deal of
political data, as well as general ethnographic information, concerning
Moroccan groups both within and beyond its administrative control.

I have supplemented the European sources with oral data collected in
southeastern Morocco over a two and a half month period in 1967 and
1969. The informants were for the most part elderly men who either had
personal or second-hand recollections of events occurring before 1912, or
who could provide descriptions of political, social, and economic institutions not available in the written sources. In general, the interviews
yielded more useful ethnographic data than historical. The field notes, as
well as tapes of some of the interviews, are in my possession. Although I
had training in standard Arabic before going to the field, I employed a
Moroccan interpreter, who translated testimony from Moroccan Arabic
dialect or Berber into French. The only written sources in Arabic I located
were a few letters (with accompanying French translations) scattered here
and there in the archives. The papers of the pre-Protectorate *makhzan*,
which remain largely unclassified and inaccessible, may one day reveal a
great deal more about Morocco's history during this period.

I Interviews

The chapter footnotes refer to interviews by number. Each interview is
identified by (1) the subject tribe or group, (2) the place of interview, (3)
the date, (4) the names of principal informants.

1. Dawi Mani', Ghorfa (southeastern district of Tafilalt), July 24, 1967, al-Hashmi ibn 'Abd al-Karim, 'Abd al-Karim Butahir, Muhammad ibn 'Amsifi, al-Hajj ibn Ahmad ibn Salah.
2. Dawi Mani', Ghorfa, July 26, 1967, Musa wuld Shaykh, Bashir ibn al-'Ayd, Sidi al-Ghazi ibn al-Madani, 'Abd al-Qadir ibn 'Ayrish.
3. Dawi Mani', Aïn Souater (small oasis south of Bouanane), August 2, 1967, Shaykh ibn al-Khayr, Khalifa 'Atman.
4. Dawi Mani', Boudenib, August 2/3, 1967, Qa'id Saddiqui Seddiq.
5. Dawi Mani', Boudenib, July 29, 1969, Musa wuld Shaykh, Hamdawi al-'Ayd ibn Sa'id, Tahri Ahmad ibn 'Abd Allah, Shahid al-Hajj al-Ma'ti, Jabbari 'Abd al-Hakim, Bakri Muhammad ibn Buka.
6. Dawi Mani', Boudenib, July 30, 1969, Shahid al-Hajj al-Ma'ti.
7. Dawi Mani', Boudenib, August, 1969, Qa'id Saddiqui Seddiq.
8. Dawi Mani', Taouz (oasis south of Tafilalt), August 6, 1969, al-Hajj ibn Seddiq.
9. Ait Khabbash, Taouz, July 27, 1967, Hamid al-Qarawi, Lahsin u-Rahma, Baha 'Ardwi.
10. Ait Khabbash, Aoufous (Rteb district), July 31, 1967, u-Rahma 'Ali u-Hassu, Lahsin n-Ait l-Hajj.
11. Ait Khabbash, Boudenib, August 3, 1967, Ba'di Brahim, Hasan ibn al-Kabir.
12. Ait Khabbash, Mesguida (Tanijiout district, Tafilalt), August 2, 1969, 'Assu Brahim Shaykh, Hada Hammu, u-Idir.
13. Ait Khabbash, Merzouga (small oasis south of Tafilalt), August 6, 1969, al-Hajj Hada l-Alla, 'Adi u-Brahim, Baha 'Ardwi.
14. Ait Izdig, Oulad Ali (*qsar* east of Boudenib), August 3, 1967, Kinsi 'Ali.
15. Idrisi *shurfa*, Oulad Abderrahman (*qsar* in Ghorfa, Tafilalt), July 24, 1967, Mawlay Ahmad.
16. Idrisi *shurfa*, Sefalat district (Tafilalt), July 25, 1967, Mawlay Muhammad Tuhani.
17. 'Alawi *shurfa*, Ksabi Moulay Cherif (*qsar* in Wad Ifli district, Tafilalt, which houses tomb of Mawlay 'Ali Sharif), July 26, 1967, Mawlay Ahmad ibn al-Mahdi, Mawlay Habib ibn Muhammad.
18. Bani Mhammad, Oulad l'Imam (*qsar* in Bani Mhammad district, Tafilalt), July 25, 1967, Lagid ibn al-Madani.
19. 'Arab Sabbah, Jorf district, July 28, 1967, 'Adl 'Ammari, 'Abd al-'Aziz, Madani ibn 'Arab.
20. Abou Am, Tafilalt, August 3, 1969, al-Hajj Muhammad Tarfas.
21. Tabouasamt, Sefalat district, Tafilalt, August 4, 1969, Sidi al-'Arabi ibn Maruf.

22. Moulay Abderrahman, Wad Ifli district, Tafilalt, August 4, 1969,
    Mawlay 'Ali ibn Mawlay Rashid (a son of Khalifa Mawlay Rashid).
23. Mawlay al-Hanafi family, Jramna (Rteb), July 31, 1967, Sidi
    Muhammad ibn al-Hasan, Mawlay al-Kabir ibn al-Maki, Hashim ibn
    'Ali.
24. Saheli *zawiya*, Saheli (east of Boudenib), July 30, 1969, Sidi Ibn
    Muhammad ibn al-Hajj 'Abd al-Rahman.
25. Boudenib, July 31, 1969, al-Hajj al-Fqih abu Kaysi.
26. Oufkir family, Bouanane, August 2, 1967, Hasan Oufkir.
27. Oufkir family, Boudenib, July 31, 1969, 'Abd al-Rahman Oufkir
    (*shaykh* of Aïn Chaïr).
28. Figuig, al-Oudaghir, September 13, 15, 1967, Mawlay Tahar ibn 'Abd
    al-Rahman ibn Jabbar, Mawlay Ahmad ibn al-'Ayd, Abu 'Ajaja
    Muhammad ibn Muhammad.
29. Figuig, Zenaga, September 16, 1967, Hajj 'Abd Allah ibn Huku, Fadil
    Muhammad.
30. Figuig, Rabat, July 20, 1969, Muhammad Jabran.
31. Figuig, Rabat, July 23, 1969, Musa Fadil.
32. Former Native Affairs officer, Meknès, September 9, 1967, Anonymous.

II Official Papers

France

Archives du Ministère de la Guerre, Service Historique de l'Armée, Section
d'Afrique et d'Outre-Mer (Vincennes).

Series A-B Algérie (40 cartons). Records of the army's political and
military action in the southern Algero-Moroccan frontier zone (*Confins*),
especially cartons 12-20.

Series C Oran (11 cartons). Documents relating to both the northern
and southern frontier regions and dealing mainly with military organization.

Series C Maroc (24 cartons). Records of the French Military Mission in
Morocco. C17 contains a large dossier on affairs in Figuig.

Series D Maroc (31 cartons). French action in Morocco 1907-1911.
Miscellaneous documents on the frontier zone.

Series E Maroc (30 cartons). E3 contains material on Tafilalt.

Archives d'Outre-Mer, Archives du Gouvernement Général de l'Algérie
(Aix-en-Provence).

Series H. An extensive collection dealing with both political and
military affairs. Many cartons, especially those in the 30H series, con-

tain documents pertaining to Morocco and to the frontier region. Since 1967 the entire Series H has been extensively reclassified. Therefore references in the chapter footnotes are in many cases no longer correct. However, the Conservateur has available a complete list of corresponding new and obsolete references.

Archives Nationales (Paris).
Series F80. Miscellaneous manuscripts on southern Oranie, Abu 'Amama, and Touat.

Archives du Ministère des Affaires Etrangères (Paris).
Maroc Nouvelle Serie. Documents pertaining to the period 1896-1912 were not made available until 1969-71 and therefore were not consulted extensively for this study. However, a check of relevant cartons in 1972 revealed mostly correspondence dealing with European diplomatic issues or copies of documents found in the archives in Vincennes or Aix-en-Provence.

Great Britain

Public Records Office. (London).
Foreign Office Political Correspondence pertaining to Morocco. Consular Correspondence (FO 174) includes the reports of the British consul in Fez. Of particular value were his descriptions of the Tafilalt-Fez date trade.

III Private Papers

Institut de France (Paris).
Fonds Auguste Terrier. Terrier was the Secretary-General of the Comité de l'Afrique Française and the Comité du Maroc, later the director of the Office Cherifien du Maroc. The collection contains a small number of documents relating to the frontier region.

Centre des Hautes Etudes sur l'Afrique et l'Asie Moderne (Paris).
The library has a large collection of unpublished 'fin de stage' studies and other monographs written by prospective colonial administrators. They vary widely in length and quality. They are arranged by number in bound volumes.

IV Official Publications

Documents diplomatiques: Affaires du Maroc, 1901-1912.
6 vols. Paris, 1905-1912.

La Martinière, H.M.P., and N. Lacroix, *Documents pour servir à l'étude du Nord Ouest africain*. 4 vols. Gouvernement Général de l'Algérie, Algiers, 1894-1897.

V Libraries

The following libraries were especially useful for consulting published literature:

Institute de Géographie, Fonds Augustin Bernard (Paris).

A special North Africa collection based on the private library of this noted geographer and historian.

Section Historique du Maroc (Paris).

Bibliothèque Nationale (Paris).

Bibliothèque Générale (Rabat).

VI Periodicals

Special attention was paid to the following journals both for reporting of events occurring in the Algero-Moroccan frontier region and for ethnographic and commercial studies:

Archives Marocaines

Bulletin de la Société de Géographie (Paris)

Bulletin de la Société de Géographie d'Alger

Bulletin de la Société de Géographie et d'Archéologie d'Oran

Bulletin du Comité de l'Afrique Française and its supplement
    Renseignements Coloniaux

Hespéris

VII Select bibliography: General works relevant to Southeastern Morocco and the frontier region

Arnaud, E., and M. Cortier, *Nos Confins sahariens: Etude d'organisation militaire* (Paris, 1908)

Bernard, Augustin, *Les Confins algéro-marocains* (Paris, 1911)

Bernard, Augustin, and N. Lacroix, *L'Evolution du nomadisme en Algérie* (Paris, 1906)

La Pénétration saharienne (Algiers, 1906)

Blaudin de Thé, *Historique des compagnies méharistes* (Algiers, 1955)

Déchaud, Edouard, *Le Commerce algéro-marocain* (Algiers, 1906)

Harris, Walter B., *Tafilet* (London, 1895)

Jacques-Meunié, D., 'Hiérarchie sociale au Maroc pré-saharien,' *Hespéris*, 45 (1958), pp. 239-70.

Jonnart, C., *Exposé de la situation générale des Territoires du Sud*, Gouvernement Général de l'Algérie (Algiers, 1906)

Le Chatelier, *Notes sur les villes et tribus du Maroc: Tafilelt, Tizimmi, Er-Reteb, Medghara* (Paris, 1903)

Linarès, 'Voyage au Tafilalet avec S. M. le Sultan Moulay Hassan en 1893.' Extracted from *Bulletin de l'Institut d'Hygiene du Maroc*, nos. 3 and 4 (1932)

Lyautey, Louis-Hubert-Gonsalve, *Vers le Maroc: Lettres du Sud-Oranais, 1903-1906* (Paris, 1937)

Martin, A.G.P., *Quatre siècles d'histoire marocaine* (Paris, 1923)

Mercier, L., 'Notice économique sur le Tafilalet,' *Renseignements Coloniaux*, June 1905, pp. 210-21.

Munholland, Kim, 'Rival Approaches to Morocco: Delcassé, Lyautey, and the Algerian-Moroccan Border, 1903-1905,' *French Historical Studies*, 5, no. 3 (1968), pp. 328-43.

Rohlfs, Gerhard, *Adventures in Morocco and Journeys through the Oases of Draa and Tafilalet* (London, 1874)

Spillmann, Georges, *Les Ait Atta du Sahara et la pacification du Haut Dra* (Rabat, 1936)

Spillmann, Georges, *Districts et tribus de la haute vallée du Draa'* (Paris, 1931)

'Le Tafilalet d'après Gerhard Rohlfs,' *Renseignements Coloniaux*, August 1910, pp. 243-57.

Tillion, Breveté, *La Conquête des oasis sahariennes* (Paris, 1903)

Trout, Frank E., *Morocco's Saharan Frontiers* (Geneva, 1969)

VIII Select bibliography: North Africa and the Sahara

Abun Nasr, Jamil, *The Tijaniyya* (London, 1966)

Adu Boahen, A., *Britain, the Sahara, and the Western Sudan* (Oxford, 1964)

Ageron, Charles-Robert, *Les Algériens musulmans et la France (1871-1919)* (2 vols., Paris, 1968)

Andrew, Christopher, *Theophile Delcassé and the Making of the Entente Cordiale* (New York, 1968)

Arnaud, Louis, *Au Temps des Mehallas ou le Maroc de 1860 à 1912* (Casablanca, 1952)

Aubin, Eugène, *Le Maroc d'aujourd'hui*, 8th ed. (Paris, 1905)

Ayache, Germain, 'Aspects de la crise financière au Maroc après l'expédition espagnole de 1860,' *Revue Historique*, 220 (1958), pp. 271-310.

Bataillon, Claude, *Nomades et nomadisme au Sahara* (Paris, 1963)

Berque, Jacques, 'Qu'est-ce qu'une 'tribu' nord-africaine,' In *Evantail de l'histoire vivante: Hommage à Lucien Febvre* (Paris, 1953)

Berque, Jacques, *Structure sociales du Haut-Atlas* (Paris, 1955)

Bourdieu, Pierre, *The Algerians* (Boston, 1962)

Briggs, Lloyd Cabot, *Tribes of the Sahara* (Cambridge, 1960)

Brignon, Jean, *et al.*, *Histoire du Maroc* (Paris, 1967)

Burke, Edmund, *Prelude to Protectorate in Morocco: Precolonial Protest and Resistance, 1860-1912* (Chicago, 1976)

Capot-Rey, Robert, *Le Sahara français* (Paris, 1953)

Carette, E., and E. Renou, *Recherches sur la géographie et le commerce de l'Algérie méridionale* (Paris, 1844)

Daumas, E., *Le Sahara algérien* (Paris, 1845)

Depont, O., and X. Coppolani, *Les Confréries réligieuses musulmanes* (Algiers, 1897)

Despois, Jean, *L'Afrique du Nord*, 2nd ed. (Paris, 1958)

Despois, Jean, and René Raynal, *Géographie de l'Afrique du Nord-Ouest* (Paris, 1967)

Drague, Georges (pseud. for Georges Spillmann). *Esquisse d'Histoire religieuse du Maroc* (Paris, 1951)

Eikelman, Dale F. *Moroccan Islam: Tradition and Society in a Pilgrimage Center* (Austin, Texas, 1976)

Evans-Pritchard, E.E., *The Sanusi of Cyrenaica* (Oxford, 1949)

Ezziani, Aboulqâsem ben Ahmed, *Le Maroc de 1631 à 1812*. Extracted

Gellner, Ernest, *Saints of the Atlas* (London, 1969)

Gellner, Ernest, and Charles Micaud (eds.), *Arabs and Berbers: From Tribe to Nation in North Africa* (Lexington, Mass. and London, 1973)

Guennoun, Saïd, *La Montagne berbère* (Paris, 1929)

Guillen, Pierre, *L'Allemagne et le Maroc de 1870 à 1905* (Paris, 1967)

Hart, David M., 'Segmentary Systems and the Role of 'Five Fifths' in Tribal Morocco,' *Revue de l'Occident Musulman et de la Méditerranée*, no. 3 (1967), pp. 65-95.

Hoffman, Bernard G., *The Structure of Traditional Moroccan Rural Society* (Paris and The Hague, 1967)

Lahbabi, Mohamed, *Le Gouvernement marocain à l'aube du XXe siècle* (Rabat, 1958)

Lesne, Marcel, 'Les Zemmour: Essai d'histoire tribale,' *Revue de l'Occident Musulman et de la Méditerranée*, no. 2 (1966), pp. 111-54, and no. 3 (1967), pp. 97-132.

Le Tourneau, Roger, *Fès avant le Protectorat* (Casablanca, 1949)

Masqueray, Emile, *Formation des cités chez les populations sédentaires en Algérie* (Paris, 1886)

Miège, Jean-Louis, *Le Maroc et l'Europe* (4 vols., Paris, 1961-3)

Montagne, Robert, *La Civilisation du désert* (Paris, 1947)

Montagne, Robert, *Les Berbères et le Makhzen dans le Sud du Maroc* (Paris, 1930)

Nasiri, Ahmad ibn Khalid, 'Chronique de la dynastie alaouite du Maroc'
   (*Kitab al-Istiqsa*),Trans. Eugène Fumey, *Archives Marocaines*, 9 and 10
   (1906)

Peyronnet, R., *Livre d'or des officiers des Affaires Indigènes 1830-1930*
   (2 vols., Algiers, 1930)

Pinon, René, *L'Empire de la Méditerranée* (Paris, 1904)

Rinn, Louis, *Marabouts et Khouans* (Algiers, 1884)

Rouard de Card, E., *Documents diplomatiques pour servir à l'étude de la
   question marocaine* (Paris, 1911)

Sabatier, Camille, *Touat, Sahara et Soudan* (Paris, 1891)

Segonzac, J. de, *Voyage au Maroc (1899-1901)* (Paris, 1903)

Taillandier, G. Saint-René, *Les Origines du Maroc français: Récit d'une
   mission, 1901-1906* (Paris, 1930)

Terrasse, Henri, *Histoire du Maroc* (2 vols., Casablanca, 1950)

Waterbury, John, *The Commander of the Faithful: The Moroccan Political
   Elite − A Study in Segmental Politics* (New York, 1970)

Westermarck, Edward, *Ritual and Belief in Morocco* (2 vols., London,
   1926)

INDEX

Abadla: plain of 32, 39, 55-6, 57, 213; village of 32, 55; map 33, 58

'Abd al-'Aziz, Sultan Mawlay: reign of 22-6; protests occupation of Touat 23; policy toward southeastern Morocco 177, 179, 181, 193, 200, 221; popular opposition to 183-4, 185, 216, 217; and 'Abd al-Hafid, 231-2; mentioned 116, 248, 270

'Abd al-Hafid, Sultan Mawlay: rise of 25-6, 231-2; and 'Abd al-'Aziz 26; reign of 26-7; *jihad* of 233, 248, 249; popular support for 234-5; and French 236, 237; mentioned 221; *see also* Hafidiya

'Abd Allah b. Rashid, Mawlay 232

'Abd al-Qadir, Amir 137, 251, 253

'Abd al-Rahman, Sultan Mawlay 114, 148

'Abd al-Salam al-Wazzani, Mawlay 146

'Abd al-Salam Tazi, Shaykh Si 218

Abou Am: market of 106, 109, 111, 121-2, 224; map 85, 108, 113, 138

Abu, Mawlay 220-1

Abu 'Amama: insurrection in 1881-82 of 21, 140-3; and French army 158-9; and *makhzan* 158, 159; and Ibn al-'Arbi al-Darqawi 162; mentioned 64, 101, 127, 171n, 197-8, 245, 253, 255

Abu Himara 24, 26, 159, 184, 249, 251

'Addi al-Mani' 51, 54, 65, 66

'adm 40

Adrar: map, 73

Agadès: mao, 113

Agriculture 35: *see also* Dates; Dawi Mani', agricultural production of

Ahansal 81n; map, 73

Ahrar 43-4, 45

Aïn-Benimathar: *see* Berguent

Aïn Chaïr (village) 38, 120, 121, 139, 239, 240; map 33, 108

Aïn Sefra: village of 107, 143, 145, 160; subdivision of 145, 177, 209; map 33, 37, 108, 138

Ait Aissa River 38; map, 33, 37

Ait 'Amr (clan) 69

Ait arba'in 52

Ait 'Atta (tribe): electoral system of

68-9; origins of 71; expansion of 71-8; mentioned 36, 39, 40, 50, 51, 55, 67, 265; map 37; *see also* Ait Khabbash; Ait Umnasf

Ait 'Aysa (tribe) 42, 44, 233; map 37

Ait Burk (clan) 70

Ait Haddidu (tribe) 162

Ait Isful (subtribe) 75

Ait Izdig (tribe) 36, 42, 59, 74, 75, 76, 77, 116, 165, 181, 233, 237; map 37, 85

Ait Khabbash (subtribe): territory of 68; social organization of 69-70; aggression in Ziz valley and Tafilalt 72-6, 166, 167; Dawi Mani' and 74, 189; aggression in Touat of 76-7; relations with *qsar*-dwellers 77-8; raiding by 112; commercial activities of 119-20, 182; Mawlay Hasan and 164; resistance of 181-3, 197, 219, 222, 243, 245-6; opposition to trade with French 190, 238; mentioned 216; map 37, 85; *see also* Ait 'Atta

Ait Mirghad (tribe) 72, 75, 77, 116, 165, 181

Ait Mjild (tribe) 163

Ait Seghrushin (tribe) 36, 38, 39, 233, 237, 240, 241, 250; map 37

Ait Umnasf (subtribe) 68, 72, 74, 75, 239; map, 37, 85

Ait Unibgi (subtribe) 68, 69

Ait Waryaghar (tribe) 51

Ait Yafalman (confederation) 72, 75, 77, 164, 165, 197, 216, 265

Ajayi, J.F.A. 263

Akka 107, 110; map 108, 113

Al-Abidat (*qsar*) 90, 95; map 91

'Alawi dynasty 17, 42, 43, 46, 51

Al-Djouabeur (*qsar*) 95

Algeciras: Act of 25, 26, 217; conference of 25, 217

Algerian settlers 142, 144, 204, 244

Algero-Moroccan frontier 34, 143; *see also* Franco-Moroccan Accords; Franco-Moroccan Protocol

Al-Hammam Foukani (*qsar*) 90, 95; map 91

Al-Hammam Tahtani (*qsar*) 90, 95;